The Gloucestershire Gentry

THE GLOUCESTERSHIRE GENTRY

JOAN JOHNSON

ALAN SUTTON
1989

ALAN SUTTON PUBLISHING
BRUNSWICK ROAD · GLOUCESTER · UK

ALAN SUTTON PUBLISHING INC
WOLFEBORO · NEW HAMPSHIRE · USA

First published 1989

British Library Cataloguing in Publication Data

Johnson, Joan, 1928–
The Gloucestershire gentry.
1. Gloucestershire gentry, to 1988
I. Title
305.5'232'094241

ISBN 0-86299-584-1

Library of Congress Cataloging in Publication Data
applied for

Jacket picture: Stanway. Photograph: Nick Meers

Typesetting and origination by
Alan Sutton Publishing Limited.
Printed in Great Britain by
Dotesios Printers Limited.

CONTENTS

ACKNOWLEDGEMENTS

I have been collecting material for this book for a number of years, during which many people have given me encouragement and help. In particular I am indebted to Mr Donald Smith, the County Archivist, Dr Nicholas Herbert, and the staff at the Gloucester Record Office; Dr Robert Bearman and his staff at the Stratford-upon-Avon Record Office; the staff at the Bodleian Library and of the Reading Room and Print Room at the Ashmolean Museum; Dr John Jones, Dean of Balliol College; Mr Bryan Rendell of Lydney; Dr Stephen Porter and Ms Kirsty Rodwell.

To the late Dr Margaret Toynbee and Mrs Hélène Dicken, who read the text and offered helpful advice thereon; to Miss Sybil Harris who produced the typescript; to Mr Alan Sutton and his staff for their cooperation throughout, I am deeply grateful.

My sincere thanks are due to the following for permission to quote from family papers: Mrs P.F. Clifford, Mrs S.W. Colchester Wemyss, Mrs P. Whitmore, the Earl of Ducie, R.M. Hale, Esq., T.D. Sotheron Estcourt, Esq., Major General J.C. Hopkinson, C.B.; to Mr Donald Smith acting as Trustee for the Blathwayt, Dutton, Kingscote and Trye papers; and to the Trustees of the Shakespeare Birthplace Trust.

I also wish to acknowledge my indebtness for permission to reproduce illustrations: Her Majesty the Queen, p. 34; The Courtauld Institute of Art, pp. 138, 210; the Trustees of the Ashmolean Museum, pp. 53, 94, 149, 232; The National Gallery of Canada, p. 99; *Country Life Magazine*, pp. 26, 116, 197; The National Trust p. 109; Mrs P. Whitmore, pp. 97, 241; Mr T. Lloyd Baker, p. 243; Mr Rupert Perry, p. 247 as well as others who have asked not to be named.

THE GENTRY'S HOUSES

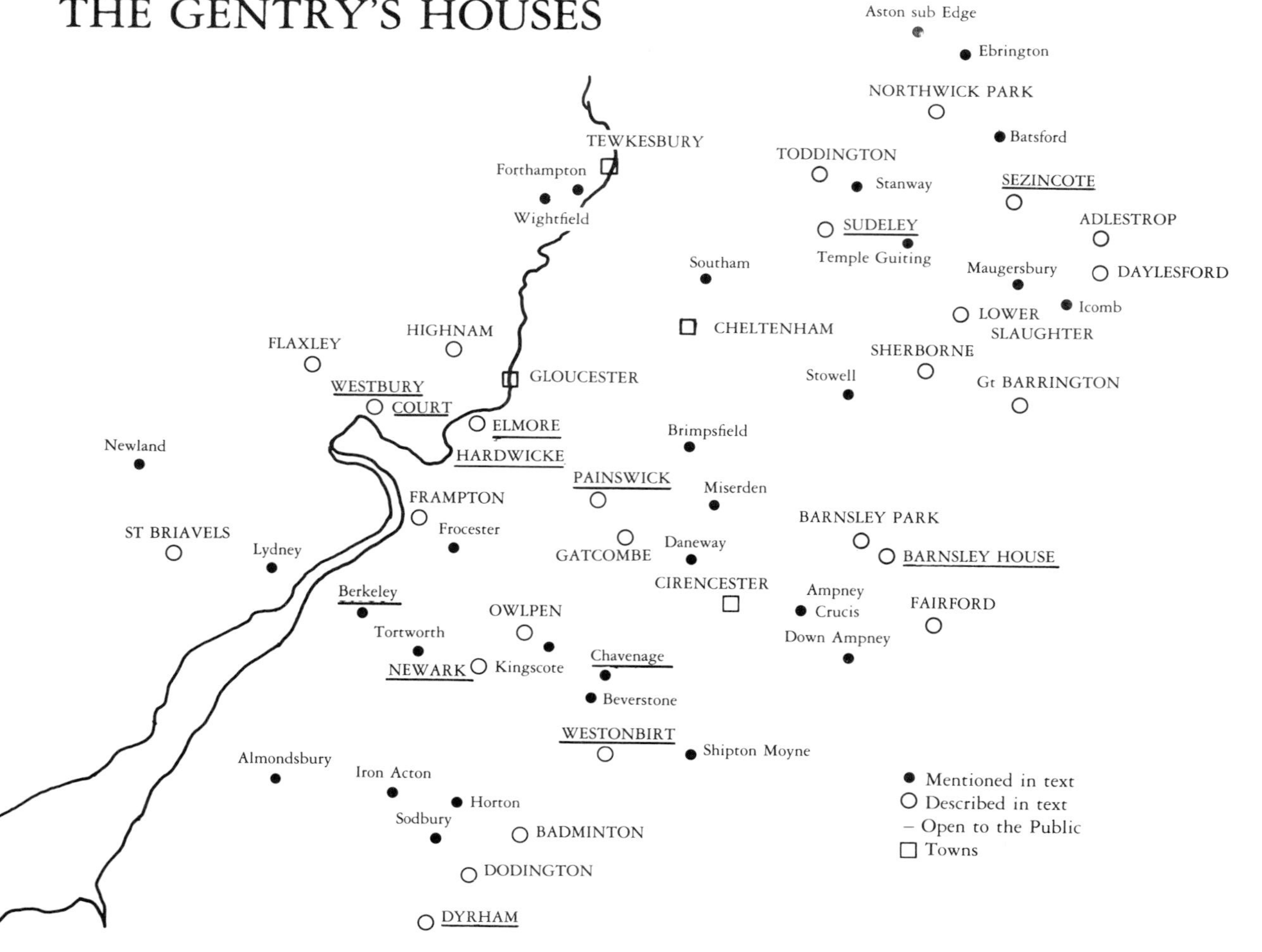

INTRODUCTION

The well-dressed hero of romantic novels, the conscientious magistrate presiding over petty sessions, the semi-literate bucolic squire – all of these at certain times and according to certain opinions have been regarded as typical gentry. This fact confuses rather than resolves the issue that, from the sixteenth century to the present day, has engaged historians and social commentators in academic investigations designed to explain the rise and fall of this class and its interim significance.

The conclusions reached by scholars have aroused interest and provoked discussion, some of it acrimonious, but so far have failed to establish absolute terms of reference that would facilitate a single, all-embracing characterization of the gentry at any given time. Between 1417 and 1685, the College of Arms, through the Visitations of the Heralds, applied its own strict interpretation of what constituted gentry status. In the 1660s, statutory rulings were issued to clarify the situation further, but because public opinion and social conventions could and did override the most rigid regulations on occasion, there have always been exceptions to the generally accepted rules. Writers during the sixteenth and seventeenth centuries were clearly obsessed with the need to establish an exact definition of a gentleman by references to wealth, possessions, behaviour and social standing, but that they were often defeated is evident from their readiness to resort to easy generalities: 'Whoever will bear the porte, charge and countenance of a gentleman, shall be accounted one.'

As a class, the gentry appear to have been most numerous and important between the sixteenth and nineteenth centuries, though their existence and significance are by no means confined to these time limits. Back beyond the sixteenth century, their origins can be found in the knightly class of the Middle Ages, but their characteristics have always been essentially non-military and modern, which helps to explain why their influence – despite its diminishing impact – has continued into the present century, and still exists today, especially in country areas. However, although it can be said with certainty that such people as were styled, or chose to style themselves, gentry were distinct as a class by the sixteenth century, even during the period when their influence was at its height the members of this class were difficult to enumerate and describe accurately. This was because the term *gentry* has been used at different periods to specify a legal category, an economic class or a status group, and always with varying degrees of comprehensiveness, being applied either with exclusive rigidity or, as in the early seventeenth century, so loosely and widely as to inspire Thomas Wilson's comment: 'Gentlemen be made good, cheap in England.'

The most outstanding characteristic of the gentry, that of being landowners committed to the care and exploitation of their estates, ensured them a place in the land-based society of pre-industrial England, while their means and social significance determined that this place should be between the nobility and the yeomanry. It is curiously anomalous though that, during a period when official forces were still trying to ensure that everyone had a place in society and stayed in it, the gentry class was noted for its changing personnel and varying qualifications. To use actual wealth or the size of estates as measuring rods to establish claims to belong to this class is not altogether satisfactory; in these particular respects, some gentlemen were better off than the nobility and some were worse off than the yeoman farmers, while others, though possessing the means to do so, deliberately avoided taking on the appearance and responsibilities of a gentleman. 'There be manie in England able to dispend a knight's living which never come into that countenance, and by their own consents' (Harrison). It is easier and more accurate, in theory at any rate, to account as gentry those who were, according to the College of Arms, entitled to style themselves knight, esquire or gentleman. Officially, the use of *esquire* was limited to the male heirs and descendants of noblemen's younger sons and the male heirs of knights. Certain officials, including sheriffs and justices, were honoured with the title during their term of office, also anyone with direct male ancestors so styled. The use of *gentleman* was limited to younger sons and brothers of esquires. To these categories were added in the 1660s army officers, naval captains, barristers, university graduates, and the mayors and aldermen of large cities; and for the first time a political overtone was added to the description: 'A person of respected loyalty to the King with a plentiful estate of lands in inheritance, and likely to be serviceable to His Majesty and his country.'

So much for the theory. In practice, from quite early on, the titles of *esquire* or *gentleman* could be assumed by anyone who wanted to pass as such, though 'to pass' necessitated having money, lands, family pride and a strong inclination to thrust oneself into the life of the locality. Writers of the sixteenth and seventeenth centuries saw clearly what was happening in their time. Lord Burleigh summarized and dismissed the matter succinctly: 'Gentility is nothing but ancient riches.' William Harrison was more particular: 'Whoever can live without manual labour and thereto is able . . . he shall for money have a coat and arms bestowed upon him by the heralds and be reputed for a gentleman ever after'; while Thomas Wilson conceded the importance of personal ambition: 'Young masters not contented with the states of their fathers to be counted yeomen, must skip into velvet breeches and silken doublet and ever after think scorn to be called any other than gentleman.' It was this last tendency that the Visitations of the Heralds, once every generation, were meant to discourage, but the heralds themselves were notoriously careless and venal, and their only sanction against pretenders – namely public humiliation – was by no means a satisfactory deterrent. After the Gloucestershire Visitation of 1623, it was reported that there were 104 'of such as were disclaymed to be no Gentlemen, within the county'; by 1682, the number of claimants disallowed had risen to 144. Daniel Defoe, writing in the early eighteenth century, was inclined to think that too much could be made of these investigations: 'We dive too deep and may indeed strike at the root of both gentry and nobility; for all must begin somewhere and could be traced to some less degree in their original than will suit with the vanity of the day. It is enough therefore that we can derive for a line of two or three generations or perhaps less.' A century earlier, Ben Jonson had already faced the fact that 'Many great men were rokked in mean cradles.'

Present interest in and concern with the problem of the gentry was first aroused by R. H. Tawney's article in the *English Historical Review* (1941) in which he suggested that the gentry first sprang into significance in the sixteenth century; they proceeded to grow in numbers and importance while a parallel decline was taking place among the aristocracy, the success of the gentry being attributed to a natural energy, enterprise and business acumen markedly lacking in their social superiors. No sooner had this theory been put forward than it was attacked by others who maintained that Tawney's argument and evidence were inconclusive, and quoted a wider range of examples to show that, though the actual personnel may have varied from time to time, the size of each class remained much the same. These also demonstrated that the qualities attributed by Tawney to the gentry were not as significant as he supposed, since some aristocrats were able to manage their affairs just as successfully as the parvenus, and that some gentry – in spite of having advantageous characteristics – failed to achieve their ambitions.

The period after 'Tawney's century' (i.e. 1540–1640) saw other people's awareness of the gentry hardening into mainly hostile attitudes. The aristocracy resented their over-anxious endeavours and successes as landowners, local officials and business entrepreneurs, and adopted an air of amused contempt to conceal a jealous fear of potential rivals. By their inferiors too, the gentry were disliked and distrusted, and as extreme political and social ideas spread among the supporters of parliament during the middle years of the seventeenth century, they found themselves castigated equally with the aristocracy for having 'suppressed the meaner sorts and deprived them of their rights and land'. For the most part, the attempts of conscientious justices, sheriffs and landowners to identify themselves sympathetically with victims of royal injustice under the first two Stuarts were overlooked by the so-called seekers after social equality and political democracy.

Since the ownership of land was a basic and indispensable requirement of their status, the gentry necessarily tended to progress at times when circumstances made the acquisition easier than usual. The break-up of baronial holdings towards the end of the Middle Ages, the dissolution of the monasteries, the alienation of Crown lands by the Tudors and the Civil Wars in the seventeenth century, all afforded opportunities to men of means who wished to become possessors of estates and simultaneously assume the social prestige and influence that went with such ownership. Thus, though their numbers were not noticeably increased, there were quite considerable changes in the ranks of the gentry during the sixteenth and seventeenth centuries, and the dividing lines between this class and those above and below it became more blurred than before. The waxing and waning of fortunes among all classes of people at this time, made it clear that the forces regulating society were no longer traditional ones, but instead were bound up with new economic developments. In the ranks of the gentry at any rate, a new pattern was emerging, according to which some families rose and fell within the space of three generations.

Although the personnel of the class and the necessary qualifications for claiming gentry status may have changed somewhat over the centuries, the personal characteristics of the gentry have remained constant. From the start, they have been landowners and mainly country-dwellers, running their estates in a businesslike fashion and constantly alert to the possibility of exploiting them. Their attitude to family and fortune has always been dynastic, and that some family lines died out and fortunes were lost was due not so much to the failure of the principle as to natural hazards such as a lack of male heirs, the marriage settlements of heiresses proving ruinous or some members of the family being extravagant, improvident or markedly inefficient. As landowners, the gentry were qualified to take up official posts locally or in a wider field, thus satisfying their natural instincts to pursue a public as well as a private career. From the fifteenth century to the present day, it has been from the ranks of the gentry that sheriffs, justices of the peace, Poor Law and school guardians, and names to head subscription lists for hospitals and charities have been drawn. And throughout, their determination to succeed and survive, and to exploit every opportunity, has developed in them a flexibility that has saved them from complete extinction even in the present century, when landowning is no longer an assured source of wealth and prestige, when opportunities for advantageous marriages within their class are becoming increasingly few, and when paid professionals have more or less replaced unpaid volunteers in public life.

In the past, after the Home Counties, Gloucestershire was one of the most gentrified areas in the country, possibly because so much land here was in the hands of the Church and the Crown after the Norman Conquest and later dispersed by alienation and sale to lesser proprietors. The county and the records of its families can provide illustrations of success and failure: estates that have not changed hands for centuries; others that in the course of a few generations have shifted from one family to another – through marriages, forfeitures and legal exchanges; of fortunes made by personal endeavour in the care and exploitation of land or more easily achieved through royal favour. There is, in short, such a wealth of material available as to enable us to follow and illustrate the progress of the gentry here from their rise, through their heyday, to their decline. Such a study can neither seek to nor succeed in establishing any new principles or ideas about the gentry, but it can prove the significance in the county scene of a class that has played a markedly important part in determining the course and nature of local history. Without the gentry, the county would have been considerably the poorer in respect of local administration and defence, agricultural improvements, industrial developments, pleasing gardens and stately homes, and artistic and cultural standards generally. Bridging the gap between the aristocracy and the poorer classes, and frequently with family links with both, the gentry cemented the bonds of local society and at the same time, because of their flexibility, were able to absorb into their ranks those who could not maintain a superior status or who wished to rise from an inferior one.

From the end of the Middle Ages until about the end of the last century, it was a social ideal in England to be 'a landed gentleman', though the implication of this changed in character as circumstances changed. Elton wrote in his *England under the Tudors* that the gentry were 'essentially not so much a class as a form of existence', which perhaps explains the difficulty of fitting them into a niche of unchanging shape and proportions. Further investigations into the subject of the gentry may well prove that generalizations about them as a class are impracticable and that the only way to get to know and understand them is to study and accept them as individuals.

CHAPTER ONE

FEUDAL ORIGINS

While making his survey of leading landowners in Gloucestershire in the early eighteenth century, Robert Atkyns commented, with some regret, that very few families flourished beyond three generations. At that point he could not know that the lines of some comparative newcomers, who had acquired estates in Gloucestershire at the time of the Reformation, were to continue to the present day; and he seemingly made light of the fact that some longer-established families had already been in possession of estates for centuries and were still flourishing. Yet it is among the latter that we must seek the origins of the class whose members were primarily significant for their military potential, but who increasingly, as time went on, came to regard their responsibilities as landowners as of greater importance than their military obligations, and comprising much more than the management of their estates.

Even before the Norman Conquest there was in England a class – the thanes – whose members held land in return for military service rendered to the king, but who also accepted as part of their role the need to serve the national and local communities in whatever way they could – attending meetings of the king's council to give advice, and the shire and hundred moots to further administration and the maintenance of law and order.

As a result of the Conquest there were no radical changes in social arrangements, save that a superior class of Normans superseded Anglo-Saxon tenants-in-chief at the top of society; and that throughout the country there was imposed a more rigid and uniform system which forced everyone into a clearly defined category, with unvarying and unvariable privileges and obligations in whatever part of England they might live. After the interim assumption of all the land by William, Duke of Normandy, in his capacity as Conqueror, some was retained by him as Crown land (in Gloucestershire this amounted to about one quarter of the county), some was confirmed in the ownership of the Church (again about a quarter of the land available), and the remainder was distributed among his followers, who became his tenants-in-chief, and those who were previously Anglo-Saxon overlords and their tenants.

William insisted on a uniform pattern of society and universal acceptance of his feudal suzerainty with the obligations this entailed, because he wanted to ensure sufficient fighting forces to safeguard his government and his newly won country. Thus

6 THE GLOUCESTERSHIRE GENTRY

The tomb of Sir Robert Atkyns at Sapperton. Atkyns produced the first history of Gloucestershire with the cooperation and patronage of gentry families. The Royal Commission on Historical Monuments

arrangements for the ownership and use of land were all geared to the provision of military service and based on the principle that those who were expected to fight had to be provided with the means of doing so. The top layer of this militaristic society was composed of aristocratic tenants-in-chief – barons whose estates were of considerable size, but usually scattered over a wide area to prevent a concentration of influence and power that might threaten the authority of the king if ever opposed to him. (William had observed, in France, the potential danger of the over-mighty subject.) Such men dominated the social and political scene, supplying qualities of leadership and a capacity to organise and direct, that were harnessed by the king to the business of government and the defence of the kingdom. Typical of these men, in Gloucestershire, were Roger of Montgomery with lands also in Sussex and Shropshire; Hugh Lupus, who was given most of Cheshire and 124 manors in other counties; William of Eu who had '115 manors in divers counties whereof 11 were in Gloucestershire'; and Roger of Berkeley, founder of the Berkeley family who was 'possest of many great Estates in Gloucestershire'.[1]

At the other end of the social scale, and comprising the majority of the populace, were the yeomanry and the peasants, some of them freemen and some serfs. It was their job to labour on the land in order to produce food and other supplies necessary to subsistence for themselves and their superiors, thus also freeing the latter for a higher role. In return for the services which tied them to the land and incidentally to the lord who owned it, these lower classes were entitled to use some of the land for their own benefit and were afforded economic and personal protection through the manorial organization that operated on the lord's estates.

Between the aristocracy and lower orders came the knightly class who, resembling the Anglo-Saxon thanes, formed the core of the king's fighting force; men with the means to equip themselves with arms, armour and a horse, and the freedom to go and fight for the king when and where he needed; and in some cases the power (derived from having dependent tenants) to bring other men with them to swell the king's army. Certainly until the end of the twelfth century, until in fact the Norman Conquest was a *fait accompli* and peaceful administration had succeeded military occupation, the knightly class – from the holder of a single manor to the near aristocrat controlling a number – was composed of men who were primarily fighters and might have few accomplishments besides.

Even as early as this, the attributes that later were to characterize an essentially non-military gentry class were beginning to accrue to the knights. Already it was usual for sons of knightly families to be sent away from home at an early age to be brought up in a strange household, where they were strictly but fairly treated, trained in the arts of war by serving the head of the household as squires, and ultimately in all probability knighted by their masters either on the field of battle or by means of a ritualistic inauguration ceremony in church; their suitability for this advancement was determined not only by their skill in arms but also by their father's status and means, and their own prospects of inheritance. Thus the importance of family background and connections was early being recognised.

Meanwhile, as a member of a baronial or knightly household, a young man would have absorbed some of the social etiquette that was becoming an accepted and acceptable part of life, in proportion as more peaceful times reduced the need for men to be in a continual state of preparedness for military activity of one kind or another. In a thirteenth-century sermon it was said: 'Peasants spoil their children and then when they are older put them to the plough. On the other hand, nobles first set their children beneath them and make them eat with the servant lads: and then when they are grown up, set them on high.'

Certainly it would have seemed wrong at the time for a man who did not know how to practice them himself to expect obedience and respect from others. Having learned patience and forbearance while carrying out menial tasks, sportsmanship from joining in ball games, hunting and hawking, and social graces from conversing with the women of the household and sharing their enjoyment of music, dancing and romantic tales told or sung by minstrels, the young squire was experienced enough to be thrown together with strangers and could be relied on to show a sense of fitness proper to the occasion. Good manners, courtesy and consideration smoothed the course of social exchange and one who knew how to behave on any and every occasion was an asset to his mentor; he might well be drawn into playing a part not merely in the family circle, but on public occasions, such as visits to other households, and attendance on the king or royal officials at meetings for the settling of legal and political business. As a result of participating therein, the prestige of these occasions rubbed off on to all who attended them, even humble squires, and thereafter redounded to their credit. To have accompanied a lord on a crusade or a foreign mission necessarily carried the greatest weight, but even a journey to London, the county town or a neighbouring castle was an added experience that might prove useful in due course.

The period between the twelfth and fourteenth centuries saw a gradual weakening of the links that bound together the various elements of feudal society, and a diminution of the latter's militaristic aspects. Primarily this was due to the changing needs of the king in respect of his army. Whereas the fighting services of the tenants-in-chief and their dependants had been sufficient for defence purposes and localised war in early Norman times, these were no longer adequate when the king had to undertake more prolonged campaigns and needed to be in a position to decide for himself the kind of fighters he took with him and for how long. As an alternative to personal service therefore, the payment of *scutage* (shield money) was introduced so that the king had the means to engage and pay for his own choice of troops; this was an arrangement that was equally advantageous to his feudatories who, though they might still *choose* to fight for their suzerain, were nevertheless freed from the *obligation* to do so. Meanwhile the personal link between the leader and his immediate followers had been weakened and even broken altogether, as also happened further down the social scale where a manorial lord similarly accepted money from his dependant tenants in lieu of their fighting services.

Another development tending to lessen the importance of military service as an essential factor in the feudal system was the fact that, as time went on, the number of really great lordships began to diminish – through death, disgrace, forfeiture or failure – while the ranks of middling and lesser landlords increased; for when the estates of a tenant-in-chief became available, they were frequently broken up and the component parts purchased or seized on by lesser owners who might have the means in hand to expand their own estates. But military service could not be fragmented as easily as estates, so small amounts of land (e.g. the equivalent of half a knight's fee) perforce had to be assessed and paid for on a monetary basis. However, though compulsory military service was fast disappearing, the number of knights and men of armigerous status was on the increase. Wars were frequent and it was on the battlefield that squires might be raised to knighthood. It was during wars also that mere squires – without waiting for knighthood – began to wear their own arms instead of those of the lord they were serving, ostensibly as a means of identification on the battlefield; this nevertheless was carried over into civilian life, there being no College of Arms as yet to investigate the right of any individual to blazon arms on his shield and surcoat.

Simultaneously, with the weakening of the rigid system that had linked particular men with particular estates and particular military obligations, a greater freedom and fluidity was developing in society. This was due to the feeling of security engendered by more efficient government, the expansion of trade and growth of towns, the increasing importance of money and the opportunities occasioned by all these for people to break out of the positions into which they had been born and change their status by the acquisition of wealth and estates and/or a profitable marriage. Already thrifty husbandmen or town merchants were alert to the advantages of using hard-earned profits or accumulated capital to add to their existing possessions, and of arranging marriages for their children that would establish links with families of inferior means perhaps, but definitely of superior social status to their own. The single-minded patience and perseverance with which such men acquired more land, acre by acre, and furthered the interest of their families, was to become one of the qualities that Tawney discovered in the sixteenth-century gentry and to which he ascribed their success.

Once released from the obligation to periodic military activity, landowners were able to give their individual attention to the running of their estates, and rapidly this came to supersede all other considerations. By the fourteenth century, on both greater and lesser estates, a system of proper management was being established. This involved a meticulous attention to detail, a fair but firm insistence on the payment of dues and fulfilment of duties on the part of tenants, a concern for the more advantageous use of land, and even an indulgence in long-term planning. Given such assiduous attention exercised by the owner personally or by his steward, it was no wonder that profits began to accrue to the successful, and that landowning, to an even greater extent than ever before, became a desirable state in itself. The gentry class had been born; for whereas in the past, land and military service had been inseparable, it was now landowning, quite distinct from military obligations, that could and did bestow a status.

Gloucestershire, even before the Norman Conquest, had a number of landowning families which, whether dignified with titles or not, nevertheless constituted the most prominent and influential element in local society; and though the majority were superseded in the local hierarchy by Normans at the time of the Conquest, they did not necessarily lose all their pre-eminence thereby. The strategic importance of the county had been evident to invaders of Britain from Roman times onwards, situated as it was on the borders of the unconquered Celtic territories in Wales, and commanding routes into the Welsh border country and the Midlands via the rivers Severn and Wye, and into the Thames valley by means of the tributary streams that rise in the Cotswolds. No less than their predecessors, the Normans were aware of the economic value of the area and its potential as a bulwark against possible invasions from Wales. Local loyalties and stability were therefore essential, and where William felt that he could rely on the status quo he left this unchanged. Wulfstan, the Anglo-Saxon Bishop of Worcester, and Aetheling, Abbot of Evesham, remained in office, and the management of their estates continued as before. Some lay landowners also continued to hold their land as tenants-in-chief, so that during the Middle Ages they could justifiably claim ancient ancestry. For instance, the same people are recorded both before and after the Conquest in possession of lands at Moreton-in-Marsh, Baunton, Rudford and Salperton; but most notable perhaps were the Tracys of Toddington whose family could be traced back to Emma, wife of Ethelred the Unready, and the le Boteler owners of Sudeley, equally long established, with whom the Tracys intermarried in the twelfth century, thus combining their lands into an extensive family holding on the western slopes of the Cotswolds that remained in their hands for centuries.

For others, roots were put down at the time of, or soon after, the Conquest, and the bestowal of land by William on his loyal followers introduced a Norman element into the top ranks of society and into the number of estate owners liable for military service and available for official duties also. The more important families had land in other counties too: 'Hascoit Musard who came in with the Conqueror was rewarded with divers Manors in Buckinghamshire, Warwickshire, Derbyshire and with six in Gloucestershire.' The lesser were given manors in Gloucestershire alone, but if more than one was involved, then they were scattered.

On the whole the new owners proved reliable, though there were a few who got involved in risings against William I and his successors, and suffered the loss of their possessions in consequence. 'William d'Eu of Badgeworth continued in possession until 1096 when he was cast into prison and his eyes put out for rebellion against the king.' The remainder proceeded to establish themselves in their new surroundings and to identify themselves so closely with the life of the locality that they either took the name of the place as their own, e.g. the Awres of Awre, Dickletons of Dixton, or else strengthened their hold on their acquisitions by renaming them after themselves: e.g. Miserden after Musard, Owlpen after Ollepen, Acton Turvil after Turberville, and Todenham 'a name derived from a Norman family which came in with the Conqueror'.

The absence of a large number of castles and fortified dwellings in Gloucestershire would seem to confirm that on the whole the countryside was fairly peaceable. Gloucester, Cirencester and Tetbury had their fortifications and there were castles at Sudeley and Berkeley; the first three have disappeared as have a number of others, a green mound, a ditch or the remains of some earthworks the only indications that they once existed. In two cases the original strongholds have been incorporated into later buildings and are now scarcely recognizable as castles. St Briavels in the Forest of Dean was designed as a keep-gatehouse, protected by a series of portcullises and had accommodation for a considerable garrison. Presumably all these measures were merely precautionary as the castle never saw any military activity and was useful rather as the headquarters of the Warden of the Forest and as a hunting lodge for the Norman and Angevin kings. Beverston too had a gatehouse and keep, the approach to which was defended by a drawbridge and a moat. The Giffards at St Briavels and the FitzHardings at Beverston were both important families owing military service to the king and with followers enough to take contingents with them when fighting was in prospect. Life in their fortified households must necessarily have been uncomplicated, unsophisticated and uncomfortable.

More characteristic than castles, as dwellings of consequential landowners in the countryside, were manor-houses, frequently stone-built halls with a central hearth, thick walls and small windows. Totally lacking in privacy and comfort at first, they were improved – as time went on and their owners felt more secure and became more affluent – by having screens introduced at each end to keep out draughts from the entrance and afford the family a place apart from the rest of the household, who lived in the main part of the hall both by day and by night. Smaller rooms might also be added, a kitchen and buttery at one end, withdrawing chambers for sleeping and sitting at the other, reached by a stairway from the raised part of the hall, reserved for the lord, his family and his guests. Thus though the 'family' life of the owner of the manor continued to comprise not merely his relatives but also all the members of his household at meal-times, and while entertainment or business was in progress in the great hall, there were periods when he, his wife and children could enjoy their own company, converse quietly or pass their time in reading and other gentle pursuits; and it was in such surroundings as these that the man whose concerns were still primarily warlike would have time and opportunities to devote himself to family affairs, the supervision of his household and estates, the entertainment of guests and the training of the young sons of his friends as squires.

On the evidence of those that remain there was a large number of manor-houses in Gloucestershire, serving as homes for landowners and administrative centres for their estates. In many cases, the original hall building has been altered and added to, so that its medieval character is no longer immediately obvious. Manors that once belonged to the Church, especially those that passed into lay hands as a result of the Reformation, suffered quite considerable changes at that juncture, as for instance Forthampton Court, originally the country retreat of the abbots of Tewkesbury, and Frocester Court which belonged to the monks of Gloucester Abbey. By contrast though, Ashleworth Court, property of St Augustine's Abbey, Bristol, was not affected so very much, and in this resembles places that had always been in lay hands and where features of the medieval structure are still easily discernible. Daneway House, built in the thirteenth century by the Clifford family, had a long rectangular hall to which a solar (withdrawing room) was added at one end, and an oratory near the main entrance – this last another indication of the owner's desire for some privacy while at his devotions or conducting important business, because it was not until much later that chapels were used exclusively for religious purposes. The hall was divided horizontally in the sixteenth century and an extra floor inserted between the ground and the high ceiling, but the roof beams still show the blackening effect of the smoke that used to rise from the central hearth in the hall below. Wanswell Court near Berkeley, home of the Thorp family, also started as a hall-house, and here again a screened passage was created near the entrance and private rooms added at the lord's end of the hall. Similar characteristic features of medieval halls can be seen at Leckhampton Court, Field Court (Quedgeley), Down Ampney House, Little Sodbury Manor, Owlpen Manor and Icomb Place – these last two perhaps, to a greater extent than the others, retaining the rather bleak sturdiness of medieval dwellings.

That the name 'Court' was given to so many of these manor-houses is a reminder of the halls having been used for meetings of the manorial court, when, under the aegis of the landowner or his steward, matters relating to the management of the estate were dealt with and disputes involving its tenants were settled. Such manorial records as remain throw light on the procedure and business of these courts. Here the customary

Down Ampney. Home of the Hungerford family for five centuries. Beyond the battlemented gatehouse was a typical medieval hall-house

practices of the manor were established and regularly confirmed: dates fixed for ploughing, harvesting, turning sheep on to the stubble or pigs into the woods, and officials chosen to supervise the tending of animals and the security of the crops. The payment (or non-payment) of rents was recorded, death dues (*heriots*) collected, and tenants presented and punished for breaches of manorial usage – keeping too many sheep, allowing houses to fall into disrepair, or failing to carry out personal services. Under penalty of fines for non-attendance, all the tenants were expected to appear at meetings of the court which afforded them opportunities of seeing their landlord and the inside of his house, and of confirming their allegiance to the manorial régime.

Another indication that the manor-house was at the hub of the estate business was the existence, in its vicinity, of great barns, farm buildings, sheep folds, dovecots and mills. Whether the landowner had one manor or more, he and his family lived, to a large extent, on the yield of the demesne land and the payments in produce made by the tenants, so there had to be places for storing grain, sheltering animals and keeping carts, tools and other farm equipment. All grain produced on the estate had to be ground at the lord's mill so that it was expedient for this to be situated conveniently for supervision. The dovecotes housed pigeons whose eggs and flesh constituted part of the manorial diet. For the most part, original farm buildings have been enlarged or replaced, though here and there some undoubtedly old structures remain – as at Doughton and Farmcote. Utilitarian dovecots, as opposed to the more decorative ones introduced in the seventeenth and eighteenth centuries, can be seen in a number of places including Quenington, Shipton Moyne and Eastington; as can also the magnificent barns that were and still are a feature of Gloucestershire estates – Chavenage, Stanway, Ablington, Ashleworth and Owlpen have good examples of these. Where soil conditions favoured them, orchards and vineyards might be planted and worked as part of the demesne, to ensure supplies of fruit, cider and wine. Certainly by the time that William of Malmesbury was writing in the twelfth century Gloucestershire abounded in these: 'A land rich in orchards . . . and planted thicker with vineyards than any other province in England; and they produce grapes in the greatest abundance and of the sweetest taste.'

As long as security remained a prime consideration, the walls of the castle or manor-house marked the confines of the life of the lord and his family; but as times became more peaceable and law and order more generally prevalent, development outside the walls was possible and life spilled out into gardens enclosed by wattle fences or quickthorn hedges. Parks, copses and woods too became regular features of estates, providing useful sources of timber and fuel as well as shelter for deer and game, and thus places for riding and hunting. Beyond its defensive ditch, Brimpsfield Castle had two parks, a great wood of beech containing 300 acres and a coneygarth of 60 acres of pasture; and at Westbury, Henry de Myners 'purchased a licence to enclose a park near his house'.

At much the same time as parks and woods were being developed as integral parts of estates, gardens for pleasure and utilitarian purposes were established in the immediate vicinity of the manor-houses themselves. Though deliberately planted and tended plots were at first the monopoly of monasteries, this was no longer the rule by the twelfth century, when the need for culinary and medicinal herbs in households aiming at self-sufficiency would have been satisfied on the spot; the desire for more space where they could relax and enjoy themselves away from the gaze of the rest of the household was also prompting the lord and his family to extend their living area out of doors into formally planned and planted enclosures adjoining the walls of the house. Here, with a measure of privacy, they could take their ease on seats of turf banked up round trees or against the fences, sewing, reading or listening to music in a setting of flowery lawns, arbours of climbing roses and shady trees. Marked off from these pleasure areas by more hedges or fences were the raised beds where flowers could be grown, and patches given over to the herbs used by the cooks in the preparation of meals, and the ladies of the household for the concoction of remedies for everyday ills and accidents.

There is no material evidence that such gardens ever existed, but we can be sure that they did. Some of the earliest writing on the subject came from the pen of Alexander of Neckham, Abbot of Cirencester, who in his *De Naturis Rerum* devoted several chapters to the growing of flowers, fruit and herbs. Although some of his pronouncements were rooted in and redolent of superstition, his knowledge of plants seems to have been based on personal observation and, if this was the case, then Gloucestershire gardens in the late twelfth century could boast of herbs such as sorrel, parsley, coriander, sage, hyssop,

St Briavel's Castle: fortified residence of the Constable of the Forest of Dean, a post of responsibility only entrusted to reliable families such as the Giffards

mint and rue, vegetables such as onions, leeks, pumpkins and shallots, and flowers such as roses, lilies, heliotrope, violets, peonies and irises. Certainly by the next century flowers were a recognised product of estates, for lands at Upton 'were bought by service of a rose at Christmas' Elmore rented for 'a bunch of gillyflower'. Moreover, in view of how many knights returned from the Crusades, having seen in the gardens of southern Italy and the Middle East flowers and fruits hitherto unknown in England, it would have been natural for them to want to reproduce these in more familiar surroundings; and to judge by illustrated manuscripts of the period, they succeeded in this, for here we can see flowers, fruit and trees represented so accurately that they must have been drawn from live examples and not just based on imaginary speculations. And did Walter Clifford of Frampton, father of Henry II's fair Rosamund, try to emulate his sovereign by reproducing in Gloucestershire the equivalent of the bower which the king had made for his mistress at Woodstock?

Although men who held land in return for military service continued to find this employing a considerable amount of their time, some were serving their overlords in other ways as well. Gilbert Marshal of Badgeworth held the office of marshal to the king; Hugh Giffard, who acquired the manor of Batsford along with a wife who was an heiress, was made Constable of the Tower of London; John Giffard of Brimpsfield was required to serve as Governor of St Briavel's Castle and Warden of the Forest of Dean;

William le Moyne held the manor of Shipton Moyne 'by serving, to keep the King's larder'; Thorp of Wanswell 'held his land for keeping the tower' at Berkeley Castle.

From the ranks of these same families, as from the Cliffords, Tracys, Guises and others of similar status as landowners, were chosen the sheriffs who represented and upheld royal authority in the county and the justiciars who were appointed from time to time to try special cases in the courts and to see that law and order were maintained generally. Such national and local positions, while not carrying high salaries, did bring perquisites in their train (food, lodging, expenses, etc.) and bestowed status on those who held them. Most importantly, public office opened up other ways of improving personal fortunes and furthering the interests of families – the kind of situation that from the Middle Ages onwards was to be one of the main explanatory factors of the rise of the gentry.

So, a survey of society during the period immediately after the Conquest would show a number of families establishing themselves as owners of estates, these varying considerably in size but all involving certain obligations of military and personal service, and responsibilities as regards the lands they comprised and the tenants living thereon. Whether of Saxon or Norman descent, these families were identifying themselves with particular localities and strengthening their hold on them by giving personal attention to their estates, assuming roles in local government and forming links with other families in the neighbourhood through marriages and the leasing or acquisition of land. Their life-style was changing gradually from that of a military camp to one more consistent with a civilized, cultured existence against the background of a family home. Coming to be more important in fact than the horse, armour and arms that had characterized a knight in the eleventh century were the gentlemanly bearing, the capacity for service and the adroitness in personal and public business that explained the continuing eminence of families such as the Guises, the Cliffords and the Tracys.

CHAPTER TWO

CHANGING FORTUNES

Between the twelfth and fifteenth centuries changes began to take place in England which affected society as a whole and in particular favoured men who had a built-in propensity for bettering themselves. These changes cannot be dated specifically nor even confined to clearly defined periods, since they were concerned with overlapping generations of people rather than particular events and were determined by the interplay of many different forces, some local, some national, some international. Thus, although certain facts were true of the twelfth century and another set of facts true of the fifteenth century, at any point between these dates and in any place, circumstances might seem to be ahead of or behind the times, and the people caught up in them deemed progressive or reactionary accordingly. Some landowners for instance were still primarily fighting men as late as the fifteenth century, whereas others as early as the thirteenth century were beginning to put the management and exploitation of their estates before everything else.

Until the twelfth century feudalism provided society generally with both a way of life and a means of subsistence. In theory, the success and continuance of the system depended on the rigidity of its structure and a universal acceptance of its working, but in practice, after this time, an element of opportunism and expediency began to creep in and was allowed to do so where changes brought advantage in their train. Those most committed to making the system work were among the first to deviate from its established usages. Lords, leasing parts of their land, accepted money rents instead of military service in exchange. The Statute of Labourers, passed in 1351 to prevent men leaving estates where they customarily worked, was broken by the landowners responsible for introducing it, in order to be sure of getting enough labour for their own needs. Cracks such as these, once they appeared in the system, subsequently widened, thus opening the way to a tide of commercialism and personal ambition. By the thirteenth century this had more or less swept away the original characteristics of a society that had been based on non-profit-making relationships and activities, and an unambitious acceptance of the status quo.

At the same time, another factor was helping to weaken the hold of feudalism on society by widening people's knowledge and increasing their competence and self-confidence. This was the gradual spread of learning downwards from the baronial and knightly classes who usually had their children educated at home, to members of the aspiring merchant classes who could now put their children into grammar schools established by the guilds, town authorities or charitable individuals. Gloucestershire was well-off in this respect. The King's School at Gloucester had been established by the twelfth century and Cirencester Grammar School by the mid-thirteenth century; Katherine, Lady Berkeley, founded a school at Wotton in 1384 and Robert Gryndour at Newland in 1443; Stow-on-the-Wold and Chipping Campden had their grammar schools by the end of the fifteenth century. Here a training in practical subjects was available, a more useful preparation for the world of business than that offered by the cathedral or monastic schools. By the fourteenth century too it was possible for boys to go on to Oxford or Cambridge to acquire a further education, still largely based on the Classics, but which could also include French, the conduct of written and practical legal business and procedure, and the keeping of accounts. In due course the establishment of scholarships made it possible for students from a wide social range to attend the universities, so that a way was opened for some to improve their chances of becoming successful lawyers or public officials, and incidentally of improving their social status. Moreover, at the end of his university course, a promising boy might be taken into the household of an eminent ecclesiastic or lay lord, where he could increase his knowledge and experience of practical affairs, e.g. the management of a household or of political business, and acquire the habits of courtesy and refinement that were already recognized as distinguishing marks of a gentleman.

Meanwhile society was developing a flexibility and mobility that it had not had before. The growth of trade, and simultaneously of the towns, the expansion of the guild system and practice of apprenticeship, were all encouraging people to extend their horizons and become less parochial in their outlook and activities. The son of a craftsman or trader in one town might be apprenticed to a master in another, even as far away as London; and still more significantly, the younger son of a country landowner, unlikely to inherit the family estate, would be placed for training under a reputable master craftsman. Thus he was introduced into a different social circle within which, in due course, he might marry – the gain on his part being a well-dowered wife, and perhaps a stake in her father's business; on hers, a link with a higher social class. Then, in a generation or two, the offspring of such a match could be found marrying back into the landowning class and gaining an interest in an estate different from that of his forebears. The story of Richard, younger son of William Whittington of Pauntley, his journey to London, apprenticeship to a master mercer whose daughter he married and ultimately his election as lord mayor, has become legendary. The Leigh and Whitmore families, who became landowners in Gloucestershire in the sixteenth and seventeenth centuries, both derived from younger sons who went to London and made their fortunes in trade. And there must have been others like them. William Harrison was evidently commenting on an established practice when he wrote in 1577: 'Merchants often change estates with gentlemen as gentlemen do with them; by mutual conversion of one unto the other.'

Another development tending to encourage social mobility was the increasing size and complexity of aristocratic and ecclesiastical households. This led to the establishment therein of a hierarchy of officials who, because office-holding was prestigious and potentially lucrative, were quickly able to improve their fortunes and status. In the

Richard Whittington. A younger son who left the family home at Pauntley to make his fortune in London

fourteenth century, William de Bradwell, after giving useful service as a steward of Winchcombe Abbey, bought an estate for himself and thus qualified to become a member of parliament. William de Cheltenham, a protégé of the Berkeleys, was helped to acquire land, nominated as a justice of the peace and a member of parliament, and founded a gentry family with extensive estates and a commitment to public service. Perhaps the most noted example of such a success story is that of John Smyth of Nibley in the sixteenth century, who started his career as a steward on the Berkeley estate, was chosen to accompany the heir to Oxford, where he absorbed the necessary experience and refinement to become a confidential servant to the family and a recorder of its history, and was ultimately given an estate by way of reward and the opportunity to rise to gentry status.

Even in less renowned households and on smaller estates, bailiffs, reeves and other officials, freed from dues and personal obligations in return for their services, were in a position to benefit themselves as well as those they served, and achieve a degree of independence beyond the reach of mere husbandmen. The Abbot of Westminster, overlord of much of the land round Moreton-in-Marsh, offered the lease of a house, and thus a superior status, to whichever of the brothers Richard or William Hodges would undertake the duties of woodward to the manorial community, a concession which enabled the family in due course to become landowners in their own right. An indication of the significance attached to being one of the entourage of an important lord, whether as a servant, a tenant or a friend, can be found among the signatures on legal documents that have come down to us from the Middle Ages. The repeated appearance of the same names argues regular attendance of the people concerned on all important occasions, and a recognition on the part of the lord that at such times it was expedient for him to have in his retinue men whose very presence contributed to his own prestige, whose advice was worth having and whose word could be trusted. The following deed, drawn up in 1250 as part of a marriage contract, is typical of many contemporary records:

> Let those present know that I, Walter of Bennecumbe, have given, granted, and by this my present charter confirmed to Henry, son of Sir Simon de Olepenne with Agnes my daughter in free marriage, all my land in Longelus which extends in length from Adam de Stut's ditch to Peter de Uley's wood; to have and to hold from me and my heirs freely and quietly, wholly peaceably. . . . Moreover, I, Walter, warrant to the aforesaid Henry and his heirs or assigns, the aforesaid land against all mortal men for ever. And, because I desire that this my gift and grant may remain firm and stable and without ill-will for ever, I have made the present charter and signed it with my seal. These being witnesses: Sir Simon de Olepenne, Nigel de Kingscote, Adam Fitz Stephen, Richard le Duc, Henry le Bret, William of Berkeley.[1]

A new factor in the situation and one of increasing significance between the twelfth and fifteenth centuries was a change in attitude to landowning and land management. Urban craftsmen and tradesmen, though perhaps the first to respond to pressures of ambition and need for material success, were not at all unique. Soon, landowners too began to regard their estates, not merely as a means of satisfying the basic needs of themselves and their families, but as vested interests and business propositions that must be made to pay, in order to provide cash to meet demands consistent with a rising standard of living – luxury foods and clothes, costly jewellery, adjuncts to domestic comfort and ambitious building projects. Thus a new spirit of enterprise began to enlighten and enliven estate management and to change what hitherto had been regarded as a fixed pattern of practice, flexibility now becoming the determinant factor of survival in bad times and of prosperity in better ones. The writing of treatises, such as that of Walter of Henley on *Husbandry* (*c.* 1240) which advocated a scientific approach to the routine of agriculture, and the carefully recorded and balanced accounts that were a feature of estate papers from the thirteenth century onwards, reflect the growing concern of landowners to increase the yield and enhance the profits of their estates. Fluctuations in the size and character of demand which in turn affected the returns on agricultural produce – wool, leather, livestock, grain, poultry, cheese – were matched by fluctuations in the amount of land actually being used, and the proportion of arable to pasture: for example, the increased prices commanded by food crops in the thirteenth century led to more land being brought under the plough at the expense of grazing; while the sure gains to be made out of wool in the fourteenth century encouraged the extension of pastures and indeed the use of hitherto unprofitable land. That the period of expansion in the wool trade coincided with the Black Death, and its aftermath of a critical labour shortage, was an additional reason for landowners, after the middle of the century, to keep more of their land under grass for the pasturing of sheep.

Other indications of a more flexible approach to the management of estates were the varying policies that were followed from manor to manor, according to prevailing circumstances. While the population was rising and there was a widespread demand for land, many owners were prepared to sell or lease part of their estates, even relinquishing their demesne, if renting this to others promised to be more profitable than working it directly themselves. A willingness to forego labour services and to enter into money-based agreements with customary tenants also showed that some landowners did not scruple to abandon feudal practice when it suited their purpose; as did their readiness to agree to the exchange and consolidation of holdings and the subsequent enclosure of these for specialised use. Such innovations were not made everywhere, because it did not necessarily follow that men belonging to a class originally geared to war wanted or were able to turn into adroit managers of land. Nor was it certain that experiments with new methods would be followed by success. As revenues from land increased, so did expenditure, and unless both were carefully balanced and continually adjusted the latter might easily and fatally outstrip the former. On the whole circumstances favoured those who, operating on a large scale, had more resources and therefore more time to cushion them against the sudden reverse of fortune that often ruined men living too close to the extent of their means; these were unable to survive even one season of poor yields, defaulting rent payers or low market prices.

Sound management of property, though undoubtedly important, was not the only factor that determined the rise and fall of family fortunes during the Middle Ages. To take marginal land into cultivation was a possible way of adding to one's acres, but the same result could be achieved by opportune marriage to an heiress or inheritance from a kinsman: just as the diminution of an estate might be the result of deliberate disposal rather than bad judgment or bad luck. Therefore, it is dangerous to oversimplify reasoning about the waxing and waning of a family's prosperity. However, two Gloucestershire families at least owed their continuing success to a capacity for good husbandry. The Tracys of Toddington, of whom we have already been aware as landowners before the Conquest, continued to hold on to their estates throughout the Middle Ages and derive a satisfying return from them. Their success was widely recognized and the quality of the wool from their flocks pastured on the western slopes of the Cotswolds acclaimed as second only to that of the acknowledged prime Herefords. Did they perhaps learn something of estate management from what went on in the neighbouring manor of Stanway belonging to the abbots of Tewkesbury? A comment made in the early seventeenth century by John Smyth on Anthony Kingscote of Kingscote indicated that members of this family too had maintained their fortunes steadily through many generations, weathering the strain of bad times and taking advantage of opportunities in good ones, always matching their undertakings to their means:

> It may be said of this gentleman and of his family . . . that he and his lineall ancestors have continued in this little manor nowe about 500 years, never attainted nor dwelling out of it elsewhere; nor hath the tide of his estate higher or lower, flowed or ebbed in better or worse condition; but like a fixed starre in his firmament, to have remained without motion in this little orbe, without any remarkable change.[2]

Meanwhile, the dawning realization that an estate might be acquired without this necessarily involving military obligations, and that mere ownership could bestow a status, was drawing into the landowning class successful craftsmen and merchants who, a generation or two before, would not have dreamed of aspiring to social promotion. 'We

Kingscote. By limiting their ambitions and commitments, the Kingscote family managed to keep their fortunes stable from the twelfth to the nineteenth century

that had our breeding from trade, though we hate gentlemen ourselves, yet are ambitious to make all our children gentlemen,' wrote Shirley. In some cases, capital acquired through business was invested in land so that this might become a family inheritance. Sometimes husbandry was added to a man's other pursuits, seemingly without the slur being attached to his commercial interests that later on, in the seventeenth and eighteenth centuries, would have labelled him a tradesman and effectively prevented his acceptance into a higher class. Perhaps it was that in the later Middle Ages so many 'business men' were in fact concerned with the marketing and manufacture of products of the land? There are examples to be found in the records of several Gloucestershire towns of men who 'had thriven so well', achieving local significance, acquiring land in the countryside and connecting themselves by marriage with old-established families. Though little detailed information about them is available, it seems likely that wool merchants such as William Grevel of Chipping Campden and John Fortey of Northleach, who could afford considerable benefactions to these towns and were commemorated by markedly magnificent tombs, had certainly achieved a status and a life-style commensurate with that of the gentry. Of Nicholas Poynter and Walter Cosyn of Cirencester we know more, as their purchases of land at Bagendon and Elkstone respectively have been recorded, also their holding of office in the town and prominence in local affairs. But perhaps the best known of the families who improved their status during the later Middle Ages were the Tames, who started out as graziers at Stowell near Northleach. They were successful enough to become wool merchants and in due course clothiers as well, acquiring land at Cirencester and the manor of Fairford, where they made considerable additions to the church and built a fine house for themselves, and ultimately achieving a title and an official position as High Sheriff of the county. Bequests in the wills of John Tame, his son and grandson – both Edmunds – indicate the size of their households and the very considerable extent of their means; and that son Edmund was able to entertain Henry VIII at Fairford, and grandson Edmund was considered fit for inclusion in the royal retinue that went to the Field of the Cloth of Gold (though in fact he did not go) were surely signs that socially the Tames had arrived. Leland subscribes to the fact that in doing so they brought success to Fairford also: 'Fairford never flourished before the Tames came into it.'[3]

Constitutional developments during the later medieval period, and especially the elaboration of governmental machinery, created further opportunities for the growing class of men who were available and willing to take on responsibilities at both local and national level. We have seen how the expansion of great households made it possible for the able and ambitious to improve their status by means of office. As time went on, posts connected with the royal household and service became more attractive than those connected with baronial establishments, because they offered better and surer prospects (baronial fortunes were apt to be precarious in politically disturbed times) and on the whole left men with more independence. The Berkeley hold over the population of parts of Gloucestershire remained powerful throughout this period and John Smyth was not the only one who, by submitting to it for a time, ultimately benefited from this domination. Elsewhere, increasingly, enterprising men sought office in the service of the crown: John le Boteler of Sudeley held the post of Lord Chamberlain to Edward II and Sir Walter Hungerford of Down Ampney that of Lord High Treasurer to Henry V.

However, although usually dependable, even exalted service could be hazardous if royal authority was in dispute. John Tiptoft, who had gained the manor of Abbenhall by marrying the heiress daughter of Robert Gryndour, served Edward IV, 'but he was then beheaded by the command of the Great Nevil, Earl of Warwick, commonly called the Make King who in this year [1470] had restored Henry VI.' Earlier, in 1465, a reverse procedure was nearly as unfortunate for the owner of Sudeley. Ralph le Boteler who served as Lord Treasurer under Henry VI 'was always for the Lancastrian line; but Edward IV attaining the crown, he [le Boteler] was apprehended at Sudeley and brought prisoner to London.' Unlike Tiptoft, he escaped with his life and perhaps could not complain since he had already done quite well out of royal service. 'He built the Castle of Sudeley out of the wars with France: he having been Admiral at sea, took Portmare, a Frenchman, prisoner; with whose ransom he built one of the towers.'

In addition to those in the household or immediate entourage of the king, further openings appeared. The extension of royal power and of royal control over government always proceeded at the expense of feudal offices and feudal courts, so men outside the baronial sphere of influence were needed to fill positions of authority in the new administrative networks: an ideal chance for those wanting to assert themselves in local affairs. Thus it was that the names of Tracy, Guise, Giffard, Whittington, Hungerford and Tame, among others, appeared in the lists of sheriffs, commissioners and justices; and as the growth of business was, in part, a search for increased efficiency, the numbers of officials multiplied steadily, coroners, jurors, verderers, constables of castles, tax collectors, etc., being needed to back up administrative experiments and advances. The proliferation of offices and work was most noticeable in the sphere of the law. As more and more of the work brought into the royal courts was occasioned by the execution of special writs and enquiries, men who had had legal training and/or experience of court procedure as members of lordly retinues were especially useful. Being landowners too, they were acquainted with local usages, boundaries and customary rights, an immediate recommendation when so much of the business of the courts turned on lawsuits concerning territorial claims.

That such men did enjoy considerable independence while engaged in the service of the crown was illustrated by the fact that some of those supposed to be upholding the law and contributing to its effectiveness were at the same time undermining it by their own lawless behaviour. As Nigel Saul has pointed out, 'where land was a measure of social standing, litigation was a constant pastime for those who lived on it'[4] and estates a permanent temptation to greedy neighbours. Many of the offenders were guilty of trespass and assault, and the victims were often their own tenants, but the jurors who should have represented the latter were disinclined to indict their superiors and thus stir up more trouble. Frequently a policy of masterly inactivity secured the result desired by the offender, since there was no machinery to enforce the attendance of an accused person and there could be no trial in his absence. When cases did reach the courts, the proceedings might be accompanied or interrupted by violence, and therefore unduly prolonged. A century before the Wars of the Roses ushered in the lack of governance that has always been regarded as one of the period's worst aspects, a certain disregard for the sanctity of law was already being shown by those who felt sufficiently insulated against the consequences of their behaviour. Dependent tenants or retained servants were more likely to partner their overlord in crime than be critical of his activities, especially as their own reputations were not always above reproach. Violence begat violence, so that an original breach of law might be compounded a hundredfold before it was finally settled. A dispute between the Berkeley and Lisle families lasted for 172 years, with relentless animosity being shown on both sides, the legal activities connected with the case paling into insignificance beside the looting and fighting that were going on at the same time outside the courts.

In spite of such disorderly lapses, however, the later Middle Ages saw the slow consolidation of the Common Law system, as all but purely estate matters and petty crimes were removed from the cognizance of the seigneurial and local courts into the jurisdiction of the royal justices, and commissioners appointed to deal with special types of case at particular times. Meanwhile, offshoots of the king's own court, the Curia Regis, were being established as courts of first instance, handling cases involving serious breaches of the peace, and as courts of appeal to settle unacceptable decisions made at local level. The men who conducted the business of the courts of King's Bench, Common Pleas and Exchequer had specialized knowledge and experience, and quickly achieved fame and status as well as considerable wealth, since judges received fees that increased in proportion to the amount of work they did. These included, from Gloucestershire, John Cassey of Wightfield, Chief Baron of the Exchequer under Richard II, Sir John Fortescue of Ebrington, Lord Chancellor, William Grevil of Arle Court and William Knight of Horton, both judges of the Common Pleas.

For carrying out special commissions, it was an advantage to use men with local knowledge or at any rate access to local sources of information, and here the landowning gentry were particularly useful. Through social contacts with each other, and day-to-day dealings with their stewards and tenants, they were well informed as to the background

Wightfield Manor. Home of the Cassey family from the fourteenth to the seventeenth century. It was a moated house partially rebuilt during the sixteenth century with materials from Deerhurst Priory

of cases and the character of the persons involved; also they had the authority to insist on and carry out the necessary formalities and to conscript lesser men of their own class to serve as jurors, witnesses, assessors and in other official capacities. Moreover, it is noticeable that in addition to the service they were thus giving the king and the country, and the benefits accruing to themselves personally, these men were acquiring a class consciousness and local identity as they met and worked together on county business, exchanged information and opinions, and made decisions of consequence to those who looked up to them for direction. This awareness of their county as an identifiable and independent community was an important factor in determining the actions and reactions of those who came together when a full session of the county court assembled under the aegis of the king's judicial representatives. Shared experience and knowledge must have produced a certain similarity in outlook among county officials and led them to maintain an appearance of solidarity *vis-à-vis* representatives of the central government. The latter, entrusted with upholding and projecting a conception of national policy, were forced to recognise that their objective could only be achieved by convincing those present from the locality of its importance to them. It was in these circumstances and at this level that the county learned of the intentions of royal authority as vested in the organs of central government, and that the representatives of the king assessed the extent and nature of local cooperation.

Ultimately, however, it was at the centre of government itself and not in any local setting that the existence and importance of the county community was recognised – that is, when representatives of the people were first summoned to parliament. In some ways these early parliaments resembled the county courts where the members were elected, for they were meetings of the Curia Regis enlarged for the occasion by the inclusion of representatives from towns and counties; in the course of a session these would be called on to subscribe to judicial decisions and enactments as well as giving their consent to levies of taxes. For the king it was vital that the majority of his subjects, even if only indirectly through their representatives, should submit to his policies; from the people's point of view, it was expedient to have some safeguard, however tenuous, against oppression. Even as early as this though, when political awareness was merely beginning to stir, potential taxpayers were inclined to weigh the cost of being represented against its advantages, so that a strong recommendation in a candidate for parliament was a willingness to bear his own expenses for the journey to and from Westminster, and for residence in London during the session. That such offers should have come from members of the landowning class was natural in view of the prominence they had already achieved in local affairs and their desire to improve on this. As with local offices, familiar names became associated with membership of parliament: Tracy, Clifford, Guise, William of Bradwell, William de Cheltenham and his son Maurice, and that of the Hungerfords of Down Ampney, Sir Thomas Hungerford being the first Speaker of the House of Commons in 1357.

The composition of early parliaments afforded incontrovertible proof of how important the landowning classes had become, in a non-military capacity, to the conduct of national as well as local government. Prospective members had to be property owners of considerable means and of knightly status, though not necessarily titled; and the right to vote was exclusive to freeholders, a narrower qualification than it might seem since most men were still copyholders, leaseholders or rent payers. Tenants-in-chief of the Crown, sitting by right of their status, formed the permanent core of the Curia Regis which was to become the House of Lords. When sessions were enlarged by the addition of representatives from counties and towns, the latter constituted the Commons. Elections conducted at a full session of the county court were not yet the scene of jobbing and jostling that accompanied such occasions in the eighteenth century, but all the same they were anything but democratic. The support of a powerful landowner who could command the votes of all his tenants, the official standing of a prospective candidate in his own locality, could and usually did decide the issue; and even in some of the towns, where rights and independence were jealously guarded, a country gentleman of independent means might well be adopted as a candidate rather than a citizen who would expect to have his expenses paid. Once established, the routine of election, journeys to and from Westminster, and working sessions in the Commons, served to strengthen the emerging élite of the county community. Their entrenched position locally gave them confidence and determination: concern for their responsibilities (with which, admittedly, personal interests were often involved) directed them along lines of moderation and conservatism.

The Hungerford Chapel and Memorial to Sir John and Sir Anthony Hungerford in Down Ampney church, reflecting the importance of this local family. The Royal Commission on Historical Monuments

The differentiation of Lords and Commons at the centre of government was a reflection of what had been happening in local society and politics. The determined attempt on the part of the crown to remove business, and simultaneously power, out of the hands of the baronial class into the sphere of royal officials had been backed by the efforts of the middling sort of landowners, ready to use service in baronial households as a means to an end, but ultimately anxious to become independent of their social superiors. By the fifteenth century, men of this class had successfully thrust a wedge into society between the owners of great estates and mere husbandmen and merchants, and taken upon themselves, not only the traditional responsibilities of feudal lords, but also the tasks created by an expanding central government.

This class was a less clearly defined one than those above and below it, and included some men who were wealthier than aristocratic lords and some who were less well off than successful farmers and merchants who chose to husband their resources rather than display them in grandiose living, and to concentrate their abilities on their own particular work rather than employ them in public service. Some aspired to knighthood and assumed the title and aims that went with this; some were content to style themselves esquire or gentleman. All were conscious and jealous of their status and independence. This helps to explain why, though they committed themselves to royal service and loyalties, the Gloucestershire gentry generally did not get involved in baronial troubles. Marcher lords like the Mortimers and Clares had manors in the county which they used as staging posts *en route* to and from Wales, yet they do not seem to have attracted much of a following locally; apart from Thomas of Berkeley and his immediate household, few were apparently aware of or concerned with events leading to the murder of Edward II at Berkeley Castle. Similarly the feud between the Beauchamps and the Despencers had no local repercussions, except in 1399 when, having failed in an attempt to capture Henry IV and restore Richard II to the throne, the Earl of Salisbury and Earl of Kent fled to Cirencester; where they were imprisoned and subsequently executed by the townsfolk led by John Cosyn, descendant of Walter, who had 'thriven so well' in the previous century. On this occasion at any rate, people were left in no doubt as to the wisdom of John Cosyn's commitment: 'For the good service performed . . . in manfully resisting those who had risen against the king', he was confirmed in the possession of the goods of the rebels and granted '100 marks to be yearly received at the Exchequer during his life'.

CHAPTER THREE

CAREERS OPEN TO TALENTS

The period between the mid-fifteenth and mid-sixteenth century was one of transition, where the end of the Middle Ages is regarded as overlapping the beginning of modern times, without there being at any point a clear line of demarcation between the two. In throwing off the strait-jacket of feudalism the country had – by the fifteenth century – made a move towards a more modern society and economy; yet it is also true that even after the middle of the sixteenth century there were spheres where customary practices remained almost unchanged and where people viewed with dismay any developments that seemed to challenge old values or to undermine the established order of their existence.

> The heavens themselves, the planets and this centre
> Observe degree, priority and place . . .
> O when degree is shaked,
> Which is the ladder to all high designs,
> The enterprise is sick.[1]

The accession of Henry VII in 1485 and the passing of the Act of Supremacy in 1534[2] were certainly signposts indicating the direction in which times were moving; but in days when there were no mass media to disseminate news, and in any case people were slow to respond to what was unfamiliar, it was a long while before the importance of events such as these was grasped and their implications fully realised. Whether from a desire to hold on to the best of both worlds or an inability to discern in which direction their true interests lay, a great number of those living in this transitional period faced the future with trepidation or hope according to their temperament, while looking back to the past for reassurance. Even the socially and politically successful, justifiably confident in their ability and good fortune, were anxious to claim ancient lineage to provide themselves with a background enhanced by tradition. This tendency is reflected in their fondness for everything relating to heraldry and the increasing busyness of the College of Arms during the period, witnessed in so many Gloucestershire manor-houses by the crop of heraldic devices in stained-glass windows, the carving of mantelpieces and the stonework of porches. However, although the attitude to change was generally

The ornate fireplace in the Oak Room at Elmore incorporating the arms of John Guise, builder of the house, and Jane Pauncefoote his wife

ambivalent, in the long run people were caught up in the tide of events and carried along by it. Where personal tastes were involved, as for instance in the matter of clothes or the furnishing of houses, the acceptance of innovations might be delayed indefinitely, but where authority demanded a speedy adjustment to new values and standards (even though an understanding of these did not necessarily follow) people were powerless to resist unless they were prepared to lose their lives in so doing. Thus the Tudor revolution in politics and the Protestant revolution in religion became *faits accomplis*.

The forces that slowly but inexorably transformed the English way of life during the sixteenth century might have taken longer to achieve results had not changes even more fundamental been affecting Europe at the same time. Thanks to the expansion of trade during the later Middle Ages which took merchants abroad in search of markets and sources of goods, England was by no means as insular or isolated as she had once been; nor, thanks to the policies of her Tudor sovereigns, was the country as able or willing to hold itself aloof from European affairs. Thus the revival of classical learning and the spread of humanist ideas, which had begun in Italy a century earlier and been carried from there into France, Germany and the Low Countries, came eventually to influence England, and in particular those people already inclined to value education, to have some degree of self-awareness and a desire to make the most of their opportunities. Among these were the gentry, now established as peaceful landowners, committed to private and public responsibilities and, while anxious to retain their links with the past, impatient with any traditional practices that might curb their ambitions. The heightened importance of the individual was one outcome of Renaissance ideas, and the widening of opportunities which political and economic developments brought in their train combined to produce a situation highly favourable to the educated, ambitious and enterprising gentleman. This explains why, during the Middle Ages, one tends to find a few names recurring in local and national affairs, whereas in the freer atmosphere of the sixteenth century new names appear in the cast list, some playing familiar roles as family men, manorial lords and public servants, others undertaking and fulfilling new commitments that arose as a result of the changing times.

Men of the sixteenth century were not aware of the Renaissance, as later generations with hindsight called the enlightening and emancipating influences that affected so much of Europe at that time; but they were conscious of widening horizons, of an urge to surmount the physical and intellectual limits imposed by medieval standards, of a power of self-determination that came from greater knowledge and experience. Scholars, and indeed all who aspired to education, seized on the New Learning with avidity and exploited its potential for material and spiritual discovery, consciously asserting themselves as individuals instead of concealing their identity behind the protective colouring of a community – be it a town, a guild or a manorial estate. Even those for whom book learning was of no interest or use began to recognize the value of basic literacy. In the past, guild regulations had required apprentices to be able to read and write: now work people of their own accord were prepared to forego the earnings of their children in favour of them first being taught to read and write, providing of course that this was possible locally. Higher up the social scale, learning – as well as a means to wordly success – soon became an integral part of gentility, socially as important as an ability to bear arms, ride or dance, since it behoved a gentleman to stand out, better than others in every way. Gone were the days when, according to Skelton, noble men

Richard Pate of Cheltenham: a local benefactor and a skilled lawyer frequently employed as a royal commissioner by Henry VIII and Elizabeth I

were able to do no more than 'hunt and blowe an horne, lepe over lakes and dykes'. 'You will bee ungentle gentelmen if you bee no schollers,' wrote Sir Philip Sidney, and a foreign observer reported: 'The stranger that entereth unto the Court of England upon the sudden, shall imagine himself to have come into some public school or the universities where many give ear to one that readeth, than into a Prince's Palace.'

It was opportune that the arrival of the New Learning coincided with both a growing desire for education and the expansion of the means to achieve this. We noted in the last chapter that some of the towns in Gloucestershire had acquired grammar schools during the fourteenth and fifteenth centuries and this process continued in the sixteenth century, even before the suppression of the monasteries and chantries gave an added impetus to the secularization of education. The personal interest of gentry and merchants led to new schools being founded in a number of other places: at Gloucester, where part of the combined fortunes of John Cooke and his wife Joan was left to finance the Crypt School; at Northleach, where by the terms of Hugh Westwood's will, dated 1559, provision was made for the establishment and staffing of a school; and at Cheltenham, where in 1574 a school bearing his name was endowed by Richard Pate, 'a very excellent and charitable man', and one of the most influential figures in county affairs at that time.

Such establishments were intended to cater for a wide range of pupils, though it was chiefly the sons of merchants and gentlemen who attended them, because even if the tuition was free, the boys had to be clothed, fed and supplied with books, candles and writing equipment which would have been beyond the means of an ordinary working family. Here, in addition to a standard education in basic skills and religious knowledge, boys were taught clear and correct speaking, and trained to mix socially and to hold their own in the community; after which they would be ready to take a step forward into either further education or responsible employment. Robert Willis, writing of his own education at the free grammar school in Gloucester, stated that 'though I were no graduate of the University, yet I had so much learning that fitted me for the places whereunto the Lord advanced me' – the places being secretary, in turn, to the Chancellor of the Exchequer, the Lord High Treasurer of England and the Lord Keeper of the Great Seal. In the foundation of all these schools, emphasis was laid on the appointment of well-qualified masters, because 'where masters achieved a reputation, there gentlemen's sons were sent'. Gentry families made use of the schools which in their turn were enhanced as a result of gentry patronage. In the event of no suitable local school being available, then a tutor might be engaged, as was William Tyndale to teach the sons of Sir John Walsh at Little Sodbury; or else the boys were sent further afield to a well-known school like Shrewsbury, Winchester, Westminster or Eton. The last seems to have been favoured by some Gloucestershire families, especially those with a more conservative attitude to religion – for example, the Pauncefoots, the Duttons and the Fettiplaces, the Gorges and the Sandys.

University and/or one of the Inns of Court was the next educational stage for a gentleman's son. Although boys who had been at Eton tended to go on to Cambridge, Oxford was more usually chosen by those whose homes were in Gloucestershire. In the sixteenth century there was no marked connection with any particular college (as there was to be with Pembroke two centuries later), but brother usually followed brother, or son a father at the same college, once a link had been established. Thus, the Hungerfords went to St John's, the Poyntzes and Estcourts to Magdalen Hall, the Tracys to Queen's and the Duttons to Exeter. Other colleges, Christchurch, Oriel and Brazenose, had entrants from the Gloucestershire families of Blomer, Huntley, Bourchier and Guise. Attendance at university only partially served an academic purpose. The average age of admission was fifteen or sixteen, the standard of tuition variable (some fathers, with foresight, provided private tutors for their sons) and, since most gentlemen students stayed only one or two years with no intention of taking a degree, study by no means monopolised their time. Classics were still regarded as of prime importance, but mathematics, languages and law were also taught, and some tutors, influenced by humanist ideas, were encouraging their students to read modern and controversial works on government and politics, whence they derived new conceptions of the state and its needs, and even solutions to its problems. Sir Philip Sidney, who embodied all the virtues that contemporary opinion deemed essential to a gentleman, wrote: 'Your purpose in being a gentleman born is to furnish yourself with the knowledge of such things as may be serviceable to your country'; and certainly though education was still a route to upward social mobility it was no longer pursued solely for private gain or self-aggrandizement.

In their free time, students seized opportunities to make the acquaintance of people who came from different parts of the country, and to establish contacts that later on might prove useful, socially or politically. The Tudor sovereigns, as well as important figures connected with government, visited Oxford and Cambridge from time to time and were entertained by university officials and students. In the course of such activities, well-spoken young men of seemly behaviour might be noticed and invited to join the retinue of a visiting personage; or, at any rate, having attracted attention, would be able to build on this at some future date. When the maintenance of a good appearance and a confident bearing constituted a potential selling-point, it was not surprising that many young men overspent on clothes, horses, hawks and hounds.

After a couple of years at university, or in a few cases straight from school or private tutoring, gentlemen's sons proceeded to one of the Inns of Court in London, primarily to become acquainted with the theory and practice of the Common Law, a necessary accomplishment for anyone destined to inherit and manage an estate and to take up responsibilities either in central government or local administration. Edward Coke, in the early seventeenth century, claimed that the Inns of Court constituted 'the most famous university for the profession of law in the world', a fact already borne out in the previous century by the increasing number of young men who went up to London to complete their education. As at university, how much they learned depended less on application and book-learning than on readiness and an ability to observe and deduce from the debates and arguments of their superiors; and, although more volumes on the law were becoming available for private use, it was legal *practice* that was of greatest concern, and indeed the fortunes of the Inns varied according to the eloquence and reputation of the exponents of law currently to be heard there. Again in common with university, a young man might expect to gain as much from the social as from the intellectual consequences of belonging to one of the Inns of Court. Members enjoyed communal dinners, acting in plays and masques, hearing and performing music together; in addition, London with its compelling interest was within easy reach, and even serious-minded students would have considered it a waste of opportunities not to exploit the pleasures available, join in public celebrations and make themselves acquainted with the latest trends. London was already becoming the hub of the nation's trade, with steadily increasing supplies of luxury goods on sale in its shops and markets. Men connected with the government or the Court, needing easy access to Westminster, were beginning to acquire houses or rent lodgings within reach, and their households were hives of activity with servants and messengers constantly coming and going, an unfailing source of novelty to the onlooker. Thus, just by being in London, young men were in the midst of a fashionable and political whirl whence they derived a sophistication and maturity that they would never have acquired at home, or in provincial towns such as Gloucester, Bristol or Tewkesbury.

Although members of the Estcourt and Brydges families went to Gray's Inn, most Gloucestershire gentlemen sent their sons to Lincoln's Inn or the Middle and Inner Temple, and in due course established family connections with them. To Lincoln's Inn went Hungerfords, Guises and Atkyns; to the Inner Temple Denys's, Duttons and Huntleys; to the Middle Temple, Georges, Overburys, Blomers and Tracys. It was expensive at all the Inns and only affluent parents could afford to send one or more of their sons there. Although the regulations forbade extravagances in dress such as velvet shoes, shirts with double cuffs and feathered caps during the hours of study, a young man might deck himself out as he pleased for social occasions, which in effect meant competing with the most fashionable of his companions. The costs of servants and service; books, lighting and heating; musical instruments, attendance at plays,

Sir Nicholas Poyntz, who had the necessary qualities and ambition to seek office at the Tudor Court and to become Esquire of the Body to Henry VII. A portrait by Holbein in the Royal Library, Windsor Castle

bull-baiting and bear-baiting; hospitality shown to friends and gaming with dice and cards; all had to be added to fees for tuition and must have involved a very considerable outlay. However, this could be regarded as an investment if the young men, on leaving the Inns, were ready to assume the responsibilities of adult life. When later some of them became justices of the peace and met at quarter sessions or the assizes, they were already acquainted, had shared the same training and been conditioned by the same influences. Those who were elected to parliament also had enough in common to give them a similarity of outlook and purpose that in the next century was to prove significant in concentrating and stiffening the opposition of the Commons to royal policy.

The accession of Henry VII in 1485, and subsequent establishment by him and his successors of firm monarchical government centred in a prestigious court, created unprecedented opportunities of advancement to any who were looking for them. The gentry for some while had shown a preference for taking service under the sovereign rather than under baronial masters, and the circumstances of the sixteenth century confirmed that this was a wise move. Politically, Tudor rule brought peace and stability to the country after the dynastic disturbances of the previous century. Economically, the encouragement and positive help given to traders and merchants boosted England's commercial expansion in Europe and her prestige at the same time. The pendulum of religious change had swung from one extreme to the other before settling into a central position towards the end of the century, but meanwhile the authority of the central government had saved the country from disastrous religious conflicts such as were currently tearing apart France, Germany and the Low Countries. Finally, as part of a policy to secure their dynasty and safeguard the country from the threat of the overmighty subject, the Tudors steadily decreased their dependence on feudal tenants-in-chief for counsel and support in government, turning instead to the gentry whose eagerness for advancement and willingness to serve made them only too ready to promise and maintain loyalty to such a useful source of favour.

'In pompous ceremonies a secret of government doth much consist.' During the sixteenth century it was widely recognised that a successful ruler needed a magnificent court to project a favourable image of himself. It served both as a stage on which he acted out his sovereign role and as a symbol of his own greatness and that of his realm. According to the occasion the court presented a domestic scene with the sovereign surrounded by his family and friends; a ceremonial set-piece, peopled by the most important and resplendent personages in the country; or a secretariat where vital government decisions were made and the initial impetus given to their execution. In all between 150 and 200 people were employed in the household departments that were concerned primarily with the sovereign's well-being, comfort and pleasure, and a proportion of these were gentry. As royal attendants – esquires of the body, gentlemen and yeomen ushers, grooms of the chamber, masters of horse – their actual duties might be light, but close contact with the sovereign gave them a personal status and potential importance as channels of approach for seekers of royal favour. Financial returns for services were not usually great or regular, but the perquisites that went with court office were considerable – foreknowledge of other appointments, grants of wardships and pensions, opportunities to give sons and nephews a start at court or to introduce daughters and nieces into a circle where they might find suitable husbands. The right education, background and bearing were essential for such appointments, especially as they involved travelling with the sovereign on royal progresses and being present on prestigious state occasions such as christenings, marriages and the reception of foreign visitors. Sir Nicholas Poyntz, whose father had entertained Henry VII at Iron Acton, was an Esquire of the Body to Henry VIII, and his son a Chamberlain of the Exchequer. Nicholas Wykes, related to the Poyntz family by marriage, served as Chamberlain to Katherine of Aragon and continued as a loyal servant of her daughter Princess Mary. Hugh Denys rose to be Chief Groom of the Chamber under Henry VII and handled much of the king's money. Sir Anthony Denny, likewise, was in charge of the Privy Purse under Henry VIII and responsible for the expenditure of large sums of money on the trappings of the king's magnificence. One of Henry's most confidential councillors, he witnessed his will and attended him on his death-bed. Later in the century, Sir Henry Jerningham and Sir John Brydges became attendants in the household of Queen Mary, and Sir William St Loe and Sir John Hungerford were similarly trusted by Elizabeth I. Sometimes advancement was furthered by a family connection and the patronage of an already established minister or favourite. Sir Nicholas Arnold, Sir Walter Denys, his brother-in-law, and Sir Giles Poole were all related to the Brydges family by marriage and owed their introduction at Court to this. The fortunes of the Kingstons and Hungerfords were enhanced considerably during the period and because of Thomas Cromwell's ascendancy. Almost invariably, young men who started their careers at Court went on to assume public responsibilities in due course as local officials and in national government, thus achieving their own ambitions at the same time as fulfilling royal expectations of some return for favours bestowed.[3]

Outside the immediate entourage of the monarch were administrative departments, such as the Chancery, the Exchequer and the royal courts of justice – all requiring secretaries and other officers; and at fairly frequent intervals special commissioners were appointed to investigate causes of unrest, promulgate a new policy or look into the conduct of local officials. Members of gentry families, with university and legal training and a knowledge of the local background, were ideal for such appointments. In Gloucestershire, as elsewhere, justices of the peace were often chosen as commissioners, but on occasion they would be joined or superseded by others if the situation so demanded. Those who collated evidence about the monasteries prior to the Dissolution were all specially appointed for the purpose from outside the county, but local people co-operated in supplying information and serving with the agents who carried out the work of destruction; the commission responsible for suppressing the chantries in Gloucestershire (1546) was entirely made up of familiar names – William Dutton, Richard Pate, Sir Anthony Hungerford and Richard Tracy. Others to whom, because of their efficiency and reliability, special tasks were entrusted included: Sir William Kingston, who was sent to York to take charge of Wolsey in 1530, and as Lieutenant of the Tower in 1536 arranged the execution of Anne Boleyn; his son Anthony who supervised the burning of Bishop Hooper at Gloucester in 1555; and Sir Henry Poole, son of Sir Giles, whose regular attendance at court proved his willingness and availability to carry out royal missions. Sir John Poyntz, Sir Henry Poole and Sir Nicholas Arnold were all members of the Council of Wales and Richard Pate of the Court of High Commission.

The concern of the Tudors for England's prestige in Europe was reflected in increasing diplomatic and commercial activity. Henry VIII's expedition in 1520 to meet Francis I of France at the Field of the Cloth of Gold was the first and perhaps the greatest of such undertakings, virtually a competition in personal accomplishments between the two sovereigns and a public display of the magnificence of their respective courts. The entire royal retinue comprised about 4,000 persons and included those of the king's household who normally ministered to his personal needs or held themselves available for other services. Of these one from Gloucestershire, Sir William Kingston, seems to have made a particularly good impression on the French: 'The Dauphin took a marvellous pleasure in young Kingston whom, after he had seen once, called him beaufils.' During the course of the century innumerable missions were sent overseas to foreign courts, to Rome and to important trade centres in Italy and the Low Countries; a gentleman with a knowledge of languages could make a valuable contribution in the retinue of an ambassador or, acting as a special envoy to carry messages, bring back replies and incidentally pick up information in the places he visited. Two of the most notable people from Gloucestershire sent overseas in the first half of the sixteenth century were Edward Fox and William Knight. The former, who came from a minor gentry family from Dursley and was educated at Eton and Cambridge, ultimately becoming Bishop of Hereford, went as an ambassador to France and Germany for Henry VIII; William Knight, educated at Winchester and Oxford, and a royal chaplain at the Field of the Cloth of Gold, carried out missions in Spain and Flanders and was entrusted with delicate negotiations in Rome at the time of Henry's divorce. As a reward for his work and to compensate for his humble birth, the king gave him a coat of arms. Knight's career well illustrates the king's avowed intention to use whom he pleased in government, regardless of their status. Other men with Gloucestershire connections who went abroad on royal business were Sir Thomas Chamberlayne, a diplomat in the Low Countries under Henry VIII and Edward VI; Thomas Leigh, a courier between London and Calais; and William Dutton who, while completing his education, was granted a passport to travel, on the grounds that he would 'prove a man meet to be hereafter employed in service for the benefit of his country.'

Although for England the sixteenth century was comparatively peaceful and the Tudors did not maintain a standing army, nevertheless skilled horsemen and fighters were much in demand, not only to take part in martial sports at Court (Anthony Kingston achieved fame through his jousting prowess in tournaments), but also to render more material aid on the occasions of Henry VIII's expeditions to France and Scotland. Sir Anthony Hungerford was knighted on the battlefield at Tournai; Sir William Denys, Sir Giles Poole, George Huntley and Sir Henry Jerningham all took their own contingents of followers to France and to Scotland. When levies had to be raised to deal with insurrections like the Pilgrimage of Grace or the Western Rising in Edward VI's reign, reliable men were needed to lead them (it was not unknown for opposing forces to throw in their lot with the rebels) and Sir William and Sir Anthony Kingston proved trustworthy in this capacity. Also, a continual supply of troops was needed to keep the peace in Ireland and, as Gloucestershire was the traditional recruiting ground for these forces, it was natural that Gloucestershire gentlemen should be put in charge of the muster. Sir Nicholas Arnold was one who both conducted the muster and took the men to Ireland, where unfortunately his soldierly qualities and knowledge of horses (he had written a treatise on horse-breeding) counted for naught against his inability to get on with colleagues, and his ruthlessness towards the native Irish. Finally, the Tower of London and other royal strongholds had to be placed in trustworthy hands. Sir William Kingston and Sir Henry Jerningham (his son-in-law) and Sir John Brydges were all Lieutenants of the Tower at different times, and the latter too was keeper of Sudeley Castle; while Sir Edward Wynter, son of the famous Elizabethan admiral, was keeper of St Briavel's Castle in the Forest of Dean.

During the course of the sixteenth century courtier-like behaviour was added, like a veneer, to the other characteristics that set apart the true gentleman from the less well-educated and less worldly experienced of his contemporaries. It is not possible to assess how many Englishmen had copies of Castiglione's *The Courtier* and deliberately modelled themselves upon its precepts. Some certainly did and their example of 'learning joined to comely behaviour' would have been influential because most ranks of Tudor society were socially imitative. Even so, growing recognition of the value of education and the extension of this to include practical skills (fencing, riding, dancing) and personal attributes (loyalty, efficiency, civility) as well as book-learning, was already producing men both useful and creditable whose employment by the sovereign set on them a public seal of approval. Gloucestershire gentry in royal service in London and elsewhere constituted a link between the county and the centre of affairs, by means of which news, fashions, ideas and values were transmitted, the status of the gentry was further consolidated, and their significance in respect of local and national affairs more widely acknowledged.

Perhaps the severest test of the strength of Tudor authority and the most demanding challenge to the loyalty of those who were benefiting from royal favour was Henry VIII's decision to end his marriage with Katherine of Aragon and seek another wife who could provide him with a son to succeed him on his throne. At the outset Henry was motivated by self-will and self-indulgence and, had Pope Clement VII agreed to a divorce, it is doubtful whether any religious changes would have taken place in England at that point. However, when the delay over the divorce proceedings drove him into a frenzy of impatience to get his own way, and this involved defying papal authority that had rarely been challenged before and never with impunity, Henry was obliged to face the possibility of excommunication and the consequent loss of his throne, unless he could be sure that he had public opinion behind him in the stance he was taking. The influence of Lollardism was still lingering in parts of the country, and the religious reform movements already under way in Europe were fuelling both anti-papal and anti-clerical feeling here (as Henry knew from the 'Supplication of the Beggars' presented to him in 1529); so any move on his part that challenged the right of a foreign potentate to override his royal authority, or the power of an establishment like the Catholic Church to make spiritual and (even more significant) financial demands of his subjects, was likely to meet with popular approval. That the divorce was accomplished, and both king and country severed from Rome with apparent ease, was a measure of the skilful handling of parliament and the clergy by Henry and his advisers, and of the willingness of a great number of people to go along with the king's carefully planned policy of 'reform'. The material benefits of a breach with Rome, the weakening of the Church's hold over their lives and the elevation of a national prince to spiritual as well as political supremacy, was all that some people desired from the situation. Those who feared and deplored the changes the king was proposing, or who would have liked even more innovations, were in a minority and, with a few notable exceptions, overawed by the legislation they were required to obey.

It was primarily the clergy who were affected by acts such as the Restraint of Appeals (1533)[4] and the Act of Supremacy (1534), though any layman involved in legal processes in the ecclesiastical courts was likely to benefit from the first (cases that were referred to Rome invariably proved long and costly) and any minister or official would have had to search his conscience before accepting the second. It was, however, the acts suppressing the lesser and greater monasteries in 1536 and 1538–39 that directly or indirectly most affected the laity, perhaps because the repercussions of these were visible and intelligible to them, whereas the doctrinal implications of the Ten Articles[5] were not. The disappearance of familiar buildings, in some cases including the church where they had attended services; the destruction of shrines which they held in reverence; the loss of sources of employment, hospitality and charity: all brought spiritual distress and social deprivation in their train; and although it is possible to overestimate the degree to which the contemporary problems of unemployment and poverty were aggravated by the Dissolution, nevertheless its unsettling effects, especially among the lower ranks of society, must be acknowledged.

Higher up the social scale the destruction of the monasteries and subsequent disposal of their estates had a markedly different effect in their sudden enhancement of the fortunes of the gentry and nobility. During the preceding century in many places, local landowners had been drawn into the affairs of monastic establishments by acting as patrons, advocates, or stewards of estates, in return for which they were allowed to lease lands which they could usefully or profitably manage along with their own estates. Although this situation had grown up without any foreknowledge of what was to happen, it did mean that gentry stewards and lessees were well aware of the value of the property that they had been overseeing or renting. The appropriation of monastic estates by the Crown and their subsequent sale made an unprecedented amount of land available and, as Henry realized, there were plenty of buyers prepared to bid highly for acres that could be added to existing holdings or form the nucleus of an estate that, for an aspirant to gentility, would set his feet on the bottom rung of the social ladder.

Initially Henry granted the monastic estates to members of his Court and Council, though evidently it was understood that these might not want to keep all they had taken on, because a licence to alienate was granted at the time of purchase. The same arrangement operated where London merchants and lawyers, presumably acting as agents, acquired considerable extents of land only to dispose of them soon afterwards. Despite widespread keenness to break into the land market, the disposal of monastic property did not involve cut-throat competition and artificially inflated prices. Some of the best estates were retained by the Crown at the time and only disposed of gradually, in later reigns. In other cases, the Crown acquired land in exchange as part of the sale transaction: thus Gloucestershire owners were able to add to their existing properties in the county by giving up land they held elsewhere, for instance, the Guises at Apsley Guise in Bedfordshire and John Pleydell at Coleshill in Berkshire. Except where Henry wanted to reward certain supporters, the initiative came from prospective buyers, knowing that the selling price would be in the region of twenty times the yearly rental value; but undoubtedly those who were already lessees of monastic holdings, and/or had ready money in hand, tended to be at an advantage. Men who were not personally

Southam Manor: inherited by Kenard de la Bere and largely rebuilt by him in the late sixteenth century with material from nearby Hailes Abbey

associated with the Court pulled strings so that they might be included in the ranks of the favoured – hence the many letters addressed to Thomas Cromwell who, as the king's vice-regent in ecclesiastical affairs, was in charge of all business connected with the Dissolution. Sir Nicholas Arnold, Sir Walter Denys and Sir William Kingston benefited in this way, also Sir Anthony Hungerford who engaged in special pleading with Cromwell to secure land for him, on the grounds that he had ten sons to provide for. Unless they chose deliberately not to do so, most of the existing holders of estates in Gloucestershire added to them at this point with the idea of making overall management easier and more efficient, and sometimes of securing extra manors that could be bestowed on younger sons who would normally not have inherited family lands.

The process of suppression began with the removal from the monasteries of valuables of all kinds – plate, tapestries, embroidered materials, jewelled relics, books – and the rendering of domestic buildings useless for future habitation. Most of the latter became quarries for local farmers and landowners bent on building new homes or improving existing ones to match their enlarged estates. In the case of Flaxley, the abbey was taken over by Sir William Kingston and incorporated into a family house. The ruins of Kingswood Abbey provided material for Nicholas Poyntz's hunting retreat at Newark. Stones and decorative sculpture were removed from Deerhurst Priory by the Cassey family who were rebuilding parts of Wightfield Manor in the 1540s. Edward Stephens used stones and glass from Bruton Priory to embellish his new house at Chavenage; Sir John Huddleston and his son-in-law Kenard De la Bere acquired tiles and panelling from Hailes Abbey when rebuilding Southam Manor. Where abbots had had residences to use as retreats, at Brockworth, Frocester, Forthampton and Stanway for example, these were taken over and used as manor-houses by the owners of newly acquired estates.

There were few complete newcomers to Gloucestershire as a result of the redistribution of land in the mid-sixteenth century; more usually, existing landowners added to what they already had. Here and there estates did pass to men with land outside the county, but usually remained of secondary importance to them. The grant of Tortworth to the Throckmortons gave them a foothold in Gloucestershire affairs, though Coughton in Warwickshire remained the core of the family estates. Sir William Petre of Ingatestone in Essex, who probably knew of their value, having been a commissioner for the dissolution of monasteries in western counties, acquired the manor of Todenham and adjoining properties, but certainly did not need more land to enhance his own importance and extend his influence. Sir Thomas Leigh was a different case. A younger son of the Legh family of High Legh in Cheshire, he had made a career for himself in London, rising from a clerkship under Sir Rowland Hill to high office in the Mercers' Guild, and finally becoming an alderman and Lord Mayor of London in 1558, at which point he was knighted. Meanwhile he had married the niece and adopted heiress of Hill, and together with Hill had purchased monastic lands at Stoneleigh in Warwickshire and at Stow-on-the-Wold in Gloucestershire. On his death Hill's share in all these estates passed to Leigh in trust for his sons, and in due course Stoneleigh was inherited by the younger Thomas, while Rowland, the elder, had Adlestrop, Longborough, Donnington, Bledington and Maugersbury. The latter was exchanged for Oddington with the Chamberlaynes in the next century, so that the Leigh holding came to comprise a continuous stretch of land between Stow and Moreton-in-Marsh, giving the family a firm foothold in the county.

There were a few yeomen like John Blomer, who bought Hatherop in 1552 and thus laid the foundation of an estate that in due course was to stretch to Eastleach, Southrop and the outskirts of Fairford, but on the whole newcomers to the *landed class* (as opposed to newcomers to *Gloucestershire*) were moneyed and professional people who had been waiting for an opportunity to raise their status. Mostly these were to be found in the towns where success in business had brought them wealth, civic appointments and public acclaim. David Atkyns, a merchant from Chepstow who bought land at Tuffley, provided his sons with a landed background as well as a good education, and the focal point of an estate that was to qualify later generations to become justices of the peace and members of the Commons and House of Lords. Richard Pate, already mentioned as a commissioner in charge of the confiscation of chantry lands, was a trained lawyer, Official Recorder for Gloucester, and a member of two Royal Councils. As well as church lands in Gloucester he bought Matson estate outside the city and built a country house there. There were also some who, in spite of aspirations to gentlemanly status, did not want to leave their familiar background and so bought what lands were available in the towns. One of these was Sir Thomas Bell, a manufacturer of caps, who acquired the site of the Blackfriars in Gloucester, adapted it as a factory where he employed 300 men and in addition built himself a house, Bell Place, pleasantly surrounded by orchards and gardens. Three-times mayor of the city and a knight, Bell was regarded with as much

Sir Thomas Leigh: who laid the foundations of estates in Warwickshire and Gloucestershire by the purchase of monastic lands at the time of the Dissolution

esteem as any landed gentleman. Richard Master, a townsman of a different kind, for he spent much of his life in London working as a physician, ended up as the owner of Cirencester Abbey lands, whereon he built a residence that was to be the home of future justices, members of parliament and other public servants.

Not perhaps particularly significant at the time, but to become so in the long run, was the transference of patronage from monastic to lay control. Before the Dissolution, it had been a common practice for laymen acting as stewards for the monks to collect tithes and transmit them to the abbeys; now the new lay owners assumed the right both to rectorial appointments and to tithes, thereby establishing the foundation of the squire–parson relationship that was to dominate rural life in the eighteenth century.

Unlike the gentry of Lincolnshire and Yorkshire who identified themselves with the risings of 1536 in opposition to the Dissolution, Gloucestershire landowners showed no inclination to prevent the destruction of local monastic establishments. Although the abbots of Tewkesbury, Evesham and Winchcombe found special reasons why their houses should not be suppressed, their protests seem to have been a formality rather than an attempt to rouse general sympathy, and certainly no local families risked incurring official disfavour by supporting them. Even the families that continued to hold conservative views of religion and remained Catholic during future reigns – Poyntz, Blomer, Poole for instance – showed no reluctance at this point to benefit from the Dissolution.

So by the middle years of the century, many old established Gloucestershire families had enhanced their prestige in the county community, achieving greater prominence in local and national life by extending their estates and thus increasing their resources and prospects for the future. Others from less prominent families, because of their education and training, had risen through royal favour to responsible, administrative posts and so improved their position socially that their sons would automatically start life at an advantage. (Office holding in itself did not necessarily confer gentility but it often did, and the title of gentleman once assumed was rarely dropped even though an office had been relinquished.) These indigenous and traditional landowners had now been joined by newcomers to their ranks, already men of means, able to bring business expertise to the management of newly acquired property, and combining ambition for themselves and their families with a commitment to public service. Those who had taken a large stake in monastic lands at the same time had assumed at least in part the territorial influence of the monks, thus reversing the medieval order where spiritual authority and values had outweighed things temporal. Members of the gentry class were now more numerous and less homogeneous than they had been, constituting a noticeable stratum in local society; beginning to merge at its upper level with the nobility whom they sought to emulate, it was still not markedly different at its lower level from the country yeomen and town merchants, many of whom were better off financially, but who – lacking estates – could not aspire to gentility.

CHAPTER FOUR

THE GOLDEN AGE OF ELIZABETH

During the first half of the sixteenth century the gentry were still moving upwards, seeking and making use of whatever opportunities occurred to speed the process. By the second half of the century some, if not all, had reached a plateau; their aim was to consolidate what they had achieved and ensure that they did not hereafter suffer any loss of favour or fortune which would endanger the prospects of their families for the future.

Although religion was no longer the dominant consideration in people's minds and the main determinant of their actions, nevertheless the changes resulting from the swings in governmental policy between the end of Henry's reign in 1547 and the accession of Elizabeth in 1558 were unsettling to all classes: a test of conscience or political acumen to the powerful; an additional and disturbing burden to humbler souls already threatened by the prevailing ills of the time – unemployment and poverty. Understanding this, Elizabeth decided that her first task must be to establish a religious régime that would be acceptable to the majority of her subjects. Members of her Council and of parliament kept her informed about the discontented minorities that her settlement created, but as long as most of the people were prepared to follow a path of moderation and give her their loyalty meanwhile, then the queen was content. The Act of Uniformity (1559) and the Thirty-Nine Articles (1571) introduced and demanded compliance with doctrines and practices that were a compromise between Roman Catholicism and extreme Protestant beliefs, but defined in such a way as to leave considerable leeway for individual interpretation; in the opening years of Elizabeth's reign at any rate, these made it possible for all who wanted peace rather than a narrowly defined religion to avoid trouble.

We noticed that at the time of the suppression of the monasteries and chantries the Gloucestershire gentry made no demur at what was happening, but acquiesced in it by aiding or serving on the commissions involved. Whatever their views on Henry VIII's breach with Rome and its implications, they had no scruples about benefiting from the destruction of the establishments with which many of them had had amicable and advantageous dealings in the past. Most seem to have been indifferent to events elsewhere also, though Sir William Kingston led a contingent of 500 men and Sir William Denys one of 60 to help suppress the Pilgrimage of Grace. During the following reign, when official policy swung to extreme Protestantism, Gloucestershire remained calm. There were no demonstrations as in Devon and Cornwall against the English Prayer Book of 1549 and, though Bishop Hooper inveighed against the 'ignorance and ungodly behaviour' of the clergy in Gloucestershire, this seems to have stemmed from a lack of ability rather than doctrinal differences and can only rarely be blamed on the religious views of patrons where appointments were now in the hands of lay inheritors of monastic estates. Sir John Brydges protected a parish priest who refused to obey the order for the removal of stone altars from the east end of the church, but this kind of situation probably did not often arise. The repeal of the Heresy Laws under Edward VI not only permitted the discussion and practice of extreme Protestantism, but also left committed Catholics free to adhere to their own faith; thus gentry living in remote country houses and employing their own chaplains were able to attend Catholic services in private, whether or not they put in public appearances at their parish church as well.

The accession of Mary in 1553 and reintroduction of Roman Catholicism, to which people were required to conform rigidly, produced a more reactionary response among the gentry than previous changes had done, but only in so far as they feared the loss of their recently acquired monastic estates. A majority found it possible, without undue qualms of conscience, to go along with official orders to abandon Protestant practices and attend orthodox Catholic services; and indeed it became clear that the destruction of symbols of the old faith had not been nearly as thorough as was assumed. From secret hiding places were brought forth missals, items of church plate, images and church furnishings, and many priests doubtless with some relief lapsed back into repeating the old Latin services, hearing confessions and celebrating the anniversaries of Catholic saints. In her household Mary already had some Gloucestershire gentlemen who now were afforded greater scope for showing their loyalty and willingness to serve, as well as complete freedom to acknowledge openly their preference for the Catholic faith. Sir Henry Jerningham was one of those who rallied to Mary's support on the death of Edward VI, raised forces in Norfolk and Suffolk (where he had estates, in addition to those in Gloucestershire) and having accompanied Mary to London was made a captain of the guard and a member of her Council. Thereafter he helped to suppress Wyatt's rebellion,[1] was entrusted with diplomatic missions to the continent and taken into the close confidence of both the queen and her husband, Philip of Spain. Sir Giles Poole was another 'safe' Catholic in attendance at Court, nominated for a place in parliament and fulfilling military duties also. Sir John Brydges, formerly Governor of Boulogne, now Constable of Sudeley Castle and described as 'one much addicted to the old religion', resisted pressures to support Lady Jane Grey and instead remained loyal to Mary; he was appointed a Groom of the Privy Chamber and Lieutenant of the Tower, in which capacity he had to undertake the safe-keeping of important prisoners such as Thomas Wyatt and the Princess Elizabeth.

By bringing pressure to bear on the sheriffs who conducted the elections and exhorting them to return men 'of the wise, grave and Catholic sort', Mary tried to ensure that members of parliament would agree to the policies closest to her heart – the return of England to the fold of the Catholic church and her own marriage with Philip of Spain. However, she failed to obtain the unanimous support she wanted. There was total opposition to the restoration of ecclesiastical property in which many members had a vested interest, and a general dislike – on patriotic grounds – of the suggestions that the queen should forego her royal supremacy over the Church and share her power over the state with a foreigner. The leader of the opposition in the Commons was Sir Anthony Kingston, a known Protestant, who both in parliament and locally in Gloucestershire organised resistance to government measures and in consequence was committed to the Tower (where he died) for 'contemptuous behaviour and great disorder'. Sir Nicholas Arnold withdrew from Mary's first parliament, was arrested for complicity in Wyatt's rebellion and deemed awkward enough to be kept in prison until the end of the reign. Sir Anthony Hungerford and Sir John St Loe as members of the Commons and justices of the peace did their best to prevent the implementation of Mary's policies and were imprisoned for this. The independence of what Mary called 'cantankerous country gentlemen' was becoming evident and obliged her to resort to measures that were unacceptable to a House of Commons becoming increasingly conscious and jealous of its power and privileges.

So when Elizabeth ascended the throne in 1558 the gentry in Gloucestershire were not as unanimous in their religious outlook as they had seemed to be under Henry VIII, but it was a measure of the success of the queen's policy that, with a few exceptions, all gave her their loyalty, and that she felt able to continue to trust in them. Whether in parliament, or locally as justices of the peace and sheriffs, the gentry chose to put their allegiance to their sovereign and the country before their religion. For Catholics, a dual loyalty to the queen in political and the Pope in spiritual matters remained possible until Elizabeth's excommunication in 1570 and the subsequent need for increasingly severe restriction on the activities of Catholics whose consciences now obliged them to put the Pope's authority above that of their sovereign. With some members of her council and the Commons agitating for more extreme Protestant features to be introduced into the Church settlement and the removal of all traces of Catholicism from the country, Elizabeth was under constant pressure to abandon her avowed preference for a middle way, and only yielded when the arrival of Mary Stuart in England gave rise to plots that threatened, not just her own life, but the safety of the country as well. The queen's reluctance to suspect disloyalty is reflected in known Catholics, such as Sir Nicholas Poyntz and Sir Anthony Hungerford, being allowed to continue in office as justices of the peace and captains of the muster; a similar trust was shown by staunch Protestant officials who exercised great discretion in dealing with neighbours and friends whom they knew to be holding, and probably practising, Catholic beliefs.

Towards the end of the reign the number of registered recusants in Gloucestershire was so low as to be suspicious, in view of how many Catholics openly declared their beliefs when laws against them were relaxed in the early years of James I's reign. A few gentlemen who could afford to had left the country during the 1570s and 1580s and gone to Rouen or Louvain, popular gathering places for Catholic refugees. Robert Poyntz, Timothy Nourse and Sir Anthony Hungerford were among these. Some chose or were obliged to remain and, except for the Pauncefootes who ultimately sold their house and estate at Hasfield, somehow weathered the increasing fines for non-attendance at church and the social restrictions imposed by the Recusancy Laws, or else reconciled their consciences with an outward conformity that kept them out of trouble. Puritanism, which represented the other extreme in religious outlook, though gaining ground in Gloucestershire during the late sixteenth century where it was popular with the merchants and craftsmen of the towns, did not appeal so much to the gentry, more perhaps because of its social than its doctrinal implications. To abandon the celebrations and customs that were an integral part of country life: to forego the pleasures and pursuits – dancing, music, drama, sports – that were essential features of gentility: to shun fashionable dress and jewellery and domestic comforts that were an indication of a man's worldly success: all or any of these would have divorced both aspiring and established gentlemen from their familiar background and sources of self-confidence. To them, the Puritans who disapproved of so much and were so fiercely outspoken in their views were as dangerous as the Catholics. The latter might defy the law and challenge the authority of the queen, but the Puritans appeared to be seeking to undermine the very foundations of the English Church, monarchy and way of life. So with considerably more zeal than when they looked for Catholic priests or harassed their Catholic neighbours, the justices of the peace were quick to break up any irregular religious meetings, prevent unlicensed preachers and teachers addressing the public, and 'search out publishers of divers shameful and infamous letters circulating in the county'. (Much Puritan propaganda was printed abroad, brought into the country and distributed by merchants and carriers, and the latest scurrilities were always available in ports such as Bristol and Gloucester and along the routes travelled by packmen.) Sir Giles Poole was particularly assiduous in reporting instances of Puritan activities to the Privy Council, no doubt because his estates included land round Cirencester, which was a hotbed of extreme Puritanism.

Political stability and the feeling of security that it engendered was the essential factor underlying the success of Elizabeth's reign. Without it normal life would have been difficult for the average citizen, and the achievements of daring seamen, enterprising merchants, gifted writers, musicians and artists, well-nigh impossible. This favourable atmosphere was largely created by sound government whose machinery Elizabeth inherited from her predecessors and proceeded to adapt to the specific needs of her own time. The trend that Henry VII and Henry VIII had started of using gentry rather than nobility whenever possible to fill responsible posts was still continuing, and indeed, without so much willing and largely unpaid help, really efficient administration could not have been achieved. At court, necessarily more ladies-in-waiting and women attendants were needed during the reigns of Mary and her sister; but in other ways as well, the character of the royal entourage changed towards the end of the century, since – after courtly graces – political wisdom and worldly experience seemed more desirable to Elizabeth than the knightly performances which had counted so much with Henry VIII. It appears also that by this time the gentry regarded it equally an honour to serve as a member of parliament or a justice of the peace as to be an official at Court. Though some might need the perquisites and favours, and enjoy the glamour that went with attendance on the sovereign, others now had well-established and profitable estates and alternative financial interests to ensure them a steady income and enable them to take on highly prestigious, even if unpaid, responsibilities.

However, there were a few Gloucestershire landowners in the queen's immediate circle. Sir Thomas Parry had become a member of Elizabeth's household during the reign of Edward VI, had been allowed to continue in attendance on her during Mary's reign, then in 1558 been knighted, granted an estate at Oakley near Cirencester and promoted to Master of the Wards and Treasurer of the Household. Later, Sir John Tracy,

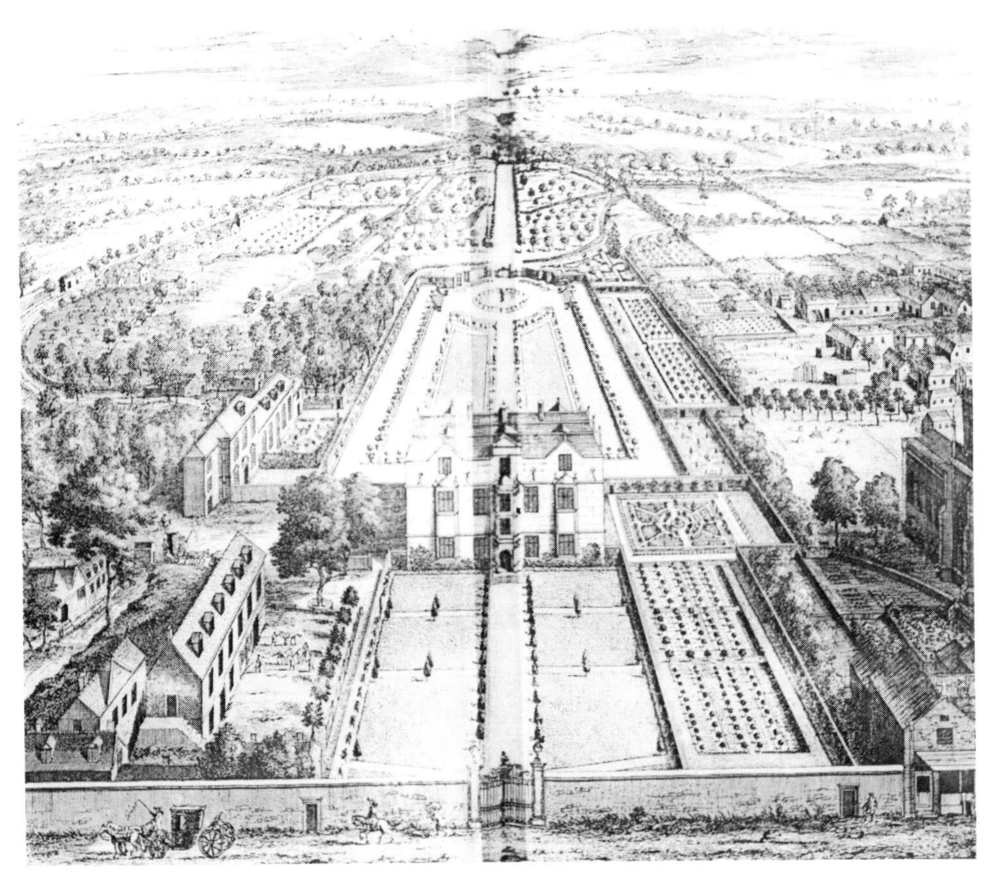

Cirencester Abbey was granted to Richard Master by Elizabeth I and was thereafter the seat of a family deeply committed to public service both locally and nationally. An engraving by J. Kip

who had fought under Essex and been introduced at Court by him, was given a post in the royal stables, not as menial an appointment as it might seem, since the stables from Henry VII's time onwards constituted one of the household departments that was directly responsible to and in touch with the sovereign. Richard Master, who studied medicine at Oxford and was admitted to the College of Physicians of 1553, became physician to Elizabeth in 1559 and continued to serve in that capacity until his death in 1588. Meanwhile he had been granted the lands of Cirencester Abbey, thereafter the centre of an estate that bestowed considerable status locally on the Master family. Sir William Wynter (of Lydney), who had survived involvement in Wyatt's rebellion, imprisonment in the Tower and a sentence of death in Mary's reign, was honoured at Elizabeth's court as an outstanding naval administrator and sea-going commander, frequently consulted on matters concerning the navy and entrusted with foreign missions. In due course his son Edward, having served an apprenticeship under Sir William, also entered the court circle and in the late 1580s, having fallen into the hands of the Spanish, became the subject of prolonged and devious negotiations on the part of the queen and William Cecil to secure his release. Though the Spaniard for whom he was exchanged was considered to be more 'valuable', his friends at the English court were genuinely anxious to have Wynter restored to them.[2]

The Privy Council was smaller after 1588 than it had been, for Elizabeth tactfully dispensed with the services of some of her sister's Catholic supporters and did not replace them; but members of this carefully chosen body continued to be the mainspring of government by ensuring the execution of policies discussed and agreed on with the queen, by using their influence in parliament to get necessary legislation passed, and directing the activities of the justices of the peace in the provinces. Except for Sir Thomas Parry no Gloucestershire men were included in the council during the reign, but some were members of two of its offshoots that extended the authority of the queen beyond the sphere of central government. The first of these was the Council in the Marches of Wales, created by Henry VIII to further the integration of Wales with England, and continued thereafter to deal with any troubles that threatened to disturb the peace of the border counties from Cheshire as far south as Worcestershire and Gloucestershire. Since potential causes of dispute most often concerned proprietorial rights, the knowledge of local people was useful and even essential in arriving at a settlement, so the council, under the presidency of the Lord Lieutenant, consisted of justices of the peace from the counties concerned: Sir Edward Wynter, Sir Nicholas Arnold, Sir John Poyntz and Richard Pate represented Gloucestershire. Ludlow was its headquarters, but the council sat in other places as well, its members making almost royal progresses to meetings and being entertained by gentry families *en route*. Its record of success reflected both the efficiency of its members and the growing tendency to resort to legal action rather than the physical assaults that had been an integral feature of life in the border counties when the seigneurial powers of the Marcher lords had been supreme. The second extension of the Privy Council – the Court of High Commission – was created in 1574 during a visit of the queen to Gloucester. It was designed to augment existing ecclesiastical courts, particularly in enforcing the laws that had had to be passed to offset the effects of the Bull of Excommunication, and to counter the growing discontent of Protestant nonconformists who were considered 'very obstinate and not obedient to the queen's majesties proceedings'. In addition to clerics, the court had a number of lay members whose local standing was likely to impress offenders, because the cases dealt with were not confined to moral lapses and neglect of duties on the part of parish priests, but included disturbances in churchyards, recusancy and claims for damages (when, for instance, an incumbent had been dispossessed). The laymen, all with legal training, included Sir Nicholas Poyntz, Sir John Tracy, Sir Giles Poole and his son Henry, Richard Baynham and Richard Pate; these attended when sessions were held in their neighbourhood or were dealing with cases of particular interest to them. Richard Pate, now a man of considerable local repute, was seemingly the most active and influential member of the court as he put in more attendances than anyone else.

Although the Privy Council and its offshoots were vital parts of the government, of even greater significance in local administration were the justices of the peace. Appointed on a temporary basis for specific purposes during the Middle Ages, the justices were turned into permanent officials by the Tudors, primarily to deal with legal business but gradually required to shoulder responsibility for all matters affecting local life, e.g., the testing of weights and measures, control of food prices, the upkeep of roads and bridges, the granting or withholding of licences to inns and strolling players, the relief of poverty and unemployment.[3] Some knowledge of the law was an essential qualification for a justice, but acquaintance with a locality and its inhabitants such as came from residing in their midst was equally desirable since his official duties would bring him into contact with all ranks of society and would demand understanding of local circumstances and an appreciation of how, as well as when, to exercise his authority. Justices of the peace were nominated by and answerable to the Privy Council, and were often summoned to London to be consulted about local affairs and to receive instructions. Thus their status was enhanced both by close association with central government and by their activities locally, and it was not surprising that there was no lack of candidates for what was a most demanding role in terms of effort, time and money. This was fortunate because, under Elizabeth, the number of justices had to be increased in proportion as their responsibilities were extended, until instead of two or three there were – in Gloucestershire anyway – as many as thirty. Whether they realised it or not, the justices were in a position to determine to what extent and with how much good grace the policy of the central government was received at local level.

The names of families that had supplied sheriffs, commissioners and royal officials in the past now appeared in the lists of justices of the peace, together with some new ones – St Loe, Leigh and Chamberlayne. Apart from the Kingstons, whose marked efficiency was coupled with an unlikeable ruthlessness, the justices, while respected as upholders of the law and general administrators and advisers, were above all local squires, familiar and neighbourly, deemed capable of finding a remedy for whatever troubles cropped up. Being human they sometimes failed, but their goodwill was seldom questioned. Fluctuations in the cloth trade resulting in unemployment, and food shortages caused by bad harvests, were serious problems during the 1590s, as was vagabondage, so that in addition to regular attendance at petty and quarter sessions, the justices were continually being called on to deal with some local crisis; and rather than appear less than efficient they dipped into their own pockets to subsidise the cost of road repairs, ease the lot of 'undeserving' poor whom they were obliged to move on to another parish, or secure stocks of food to resell at reasonable rates to local needy persons. The prototype of the eighteenth century justice whom Addison portrayed in Sir Roger de Coverley was already in existence by the end of the sixteenth century.

As in the previous century, because of their landed and knightly status, the Gloucestershire gentry were also involved in parliamentary activities. All of them, before becoming members, served as sheriffs at some point, with responsibility for conducting the elections and on occasion even determining the outcome. The shrievalty was not an office to be enjoyed. Much of its powers and privileges had been shorn away by now and only the burdens of tax collection and preparations for elections and the assizes remained. Moreover it could be an expensive experience, as a newly elected sheriff might well be saddled with making up the tax arrears of his predecessor, and during his year in office would certainly be the poorer after a visit of the assize judges. Although now and again one asked to be exempted from appointment, most aspiring gentlemen reckoned that the outgoings for the year in office were well-spent in terms of the insight gained into county politics, and when they in turn sought election they were already aquainted with their potential supporters and knew how to manipulate them to advantage. As yet it was not (as in the eighteenth century) the use of bribes and intimidation that secured a favourable result, but the calculated timing and location of the election, revealed to friends but kept secret until the last minute from rivals. In such matters the sheriff was omnipotent.

Of all appointments, membership of parliament seems to have appealed most to country landowners during the latter half of the sixteenth century. This is borne out by the large proportion of gentry in the Commons which outnumbered the combined total of royal officials, lawyers and burgesses. By training, temperament and outlook they were certainly suited to the responsibilities they had undertaken; some Gloucestershire members attended sessions for twenty and thirty years and then relinquished their seats to their sons. Sir Nicholas Arnold who was first elected in 1545 was still in the Commons in 1572; meanwhile Sir William Kingston had been succeeded by his son Arnold, Sir Giles Poole by his son Henry, Sir Nicholas Poyntz by his son John and Sir John Tracy by John Tracy II. This repetitive pattern of returns reflected the conservative nature of county society and mutual satisfaction on the part of both members and their supporters. As there were not always as many seats as there were candidates wanting them, Gloucestershire gentlemen might offer themselves as representatives for neighbouring counties or for borough seats in the county and elsewhere; their willingness to pay their own expenses was a powerful recommendation. Sir Nicholas Arnold was given a present of wine by the burgesses of Gloucester for remitting his wages while representing them; and when Giles Estcourt applied to the mayor and burgesses of Poole for the nomination of his son as their member of parliament, he undertook 'to discharge the place without any charge unto them.' On the whole, Bristol, Tewkesbury and Gloucester preferred their own burgesses as candidates (Richard Pate was returned on the strength of being Recorder of the city, not because of his estate at Matson), but Cirencester was ready to accept country gentlemen as were the new boroughs being created during Elizabeth's reign on Crown lands in Cornwall, Devon and Dorset.

We noted that even before the end of the fifteenth century a conscious concern for their country (i.e. the county) and an identity of interests was producing a coherence among members of the Commons. By the end of the sixteenth century, after many years of working together in London and Gloucestershire, this unity was much stronger. Respect was shown and support given, on an exchange basis, for each other's particular commitments, and the leadership of men of experience accepted. Sir Nicholas Arnold, who had not been an easy colleague in his early career, was looked up to as an elder statesman in the Commons during the 1570s. The widening interests of the gentry were reflected in the committee work undertaken by them in parliament and carried out by commissions in the county. Sir John Poyntz, Sir John Hungerford and Sir John Tracy (the elder) were all interested in the Gloucestershire cloth trade. Thomas Chester concerned himself with the trade of Bristol and Gloucester, and Sir William Wynter with encouraging fishing as a means of promoting shipbuilding and seamanship. Sir John Poyntz and Sir John Tracy, perhaps because of their interest in the cloth trade, also concerned themselves with the working of the Poor Law regulations and the control of food supplies and prices in times of shortages. Meanwhile Sir William Wynter and his son kept a watchful eye on developments in the Forest of Dean involving enclosures, encroachments and new mining projects, partly out of a desire to preserve the country's main source of shipbuilding timber and partly because their own estates lay in the area.

We have stressed the comparative peace and stability of the country during the sixteenth century. The few rebellions that occurred were speedily suppressed and on the whole their repercussions were limited to particular localities. An even tenor of life suited most people because it safeguarded their means of livelihood. During the first half of the century a number of Gloucestershire gentlemen took up arms to serve Henry VII and Henry VIII in expeditions abroad, but when there was a lack of such opportunities later in the century, most of them found satisfaction in more peaceful pursuits. Sir William Wynter was one of the few who revelled in excitement and took to voyages of discovery and privateering – the latter proving a lucrative calling which afforded the means to build a new house, Whitecross, on the family estate at Lydney. His son, Edward, also found it intolerable to be inactive, and wrote in 1587: 'Because I despair of any new putting again into the field this year, I am resolved to repaire with all speede to the King of Navarre who – as I hear – useth such gentlemen as come to him honourably. I am resolved to live in the wars for a time or else to travel for a year or two.'

However, when Spain declared war on England in 1588 and this country was threatened with invasion, even the most peace-loving gentlemen were ready to rally round with financial contributions and personal commitments. It was ultimately the responsibility of the Lord Lieutenant – Lord Chandos in Gloucestershire – to put the county into a state of preparedness in the event of a crisis, but the practical aspects of mustering the militia were in the hands of the justices of the peace. During an earlier emergency Sir Nicholas Poyntz and the rest of the justices were responsible for 'putting in readiness the 300 soldiers required and placing them under the command of Captain Baskerville to be conducted to London'. In 1588 Sir Nicholas, together with the younger Sir John Tracy, was actively involved again with the muster at the time of the Armada. Everyone, with the exception of the very poor, was expected to contribute, according to their means, to the cost of equipping the mustered men, so the landed gentry had considerable obligations to supply weapons and armour and most importantly, horses (every owner of a park was required by law to keep at least two mares for breeding purposes). The gentry also, because of their status, gave large sums to the Armada subsidy – £25 for the most part, as much as £50 in some cases; and while, on land, they waited in arms to repel any Spanish invaders, Sir William Wynter, his son Edward and nephew John were at sea helping to turn the Armada off course and secure an English victory. In general the Elizabethan muster has been criticized as badly equipped, poorly trained and not very well supervized, but it must be acknowledged that from the point of view of the government it was cheaper than a standing army would have been, and commanded by men used to being in a position of authority and habitually obeyed and respected. Sir Thomas Throckmorton was an exception in his blatant mismanagement of the muster and misuse of his powers over it.

During the late sixteenth century political stability, religious peace (for a majority at any rate) and national security, all combined to produce a situation favourable to comfortable living and the enjoyment of material possessions and worldly pleasures, on which those who could afford aimed to spend their money. For many of the socially ambitious, the initial period of effort was now over and a point had been reached when expenditure could be substituted for saving and display for restraint. The care with which gentry estates had been built up and their resources husbanded was already

Sir William Wynter's ship, the *Vanguard*, engaging the enemy during the campaign against the Armada. Inset: Sir William Wynter of Lydney

bearing fruit, and landowners were in a position to reveal in their standard of living the sufficiency of their means, as well as a knowledge of fashionable trends in architecture, furnishings and dress. Whereas in the past men of means had built castles or fortified manors for the protection of their families, and as a symbol of territorial rights, now they built country houses to provide a setting for their social life and administrative duties, and to reflect their aesthetic taste.

Gloucestershire had never abounded in great nobles, and during the sixteenth century only the Duke of Buckingham and the Berkeley and Brydges families represented a social superiority that was so often the object of gentry admiration and emulation. Edward Stafford, Duke of Buckingham, a proud and ambitious descendant of the Plantagenets, was disgraced in 1521 before his dream of a 'royal' castle at Thornbury had materialized; and, for lack of a successor to complete it, the half-finished building remained as a reminder of Tudor resentment of the over-mighty subject. It also was an indication of changing styles in architecture, since behind the fortified gatehouse and battlemented frontage – completely medieval in character – lay a series of state apartments, a long gallery and a privy garden that were in keeping with the residences

Sudeley Castle. Remains of the Tudor buildings where Katherine Parr lived and where Elizabeth I stayed three times during progresses in Gloucestershire

in the new fashion, for example, Richmond Palace and Hampton Court, built by Henry VII and Henry VIII. Berkeley Castle, the powerhouse of Berkeley influence in the southern half of the county, remained throughout the century a military stronghold that could not easily be altered; as times became more peaceful, however, considerations of comfort began to take precedence over those of defence, the family's quarters being made more homely and sufficiently convenient for the entertainment of the queen in 1574. Sudeley also kept its military importance, but was modified to a much greater extent than Berkeley. In 1547 it passed into the hands of Thomas Seymour, who had married Katherine Parr within a few months of Henry VIII's death and now wanted to adapt the building to accommodate the widowed queen's huge household. A number of new rooms had to be introduced, the chapel fitted out in keeping with Katherine's firmly-held Protestant beliefs and practices, and the banqueting hall enlarged. After the death of Katherine in 1548 and the disgrace and execution of her husband, Sudeley was transferred to Sir John Brydges, whose son Edmund, Lord Chandos, made further alterations, completely rebuilding the outer court to comprise guest suites and a long gallery above; and though Thomas and Katherine had never presided over regal gatherings there, the castle did in due course provide a setting for the visits of Queen Elizabeth during the lifetime of Edmund's son, Sir Giles Brydges.

It was the innovatory domestic features in the houses of their superiors that attracted the attention of the gentry who were more prepared and able to spend money for personal ends than they had been previously. Some sixteenth-century buildings have disappeared completely and others were greatly altered at later dates, but enough individual features survive to enable us to piece together a picture of a typical country house of the Elizabethan period. Each feature would contribute to the overall impression the owner wanted to convey, of a home lived in and enjoyed, simultaneously embodying new ideas, new wealth and everything suited to an energetic and expensive life-style. Gentry such as the Guise, Poyntz, Estcourt, Hungerford, Kingston and Tracy families, involved in service at Court or at any rate spending part of their time in London on parliamentary and legal business, were naturally acquainted with new building developments in the capital and Home Counties, where architectural styles imported from Europe were popular and being carried out by foreign workmen – many of them refugees from France and the Low Countries. It is unlikely that any of the latter travelled as far as Gloucestershire, but local craftsmen may well have had plans to follow, taken from the many architectural books being published at the time. They would have been expected to produce approximations to these when adding exterior and interior decoration to buildings that were basically vernacular in style.

The site of the residence of an important landowner had still to be a commanding one, even if no longer primarily for reasons of defence, and where new foundations were being laid, this was a significant factor. Stowell Park (near Fossebridge), built *c.* 1600 for Sir Robert Atkinson, Recorder of Oxford, is notable in this respect for it stands in extensive grounds above the Coln Valley with superb views in all directions. Equally noteworthy is Newark Park, the 'new work' of Sir Nicholas Poyntz, who after 1550 transformed his hunting lodge overlooking the family's deer park and the Vale of Gloucester into an elegant residence, perhaps to provide a retreat from the demands of court life. Unlike most Gloucestershire buildings of the time, Newark was not vernacular in style but owed much to court influence, not surprisingly, since four generations of the family had been in close attendance on the Tudor sovereigns and entertained both Henry VII and Elizabeth in the family home at Iron Acton. Built with stone from Kingswood Abbey, it satisfied the current fasion for symmetry, was lit by many windows, furnished with fireplaces in the principal rooms and had two upper floors consisting of single apartments for banquets – not the sumptuous feasts of medieval times, but small private gatherings for repasts of fruit, sweet dishes and cakes. Another late sixteenth-century building, aesthetically (as well as strategically) situated, was Matson House built *c.* 1575 for Richard Pate on the site of a manor that had belonged to Llanthony Priory. The house, overlooking Gloucester, was on Robinswood Hill close to the reservoir supplying water to the city (hence its importance to Charles I when he was laying siege to Gloucester in 1643); it had a gabled roof, mullioned windows and 'a multitude of chimneys' which William Harrison, in his *Description of England*, mentioned as a characteristic of Elizabethan buildings.

Having commanded attention from afar, a gentleman's house continued to impress at

Newark Park. The 'new work' of Sir Nicholas Poyntz, a hunting lodge transformed into a comfortable retreat from court life and a place to entertain friends

closer quarters. Detached gatehouses or elaborately ornate porches greeted those who arrived before them on business or pleasure bent. They were decorated with heraldic devices and coats of arms (often only recently acquired), with dates and initials that confirm who erected them and when. Builders in Gloucestershire were fortunate in having skilled masons available locally, as well as abundant supplies of stone that could be sculpted into the designs they favoured. The gateway at Shipton Moyne and the porches at Chavenage, Ablington Manor, Down Ampney and Horton Court all emphasized the importance of their owners and, although it was not built until early in the seventeenth century, the great gatehouse at Stanway House – as much Elizabethan as Jacobean in style – is perhaps the most outstanding local example of what was a typical feature of a Tudor country house.

Indoors, similar designs were used to draw attention to the new fireplaces, which dominated the rooms where they were introduced, as well as providing a hitherto unknown source of warmth therein. Pillars of marble, or of stone simulating marble, supported massive overmantels made of wood or stone with strapwork decoration, caryatids and coats of arms. Elizabethan love of pageantry came into its own here, for the carving was gilded and painted so as to be brought to life by the glow of huge log fires and the light of candles. Of the fireplaces that remain, that in the Oak Room at Elmore Court is one of the most magnificent, still retaining its colouring and the arms of the Guise and Pauncefoote families; a similarly grand fireplace at Somerford Keynes bears the arms of the Hungerfords. At Upper Swell and Chavenage, marble inlays instead of paint achieve variations in colour and point to the trouble taken by the builders to obtain unusual materials.

The other new features introduced at this time were oak staircases, leading straight out from the main hall and necessitated by the increasing number of rooms that had to be reached now that the family had their own private quarters upstairs. These stairways were serviceable rather than elegant, but their wide, shallow steps gave an air of spaciousness and dignity; and together with elaborately carved newel posts and balusters, they afforded an impressive approach to the rooms where the family lived and entertained. Such staircases can still be seen at Elmore and Whittington Court, but in many places eighteenth-century improvements led to these features being replaced by others of more elegant design and intricate structure.

Banqueting rooms, galleries and private chambers, reached by important stairways and heated from disproportionately large and elaborate fireplaces, were decorated with friezes (of dragons at Elmore, sphinxes at Upper Swell, painted designs at Iron Acton), plastered ceilings and panelled walls. Westbury Court was described as having 'a faire dining room curiously wainscotted'; the dining room at Stowell Park was also panelled; and most of the rooms at Frocester Court had 'waynscot'. Large windows, often room height, were 'well glassed' and hung with curtains; 'fair pieces of Arras' and tapestries, rare as yet, but fashionably desirable, hung on the walls. All rooms had more furniture than ever before, including massive bedsteads and chests where quilts and linen could be stored, stools and upholstered chairs, and cupboards for the display of pewter, brass and silverware. That the gentry had such possessions and valued them is evident from itemized lists in wills and inventories.[4]

As well as being family homes, gentry houses served as offices where estate and other business could be conducted. Separate rooms were often provided for a clerk and a steward to work, for workers to eat, and for produce to be processed and stored. The mention in inventories of granaries, haylofts, dairy-houses, cheese chambers, malting-rooms and brewhouses indicated that throughout the county landowners were diversifying their farming activities, combining dairying with pig-breeding on the flat, heavy soils of the Vale of Gloucester and arable farming with grazing on the slopes of the Cotswolds. It is interesting to note that before the end of the century a number of agreements had been made in Gloucestershire between landowners and their tenants whereby all parties benefited from the consolidation of holdings into enclosed plots, on which a variety of crops might be grown or livestock carefully bred and tended. In the Forest of Dean, although timber remained the prime source of wealth, iron and coal were becoming increasingly important to those who had estates there and who frowned on any intruders seeking to 'build unnecessary cabins and cottages . . . and taking this place for shelter to cloak their villanies', that is, making clearances for farming, mining and charcoal burning. Landowners' other business interests – the marketing of estate produce, investments in trading ventures, the management of urban properties in Gloucestershire towns and in London – would all have been handled by their clerks and stewards, though already when any legal issues were involved, as happened with increasing frequency, these matters would be referred to London advisers.

Finally, the gentry used their houses for entertaining friends, important acquaintances and sometimes royalty. To have money and to spend it was becoming one of the distinguishing marks of a gentleman; there was no more impressive form of expenditure than gestures of hospitality wherein material wealth could be gauged by the furnishings of rooms and tables, and culture and wit by the devices used to tempt the appetite (banquets often consisted of a succession of fanciful dishes) and to keep boredom at bay. Only nobles like the Duke of Buckingham or Lord Chandos could afford resident musicians and entertainers; but with or without the aid of professionals, there were seasonal celebrations in most households and these might be performed elsewhere as well for others' benefit. In the Gloucester Borough Records there are references to payments:

> To Master Kingstone's Players.
> To Master Arnold's Servants on May Day at the bringing in of may.
> To one that brought golden sommes from the Lord of Misrule at Highnam.[5]

Local waits and mummers would be available at Christmas and Whitsun and for celebrating family christenings, marriages and the heir's coming of age, occasions which would also provide pleasure for neighbours and dependants who were usually drawn into the feasting and revelry. Groups of professional entertainers belonging to the queen and important nobles also visited Gloucestershire. The players of Lord Dudley, Lord Hunsdon, Lord Strange and the earls of Warwick, Leicester and Sussex were there at various times in the late sixteenth century. These included actors, musicians and dancers who were grateful for opportunities to earn extra money when not needed by their employers. The open spaces of market squares or inn yards made ideal settings for performances, but the halls and courtyard approaches of country houses were equally suitable; gentlemen familiar with entertainments given at the royal court or in noble households would have appreciated opportunities of sharing similar experiences with their families and guests, the difference between these and the bucolic efforts of local talent emphasising the increasingly sophisticated tastes of men whose experience was no longer limited by parish boundaries.

Long galleries indoors, bowling alleys outside, and flower gardens with well-shaded walks provided areas for gentle exercise, and women especially must have appreciated congenial surroundings where they could indulge a liking for domestic gossip, needlework, or flowers and herbs. Many Elizabethans took an interest and pleasure in gardens. Francis Bacon reckoned that even greater skill was needed to make a garden than to build a house, and John Gerard asked: 'What greater delight is there than to behold the earth apparelled with plants?' Men who had studied at Oxford or Cambridge, visited London on business and travelled abroad were inevitably familiar with contemporary fashions in horticulture and, while not seeking to emulate the grand effects and symbolism of the gardens that surrounded Tudor palaces or prodigy houses of important courtiers, they nevertheless wanted to be up to date. So they planted flower beds, herb gardens and orchards, and added interest by terracing the ground near the house, arranging hedges and trees to provide shade and pleasing vistas, and introducing features such as dovecots and banqueting houses.[6] Although some idea of the past may be gained from the present layout of the grounds at Sudeley or Thornbury, there are few remains of the gardens that surrounded the more modest dwellings belonging to the gentry. The terraces at Upper Slaughter Manor, Snowshill and Owlpen may well resemble features of the original gardens there; and a contemporary watercolour of Chipping Campden house, built in the early seventeenth century by Sir Baptist Hicks,

Sixteenth-century ironwork: the dragon weather vane on the stables at Newark

A stone sundial found at Iron Acton, engraved with the initials of Nicholas Kratzer, Henry VIII's horologist

shows banqueting houses (the only part of the building still standing) at each end of a raised terrace. The dragon weather-vane on the roof at Newark is sixteenth-century work, and a stone sundial found at Acton Court, dated 1520 and engraved with the initials of Nicholas Kratzer, Henry VIII's horologist, is interesting on two counts: it is believed to be the earliest specimen of its kind found in England, and would seem to indicate that courtiers like those from the Poyntz family were indeed influenced by what they saw in London.

For those who enjoyed more active pursuits, hunting, hawking and fowling were available. According to Leland, 'every considerable landowner had his paled park' and Christopher Saxton's county maps of the late sixteenth century illustrated this. Certainly there was a large number of parks in Gloucestershire where deer were kept and hares could be coursed, and gentlemen without such amenities could lease hunting rights from those who did have them. Thus all might claim to fulfil Roger Ascham's requirements of their class, namely 'to ride comely . . . to shoot fairly in bow or surely in gun . . . to hawk, to hunt, to play at all pastimes used in open place containing either some fit exercise for war or some pleasant pastime for peace.' The horses needed by the gentry to fulfil their military obligations were also useful for hunting; they had dogs and hawks too, and weapons – bows and arrows at first, though fowling pieces were widely used by the end of the century. Not everyone could emulate Sir Henry Berkeley who sent abroad for horses, dogs and falcons, but most were prepared to spend considerable sums of money on acquiring them. Deer for stocking parks and animals for breeding purposes were exchanged between friends, and those who had any links with Ireland negotiated for dogs and horses to be sent from there.

From Norman times onwards hunting had been one of the chief attractions that Gloucestershire held for royalty, and during the sixteenth century this was still high on the list of entertainments offered when the Tudor sovereigns visited the county. Although all the necessary trappings of the chase had to be provided, together with elaborate alfresco meals, these must have cost far less than attempting to stage masques and plays which called for expensive costumes and ingeniously contrived effects such as might bear comparison with those offered by nobles like the Earl of Leicester for the diversion of Queen Elizabeth. Only at Berkeley and Sudeley could such productions have been afforded and only these two establishments could provide suites of rooms for accommodating the queen and her retinue. How families with adequate but not unlimited means – like the Poyntzes, the Tames, the Hungerfords and the Huntleys – were able to manage during royal visits is not recorded, and it would be interesting to know how the Tudors themselves really felt about what must have seemed rather unpretentious hospitality. Henry VII, who had expressed a dislike of fuss when he visited Gloucester in 1486, probably did not mind his quiet reception at Iron Acton by Sir Robert Poyntz. Henry VIII apparently felt so much at home with the Tames at Fairford that he bestowed a special grant of arms on John Tame, knighted the latter's son Edmund and invited him to join the royal retinue at the Field of the Cloth of Gold. Elizabeth visited Gloucestershire three times in the course of her reign and on each occasion stayed at Sudeley, where she was sumptuously entertained. Some of her other lodgings must have been much less grand and that she was reported to have spent a night 'with great humanity' at Frocester as the guest of George Huntley sounds as if there may have been some condescension on her part in accepting his hospitality.

Elizabeth Brydges, daughter of Sir Giles, painted in the dress she wore in the masque performed before Queen Elizabeth in 1589. A portrait by Hieronymus Custodis. Woburn Abbey

In their means, life-style and significance as individuals, the Gloucestershire gentry advanced considerably during the course of the sixteenth century. Education and training and an introduction to royal service and court life smoothed the rough edges of those who came from rural backgrounds. Travel to and from London, and an acquaintance with new fashions and ideas, supplied a veneer of self-confidence and the worldly experience necessary for social and business success. Involvement in local administration and governmental responsibilities brought recognition to those concerned, as important figures in local and national politics. Favourable circumstances had been seized by the enterprising and exploited to the full. In some cases marriage links with established families like the Berkeleys and Brydges, or the patronage of a public figure such as Thomas Cromwell, gave an initial impetus that helped to bridge the gap between mere local existence and life in a wider world; once the initial step had been taken, families like the Poyntzes, Kingstons, Arnolds and Hungerfords gathered their own momentum and in turn were able to extend a helping hand to others who came within their spheres of influence and activity. The century proved that older families – Guise, Tracy, Kingscote, for example – were just as likely to run their affairs competently and profit thereby as newcomers to the landowning class, whose success in other spheres had provided the means to buy gentlemanly status, as in the case of the Pates, Wynters, Leighs, and Chamberlaynes. It was also shown that without diversifying their interests or sources of revenue a family could survive, as the Kingscotes did, 'like a fixed starre'; nevertheless by the end of the century, as much perhaps for the sake of excitement as for that of gain, there were men like the Tracys, the Wynters, the Stephens and the Romneys (of Tetbury) beginning to take an interest in overseas ventures (the Levant, Muscovy and East India Companies were already in existence and commanding attention) and to invest in urban property (as opposed to acquiring more farming land) and new industrial ventures. Though ownership of land was still the prime qualification for social significance and political power, it was no longer necessarily the sole source of a family's means to maintain its status.

CHAPTER FIVE

A NEW DYNASTY AND A NEW AGE

For many, and perhaps the gentry most of all, the sixteenth century had proved stable, prosperous and progressive, bringing in its train social and political successes that – in popular estimation – were linked with the nature of Tudor rule and the trust that existed between monarchy and nation. Even in her declining years Elizabeth still fired popular imagination and inspired loyalty, and so long as she remained queen the majority of her subjects regarded her authority as indisputable. The accession of James I in 1603 ushered in, not only a new dynasty, but also a new conception of monarchy derived from the theory of the Divine Right of Kings, which was to distance the first two Stuart sovereigns from most of the people, and lead them, in time of crisis, to resort to the use of prerogative power rather than an appeal to the nation's loyalty.

Initially any successor to Elizabeth was likely to seem unsatisfactory, but James Stuart, with his Scottish accent, uncouth manners and impatient attitude to things English, was doomed to mistrust and unpopularity. Moreover, his high-handed way of dealing with problems, or alternatively of dismissing them as of no account, disinclined people to concede that few of them were of his own making, most being a legacy from the previous reign or a product of the times. Elizabeth's success as a sovereign had been the result of conscientious application and an astuteness in papering over cracks that were now too wide to be concealed, as for instance the essential impermanence of her religious settlement and an insoluble and deepening financial crisis. New developments, also outside James's control, were changing the situation in Europe, a new conception of royal service and an unprecedented spirit of self-confidence in the nation that made people more critical and independent in their attitude to authority than they had been under the Tudors. Even Charles I, who succeeded James in 1625 and who, having had an essentially English upbringing, was a more cultured and reserved person than his father, did not measure up to popular expectations. He was competent to deal with neither the financial crisis that – as a result of James's extravagance – far exceeded any the Tudors had to face, nor the frustrations of those of his subjects who found their social aspirations blocked, or whose Puritanical zeal, restrained under Elizabeth, had been brought to boiling point by James's distrust of their anti-monarchical sentiments and by Charles's own hatred of their nonconformist practices.

In addition to a new dynasty, the period between the accession of James in 1603 and the outbreak of war in 1642 brought other changes that affected the country socially and economically. The rise in population, so marked during the previous century, still continued, as did inflation, though both had passed their climax by now. For those capable of taking advantage of them, there were opportunities in the expansion of trade at home and abroad, and in new industrial enterprises which brought material benefits and a higher standard of living. However, the gap between the successful and the unfortunate was widening, so the problems of poverty, homelessness and food shortages were no less than they had been, and for people with a social conscience they caused increasing anxiety in the face of which the extravagant demands of the early Stuarts for money seemed inexplicable. For the gentry who thrived on them, the challenges of the early seventeenth century were different from those of the sixteenth and called for a different approach – considered rather than impulsive, intellectual rather than emotional. Conscious of their influential position in local and national affairs, their patriotism bound up with the idea of service to the county community, they were eager to participate in government, regarding parliament as the safeguard of liberty and the people's rights, and their own administrative roles as the mainstay of peace and stability locally. Their willingness to serve had admittedly been exploited by the Tudors, but it was recognized and rewarded as well, and they had been led to feel that it was the combined efforts of monarchy and people that had achieved success. Now the situation was changing, since as they became better acquainted with Stuart policy and principles, members of parliament and local officials began to doubt whether their own aims for the community and preferred means of achieving them were the same as those of the monarchy. But James I and Charles I, whether they acknowledged it or not, needed faithful followers to uphold and justify their actions to the nation: at critical times, a failure to convince public opinion of their good intentions not only widened the gap between monarchy and subjects, but also caused the beginning of a rift in the ranks of the gentry – some, for personal reasons and as a matter of principle, being prepared to go along with royal policy, others, seemingly influenced by the same factors, persuaded that their duty lay in opposition.

The new concept of royal service that resulted from James's accession was a two-way process. The chivalrous attitude underlying the loyalty of Elizabeth's courtiers and officials would have been irrelevant under a male sovereign; but a more attractive personality than the first Stuart king might have inspired some liking and respect, and more discerning judgement on his part created a desire in his subjects to harness their abilities to his service. As it was, very many potential supporters were alienated from the king and his court and chose to make their respective counties the scene of their social and political activities. James, for his part, made no deliberate effort to win the hearts and allegiance of his subjects – not even the nobility and gentry who might have formed a useful entourage and body of support. In his estimation, a king by Divine Right should be obeyed and served anyway and, because his authority was supreme, he saw no need to maintain close personal links with members of his council and thus with the House of Commons, or to ensure that those whom he took into his confidence were reliable and worthwhile. Though a learned theologian and an intellectual himself, James did not value literary or artistic ability in others, and culturally his court was something of a desert. His wife, Anne of Denmark, was fond of clothes, jewels and showy

Sir Thomas Overbury of Bourton-on-the-Hill. An adviser of James I who fell from favour, was imprisoned in the Tower and died there

entertainments and was responsible for establishing the tradition of court masques that in the next reign were to become one of the chief bones of contention between royal supporters and their critics. But these occasions were for courtiers alone and, as James made few progresses beyond the Home Counties, no presentations of plays, speeches, dancing and music took place in stately homes or the countryside generally, such as had entertained his Tudor predecessors and all who could crowd round to watch. Indeed, the only pleasure that James shared with his subjects was hunting, and his passion for this determined where he visited and his valuation of the hospitality offered. In view of the excellent facilities for the chase in Gloucestershire, it is surprising that he did not undertake a journey to sample them. Seemingly the south-eastern counties and Oxfordshire satisfied his needs.

Generally, the qualities that James looked for in his courtiers and counsellors were an attractive appearance, an unquestioning acceptance of his opinions and a willingness to pay obsequious homage, no matter how insincere this might be. It was men like Robert Carr, Earl of Somerset, and George Villiers (later Duke of Buckingham) who commanded the king's attention and favour; there was no place in his immediate circle for the bluff active types who had served Henry VIII, nor the accomplished and experienced gentlemen of Elizabeth's court, all of whom had expected more to be demanded of them than an outward show of seemliness and servility. In contemporary eyes, the imprisonment of Sir Walter Raleigh on a charge of treason reflected James's contempt for a brave soldier and seaman, a loyal servant of the Crown and a national hero; that Raleigh's ultimate execution was carried out at the behest of a foreign favourite at court (the Spanish ambassador, Count Gondomar) further heightened the enormity of this political blunder. Undoubtedly there were worthy souls serving the king to the best of their ability,[1] but these were not the ones singled out for attention and promotion, and the example of one Gloucestershire gentleman underlines how precarious royal favour could be. Sir Thomas Overbury, who came from a legal family owning an estate at Bourton-on-the-Hill, was a member of the Court and confidential adviser to Robert Carr until the latter proposed marriage to the Countess of Essex. Overbury, who queried the validity of the latter's divorce from the Earl of Essex, did his best to dissuade Carr from his plan, thus antagonizing both his friend and the king who, anxious to promote the cause of the lovers, had helped to secure the divorce. Overbury refused to change his views and to be removed from the scene by accepting a diplomatic post abroad, and so found himself a prisoner in the Tower where he died, poisoned, a victim of the countess's malice.

The other useful attribute for anyone with ambition at the court of James I was an ability and willingness to lend money to the king and his favourites. Even allowing that James, as a family man with an extravagant wife, an heir to prepare for kingship and a daughter to marry off, needed much greater resources than his unmarried predecessor, nevertheless his expenditure far exceeded the bounds of what seemed reasonable or could be met out of the usual sources of royal revenue. His courtiers too, because of extravagance or fluctuating fortunes, needed to be able to raise money quickly from time to time, so willing money-lenders were a godsend. Although only the very rich could afford to advance loans that might long remain unpaid, a creditor was nevertheless in a position to demand and expect favours which might be worth more to him than the actual money. The Hicks family (father Robert had been a Gloucestershire yeoman who migrated to London and became a successful mercer) had prospered under Elizabeth when Robert's eldest son Michael was appointed patronage secretary to William Cecil and member of parliament for Truro. With many contacts at Court and among the nobility, he was able to secure an entrée to the same circle for his youngest brother Baptist and to put business in his way. By the beginning of James's reign, as well as 'supplying the court with silks and rich mercery wares', Baptist was a successful banker lending money to any who needed it, including the king, whose debts to him within a few years amounted to £16,000. In letters to his brother, Baptist complained: 'I fynde Scottyshe men are fayre speakers and slow performers. Being rydde of them, I will crosse them out of my books.' All the same, his fortune was large enough to finance the purchase of an estate at Chipping Campden and the building of a house there, to buy his way into the peerage in due course and to spend large sums on charitable undertakings locally. Another family wealthy enough to oblige the king and his courtiers with loans was that of Sir William Courteen who acquired an estate in Gloucestershire at Lower Swell. The son of a Dutch Protestant refugee, and working in conjunction with his father, brother and brother-in-law, Courteen started his career as a tailor and by the early years of James's reign also had vested interests in trade with the East and West Indies, colonization and the less reputable pursuits of bullion smuggling and money-lending. With royal debts to him amounting to £200,000 it is not surprising that Courteen's questionable activities escaped official censure. A third family that received favours for having helped the king financially were the Whitmores. William, a younger son, left his home in Shropshire in the late sixteenth century to seek his fortune in London. Conscientious pursuit of the trade of a silk merchant and marriage to the daughter of a city alderman drew him into the business community and ultimately into the court circle. In 1611, in return for his services, he was granted the manor of Lower Slaughter and other estates in Gloucestershire where, in due course, his descendants were to play an influential role.

With the accession of Charles I the character of the Court changed radically. In place of undignified licence, convention and restraint prevailed, and only the well-educated, cultured and gently mannered qualified for access. Charles, being a shy person with little desire or capacity for close friendships, was determined to preserve some privacy for himself and his family, into which not even the most trusted adviser could hope to intrude. Influenced, it is said, by what he saw of rigid protocol at the Spanish Court during his abortive wooing of the Infanta in 1623, Charles hoped to run his own court along similar lines – piety, propriety and good taste being the desirable features of behaviour there. This should have inspired respect and even admiration in his subjects, but the new image had a similar effect to the old, of rousing resentment and jealousy among those who were not members of the charmed circle, and widened even further the gap between Court and country. Under James, both worthy and worthless counsellors and officials were regarded with dislike because of the sources of their favour. Under Charles it was suspicion that prevailed. Reserve could seem like secrecy, a devotion to religious duties savour of Romish practices (a fear heightened by the Catholicism of Queen Henrietta Maria) and the cultivated manners and tastes of those closest to the king, mere affectations that could be both irritating and insulting to outsiders.

Two Gloucestershire gentlemen in the king's confidence were Sir John Wynter and Endymion Porter. Both worthy of trust and of promotion, they nevertheless aroused mistrust and even dislike amongst other county landowners and those over whom they had authority. Sir John Wynter, grandson of Admiral Sir William Wynter, inherited the family home and estate of Lydney, and also the iron furnaces – fuel for which he was allowed to obtain from the Forest of Dean according to a special agreement with the Crown. Much influenced by his cousin the Marquess of Worcester whose Catholic faith he shared, he was drawn into the circle round Henrietta Maria at Court and in due course became her secretary. When the Long Parliament met in 1640, in spite of his family's reputation for patriotic service, Wynter was singled out for abuse and his removal from Court demanded on the grounds that he was 'a person of ill-fame and disaffected to the public peace and prosperity of the kingdom – a busy promoter of those mischiefs and grievances which had produced great dangers, distempers and fears.' Admittedly, some of this hatred was caused by Wynter's activities in the Forest of Dean (to be discussed below), but as other gentry landowners were involved in similar ventures, there must have been something more personal in the Commons attack – presumably jealousy of Wynter's close contacts with the king and queen, and fear of his Catholicism.

Endymion, son of Edmund Porter, a Gloucestershire landowner of Aston-sub-Edge, had been taken to Spain at the age of eighteen by his grandfather, an interpreter with the embassy of the Earl of Nottingham. During his time there, Endymion perfected his knowledge of the language, made contacts with Spanish diplomats and, most important of all, acquired a love of the arts for which Spain was the chief centre in Europe at the

Endymion Porter of Aston-sub-Edge: country gentleman, courtier and connoisseur. A portrait by William Dobson

time. On his return he took service under the Duke of Buckingham and, in view of his knowledge of Spain and Spanish, it was natural that he should be asked to accompany the duke and Prince Charles when they went to Spain in 1623 to arrange a marriage between the prince and the Infanta Maria Anna. While there, Porter became aware that the prince shared his own enthusiasm for the arts, and from then onwards he became the latter's chief adviser and agent in the creation of the royal picture collection, as well as his supporter in encouraging painters such as Van Dyck and Rubens to come to England to practise their art here. To many, patronage of the arts in any form was not only financially wasteful, but also morally reprehensible, so as Porter was making his own collection of pictures at the same time as helping the king, they were regarded as equally blameworthy. Porter's contacts with Spain had always been highly suspect in the eyes of those for whom that country still represented a threat to England in respect of trade and religion, and his acceptance of favours from the Duke of Buckingham further blackened his reputation. Yet in fact he was a family man at heart, always torn between his duties at Court and a longing to be at home with his wife and children, and the perquisites of attendance on the king were a necessary supplement to the revenue from his estate if he was to maintain his household in comfort.[2]

So it was by association rather than because of any real weakness or wickedness that many of the servants of James and Charles were condemned. To accept titles and concessions from unpopular sovereigns or their favourites (both Carr and Buckingham were lavish in their gifts to followers) roused jealousy in those not so favoured, and contempt in those who believed that, instead of being the hub of government, the Court had become a centre of frivolity while the real work of administration was being done elsewhere. By 1640, the rift between Court and country had become wide and visible, and morals were being drawn from the situation – court and city life were associated with vice while virtue prevailed in the country: 'The country hath constantly a blessing for those for whom the court hath a curse.' Clarendon even hinted that herein lay one of the causes of the Civil War:

> There was a people – who by good husbandry, clothing and other thriving arts had gotten very great fortunes: and by getting into the gentlemen's estates, were angry that they found not themselves in the same esteem and reputation with those whose estates they had.

However, in the case of the gentry in Gloucestershire, though some of the rising clothiers did indeed espouse the parliamentary cause, they had stronger reasons than mere social jealousy for doing so.

Sir John Wynter was a Catholic. Endymion Porter (mistakenly) was suspected of being one. How could anyone who had been in Spain and had friends there retain their adherence to the Church of England? But dislike of royal favourites on the grounds of their religious beliefs was, however, not so much personal as a reflection of unease and dissatisfaction with the trend of religious affairs generally. Although it could never have secured lasting and unanimous support, Elizabeth's *via media* had satisfied a majority of people in so far as it had left them considerable scope in interpreting and practising their beliefs. The restrictions that were enforced towards the end of her reign – to combat Catholic plots and muzzle Puritanical pamphleteering and preaching – only affected the extremists and even they were prepared to bide their time. They were confident that a new sovereign, especially if it were James of Scotland, could and would ameliorate their lot – the Catholics because his mother Mary, Queen of Scots, had died on account of her religious affiliations, and the Puritans in view of James having been brought up under the aegis of the Presbyterian church in Scotland, of which he was presumed to be a conforming member. James's first actions on reaching England confirmed the hopes of both factions: the Recusancy Laws against the Catholics were relaxed and the Hampton Court Conference was summoned to allow the Puritans to air their grievances. As a result his subsequent about-face was all the more difficult to accept. It was, however, inevitable that the revelation of an unprecedented number of non-church-going Catholics should fan James's terror of plots and assassination, and that the Puritans' declaration of their wish to free the English Church from royal and episcopal control should remind him unpleasantly of the humiliations he had suffered at the hands of Presbyterian elders.

Later, in spite of the Gunpowder Plot of 1605, James showed himself less adamantly opposed to the Catholics than to the Puritans. His friendship with the Spanish ambassador and attempts to influence the course of the Thirty Years War through an alliance with Spain (to be cemented by Charles's marriage with the Infanta) naturally led to discussions of toleration for Catholics in England, and a token show of leniency towards them that rearoused in many English hearts the Protestant fervour with which they had fought the Spanish war under Elizabeth. Charles's marriage to Henrietta Maria of France in 1625, and the subsequent establishment of an influential Catholic clique round her at Court, further heightened suspicions; it was not surprising therefore that the attempts of William Laud – after his appointment as Archbishop of Canterbury in 1633 – to restore 'the Beauty of Holiness' to the English Church should be interpreted as pro-Catholic and used by his Puritan opponents to fuel public fears and hatred. Certainly nothing was further from the thoughts of Charles and Laud than a reconciliation with Rome or a revival of what had been termed 'superstitious practices' at the time of the Reformation, but they did consider that an altar table decently railed in at the east end of the church, services enriched by ritual and music, and well-tended church buildings were essential to the dignity of England's established religion; it was to this end that the new Archbishop issued orders for all bishops to enforce uniform practices throughout their dioceses. Members of the court circle who attended services in the new Catholic chapel at St James's and Catholic gentry who practised their faith privately in their own homes were not affected by the reforming zeal that inspired official policy; but any congregations that had come under the influence of extreme Protestant parsons and lecturers resented interference with the way their churches were being maintained and used, and where lay patrons had been instrumental in appointing conscientious incumbents who put sermons before ritual, potential supporters of the king and his policies were lost.

It was, however, not so much the official measures in themselves that distressed people generally, as a fear that these were intended to pave the way for a return to a faith which, in the minds of patriotic Englishmen, was synonymous with foreign domination, and possibly the wholesale massacre of Protestants. Known recusants had been tolerated at any rate by their neighbours for nearly half a century, but a newly conceived belief in the existence of hundreds of *unknown* Catholics and their sympathizers led to the spread of many wild rumours of plots, and suspicion of anyone who was not prepared to condemn openly the principles and practices of the king, his courtiers and the archbishop. The wives of both James I and Charles I were practising Catholics and seemingly the foreign policy of both monarchs was concerned with achieving an alliance with France or Spain, thus making it difficult for English patriots to separate religious from political prejudices and to believe that a Catholic might still be a loyal Englishman. Recusants were not allowed to have weapons (though obliged to arm and pay a substitute to represent them in the muster); nevertheless it was believed that gentlemen like Sir John Wynter had stores of weapons in their houses and followers ready to use these against Protestants, given a signal for a general rising. However exaggerated and unfounded these rumours may have been, Puritan propaganda made it impossible for people to ignore them or reserve judgement, and many gentlemen, including those in responsible positions, whose fundamental loyalties were to the king and the established church, threw in their lot with the neighbourhood. They rejected 'innovatory practices' in religion in favour of retaining a *modus vivendi* that had been worked out over the years and constituted a familiar, undemanding background to everyday life.

In economic as in religious affairs the Gloucestershire gentry had the well-being of the county community always in mind, and because of their involvement in local affairs they were alive to current trends in agriculture and trade, and sensitive to the needs of their neighbours – be these for the control of market supplies and prices, the investigation of illicit practices, or the suppression of unrest in times of food shortages. The Tudor Council had favoured the use of benevolent despotism in attempting to deal with social and economic problems, but it had left the justices of the peace to interpret and carry out its instructions to the best of their ability. There was little the council could do if the justices proved uncooperative, so just as in judicial matters, the latter determined the nature and extent of governmental control over economic affairs. Although in their houses and standard of living generally the gentry had gradually been distancing themselves from their tenants and dependant labourers, nevertheless they still shared with the latter a common interest in the land and its potential for exploitation; they also shared with merchants and craftsmen a concern for the cloth industry in Gloucestershire, and the expansion of trade with London and overseas markets.

During the early years of the century, in spite of the recurrence of bad harvests which brought serious hardship to poor families, farming in the county was progressing. The estates of the gentry, enlarged and consolidated during the previous century and now being run with greater efficiency and profit than ever before, kept the owners' families in comfort and provided employment and a means of subsistence to many dependants; and for all surplus produce there were markets, not only in the immediate vicinity, but also in expanding towns such as Gloucester, Tewkesbury and Bristol and as far away as London. Innovatory experiments with crops and farming practices were quickly copied and even enclosures, consistently decried during the sixteenth century, were now being made by voluntary agreement among village landowners. The attempts of Charles's councillors during the 1630s to reinforce the Elizabethan statutes against depopulation and the conversions of tillage to pasture (once believed to be the inevitable consequences of enclosure) met with opposition where self-interest and the advantages of innovation had brought about a change in public opinion which was shared by the justices. When the initiative to enclose was taken by an important landowner, the result might be different. Sir William Petre in the 1590s had effected an enclosure at Todenham with the amicable cooperation of his tenants, but when Endymion Porter tried to enclose some of his land at Aston-sub-Edge, he found it impossible to get all his tenants to agree to this, although initially they had promised to do so. However, it is feasible that Porter's activities, like those of Sir John Wynter in the Forest of Dean, roused resentment not so much because of any inherent disadvantage therein, but because they were being carried out by a royal favourite.

Charles's Council was also unable to get its own way over the banning of tobacco-growing in Gloucestershire. This had been started during the 1620s in several areas, but chiefly round Winchcombe and Cheltenham, to satisfy local needs more cheaply than imported supplies could do. Though the amount grown must have been small, even this slight infringement of the Virginia Company's monopoly was considered reprehensible and, when local magistrates failed to carry out orders to stop it, troops were sent to uproot the crops. To what extent the gentry were involved in growing the forbidden plant is not known, but they certainly sympathized with those who were doing so and the solidarity of local opposition caused astonishment in London:

> We could not have believed that after so many commands of his Royal Majesty any man could have presumed to have planted or maintained any English tobacco, until we have lately been informed that in the county of Gloucester there is great quantity of tobacco planted and continued, contrary to these strict prohibitions.[3]

More often than not, the efforts of landowners to improve the output of their estates by whatever means were recognized and accepted as generally advantageous. However, a hostile reaction usually met any attempts to exploit the land for purposes other than agriculture and to ignore communal rights in doing so. The timber, iron and coal in the Forest of Dean had long been a source of income to landowners and to small communities of miners, charcoal-burners and the like living in the area, some of whom claimed customary rights to settle, make clearances for farming and dig for coal wherever they liked. Thus royal concessions to landowners such as Sir John Wynter and Sir Baynham Throckmorton, which allowed the enclosure and subsequent use of land for mining and tree-felling, led to immediate and violent protests. The Coleford riots of 1631 against enclosures and proprietary mining involved between 500 and 3,000 persons, armed with guns and pikes, who 'in a warlike manner with sound of drums and ensigns displayed' entered the forest, broke open enclosures, burned houses and filled up ditches and coalpits. Their ringleader was described as a 'professional rioter', so presumably there had been other occasions when his services were called on and, since by 1640 Sir John Wynter had acquired most of the land in the forest, it was probably only the outbreak of war that prevented further serious protests against him and other receivers of royal concessions.

The spinning and weaving of wool and the sale of woollen cloth had been important sources of employment and wealth in Gloucestershire for many centuries and the first two had become an indispensable adjunct to farming as a source of revenue during the winter months and hard times; the money earned thereby could make all the difference between subsistence and destitution. Justices of the peace, responsible for administering the Poor Law, were only too well aware of the importance of rural industry. They were therefore anxious to mitigate the effects of fluctuations in the cloth trade, in which a slump immediately led to cottage workers being laid off with consequent heavy demands for relief out of the local rates. However, the first three decades of the seventeenth century were adverse for the clothiers because war in Europe was seriously interfering with the usual channels of trade and neither James I nor Charles I took the same interest in commercial affairs as the Tudors had done. Indeed the clothiers blamed their falling sales on the monopolistic control of the Merchant Adventurers over the export of cloth and on the government for upholding this, and it is not surprising therefore that any official move – even if well-intentioned – was regarded with suspicion. During the 1620s and 1630s the Royal Council, at the instigation of the Merchant Adventurers, tried to push up the sales of cloth by insisting on the stricter enforcement of regulations concerning the quality of goods being produced. The appointment of special commissioners to this end proved abortive as the clothiers believed that only by cutting costs of production (and thus prices) through the evasion of statutory regulations could sales be increased. They were supported in their attitude by local justices of the peace and in particular by Nathaniel Stephens, who was so persistent in his obstruction of the commissioners that in the end he was prosecuted for his conduct in the Court of Star Chamber.

Other orders of the Council, more particularly concerned with the prevention of unemployment and popular unrest in the clothing districts, were similarly opposed by the justices in support of the clothiers, on the grounds that the latter could not be expected 'to prevent mutinies by employing their people a month longer . . . without the sale of their cloths'. Again, when in 1630, because of a food shortage and the careful monitoring of supplies, the clothiers were accused of using oatmeal to thicken their cloth, the justices quickly leapt to their defence, informing the Council that 'the greatest clothiers protest they have not used a peck of oatmeal in a week and most of them, none.' Although as yet there were no clothiers among the Gloucestershire gentry, some of the latter had a vested interest in the cloth trade as suppliers of wool, owners of fulling mills and landlords of spinners and weavers, and their sympathy with the clothiers was whole-hearted. However, this did not shake the popular conviction that Charles and his advisers were ultimately responsible for the clothiers' misfortunes, so at the outbreak of war, though some of the justices who had befriended them espoused the king's cause, it was reported from Painswick: 'There is scarcely one of all these clothiers but have both lent money and do maintain soldiers upon their own charge *against* His Majesty.'

In respect of the economic situation, local authorities were more knowledgeable and perceptive than the bureaucrats at Whitehall and, as long as they were left to execute the law and conciliar orders at their discretion, they found it possible to reconcile local interests with their official commitments and loyalties. But when they were saddled with fiscal responsibilities, their position was quite different and they found themselves faced with an insoluble dilemma – as to whether they could and should serve the king if this meant losing the respect and trust of their neighbours, and repudiating their own conception of and reverence for the law. Believing in parliament as the ultimate safeguard of the nation's liberties and the supremacy of the law, they found it difficult to subscribe to the collection of irregular impositions that were demanded by the king to obviate the need for parliamentary subsidies.

The first challenge of this kind came in 1626–7 when Charles ordered the collection of a Forced Loan from all those liable for a parliamentary subsidy together with others deemed able to pay. As no one supposed the money would ever be repaid, this was virtually the same as a subsidy except that it was assessed at five times the usual rate. In Gloucestershire the justices of the peace were deputed to collect the money. A number of these – John Dutton, Nathaniel Stephens, Sir Robert Poyntz and Henry Poole for instance – refused both to levy the imposition and to pay it themselves, and the first two were imprisoned for this; some, like John George of Cirencester, paid their own contribution but dragged their feet over making demands of others. In the end, a proportion, but not the whole, of the hoped-for amount was realized, though recalcitrants were threatened with being conscripted or having soldiers billeted on them. It was noticeable, however, that these penalties were not imposed on the gentry, presumably for fear of antagonizing even further such an influential class.

Another method of raising money – Distraint of Knighthood – was tried out a few years after Charles's accession. It was usual for as many gentlemen as possible to attend the coronation of a new sovereign and for those suitably qualified, but as yet untitled, to be knighted at this time. It was not surprising that from as far away as Gloucestershire some chose not to attend and, in view of the services required of men of knightly status, that some should deliberately seek to avoid the honour. Nevertheless in 1630 commissioners were appointed to investigate the means of estate owners, and those who were found to have had land worth £40 a year or more at the time of the coronation and to have been absent from the ceremony were fined. Thomas Daunt of Owlpen had to pay £10, rather less than if he had been a justice of the peace, and definitely less than a knighthood would have cost him.

Knighthood fines once imposed could not be repeated. Ship Money was a different matter. The first levy, ordered in 1634, was received quietly in Gloucestershire because both Gloucester and Tewkesbury had subscribed to the tax on previous occasions; this was despite the fact that, strictly speaking, being river ports, they were inland rather than examples of the coastal places expected, by means of the levy, to finance the building of ships for protection against piratical attacks. Three subsequent levies in 1635, 1636 and 1637, which fell on the whole county, ran into trouble, partly because of complaints about the assessment (which was in fact fairer, though it ran contrary to traditional assessments for subsidies) and partly because the deputy lords-lieutenant and justices of the peace refused to cooperate with the sheriffs ordered to make the collection, thus setting an example for others to follow. Edward Stephens lost his shrievalty and Nathaniel Stephens and Henry Poole were removed from their offices as justices for refusing to pay the levy. A few, like William Leigh, felt they had an obligation to try to carry out the collection even against overwhelming odds, but by 1638 (in spite of the judgment in favour of the king in the test case against John Hampden in 1637) there was such serious and widespread opposition throughout the county that even the most conscientious officials had to admit defeat. Indeed they had reached a point where the interests and well-being of the county community overrode personal considerations of loyalty to the government. When in 1639 a last attempt to raise a non-parliamentary levy was made by the king to help finance the war against the Scots, a collection in Gloucestershire was totally impossible because no one was willing to act as either an assessor or a collector.

In 1640 Charles was obliged to summon his first parliament since 1629. During the interval he had ruled with the help of his ministers and the Royal Council, but an insufficient revenue and the gradual withdrawal of cooperation by local officials was already hampering administration when the threat of invasion by the Scots (to secure the right to practise their Presbyterian faith) created a financial crisis that could only be solved by parliamentary help. In view of the circumstances the king expected the representatives of his English subjects to rally to his support, but he failed to realize just how much opposition some of his policies had aroused, and to what extent the loyalty of the trained lawyers and experienced local officials, who made up the Commons, had been strained. It was to be expected that in the towns in Gloucestershire, where Puritanism was strong and where attempts to regulate the cloth trade had been most keenly felt, public opinion should be against the king, and burgess members were indeed strong supporters of the parliamentary opposition. That gentry members should also take an opposing stand was more surprising, and an indication of how much policies that ran counter to local feelings had been resented. Because of his legal training and previous parliamentary experience, John George, who had property in Cirencester, Baunton and London and court connections through holding office as Clerk of the Wardrobe, took particular exception to irregular financial levies and was returned for Cirencester to represent this view. The successful candidates for Tewkesbury were both gentry from outside the borough and strongly parliamentarian in sympathy. Edward Stephens, already mentioned for his opposition to Ship Money, was a landowner of Chipping Sodbury and, as a sheriff, justice of the peace and captain of the Trained Band, an active participant in county affairs; Sir Robert Cooke of Highnam, a receiver at the Court of Wards and a man of considerable means and status in both London and Gloucestershire, was also committed to opposing the king. Gloucester city too elected a landowner for one of its members: Henry Brett of Hatherley. With estates in the county and town properties in London, a position in the office of the Lord Chancellor, marriage connections with the latter and with the Duke of Buckingham, Brett was nevertheless as critical of royal policy as his fellow burgess member Thomas Pury, the self-made lawyer and fanatical devotee of city interests, whose 'custom of sitting in church with his head covered endeared him to the Puritans'.

Even more surprisingly, the knights of the shire were also parliamentary supporters. Throughout the years of the king's personal rule, Nathaniel Stephens had been noted for his firm rejection of the policies he had been expected to implement as a justice of the peace. A prosperous landowner (his family had become wealthy through sheep-farming), he had many friends among the clothiers of the south Cotswolds and the Puritans of the clothing towns, and seems to have had more in common with them than with other landed gentlemen, some of whom strongly disapproved of him. Indeed, during the election Sir Robert Tracy, whose family was traditionally loyal to the monarchy, entered the contest and threw all the weight of his influence against Stephens. 'Apprehensive of foul dealing and undermining practices and having the advantage of the Sheriff's power (who is a relative) Tracy not only put back divers of Stephens' voices, but adjourned the court and continued the election at Winchcombe, conveniently situated for his own, but inconvenient for the repair of Mr Stephens' supporters!' Nevertheless the latter prevailed, in spite of being no better than 'a pack of deprived, silenced or puritanically affected clergymen'. The other knight of the shire was John Dutton of Sherborne. A close friend of Endymion Porter and a frequenter of the royal Court where his brother Ralph was a gentleman of the Privy Chamber, Dutton held independent views and was no blind supporter of the king's policies. Inclined to Puritanism and a firm opponent of unconstitutional practices, the trend of his sympathies was necessarily significant in the county where his great wealth and local influence marked him out as a person of importance.

Of the elected members for Gloucestershire constituencies this left but one gentleman who entered the Commons committed to upholding the king's cause, namely Sir Theobald Gorges of Cirencester. A trained lawyer concerned with the issue of Chancery writs and an Usher of the Privy Chamber, his interests were divided between London and his country estate, but his marriage into the Poole family of Sapperton drew him into a section of local gentry society that was strongly anti-Puritan. Whether through indifference or positive disinclination, Gorges was frequently absent from parliament and so made little contribution to the royalist cause.[4]

In 1640 therefore, to judge by its members, it would have appeared that Gloucestershire was an area almost totally committed to opposition and to a political campaign designed to remove the king's unpopular ministers, put a stop to arbitrary policies and introduce safeguards against future ventures into non-parliamentary and unpopular government. But in the two years that were to elapse before the outbreak of civil war in 1642, some of the members began to have second thoughts about the implications of opposition that threatened to go much further. John Dutton, like Sir Theobald Gorges, absented himself from the Commons on numerous occasions until, two years later, in 1644, he was voted out of his seat. John George and Henry Brett similarly detached themselves from active attacks on the king's policy. The recognition of the ultimate ends of the more extreme parliamentary members drew a majority of the landed gentry together once more to defend what they considered to be the traditional principles of life in their community. Whereas in the 1630s the king had been accused of innovatory policies, now it was his opponents who were considered revolutionary and a threat to those accepted pillars of English society – the monarchy and the established Church. Only the more confident and committed parliamentary men and Puritans were prepared to take opposition to the lengths of armed hostilities in pursuit of their aims, namely a dis-established, non-episcopal church and a form of government in which the king would be without any practical power at all. The remainder, naively as it turned out, still hoped that counsels of moderation would prevail to turn the country back from the brink of war.

CHAPTER SIX

A CLASS DIVIDED BY WAR

Although Gloucestershire was affected directly by only four main events during the course of the Civil Wars – the siege of Gloucester (1643), the capture of Bristol (1645), the battle of Stow-on-the-Wold (1646) and the flight of the royalist troops from Worcester (1651) – nevertheless throughout the years of military activity the county suffered from the passage of armies belonging to both sides; attempts to subdue and hold strategic points like Cirencester and Tewkesbury; and frequent skirmishes in the vicinity of country houses, from which quite small garrisons were able to operate, terrifying those who lived in the area, friend and foe alike.

There were military and economic reasons why both the king's supporters and the Parliamentarians were anxious to control the county. In the early stages of the war the Royalists could count on support in the south-western counties, Wales and parts of the Midlands, and it was vital that they should maintain contacts between these areas and keep them linked to the king's headquarters at Oxford. To their opponents it was equally vital to sever these lines of communication and to isolate royalist areas as a first step to subduing them. Some of the towns in Gloucestershire, as well as straddling main roads, also controlled river crossings – Lechlade, Cirencester, Gloucester and Tewkesbury for example – and this constituted an additional reason for wanting to occupy them. The county also had important ports: Bristol with a considerable volume of sea-going trade and links with Europe; Gloucester, having coastal links with other Severn ports and South Wales; Tewkesbury, controlling the river routes along the Severn into Wales and the Avon to the Midlands. Traditionally Gloucestershire was the area for recruiting men and assembling supplies for Ireland, with administrative machinery geared to this. Moreover it was an area dotted with country houses capable of being garrisoned, and where there were stores of weapons and food. And, most important of all perhaps, was the fact that in spite of the decline in the cloth trade the county was a prosperous area with well-stocked farms, resources of raw materials – leather, timber, iron, coal – and a number of established market centres that normally satisfied the domestic and industrial needs of local people and buyers from further afield. 'We are credibly informed that at Cirencester, Stroud, Minchinhampton, Tetbury, Dursley, Wootton and Chipping Sodbury, great quantities of cloth, canvas and locherame are to be had for supplying the great necessities our soldiers have of suits,' wrote the king to

Matson House. The home of the Selwyn family used by Charles I as his headquarters during the siege of Gloucester

his nephew Prince Rupert in 1643. And from his base at Matson House during the siege of Gloucester, he sent to Sir Baynham Throckmorton in the Forest of Dean for timber, coal, twenty small boats, 'forty miners to repair our train of artillery and a smith with an anvil, bellows and fitting instruments to work'. As he had failed to secure valuable arsenals in London, Portsmouth and Hull, the smiths and forges in the Forest of Dean were vital to Charles for keeping his troops supplied with cannon, ammunition, pikes and swords.[1]

In 1642, when the proceedings of the Long Parliament had been halted abruptly by Charles's attempt to arrest the five leaders of the opposition in the Commons, war was neither expected nor wanted. Those most closely involved in the quarrels that had arisen between the king and Parliament still believed that a political settlement might be reached, and meanwhile, along with the remainder of the country, they were prepared to sit back and wait on events. To everyone, rich and poor alike, the security of their local community and traditions was of prime importance and only when this seemed threatened could people be persuaded to take up arms and fight. As time went on, neutrality, especially in persons of consequence, began to be considered an evasion of responsibility and, as each side sought to recruit support, propaganda was especially designed to shame people into action; the gentry, now established as natural leaders in county affairs, consequently came under the greatest pressure. Christopher Guise removed himself to London, 'finding it very difficult to stay in the country and not engage myselfe in some party which I did not like.'[2] Those with puritanical ideas were exhorted to do the work of the Lord by taking up arms against 'that garbage of the land made up of Jesuits and Papists and Atheists – with that bloody and butcherly generation commonly known by the name of Cavaliers'; while the king tried to persuade his followers that to be called Cavaliers or Royalists was no disgrace since such names signified 'a gentleman serving his King on horseback . . . daring to adventure all for the eternal reward of a justly acquired honour'. However, there is no doubt that even when they had searched their hearts and decided on a particular line of action, many men on both sides abandoned their neutrality with reluctance and regretted the duties forced upon them. William Waller, one of the parliamentary commanders in Gloucestershire, in a letter to his friend Sir Ralph Hopton fighting on the opposite side, summed up their dilemma:

> That great God, which is the searcher of my heart, knows in what a sad sense I go on this service and with what a perfect hatred I detest this war without an enemy; but I look upon it as the work of God which is enough to silence all passion in me. We are both upon the stage and must act those parts that are assigned to us in this tragedy.[3]

To whichever side they gave it, the support of the gentry was invaluable. Their background, education, training and experience fostered powers of leadership; moreover, all had learned to ride, been trained in the use of arms and become accustomed to an outdoor life while looking after their estates, travelling to the county town or to London on business, or amusing themselves in hunting and other sports. Some had already done military service abroad or in Ireland, or at any rate been involved in summoning and drilling the muster; while others in their capacity as justices of the peace, sheriffs and deputy lords-lieutenant were used to exercising authority and expecting obedience. The barns and stables on their estates were filled with grain, cattle and horses; those with trade interests had stocks of wool, leather and cloth; and holders of property in the Forest of Dean controlled supplies of iron, coal and timber there. Above all, at a time when, except for the main roads, travel had to be across open country via unsignposted tracks, the gentry's knowledge of their own and their neighbours' estates, and their connections with tenants and local workers, gave them a fund of inside information that was indispensable when it came to recruiting support and making use of the terrain during surprise attacks on the enemy.

As there was no standing army in the country at the outbreak of war in 1642, both the king and his opponents realised the importance of gaining control, as quickly as possible, of the militia men in each county and whatever arms were kept in store for their use. The king's Commission of Array and Parliament's Militia Ordinance met with mixed receptions according to the trend of local sympathies; Lord Chandos, Lord-Lieutenant of Gloucestershire, for instance, was prevented from reading the Royal Commission in Cirencester and narrowly escaped with his life at the hands of the irate townspeople. On the whole though, from whichever side the appeal came, the militia men were reluctant to respond, and much more successful were the efforts of individual landowners who used their influence to persuade tenants and neighbours to join them in

Hidcote House. The home of Hastings Keyt, a Royalist killed in battle. A pen and ink drawing by Miss M.S. Smith

defensive measures. Members of parliament left Westminster and returned home to do likewise. In Cirencester, Gloucester and Tewkesbury there was already enthusiastic support for the parliamentary cause, and for the time being their respective members assumed authority for organising the townsfolk into a state of readiness to defend their homes and neighbourhood. The avowed Royalist, Sir Theobald Gorges, seems to have distanced himself from affairs in Cirencester at this point. Meanwhile, out in the country, without openly aligning themselves with either side, the gentry were putting their houses into a state of readiness for a war they did not want and the ultimate consequences of which no one could have foreseen at this juncture. Valuable plate and jewels were stowed away, arms brought out and refurbished, and stores of food and household necessities measured against future needs. Where it was possible to strengthen houses against attack, this was done; remaining medieval features like moats, gatehouses, battlemented roofs and shuttered windows – little valued during the 'great rebuilding' of the sixteenth century – now came into their own again, but the comfortable new homes that were in fashion under Elizabeth revealed their shortcomings as strongholds. Contemporary lists of garrisons included almost every country house of any size and indicate that household servants and dependant tenants must have been conscripted into this service.

As pressure on the gentry mounted to commit themselves to one side or the other, some left their homes and families to take an active part in the fighting. Along with many others, Endymion Porter, Noel, son and heir of Sir Baptist Hicks, Sir Edward Bray (of Barrington) and William Chadwell (of Broadwell) joined the king at his headquarters in Oxford. So did John Dutton, though he claimed later that 'he was compelled to adhere to the party there for the preservation of his house and estate.' Others, with attendant groups of servants and dependants, while preferring to remain in the county, were ready to join royalist forces in action there, for example, at the storming of Cirencester and siege of Gloucester; Sir Edward Hale, Sir Humphrey Tracy, William Cooke and Sir Robert Poyntz were among these. Sir John Wynter, 'the scourge of the Forest', was a lone campaigner. He turned his house at Lydney into a base for operations, and used it to maintain his hold over the Forest of Dean and to neutralize the attempts of Edward Massey from Gloucester to bring the whole of the Severn Valley between Gloucester and Tewkesbury under parliamentary control. Sir Baynham Throckmorton of Clearwell led a company of horse, some of them his own followers, actively supporting other royalist forces in the border country round Worcester. John Keyte of Ebrington, at his own expense, raised a company to fight for the king's cause in the north Cotswolds. His two brothers likewise were Royalists and the younger one, Hastings, lost his life while serving under Sir Jacob Astley in the battle of Stow. On the parliamentary side, Sir Robert Cooke, Thomas Hodges, Edward Stephens and John George opted for service in the field, actively encouraging resistance in the towns where they were known and respected, and endeavouring to wipe out country-house garrisons that were a constant source of irritation and harassment to parliamentary troops operating in the county. Nathaniel Stephens made a stronghold of his house at Chavenage, and frequently joined Massey in sorties from Gloucester aimed at capturing royalist bases like Beverston and Sudeley. Richard Aylworth, from his family estate on the outskirts of Naunton, kept watch over the approaches to Stow-on-the-Wold and interrupted the passage of royalist troops along these. Richard Deane of Temple Guiting, who joined the parliamentarian forces under Essex at the siege of Gloucester, rapidly became an artillery expert and started on a meteoric rise to authority in both the New Model Army and the Commonwealth Navy.[4]

Nor must the women's efforts be overlooked. The wives of men away from home were necessarily left to take responsibility for the management of estates and the defence of houses and their occupants – no mean task as increasing numbers of troops of both sides became involved in marches and counter-marches throughout the country, all needing shelter from time to time and some bent on provocation and plunder. If a husband died – as, for instance, Sir Robert Cooke and Sir Edward Hale – then the family and household might well become a target for predators from both sides. A husband taken prisoner would be released if he was prepared to compound for his 'delinquency' and promise to withdraw from the fighting, but only then could he return home. Some, rather than remain inactive, fled abroad and became an added charge on already overburdened estates. Any recorded incidents indicate that wives were ready and able to face the demands made of them. Lady Wynter, threatened with fire and sword if she did not surrender Lydney to Edward Massey, rejected assurances of 'good usage and protection' and defied her attacker with 'a courage answerable to the undertakings of her husband':

> Sir: Mr Wynter's unalterable allegiance to his King and sovereign, and his particular interest in this

> place, hath by His Majesty's commission put it into this condition which cannot be pernicious to any but to such as oppose the one and invade the other; wherefore rest assured that in these relations we are by God's assistance resolved to maintain it, all extremities notwithstanding. Thus much, in Mr Wynter's absence, you shall receive from Mary Wynter.[5]

The wife of Sir William Guise, left alone at Elmore when her husband fled to Wales to escape the attentions of Massey, was beset by a parliamentarian troop from Gloucester. Finding that they were going to be refused entry, the latter pretended to be followers of Prince Rupert and demanded food and shelter. While Lady Guise was still hesitating, some scouts went round the back of the house, discovered the kitchen door open, entered and, in spite of the efforts of the household to resist them, took away what money, plate and useful commodities they could lay hands on. Lady Guise's vehement protests about the episode led in due course to Massey ordering that the property should be returned.

Another woman who had responsibility thrust on her was the wife of Sir Robert Cooke. Because of his parliamentarian sympathies Cooke received too much attention from royalist troops in his home at Highnam, and so left with his wife and family to take up residence in Gloucester. Shortly afterwards he died, and his widow petitioned 'to be exonerated from rates and taxes and asked for the payment of her husband's arrears'. These requests were refused and she was obliged to vacate the house in Gloucester and live in want until her eldest son – a known Royalist – changed sides and paid a fine to recover the estate. More fortunate than any of the foregoing was the widow of Sir William Leigh of Longborough and Adlestrop who, during the imprisonment of her son and heir, assumed responsibility for managing the family estates. In her house at Longborough, Lady Leigh sheltered and entertained any passing Royalists, from whom she eagerly demanded news of the king's fortunes. If none came to Longborough she would send her servants down to the Fosseway to pick up reports from travellers there. Although she was an extremely formidable woman, it was probably not this fact so much as the distance of her household from frequented roads that enabled her to continue unmolested in her overt Royalism throughout the war.[6]

The plight of Lady Cooke highlights one of the problems that arose in some families when the menfolk chose sides but not always the same one. That father and son, or two brothers, might have different loyalties indicated how deeply they felt about the issues at stake. In spite of Sir Robert Cooke's whole-hearted support of Parliament and of Edward Massey in Gloucester, the family was denied sympathy and consideration because of his son's loyalty to the king. How readily in the end William Cooke made his peace with Parliament is not recorded, but the pressures to do so must have been considerable with his widowed mother and the rest of the family homeless and virtually penniless until some revenue from the Cooke estates was restored to them. William Chadwell of Broadwell, a member for a Cornish borough, supported the king in parliament until 1642 and joined the latter at Oxford when hostilities started. He acted against the wishes of his father who was 'in displeasure with him for his delinquency' and much aggrieved when his son's behaviour had to be compounded for, later. In this case both father and son stuck unwaveringly to their principles and would not be reconciled. A similar situation obtained in the Kingscote family where father Anthony, a strict Puritan, was so outraged as to list in his will the sins of his son and heir

Highnam Court: home of the Cooke family. Badly damaged during the course of the wars, the house was rebuilt by William Cooke during the 1650s in the style of Inigo Jones

Christopher who 'stood ill affected . . . and did adheere to the popish Army, the enemies of God, his Church and this Nation,' that is, he supported the royalist cause.

In the Whitmore family, Sir George (with property in London and an estate at Lower Slaughter) was an ardent Royalist. While Lord Mayor of London (1631–2) he had entertained Charles and thereafter lent him considerable sums of money. At the outbreak of war he was imprisoned for his loyalty and his property sequestrated; at his death in 1645, his son Richard inherited debts and an encumbered estate for which he was obliged to compound in spite of being 'well affected to Parliament'. Another case of the 'sins' of the father being visited on the son was that of Sir William Guise, who, though a Royalist at heart, by trying to remain neutral in the struggle and thus save his family from attack, only succeeded in intensifying the wrath of both sides against him. His son and heir Christopher, who also had avoided declaring his loyalties at the outset, openly espoused Parliament in due course, yet undertook to argue his father's case before the Committee for Compounding. Father and son seem to have remained on fairly amicable terms, though it must have taxed the ingenuity of the latter to the utmost to explain away his father's ambivalent actions.

In the Dutton family Sir Ralph made no secret of his royalist sympathies and 'beat upon a drum in Gloucestershire and Herefordshire for soldiers for the King'. His property was quickly earmarked for sequestration, but he refused to appear before the committee to compound his delinquency and pledge adherence to Parliament. He was therefore ordered to be arrested, but he managed to elude his captors, swam the Severn and escaped abroad, though he never returned to or recovered his estates. His elder

The hunting lodge at Sherborne: built to afford a vantage point for watching deer being hunted in the park. Some of the deer were given to John Dutton by Cromwell in return for his support

brother, John Dutton, managed more successfully. A persistent opponent of the king's policies during the 1630s and an avowed supporter of Parliament in the Commons (1640–1642), he nevertheless offered to lend the king £50,000 at the outbreak of war, joined him for a while in Oxford and raised a force to help the Royalists at the siege of Gloucester. He subsequently claimed that he had been blackmailed into doing these things, but this seems doubtful. After 1642 he began to absent himself from parliament and was voted out of his seat for this in 1644, though he was still subscribing to the parliamentary war effort and remained on friendly terms with many prominent Parliamentarians including Cromwell. Two letters testify to this. In 1655, writing to the Committee of Sequestration on Dutton's behalf, Cromwell stated:

> These are to let you know that the gentleman hath given so many real testimonys of his affection to the government and so to my person in particular so constantly for many years past, that noe man that I know of in England hath done more.

And in the same year he wrote to the chief ranger of Wychwood Forest, ordering him

> To serve unto John Dutton Esq so many bucks of this season and so many Does of the next season as he shall require of you. And at any time he shall think fitt either to hunt or to course with his Greyhounds, you are to be assistant to him herein.[7]

Doubtless Dutton's great wealth enabled him to meet any demands that might be made of him – friendly or menacing; and for the rest, his honest and attractive personality seems to have recommended him to everyone with whom he had dealings.

According to the propaganda of both sides, the conduct of their own supporters was unfailingly commendable, that of their enemies deplorable and outrageous. Since most of the rank-and-file combatants at the start of the war were unused to weapons and fighting, and their leaders – though skilled in arms themselves – inexperienced in enforcing military discipline on others, there was inevitably a great deal of confusion which heightened popular feelings of uncertainty and fear of the unknown. The inbred confidence of the gentry on the royalist side was reflected in so-called *Cavalier* conduct – a careless and carefree attitude to events, high-handed dealings with opponents, reckless courage in the face of danger. Sir John Wynter's exploits in the Forest of Dean were reminiscent of the activities of his father and grandfather during the war against Spain in the previous century: his spectacular escape from an ambush by leaping his horse over a cliff into the River Wye, and the burning of his house at Lydney rather than allow it to fall into the hands of the enemy, were suitable incidents to be inscribed in legend. So was the conduct of Sir George Brydges who had three horses killed under him at the battle of Newbury (1643) before withdrawing from the fray. On the parliamentary side, the sobriety and single-minded pursuit of God's purpose inculcated by Puritan doctrines led to *Roundhead* stubbornness and complete intransigence when policies were being formulated, prisoners dealt with or setbacks accepted. The Gloucestershire landowners who sided with Massey, joined him in Gloucester and shared the hardships of the siege there, were all fired with the courage of their convictions. Richard Deane, who rose to the rank of major-general in the New Model Army and admiral in the Commonwealth Navy, did so because of his great courage in battle, unswerving loyalty to his commanding officers – Essex, Fairfax and Cromwell in turn – and a total dedication to the parliamentary cause. This last convinced him of the necessity for the death of the king, and led to his being appointed one of the commissioners to try Charles and to his signature appearing among those of other regicides on the royal death warrant. That his body lay in state after he was killed fighting the Dutch fleet at Solebay (1653) and was then buried with pomp in Westminster Abbey was an indication of his standing with fellow supporters of the Commonwealth.

As well as outstanding examples of partisanship, there were on both sides many who, without going to extremes, hung on to their political principles and to their own sense of decency and moderation. Some endured long periods of imprisonment and separation from their families with fortitude. Though it was increasingly Royalists who suffered in this way as events turned against them, nevertheless while the king held Oxford and parliamentarian prisoners from Gloucestershire were taken to the castle there, the taunts of their captors and the crowded conditions in which they were kept called for all the powers of endurance they could muster. On both sides too, there were those who treated prisoners with fairness, sheltered the sick and injured in their homes regardless of what uniform they were wearing, and helped their tenants and dependants in times of hardship and distress. That the truth of what happened probably lay somewhere between the extremes of contemporary assessments may perhaps be illustrated by two accounts of the taking of Cirencester given by 'eye-witnesses' and included in Washbourne's *Bibliotheca Gloucestrensis*. The Parliamentarian whose account is given maintained that

Chavenage. A new house built by Edward Stephens of Eastington in the late sixteenth century, and used as a Parliamentary base by Nathaniel Stephens during the Civil Wars

the prisoners taken and carried to Oxford were stripped, kept locked up at night without food or water, and all – including the old and wounded – made to walk by day up to their knees in mud, while their captors rode on horseback. It was also claimed that many were promised their freedom in return for sums of money but never released when these were paid, and 'that one of their friends that had a free pass promised him into the town with the money had very much ado to escape killing or imprisoning.' The Royalist said that those involved in the defence of Cirencester had been largely the poorer country people 'violently fetched from their houses . . . and dragged from their ploughs', brought to the town and kept there under duress; and that having been told the king's supporters were 'but a rabble of poor ragged fellows, they were amazed to see such gallant gentry come upon them and discover how merciful they were in granting quarter.' A notable example of moderation ultimately prevailing was the case of Nathaniel Stephens who, until the time of the king's imprisonment in 1648, had been implacable in his opposition to the Royalists and indefatigable in promoting the parliamentary cause in Gloucestershire. As one of their closest friends and allies, it was assumed by Cromwell and Ireton that Stephens would support them all the way through the king's trial and execution, but though they visited him in his home at Chavenage and did their utmost to persuade him to this end, Stephens firmly refused. It says much for the respect these men had for each other that this incident made no difference to their relationship afterwards.

In the opening stages of the conflict, before any overall national strategy superseded fragmented local efforts, it was the fulfilment of the everyday needs of garrisons and the tit-for-tat attacks on these and on passing troops that determined people's behaviour and the impact of the war on the countryside. As the fighting continued both sides directed the activities of local forces towards what they hoped might end in a decisive victory, but in due course it was clear that the Royalists were losing ground and Parliament gaining the upper hand. The former therefore became more despairing in their efforts, the latter more determined and calculating in the moves they made. Inevitably, as shortages of all basic necessities and of supplies for the war effort became acute the troops ranged further afield and their conduct became less scrupulous in seeking to satisfy their needs. Sir Henry Bard, in charge of the royalist garrison at Chipping Campden, proclaimed to the people living in the area:

> Know that unless you bring unto me the monthly contribution for six months, you are to expect an unsanctified troop of horse among you, from whom if you hide yourselves, they shall fire your house without mercy, hang up your bodies wherever they find them and scare your ghosts.

And at Chipping Norton:

> A great party of Cavaliers came into the town where they quartered and at their going thence, to show their impartiality (though there was but one Roundhead in the town) they plundered every house therein of whatsoever was of value and took 200 sheep and above £40 from one man.

Meanwhile, the Parliamentarians were systematic in the desecration and sometimes destruction of churches, and thorough in searching out everything of value from the houses they stormed and rendering the latter unfit for further use in the war. Although, for the most part, Royalists once committed to the cause gave their plate to the king for minting coins and sold other articles of value to meet their own expenses, nevertheless their enemies found it hard to accept that houses – once centres of gracious living and generous entertainment – were not packed with goods worth plundering; if these could not be found, then attackers took anything they could carry off, even to the extent of leaving a family without basic necessities and clothing, and a house with doors and windows shattered beyond repair.

Commanders on both sides issued orders forbidding looting and the destruction of crops in the field, fixing the rates to be paid for the billeting of troops and guaranteeing the validity of passes issued to those who needed to travel on public or private business. To what extent any of these were observed depended entirely on the integrity of officers and the extent of control they had over their men; as the fortunes of the Royalists declined, so did the morale of their troops, while on the parliamentary side the discipline of the New Model Army gradually extended to all forces and the regular payment of wages ensured better control. Nevertheless, even those who kept careful accounts of money owed to them for billeting and supplies were never repaid in full, and many found it more expedient and cheaper to try to buy immunity from the visitations of passing troops; some also preferred to stay at home rather than risk the hazards on the roads. The record kept by William Guise of Elmore gives some indication of the range of goods taken from him at different times: plate, horses, 'household stuffe, 100 pairs of pistolls, two carbines, ten swords, saddles and all other furniture of arms for the riders' bodies', and one iron chest worth £10. The accounts of John Chamberlayne of Maugersbury reflect the consequences of living near a main road – the Fosse Way – used by the troops of both sides, and at the same time indicate the very considerable resources of a country house and its estate.

When my Lord of Essex, his army marched to the relief of Gloucester, they spent me in household Provision of Bread, Beer, Cheese, Meate and Provender	£ 6
Quartered upon the Breaking up of Gloucester siege, 20 men and horses of the King's army, 3 days of which comes to	£ 4
I had corn upon the ground spoiled by the two armies: Prince Rupert facing my Lord of Essex at Stow, at least	£40
When Sir Wm. Waller chased the King's army toward Worcester I quartered the King's men, 43 men and horses one night	£ 2 17*s*. 4*d*.
The next day I quartered of Sir Wm. Waller's army 30 officers and about 40 horses & 120 foot soldiers, 5 days which comes to	£27 10*s*. 0*d*.
About 10 days after the King's army returned and then his army spent me in provision for horses and men	£ 6 0*s*. 0*d*.
When Sir William Waller lay at Stow the carriage horses were turned on my corn and did me at the least £30 worth of hurt	£30 0*s*. 0*d*.
Besides . . . I have lost 17 Plough Horses taken out of my teams upon the land, and many times paid great sums of money to stave off quartering and for post horses, to avoid other charges incident to war which I reckon not.[8]	

Chamberlayne was a Royalist, but had he been a Parliamentarian he would still have suffered visitations from both sides – unannounced, at irregular but frequent intervals and always costly. The taking of horses was a marked feature of hostilities in the county and a serious loss to landowners who, as well as for pleasure, used their horses for travelling and for carriage and draught purposes in the fields.

More difficult to assess and to put right was the damage done to roads and bridges by the passage of trains of artillery, supply wagons and horses, and to fields and to field paths, by troops of cavalry dashing indiscriminately by the nearest route in pursuit of the enemy or to get from one place to another. Again, though local men, fighting in the ranks, deserted at harvest time to try to save food crops and fodder, and landowners did their best to keep their estates functioning, there were serious interruptions to the usual routine and incalculable inroads made into stocks of cattle and sheep, supplies of seed, etc., so that each year revenues from land diminished while the need for increased returns grew more urgent.

As has been said, the burden of billeting and supplying troops fell on everyone and neither compliance with demands nor payments for immunity were a guarantee against further molestation, but as the forces of Parliament gained the upper hand, so heavier penalties were imposed on those they regarded as their enemies. Although from the start they had control of London – the hub of administration and trade – and in due course were able to enforce regular taxation on the whole country, nevertheless the wages and equipment of the army and the expenses of government called for more money, and who

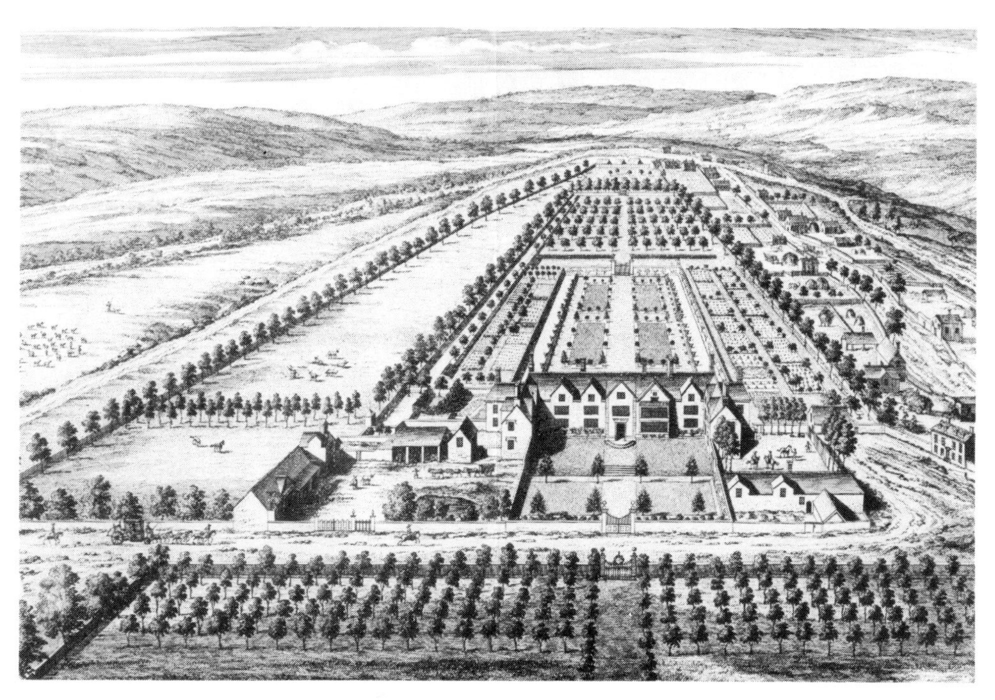

The house and estate at Maugersbury, with evidence of the farming activities that enabled John Chamberlayne to bear the burden of wartime requisitioning. An engraving by J. Kip

better fitted to supply this than the Royalists whom they regarded as responsible for the war? In the first place, a Central Committee was set up in London to bring under scrutiny the estates of Royalists and Papists. Then committees answerable to it and composed of local members of parliament were appointed in each county and directed to take action against any who could be proved to hold offending loyalties. The delinquent was required to make a confession of his guilt, give a full account of all his assets and thereafter pledge his adherence to Parliament; then, according to the degree of his guilt, he was fined and allowed to recover a portion of his estates from which the revenue was to be divided between himself, his dependents and the informer who had denounced him. In 1645 further ordinances were issued, adding to the list of potential delinquents anyone giving voluntary contributions to or raising troops for the Royalists, or robbing or plundering parliamentary supporters.

In Gloucestershire the committee proved markedly assiduous partly because so many of the members were staunch Parliamentarians and partly because the Speaker of the Commons and leading member of the Central Committee was William Lenthall, Recorder of Gloucester. Under such circumstances the discretionary powers left to the local committee were used anything but fairly. It was reported:

> One extravagant word spoke by one man is enough to confiscate the goods of a whole family to the Parliamentary soldiers. The gentry have been our masters a long time and now we may chance to master them.

And Christopher Guise, himself a Parliamentarian, who conducted his father's case before the Central Committee, complained that the rules kept being changed:

> Since our coming to attend this committee there have been many new orders which press hard upon those who are under the sense of delinquents, so that now either words against Parliament or going into the King's quarters upon any pretence whatsoever is enough to condemn a man.

As it was known to be in the power of the committee to do what it wished with an estate and its revenue, there were opportunities for the unscrupulous to profit from 'informing'. The shabby treatment meted out to William Guise was occasioned by the desire of some army officers to have his estate allocated to them, for which purpose they were prepared to go to any lengths and twist any evidence. Christopher Guise, not without reason, congratulated himself on winning a respite for his father in the end. Sir Edward Hale, having been taken prisoner in 1643, was not in a strong position to argue his rights and had his effects confiscated to help defray the expenses of his captors in Gloucester. Sir Baynham Throckmorton, after his capture and imprisonment, had to part with much of his estate in order to raise money to pay the fine imposed on him; and the Pooles of Sapperton sold all their property to meet their debts. Henry Cassey and his son Thomas of Wightfield, offending doubly by being Catholics as well as Royalists, had their estates wholly sequestered for seven years, during which time they had no means of avoiding debts for fines and taxes. Army officers again had designs on the estate of Sir Richard Ducie and reported him for shooting at them from his house and refusing them admission. Unwilling, and perhaps unable as well, to meet the fine imposed on him, Ducie was warned that if the payment was not forthcoming promptly, it would be 'assigned to some of the troops for their pay: who being necessitated and already enraged for want of pay, will – you may presume – be but harsh collectors.' The fines imposed on proven Royalists in Gloucestershire ranged from single figures in respect of modest estates to large amounts paid by important landowners such as Sir Maurice Berkeley, £1372, John Dutton, £5216, Sir William Master, £1483, and John Chamberlayne, £1246. To all, except perhaps Dutton, they presented a problem that dogged them for years, because their wealth was in land and produce, not ready money, and to make their estates more profitable under war conditions was an impossibility. One Royalist more fortunate than the rest was William Leigh – imprisoned at Gloucester because 'in accordance with his loyal principle of obedience', he had carried out his duties as sheriff in trying to collect Ship Money, and had openly thrown in his lot with the king in 1640. His gaoler was Thomas Pury – the fanatical Puritan member of parliament for Gloucester – from whom he could have expected no mercy, except for a chance meeting with Joanna Pury who promptly fell in love with her father's prisoner. She got permission to marry him and then used her influence to secure his release and the return of his estates. Any suspicion of opportunism on the part of Leigh must be dispelled by the great happiness of his married life with Joanna. They had a number of children, built a new home for themselves at Adlestrop, and together enjoyed their pets and their garden (reputed to have the finest bowling green in the country), visiting and entertaining their numerous friends. Whenever William was away from home he wrote regularly to Joanna, always in terms that reflected his affection for her and their children:

> My deare Harte, I hope by this time you have found some good effects of the Physicke you have taken and that I shall finde yr melincholy humours well spent and that you have gained a cheerful harte; and be confident that there shall be nothinge wantinge on my part that may conduce thereto. And as I take my greatest delight in this Worlde in you and next in our Children, the pledges of our Affection, I beg you will have a greate care and bee not boulde in your going into the fresh air . . . and when you do go abroade, be sure to be well clothed lest you catch colde.[9]

The major events of the war that took place in Gloucestershire all presaged a victory for Parliament. Tewkesbury, having been fought over and exchanged eight times between the two sides, was finally garrisoned by parliamentary troops. Gloucester, successfully defended against the king in 1643, continued as a base for sorties into the Forest of Dean and Cotswold areas which steadily destroyed the garrisons holding out for the king. Sudeley Castle, the chief royalist stronghold in the county, used as a base and headquarters by Prince Rupert, was besieged and taken in 1644 and thereafter became a parliamentarian garrison. The taking of Bristol in 1645 was a heartening victory for Parliament; and finally, the defeat of the Royalists at Stow-on-the-Wold in 1646, which prevented Sir Jacob Astley from reaching the king at Oxford with reinforcements, brought the first Civil War to an end, so conclusively that there were only flickers of royalist support in the county during the renewed hostilities of 1648 and no marked reaction to the execution of the king in 1649. Two years later, when Prince Charles marched from Scotland to Worcester in an attempt to regain his father's throne, still no positive support came from Gloucestershire. This, however, may not have been due to indifference or apathy, but rather to the extreme efficiency of parliamentary officials who were quick to imprison leading Royalists, to put Gloucester and other towns into a state of defence, and, because of the need for troops in Ireland at the time, to seek out and send away 'all those who were suspected of attachment to the King or disaffected to the existing government'.

For both the victors and the vanquished the ending of the king's constitutional authority left a question mark over the future. So far as the victors were concerned, Charles's desperate attempts to hold on to power – extending to collaboration with the Irish Catholics and Scottish Presbyterians, a willingness to seek help from abroad and the precipitation of a second civil war – had justified the extreme measures taken against him, even though at this point no clear plans existed for introducing an alternative form of government. Cromwell, Charles's most bitter critic and opponent since the days of the Long Parliament, and the chief instrument of his defeat, was to discover that a compromise with the past, involving government by the members of the Parliament remaining after Pride's Purge (the Rump), was not what the victorious forces desired; and that, as Marvell wrote, 'The same arts that did gain / A Pow'r must it maintain', therefore only experiments acceptable to the New Model Army would prove at all feasible. Even this policy had its pitfalls, since many who had opposed the king and his policies had done so to strengthen the power of parliament in the constitution, not to replace it with military rule. Thus, inevitably, quarrels broke out between the Rump and the army, and even between different factions in the army itself. From the point of view of the vanquished, whether they had been active participants in the war or passive sympathizers, even the death of the king could not destroy the monarchy – hence their immediate recognition of Prince Charles as their rightful ruler and a continuing hope among them that sooner or later a familiar form of government would be re-established.

Meanwhile, for the gentry at any rate, it was a case of deciding what course would be most in accordance with their consciences and principles: to follow Charles II into exile abroad; to stay in England and – if they were Royalists – accept the penalties of sequestration and exclusion from office; or to recover and re-establish their influence in local life by taking the required oath of allegiance to the Commonwealth and carrying out administrative responsibilities under its aegis.

The efforts of the various Commonwealth parliaments, and of Cromwell himself when no parliament was in session, were directed at moral, religious and administrative reforms, and in respect of the first two at any rate the intrusion of central government into the local situation was as much resented as Laudian measures had been. The banning of the use of the Church of England Prayer Book, services and practices, and the exclusion of all but dedicated Puritan preachers from church livings, together with a strict observance of the Sabbath, while encouraging traditional church-going, for many turned this into a joyless undertaking unrelieved by sports on the village green, tippling in the alehouse and idle relaxation that had formerly been acceptable ways of spending the rest of Sunday. Only the most extreme Puritans felt happy under such a régime. Where gentry families could afford it, they employed dispossessed clergy as private chaplains, or tutors for their children, so in some houses the familiar services were read and books of devotion used, despite official regulations and the risk of some zealot or disgruntled dependant 'informing'. Bishop Juxon, who retired to Little Compton on the borders of Gloucestershire and Oxfordshire after attending Charles I at his execution, held services regularly for the Jones family at Chastleton, and was a welcome visitor in the homes of the Chamberlaynes and Leighs at Maugersbury and Adlestrop. When, in addition to prayer book services, celebrations of Christmas, Easter, Whitsun and patronal saints days were also forbidden – landmarks not only in the Christian year but in the farming year as well – real deprivation was felt, since these were occasions when both in town and country, and regardless of class, people shared the feasting and entertainments involved. As much as any other move made by the Commonwealth governments, attempts to regulate people's behaviour by order and to condemn as immoral what were always regarded as harmless diversions, had a destabilizing effect because they challenged traditional customs and values. In the Cotswold area the suspension of Dover's Games, held at Whitsun near Chipping Campden, was widely resented. Though condemned by the puritanically-minded during the 1630s as wicked and licentious, they had given pleasure to gentry and commoners alike; and to judge by a contemporary print of the occasion, the participants were much more likely to end up with bruised shins, sore heads and aching muscles than corrupted minds and morals.

In the sphere of administration, locally at any rate, there was less disruption than might have been expected. For the first few years of the war, justices of the peace who were not actively engaged in fighting or imprisoned continued to meet and deal with their customary business. By 1645, only men acceptable to Parliament were left in office and any vacancies filled by nominees whose politics and religion were considered sound. John Stephens of Lypiatt was one of the latter. He belonged to a lesser gentry family, had trained at the Middle Temple and been nominated as a deputy lord-lieutenant in 1640. His parliamentary sympathies were well known and, while taking no active part in the wars, he served on a number of commissions in the county including those for the assessment of taxes and for sequestration. Another of the lesser gentry to come to the fore at this point was Captain John Crofts of Lower Swell. Having fought as an officer in the parliamentarian army, he then became involved in civil administration, serving on the same commissions as John Stephens, and was later appointed a captain of militia. He was related by marriage to William Leigh of Adlestrop and this may have improved his standing among the local gentry and helped to secure him a seat in the parliaments of 1656 and 1658. During the 1650s Cromwell was faced with a choice. He could either obtrude the authority of the central government into local affairs by attempting to control the activities of the justices of the peace and sheriffs, thus repeating one of the mistakes of Charles I in the 1630s; or he could leave the localities a larger measure of independence, thus ensuring their co-operation. It was this second policy he decided to follow, with the result that, except for the year of direct military rule in 1655 when his major-generals, backed by troops, took over every aspect of local administration, affairs in Gloucestershire gradually reverted into the hands of men from families long associated with local government. Nathaniel and Edward Stephens, Thomas Hodges, Henry Brett and Christopher Guise – already *persona grata* with Cromwell because of their support for the parliamentary cause – all continued to play a leading role in the county during the 1650s; and as justices of the peace they were joined from royalist families by Sir John Howe and his son John Grobham Howe, also Sir Baynham Throckmorton. In writing his *History of the Great Rebellion*, Clarendon expressed surprise that members of families whose relatives had been ready to risk and even lose their lives fighting for the king's cause could consider compounding for their delinquency and cooperating with the Commonwealth régime, but short of going into exile with Charles II there was little to be done at that moment. Concern for their estates, always a characteristic of the gentry, persuaded them to favour the expedient of recognising the reality of the situation, bowing to overwhelming odds and biding their time. At least this way they escaped the boredom and helplessness that overtook those who went abroad, and in so many cases led to cynicism and a dissoluteness that made them unreliable and unfit for responsibility later on.

Thus by Oliver Cromwell's death in 1658 the administration of county affairs was in the hands of familiar and experienced people, deliberately being left with a considerable amount of discretionary power; and once more we find this power being exercised as it was during the 1630s, with prime consideration being given to local interests and local opinion. For instance when, to protect colonial trade, Cromwell followed Charles I's policy of trying to ban the cultivation of tobacco in Gloucestershire, the growers petitioned against the order and then ignored it, successfully defying the troops sent to destroy their crops, because, as the latter's officer reported, 'Some of the county troop are dealers and planters . . . and the Justices rather hinder than help us.' Again, licences were issued to alehouse and innkeepers, although such places, as well as encouraging the intemperance so much deplored by the Puritans, were known to afford cover for meetings of potential plotters. In some areas too, when it suited the inclinations of the justices, Sabbath-breaking and field sports were allowed to pass unchecked. As local authorities had failed to take cognizance of them, Bishop Juxon, who whiled away some of his retirement in keeping hounds, was reported to Cromwell for the dual offences of having coursed his pack through Chipping Norton churchyard, during a Sunday service. On this occasion even the highest authority was inclined to turn a blind eye and dismiss

Sir Matthew Hale of Alderley: an eminent lawyer who served the Commonwealth government and later became Lord Chief Justice under Charles II

the complaint as frivolous. 'Let him enjoy his diversion of hunting unmolested so long as he gives my government no offence.'

When it came to parliamentary elections, events took a similar course. After Cromwell dissolved the Rump in 1653, he summoned an assembly of godly men, chosen from church congregations, to help him govern the country, and three new names appeared representing Gloucestershire: John Crofts, William Neart and Robert Holmes, all former parliamentarian soldiers. In spite of its good intentions, Barebones Parliament ('The Rule of the Saints') lasted less than a year and its members achieved little, through lack of political experience. Elections to the first and second Protectorate Parliaments in 1654 and 1656 resulted in a familiar pattern emerging among the membership, since the franchise and the qualifications for election excluded, as in the past, all but property owners. Not surprisingly therefore, although John Crofts remained, we find George Berkeley, Matthew Hale, Sir John Howe, John Grobham Howe and Sir Baynham Throckmorton among the Knights of the Shire. Of these Hale represented a family of growing importance that had added to its lands at Sapperton when the Pooles were obliged to sell their estates there. The son of a barrister, Matthew was educated at Magdalen College, Oxford, and Lincoln's Inn, in both of which places he had indulged his taste for the theatre and sport. Nevertheless, from his training he derived a great knowledge of and reverence for the law, which in time overrode all other considerations. Though a Royalist by upbringing and inclination, he took an oath of allegiance to the Commonwealth in its early days, thereby qualifying for appointment to a Committee for Law Reform, membership of parliament and of the Judiciary. The Howe family too was in the ascendant. Already owners of land at Little Compton and Withington, the marriage of grandfather John with heiress Joan Grobham brought an accession of land and wealth to the Howes which in due course was to enable them to purchase yet another large estate at Stowell Park. John Grobham Howe was a trained lawyer, a justice of the peace and served on various local commissions before becoming a member of parliament. Sir Baynham Throckmorton (the second of that name), whose father had been obliged to sell some of the family estates in the Forest of Dean to meet his sequestration fine, had been brought up as a Royalist but to retain his influence in local affairs was prepared to serve under the Commonwealth. Like his father, he took a keen interest in the Forest of Dean and its resources, but he was on better terms with the colliers and forest dwellers than his father had been, so that both his authority and his own undertakings in the forest roused less resentment.

Even if not to others, to those who were members of parliament it must have become clear during the late 1650s that the aims of the Lord Protector and the New Model Army which had promoted him to that position had already been undermined by the trend of circumstances and public opinion. A régime backed by military power was proving even more unpopular than non-parliamentary monarchical rule; taxes necessitated by the upkeep of an army and navy engaged in foreign wars (though admittedly these were being used to defend the country from foreign interference) were just as much resented as those once believed to be financing the collection of works of art or court masques; and an assembly that did not include an Upper House and was not summoned by a duly crowned king could never be considered an orthodox parliament. Although Oliver Cromwell did not accept the crown when it was offered to him, the mere fact that the thoughts of some of his supporters were proceeding along these lines indicated that, so far, their suggested innovations had not worked and that opinions throughout the country were veering in favour of a return to the old and tried constitution.

After Cromwell's death in 1658 and the succession of his son Richard to the position of Lord Protector, a contemporary report stated: 'During the brief government of Richard, the Royalists in Gloucestershire were very industrious because it became apparent that matters were likely to run into confusion and a favourable opportunity might be at hand. John Howe Esq of Stowell was exerting himself for the king.' Nor was John Howe the only opportunist. Throughout the county leading public figures were in touch with Charles II and his advisers, exchanging information and making plans for a Restoration as soon as this seemed practicable. The widespread refusals in 1659 and 1660 of 'Lords, knights and gentry of the county of Gloucestershire to collect or pay any taxes imposed by an unconstitutional assembly' offered challenges that the Army Council was powerless to meet. The anarchy that followed Richard Cromwell's abdication was such as could only be remedied by outside intervention, and this was to materialize in the person of General Monck who led his forces from Scotland to London;

imposed his authority on the factious army leaders; dismissed the members of the Rump whom they had reassembled; and ordered the election, along traditional lines, of a new parliament which he then directed to send an invitation to Charles II to return.

So far as social issues were concerned, the weaknesses of the Commonwealth régime had been evident to the county community for some while. The ideals of Oliver Cromwell and his followers, though compelling enough to themselves, were too extreme to appeal to and captivate the imaginations of the majority of the English who, as Elizabeth I had divined, really preferred compromise and the middle way. As the fears engendered by war subsided and it was clear that the gentry – the accepted leaders of county society – were conforming to the existing régime only as much as seemed expedient, then a general lack of enthusiasm became apparent. It was overlooked that the parliaments summoned by Cromwell and the council appointed to help him were responsible for introducing some long-needed reforms in the legal and fiscal systems, and economic measures to boost overseas trade; and as so often happens under a new régime, many aspects of the previous one assumed an attractiveness they had never had at the time. The grievances that had precipitated the crisis of 1640 were forgotten and what people wanted was a return to an unregimented way of life with their interests being cared for by known and trusted local men. Meanwhile, as farmers, traders and craftsmen gradually resumed their daily routine of work, the gentry too were returning to the kind of life they had led before the wars, short of money in many cases, always under surveillance if they were known to have royalist sympathies, and taking care whoever they were to conform in speech, dress and behaviour with what was officially demanded of them.

Nevertheless by 1660 some Gloucestershire gentlemen had begun to travel again on estate and personal business. In 1656 Christopher Guise wrote: 'I betooke myself to visites and recreative journeys to Bath and elsewhere'; and in 1658, his wife being ill and in need of skilled medical attention, 'towards London wee went . . . and my sicke wyfe desiring itt, wee took in Windsore in our way . . . and so on to Tunbridge.' When able to do so, many gentlemen were buying clothes and household requirements for their families; they were also acquiring horses to replace the hundreds that had been requisitioned during the wars, and building up and coursing packs of hounds. Rather unexpected in view of the expense involved, and because it had to be done overtly, was the amount of building that was going on during the 1650s. Nor was this confined to the repair of war-damaged houses. At Highnam, William Cooke embarked on rebuilding his father's house, left uninhabitable after Royalists and Parliamentarians had fought over it in the early stages of the war. The new dwelling was built in brick with stone facings for doors and windows, and closely resembled houses built by Inigo Jones, though it was not his work but probably that of one of his pupils. John Dutton, whose great wealth even the combined demands of both parties during the wars had not noticeably diminished, arranged for the family seat at Sherborne to be refronted and new wings added, and for a lodge to be built in the park nearby to serve as an observation post when deer were being coursed there. For its purpose the lodge was unusually well-built and attractive, with a ground-floor entrance hall and one large room above opening out on to a balcony overlooking the coursing ground whence the company might watch the sport in comfort.

Valentine Strong, a local stone-mason, may have been responsible for the work done

Lower Slaughter Manor, designed and built in 1655 by Valentine Strong for Richard Whitmore. A drawing from the family's collection

at Sherborne; it is certain that he was commissioned by Richard Whitmore to plan and build the latter's new house at Lower Slaughter. According to the contract drawn up in 1655, Strong was to provide from his own quarries 'all such free stone as shall be necessary for the making of doors and windows'; and his honesty as well as sound workmanship was put at stake, since for his efforts he was to receive '£200 of lawfull English money with an extra £10 if the said Valentine Strong shall say that his work doth deserve the £10.'[10] To make room for the new house a small manor was swept away and only its splendid sixteenth-century dovecot left to enhance Strong's square-built mansion, contemporary in style, with fine fireplaces and plastered ceilings that have survived until today. Time has certainly proved that Strong deserved his additional £10. Shortly before this, in 1650–52, William Clifford had arranged to have a new house built at Frampton-on-Severn. Although this was pulled down a century later to make way for a more up-to-date dwelling, a drawing of it remains, showing a tall building with a steep-pitched, gabled roof, many chimneys, two unlikely-looking bay windows on each side of the front door, and an arched entrance set in the high wall surrounding the garden. Some abnormally tall trees behind the gateway dwarf the proportions of what was probably a very comfortable family home. Household accounts which record the employment of local masons and carpenters, the purchase of tiles, bricks, nails and

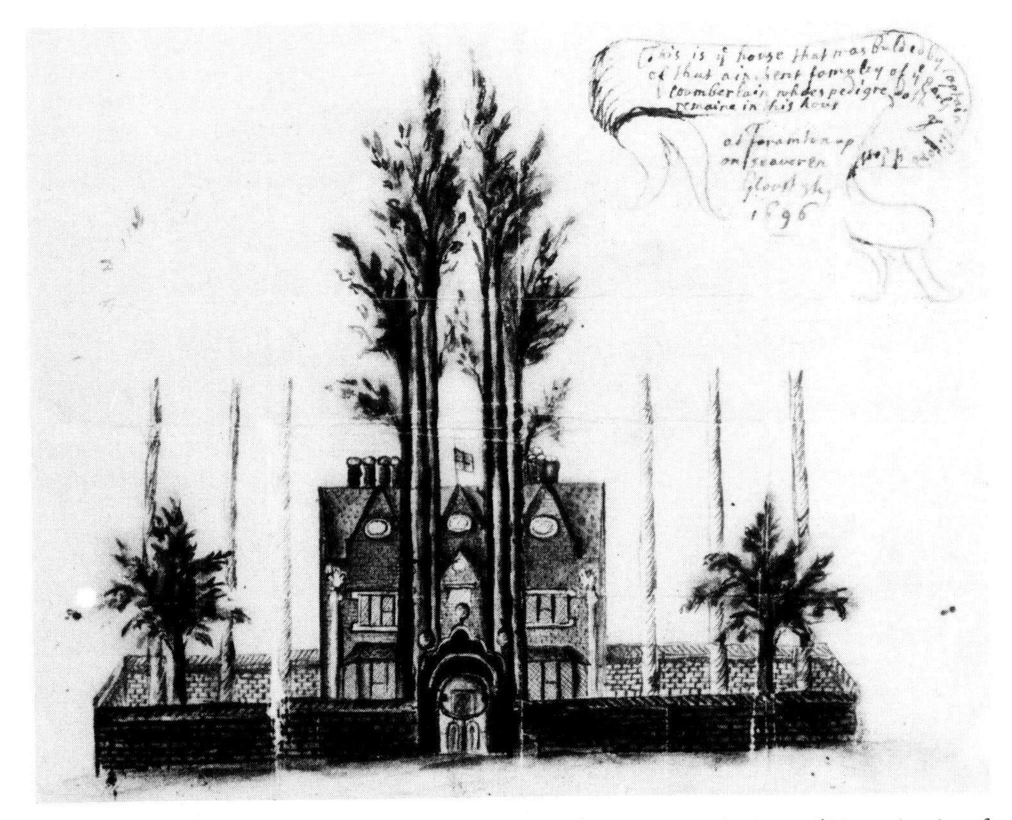

Frampton Court. A curious picture of William Clifford's new house, built *c.* 1650 on the site of an older manor

other materials locally, and the carriage of much of the necessary timber from Berkeley by river, would seem to indicate the availability of supplies and labour and fairly normal working conditions in the area at the time.

An account of the war period in Gloucestershire would not be complete without some mention of Edward Massey. Although he was neither born and brought up in the county nor associated with it until the start of hostilities in 1642, his career from that point onwards was so closely bound up with events in the area as to be an integral part of local history. A trained, experienced soldier, both courageous and enterprising, he pursued a career consistent with his conscience and ambitions; and as his portrait by Sir Peter Lely shows, he was a commanding and confident figure, well able to dominate his surroundings. He joined the king's army at the outbreak of war, but finding that the opportunities of promotion were slight, he moved over to the parliamentarian forces to become a lieutenant-colonel in the army of the West. This brought him to Gloucestershire and led to his taking charge of the defence of Gloucester during the siege of 1643, the successful outcome of which was largely due to his ingenious tactics and his ability to inspire the inhabitants to hold out against overwhelming odds. For the next

Edward Massey who successfully defended Gloucester against royalist attacks. A portrait by Sir Peter Lely in the National Gallery of Canada

three years he campaigned against royalist garrisons in the county and assisted other parliamentarian troops in the West; then was elected to parliament as a member for Gloucester. However, as a Presbyterian and one anxious to uphold parliamentary as opposed to military rule, he offended fellow members with independent religious views and former colleagues in the army, and was obliged to flee abroad where he later took service under Charles II. He accompanied the latter during the Worcester campaign where he was wounded, taken prisoner and lodged in the Tower pending trial; this he avoided by escaping and returning to Holland. In 1659 he came back to Gloucestershire secretly and was one of the leading figures among the gentry who were then beginning to plan the Restoration. Betrayed, captured, but once again managing to escape abroad, he remained there until the following year when he returned to take up his seat in parliament as a member for Gloucester, which he remained until his death in 1667. He was knighted by Charles II in 1660 for his services to the royalist cause, and in spite – or perhaps because – of having driven them to extremes of suffering during the siege of 1643, he never lost the support of the anti-Royalist Gloucester inhabitants. A solitary, independent figure (he never married) he was willingly drawn into their plans by the Gloucestershire gentry in 1659, who seem to have recognized in him a courage and determination on which they could rely.

CHAPTER SEVEN

POST-WAR RECOVERY

All over the country the return of Charles II and the restoration of the monarchy were greeted with rapturous delight. With the exception of those who opposed this turn of events on ideological or religious grounds, people in all walks of life were filled with a sense of relief and optimism, confident that the events and experiences of the past eighteen years could be wiped from memory at will. Borough and parish records bear witness to the ringing of bells and lighting of bonfires; rewards given to those who 'proclaimed the King' and repainted the royal arms in churches and on public buildings; and money spent on feasts and festivities. From Gloucestershire, representatives set off for London to take their seats in the reconvened parliament that was to ratify the conditions with which Charles's return had been hedged about, and in due course they were followed by members of the gentry, eager to pledge their allegiance at the king's coronation, and in some cases hopeful that past gestures of loyalty and the losses these had entailed might be recognized and recompensed. While the initial euphoria lasted, few people perceived any inherent difficulties in the situation, nor were they prepared to acknowledge that the passage of time – however short – leaves an indelible mark on people's lives and outlook.

Only gradually, as the Convention finished its work and was succeeded by an orthodox assembly – the Cavalier Parliament – summoned by the king, did it dawn on people that statutes might be repealed without their effects simultaneously being wiped out; that the army might be disbanded but the harshness of military rule still be felt; and that the differences of opinion that arose between neighbours, and the hurts mutually inflicted during the course of the wars and years of the Commonwealth, were in many cases proof against the Christian urge to forgive and forget. For many, bitter disillusionment set in as the king's means of rewarding the faithful dried up, and legislation – the Act of Indemnity and Oblivion,[1] designed to heal the rift between the king and his former enemies and alleviate all fears – merely underlined the ease with which past disloyalty could be glossed over, while unselfish and unstinting service was denied its due reward. Financial debts were a matter of honour yet beyond the king's resources to repay in kind. Titles or official appointments were the most that his creditors could expect, and even these were limited by the number of vacancies available, and a lack of experience to fill them on the part of many who aspired thereto.

Christopher Guise 'did lend the King a large sum of money in his exile which he could never get repayed but by a title of Barronet which he was told was the only recompense he had to expect for that service.' The recovery of material losses in land and goods was restricted to what was legally feasible, namely the return of what had changed hands without legal sanctions; where some form of purchase had taken place or where forcible seizure could not be proved (virtually an impossibility after so long) then the status quo had to remain – a galling situation for those condemned to watch former enemies enjoying what must have seemed like ill-gotten gains. The wrath with which members of the Convention insisted on excluding regicides from the general pardon, and ordering sentences of execution to be carried out on both the living and the bodies of those already dead, far exceeded the hatred felt by the king against the agents of his father's death and his own miserable years in exile, and was a reflection of Royalists' determination to avenge their humiliation at the hands of the New Model Army.

Some people in all classes continued to look back, pointlessly longing for a return of old times or equally unprofitably grieving over the events of the Interregnum; but as has already been noticed, many – even before the Restoration – had turned their backs on the past and begun to make the most of contemporary opportunities. In Gloucestershire, among the carriers, the blacksmiths, the leather-workers and the clothiers, there were those who had actually prospered during the wars, and subsequently, by catering for the needs of the parliamentarian armies and garrisons. For the gentry, whose main source of wealth was still their land, now encumbered with debts and still below pre-war standards in respect of numbers of cattle, horses and sheep and levels of productivity, the need for higher revenues was urgent if they were to offset losses and continue to maintain their accustomed way of life. To begin with, the improvements had to be achieved by better management of their estates, involving a reduction in running costs, an insistence on efficiency and a willingness to consider potentially profitable innovations. Unlike the king, whose feudal rights had not been restored in 1660, landowners who were also manorial lords continued to exercise customary control over their estates. Sir John Newton of Bitton was careful to ensure that he received his due heriot on the death of a tenant; Maynard Colchester at Westbury retained payments in kind as part of his rents – capons, geese or 'Fat Hens'; while the Leighs at Adlestrop insisted on corn being ground at their mill, and kept alive the old carrying service, one of their tenants having to bring yearly 'a ton of Coal from Tewkesbury or Evesham to the Manor House of Adlestrop, the lord to pay the price of the Coals at the place where bought.' By now, in a number of places, strip-farming in open fields according to a communal agricultural policy had given way to consolidated holdings, being worked at will by individual tenants; nevertheless manorial courts continued to meet to ensure that remaining responsibilities to the community were still being fulfilled – the maintenance of hedges, clearing of ditches, removal of rubbish and adequate fencing-in of stock. When the death of a tenant or the culmination of a lease made it possible, landlords entered into new contracts fixing rents at a higher rate than before, and inserting specific provisos as to the management of the holding, which included 'dressing the land with lime and dung according to husbandry'; a rotation of crops; the addition of trees to existing stands; and the maintenance of 'a nursery of stocks', especially of crab apples. Demesne land too was leased out so that owners were relieved of the anxiety, burden and incidental expense of farming it themselves. Sir John Newton's father adopted a policy of 'the greatest frugality' where his tenants were concerned, and the son followed suit. Writing to his agent, he recalled his father's customary practice and expressed surprise 'that you should give encouragement to ye Tenants for to apply to me to New Build their barns and buildings. You should have at first called upon them, before their Buildings was so badd, to have repaired them and then ye winds would not have damaged them so very much.'[2]

It is clear from surviving records, which become more numerous towards the end of the century, that much more careful accounts were now being kept by conscientious stewards entrusted with wide and varied responsibilities by their employers, who even in absence expected to be kept well informed of the state of affairs. Sir John Newton insisted on knowing *everything* and presumably was not surprised to hear from his agent: 'Two things here goe not well – first the Pole-Evil is broke out again in the Mare that had it two years since: then the Clock is out of order and without youre [leave] I dare not let any countrey workman medle with it.' A longer letter, also dated 1685, lists further worries:

> I have by the carrier this day sent what you ordered, together with a dozen bottles of ale . . . they are all together in a small hamper. By the same return comes the gardener too, being forced to execute the commission you gave me of parting with him, by reason he went out on Monday last without my leave and stayed out four days . . . Besides, he designed to leave us at Christmas, and since he was able to work, went every afternoon to the alehouse. I never said so much as 'I'll you do' to him nor refused him help, neither did he ask for any tools. Dame Clinton is in the ladies' condition and as forward so that should I discharge her, I might be guilty of murdering her child. For visitors who would stay all night, I use this remedy. Two tenants dined here and their business being done, I ordered the servants to let them know there was no lodging, but they unwilling to be gone, put it to the hazard, so I let them fairly sit in the kitchen all night.[3]

At the same time, the employers themselves were keeping detailed personal and business account books and treating them almost like a confessional, entering notes of self-congratulation, anxiety or explanation at the close of each year according to how close to a satisfactory balance their figures had worked out. A discrepancy that could be attributed to extra journeys, a family funeral, or a son's expenses at college was apparently acceptable.

By chance, but most fortunately, the need to make estates more profitable coincided with other significant developments. The seventeenth century saw the start of a fashion in 'improving' books on agriculture, and after the Restoration these were implemented by periodicals such as Houghton's *Agricultural Newsletters*. Inventories of library books and subscriptions to periodicals recorded in personal accounts indicate that the owners of even modest estates were sufficiently interested in the business of management to read about as well as practise it. At the same time, the establishment of the Royal Society (1662) made a considerable contribution to innovatory and improved methods, and the recommendations issued by its various committees encouraged experiments with new tools and equipment, and new crops. As Houghton reported in one of his Newsletters:

> Since His Majesty's most happy Restoration, the whole land hath been fermented and stirred up by the profitable hints it hath received from the Royal Society, by which means parks have been disparked, commons inclosed, woods turned into arable and pasture land improved by clover,

> sainfoin, turnips, coleseed, parsley and many other good husbandries, so that the food of cattle is increased as fast if not faster than the consumption.

And if any further impetus to increased output was necessary then it was provided by the payment of government bounties on surplus wheat, barley and rye available for export in years of plenty. This was not intended as a subsidy to encourage arable farming, since it only operated when grain prices on the home market were low, but it afforded a good reason for maintaining steady production and helped to offset the land tax introduced under the Commonwealth, which continued after the Restoration and fell exclusively on the landed classes.

Thus, by the end of the century, the look of the countryside reflected the changes that were taking place. The continuing process of consolidation and enclosure was producing small fields outlined by ditches, walls or hedges. Celia Fiennes and Cassandra Willoughby, both journeying during the 1690s, commented on the attractiveness of the hedges in Gloucestershire and Herefordshire and on the large number of pear and apple trees included in them, a point also made twenty years later by Daniel Defoe. The new emphasis on manuring with anything that came to hand – sewage, rags, burnt turfs – and the planting of root and fodder crops in what would otherwise have been fallow land, meant that there were fewer areas lying idle and unproductive, and many more farms combining animal husbandry with arable. Owners of estates in the Cotswold area – the Leighs and Duttons for example – and in the Severn Vale – the Cliffords at Frampton, Colchesters at Westbury and William Blathwayt at Dyrham – were equally interested in buying and selling animals as well as grain and dairy produce at local markets. Experiments in draining and irrigation also increased the amount of land in use, as Christopher Guise reported of the family estate at Elmore:

> Situated upon the banke of the river Severne upon a pleasant hill of gravell, but otherwise an ill ayre in the winter and springe as being surrounded with meadows overflowen, which beginning to dry in March have very ill disposition in the ayre: this objection is now effectively removed by the large draines and sluices, since which it is become as healthy as pleasant.

The thriving character of local markets and fairs and the variety of goods on sale there, noted by Thomas Baskerville on his journeys round the county during the 1670s, indicate that, however prolonged and profound the effects of the wars on individuals, in general there had been a rapid recovery afterwards, with produce from estates and smaller farms being available for disposal along customary channels. Lechlade had its great fair 'for cattle, cheese and other commodities more especially sage cheese in various shapes and colours'; at Cheltenham there were lambs, cattle and 'an abundance of horses for the cart'; and at Tetbury wool, yarn and mutton. Tewkesbury's specialities were even more diverse – carrots and other garden stuff, and mustard 'made into balls which may be carried with little trouble where you please and when you have occasion for that sauce, you dissolve it in vinegar or verjuice.'[4]

In exploiting the agricultural resources of their estates, landowners were also drawn into non-agricultural commitments since so many of their products in fact constituted vital raw materials for industry – leather, wool, barley (for brewing), timber, and bark (for tanning). This was no new development, but the growing demand for consumer goods in the second half of the seventeenth century led to an expansion of industry, and thus a wider market for raw materials. The tendency in the sixteenth century for the object of estate management to switch from mere subsistence to producing a surplus now speeded up. As well as dairy produce, bacon, poultry and eggs being sent to local markets and increasingly to London, landowners aimed to become regular suppliers of materials to the clothiers in the Stroud valley, the brewers of Bristol, Tewkesbury and Gloucester, the tanners in the nearest market towns, shipbuilders in ports along the Severn, and furniture and tool-makers in the county and as far away as the Midlands. Also regarded as legitimate products for exploitation were coal, iron and stone. As owners of estates in the Forest of Dean, Sir John Wynter, Sir Baynham Throckmorton and the Boevey family at Flaxley were already accustomed to deriving profits from coal- and iron-mining; great hopes were expressed in 1700 of the coalworks at Bitton, and Thomas Baskerville noted that, at Pucklechurch also, John Denys, his brother and his mother were benefiting from mining: 'They have a good estate in lands and coal mines and do keep a plentiful house. At a mile distance from their house they have a pretty little park with a fine lodge and some deer in it.' The extended use of coal for domestic purposes as well as a substitute for wood in soap- and sugar-boiling, glassmaking, brewing, tin- and iron-smelting made increased production all the more desirable.

At the same time, there were profits to be gained from the increasing need for iron, now being used in more sophisticated equipment for forges, furnaces and mines as well as tools and machinery for agriculture. Sir John Wynter was typical in his attitude to the resources of his estates. Aggressive, inventive and enterprising, during the 1660s and 1670s he threw himself into entrepreneurial undertakings with the same gusto that he had attacked parliamentarian forces in the Forest of Dean during the wars. Although his exploitation of the forest continued to be resented by local people, his knowledge and skill were admired far afield and were enlisted by miners in new workings elsewhere. He also played an important part in launching the syndicate of proprietors living in Gloucestershire, Shropshire and the Black Country that led to their pooling knowledge and combining operations to facilitate the extraction, transport and marketing of the products of their mines. In addition to having access to coal and iron deposits in the Forest of Dean, Wynter had quarrying rights including 'liberty to dig and get limestone, tilestone and other stones and to make and get millstones and grindstones, also stones for cider presses, window-stones and paving.' Thus at a time of increasing demand from private builders and industrial developers, he was able to supply a variety of needs locally, in neighbouring counties and in the Midlands. Similarly, in the Cotswold area a number of estate owners had their own quarries whence came the stone for renovating or rebuilding their houses and repairing parish churches. At Barnsley the quarries were said to produce 'a very excellent kind of white freestone almost equal to that of Bath', which explains the pleasing uniformity of the two great houses there, Barnsley House and Barnsley Park, and many of the dwellings in the village itself. Farmington Quarry provided John Dutton with materials for Sherborne House as well as for his hunting lodge in the park and homes for his workers. Likewise, at Snowshill, Aylworth and Great Barrington, useful supplies of stone being exploited by estate owners produced manor-houses and estate villages that literally grew out of the local earth.

More efficient administration and increased production, while providing a sound basis for estate management, would not in themselves have been enough to finance the innovatory experiments begun in the late seventeenth century nor to subsidize the enhanced standard of living of most of the gentry at that time. A new and fairly rapid means of augmenting revenue was needed (as opposed to loans that afforded only short-term aid) and this was found in the return on investments. Fortunately for those willing and ready to show enterprise and run risks, the period provided favourable opportunities in the new companies being developed to exploit England's expanding empire and overseas trade. The Navigation Acts, introduced during the Commonwealth period and re-enacted after the Restoration, created highly favourable conditions in English and colonial ports for their own shipping, and restricted colonial imports to goods bought in England, thus promising to save traders from foreign competition. Even so, ships, colonial settlements and port establishments overseas needed protection, and this called for large amounts of capital over and above what was spent on filling the ships with cargo. The Joint Stock companies were founded to raise these sums and quickly attracted money, not just from merchants, but from a wide public including gentry families.

The first of these companies were the East India, the Royal African, the Hudson Bay and the Levant, and the success of one voyage was enough to inspire increased confidence and hope in the next. Gentlemen who went up to London on business acquired information there about prospects for investment; those who had connections with merchant families through business or marriage would be given favourable tips; and so promising did the fortunes of the companies seem, that younger sons of gentlemen with few prospects of inheriting family estates became apprentices, primarily with the object of making a living, and then of achieving more lucrative posts in the long run. (They had examples before them like that of Sir Josiah Child, who rose from a lowly clerkship to become Governor of the East India Company.) By the end of the century, the Stephens and Romney (of Tetbury) families among others had investments in the East India Company; members of the Bathurst, Curtis-Hayward and Codrington families were working in the West Indies where Christopher Codrington 'inherited a great estate . . . and much increased the wealth of his family. He died Governor of the Leeward Islands.' Sir Edward Wynter, a great-grandson of Admiral Sir William Wynter of Armada fame, spent much of his life in India in the service of the East India Company, ably abetted by an elder brother in the London office of the company. Family property in Jamaica was inherited and managed by Edward's son. The Leighs of Adlestrop and Chamberlaynes of Maugersbury, connected by marriage with Sir James Brydges, a representative of the Levant Company in Constantinople, and with Sir Josiah Child, were given guidance by them about investments. William Sandys of Miserden chose ventures nearer home to invest in. He was particularly interested in river navigation and involved himself in schemes to improve the passage of ships on the Wye, the Avon and the upper Thames. The rapidly increasing value of urban property – especially in London – also promised a steady return on investment, since the demand for business and residential accommodation far outstripped the supply. During the rebuilding of the city after the Great Fire (1666), not only Cotswold stone and Cotswold craftsmen were involved, but a number of Gloucestershire families acquired properties in the capital, which brought in a small income in rent. The great age of speculation was yet to come, but already some families were taking a keen interest in their investments, to judge by references to these in letters, and making use in their knowledge of the movement of ships and nature of cargoes to obtain goods such as china, wood and fabrics for their homes, seeds and plants for their gardens. In 1693, 'the contents of a Box directed for ye Hon William Blathwayt and put on board ye *Samuell*, Tho Harrison Commander', included peach stones, tulip tree cones, sassafras berries, gum trees and, at the same time, 'Two Rattle Snakes [were] put on board in a cage, directed as above.' Whether the latter survived long enough to be delivered at Dyrham is not recorded.

Although the Restoration of 1660 did not bring complete political stability as had been hoped, nevertheless the later years of the seventeenth century were quiet enough to restore confidence to the minds of the majority of people and to re-establish an even tenor in their lives. To the gentry, many of whom had been uprooted and all of whose lives had been disrupted to some extent as a result of the wars, domestic ties were now stronger than ever. Devotion to their families and estates was the more intense because it was based on greater knowledge and experience than they had had before, and represented a conscious choice in favour of life in a familiar setting, as opposed to the challenge and change of making their way in a wider sphere. Moreover the experience of a strong central government under the Commonwealth régime had made it seem all the more important that some measure of autonomy and a local identity should be retained by the county. The resumption of administrative responsibilities by the gentry during the late 1650s, and the acquiescence of the county community in this, established a situation that was continued after 1660; it was facilitated by the fact that the interests of the two noble families in the county – the Berkeleys and the Beauforts – were now centred more on London and national politics than on the affairs of the county, which left the gentry to exercise undisputed leadership locally.

Much though they had disliked enforced absences from home during the wars, there was no doubt that the gentry had gained from them by having their horizons and social contacts extended. Many of the younger generation now tended to branch out and seek a career for themselves in the army, the navy or commerce, and to better themselves through independent efforts rather than seeking the favour of social and political superiors, or remaining a charge on family revenues and estates. Of course, patronage still continued and was important, but not so much the patronage of the Court and of great men, as of family connections. Wherever possible, advowsons were exercised exclusively in favour of younger sons or nephews. The Leighs at Adlestrop jealously reserved the living of Broadwell with Adlestrop for members of the family. In the mid-seventeenth century William Leigh had no son available, so Augustus Martyn – a cousin – was appointed. Later Theophilus Leigh wanted the living for his son Theophilus, and to ensure this appointed a brother-in-law, Dr Henry Brydges, to hold it until the young man was old enough to assume the responsibility himself. Dr Brydges amongst other appointments acted as Visitor to Balliol College, Oxford, and in this capacity was undoubtedly helpful in the election of the younger Theophilus as Master of the College. Another member of the Brydges family, Henry's brother James, as Paymaster of the Forces under Anne, secured an army appointment for Theophilus's eldest son James, and in due course – it was anticipated – would use his influence on behalf of a younger son Henry, according to a letter from Theophilus to James:

I must desire you in the meantime to entreat your Uncle Brydges's interest to get him (Henry) the

> Queen's letter to go to sea in some ship of war. If my brother has interest with any of the Commissioners of the Admiralty, it will be easily obtained.[5]

Even more significantly than in place-seeking, ties of kinship operated in the sphere of marriage. Families still intent on recouping losses suffered during the wars needed, more than ever, profitable marriages for eldest sons and for daughters whose connections might well be valued more highly than their dowries. It had always been a characteristic of the gentry to marry advantageously, in the locality preferably if this would help to extend or consolidate properties, or into a different area if suitable contacts or contracts could be achieved. William Blathwayt gained a foothold in the county as well as estates and a settlement of £10,000 when he married Mary Wynter. The Clutterbucks, already an established family in the county, improved their status by linking their fortunes with those of the Cliffords. We became more aware of behind-the-scenes negotiations from the seventeenth century onwards because more records of these have been preserved. There is a note of near desperation in a letter sent in 1696 from John Estcourt, 'his loving although very aged uncle', to his nephew urging him to make a visit soon, since there is a prospect of marriage that will ensure money and land staying in the family. 'The elder of the Sisters is dead and was buryed about St Thomas day last and now our Cousen Anne is possesst of all: seeing your and your Brother's wives are dead, I wish that you both would come speedily to us and endeavour to obtain her love to be a Wife to one of you: a thousand pounds yearly is worth the getting.'[6] Probably few young people were pushed into marriage against their will, but, after parents had indulged in considerable preliminary skirmishing designed to remove any material hindrances there might be to the match, dutiful sentiments even if not fear of reprisals must have persuaded some young people to submit to the wishes of their elders, where personal emotions were not actively involved. To cite just one example of a complex network of local relationships – the Leighs and Chamberlaynes became neighbours and friends when they settled in the Stow area in the sixteenth century, and subsequently intermarried. Then, members of both families married into the Brydges family of Sudeley and Wilton, and thus became connected with various Herefordshire families. Meanwhile the Brydges had also established links with the Atkyns of Sapperton and the Bourchiers of Barnsley, so that over a wide area all the leading families were related. Both a cause and an effect of these connections were the frequent inter-family visits that took place. Except in the winter, when travelling conditions made it difficult, husbands and wives separately or together went to stay for quite long periods with relatives; and children were sent to grandparents when births were due or there was serious illness in their own household. This was certainly a regular occurrence in the Leigh and Brydges families:

> Twice every year Mr and Mrs Leigh [Theophilus and Mary] with a coach full of little children failed not to meet Lord and Lady Chandos at Moreton [-in-Marsh] (for they always travelled up and down to town in the Hereford coach) and in this meeting an exchange of children was often made on my Lady's part, for some of her grandchildren were always with her.[7]

It was during such visits that marriages were planned, and prospective brides and grooms – even while still children – made their first acquaintance with each other.

In preparation for careers, sons of gentlemen were receiving much the same kind of

William Blathwayt and his wife Mary Wynter. By this marriage, the Wynter estates at Dyrham came into the possession of Blathwayt and gave him a foothold in the county. Portraits by Sir Godfrey Kneller

education as in the previous century and, though perhaps more had private tutors at the start, they went on to university and the Inns of Court as their fathers had done. For younger sons not intended for public office or the church, a thorough grounding in the Classics was no longer as essential as in the past. A grasp of foreign languages and mathematics might prove as useful; while social graces and attainments such as riding, fencing and dancing were definitely desirable, though not to the exclusion of other qualifications: according to Theophilus Leigh, who commented on a nephew's training, 'Fine feathers make fine birds. Riding the great Horse and Dancing may make him a Beau but I doubt will conduce little to making his fortune in the world.' A good local grammar school still attracted the patronage of the gentry. Christopher Guise recalled being sent to 'Lord Berkeley's free schoole at Wootton Underedge where I spent some yeares as to my studyes in a course profitable enough . . . here I found myself on the playne ground without any advantageous rise of alliance or prominence of extraction.' The four brothers of William Clutterbuck were educated either in a small private school or else boarded with a master who taught them, since bills paid to one Robert Walters for their schooling included tabling (boarding) as well as books, inkhorns and ink, paper and quills. Matthew Hale was brought up by a guardian and taught by the vicar of Wotton until proceeding to university.

A number of young men from Gloucestershire families continued to go to Oxford, though the reputation of the university in the late seventeenth century was anything but predominantly academic. Christopher Guise had commented that in his day 'the vice of Oxford scollars is their frequenting tippling houses', and his son William could have made the same observation when he was up. He might have included many of the fellows and college officials in the stricture, since in spite of the efforts of Dr Fell (Dean of Christ Church and Bishop of Oxford during Charles II's reign) to enforce some standards of sobriety and studiousness, much time and money were spent on dress, entertainment, hunting and sport. The Tory and High Anglican tendencies throughout the university were other grounds for suspicion among families which had supported Parliament during the wars or become disillusioned with the Stuarts after the Restoration. Nevertheless, although contemporary accounts highlighted the ills that abounded there, Oxford during this period produced many able lawyers, churchmen and politicians.

Among the lawyers was Matthew Hale, who had played a leading part in the affairs of the county during the Commonwealth and was knighted and promoted by Charles II to be Chief Baron of the Exchequer and Lord Chief Justice. 'He carried himself so uprightly as to be equally admired and esteemed by all ranks and conditions of men.' Also eminent in the legal sphere was Sir Robert Atkyns, Recorder of Evesham and Bristol, and a judge of the exchequer as well as a zealous member of parliament who refused to become a paid supporter of the king. 'I will not accept anything for my attendance in Parliament. I did take occasion upon this to advise my country [constituency] that those who took pensions were not fit to be sent up to Parliament again.' Almost all the post-Restoration Gloucestershire members of parliament and justices of the peace were Oxford men. These included Sir John Guise, Sir Ralph Dutton, Thomas Master, John Grobham Howe, Sir Baynham Throckmorton, and members of the Bathurst, Blomer, Leigh, Chamberlayne and Bourchier families.

Nor was all the money available in Oxford being squandered on fleeting pleasures. The late seventeenth century was a time of considerable architectural achievement, with St Mary's Church and many college chapels being restored or rebuilt, common rooms and halls improved with panelling and carpets, new libraries and quadrangles added, gardens laid out, and the university as a whole enriched with the Ashmolean and Sheldonian buildings. The latter was, however, a direct result of student licentiousness, since it was designed as a secular setting for the annual Encaenia, usually marked by an outbreak of buffoonery unfitted to the traditional venue of the occasion which was St Mary's Church. Cassandra Willoughby, who went to Oxford in 1695 to visit her cousin William Leigh, mentions having been shown among other places 'ye Theatre' (the Sheldonian); the chapels at Queen's, Lincoln and Trinity colleges; the libraries at St John's and Queen's, the latter 'then a-building'; 'the Physick Garden, and John Tredeskins his Rarities', which were housed in the Ashmolean building and inevitably of special interest to the daughter of Francis Willoughby the famous naturalist.[8] Whether consciously or not, Oxford students were in a position to observe the work of the leading architect of the period – Sir Christopher Wren – in the Sheldonian Theatre, Trinity College chapel and Tom Tower; of outstanding craftsmen in wood and metal – Grinling Gibbons, Thomas Robinson and Paul de Lamerie; of garden-makers and plantsmen – Robert Morrison, the first Professor of Botany at Oxford, Dr Plot, keeper of the Ashmolean and recorder of the Natural History of Oxfordshire, and Jacob Brobart father and son, in turn keepers of the Physic Garden.

The Inns of Court also continued to attract as a final stage in formal education. For some, moving to London was a continuation of university life; others were plunged into this adult experience after being taught in a local school or tutored at home; but most had been preceded by a father, uncle or brother – the De la Beres, Stephens, Aylworths and Duttons at the Middle Temple; Hales, Howes and Atkyns at Lincoln's Inn – and so were not entirely unprepared for what lay ahead of them. William Guise at Lincoln's Inn found, like his father, that except for the single-minded academics 'London will yield diversions enough to keep a man from study'. As in the past, this was not necessarily a bad thing, since the contacts made at this stage might prove useful in the pursuit of a career. An acquaintance also with the latest fashions in dress, deportment, architecture, literature, etc. could shape tastes and opinions, and help to develop a capacity for social leadership that would stand a gentleman in good stead on returning to his native county.

Additionally, for those who could afford it, foreign travel was now coming to be regarded as part of the educational process. The rigid routine of the Grand Tour had not yet been fully established, but its characteristics were already emerging – the tendency for France and Italy to head the list of countries visited and for young men to go abroad with letters of introduction to family acquaintances, English agents or prominent social and political figures who could provide an *entrée* into desirable circles. How much real benefit a young man derived from his travels varied enormously according to the company he kept and the expectations of his family. A conscientious tutor or sober companions, though not exciting, might nevertheless ensure serious sightseeing, a programme of improving reading and the learning of foreign languages. A father like Theophilus Leigh expected and indeed received regular letters from his son William written in the language of the country he was in and with reliable comments on current affairs in them; but other young travellers, insufficiently supervised, met the wrong people and often got involved and out of their depth in gambling or undesirable love-affairs. Again, the serious-minded came back with impressions of fashionable architecture and gardens, and with the start of collections of books, prints and sometimes pictures. As yet it was not primarily nor exclusively Italy which influenced them; indeed some were more impressed with Louis XIV's grandiose building schemes or the artistic achievements of the Dutch. But the sum total of their experience was to enrich their imaginations and, in some cases, inspire a desire to produce English versions of what they had seen abroad when they embarked on building projects or garden-making for themselves. The value of such experience was recognized by the architect Sir Roger Pratt, who advised those who were planning to build: 'If you are not able to handsomely contrive it yourself, get some ingenious gentleman who has seen much of that kind abroad, to do it for you.' A letter from William Leigh to one of his former tutors gives a clear and comprehensive summary of his tour and refers to another undertaking often required of travellers abroad, namely the making of purchases for people at home:

> You desire me in yours to make a small collection of the several coins of the countries I pass through. I wish I had known your mind at my first going abroad and then I had been in a condition to have complied with your request . . . Let me give you a brief History of the ramble I have made since I left

> you. I have seen this [Utrecht] and North Holland: the great part of Germany which contains those principal cities viz. Berlin, the residence of the king of Prussia, Dresden of the Elector of Saxony, Lipsick [Leipzig], Prague, Vienna; from this last I past the Alps over the Tyrol for Italy. I resided half a year in Rome and a month in Naples and am charmed with both: the prodigious number of Curiosities in the first and the admirable situation of the last are equally surprising.[9]

Education, travel and social contacts worked together during the seventeenth century to make the gentry classes less extrovert and less aggressively ambitious than they had been in the previous century. With increasing means at their disposal, a greater willingness to spend and many more consumer goods available, they began to achieve more refined comfort domestically and a wider range of interests in their public life than had previously satisfied them. The urge they had felt in the late sixteenth century to improve their houses and gardens was still there, much encouraged by personal acquaintance with the work of well-known architects; by information and recommendations given by family connections and acquaintances in Gloucestershire and elsewhere; and by the availability of the means (e.g. wood, furnishing materials) to realize fashionable and luxurious effects. After the Restoration of 1660 a number of houses were enlarged and improved, and turned into considerably more than the 'proud ambitious heaps and nothing else' which had been Ben Jonson's description of gentry houses in the early seventeenth century. New stabling, barns, dovecots and garden rooms or gazebos were added outside, while inside improvements included: many more fireplaces installed; walls panelled to exclude draughts – though Owlpen and Chavenage had tapestries, and some rooms at Dyrham were hung with gilt leather; closets attached not only to bedrooms but to living-rooms as well, and used for reading and writing; and servants' quarters arranged to ensure complete privacy for the family. Not many completely new houses were started during this period, but an outstanding example of new building and an elaborate new layout of grounds was introduced at Badminton, the family home of the Somersets, later Dukes of Beaufort, which replaced their former seat, Raglan Castle, destroyed during the Civil Wars. The house was contemporary in style and consisted of a great central block with wings and outbuildings, large enough to accommodate the family, their guests and the huge staff needed to maintain an aristocratic life-style. The surrounding grounds were even more impressive because of their extent. Cassandra Willoughby, who visited Badminton in 1697, commented: 'From the top of the House the Ground appears so far as you can see, all smooth like a Bowling Green; there is not a hill nor anything to bound your Sight, tis indeed the noblest flat I ever saw.' She also noted the avenues lined with trees, radiating in all directions: the 'Arbour-like walk to the Wilderness . . . so close-shaded on the top that it kept us free from a very fierce shower of rain'; and nearer the house, many greenhouses 'very neat and very fine' and nurseries for bringing on plants.

Such an edifice and grounds were of course beyond the means of mere gentry, but Badminton was visited by many prospective builders and renovators seeking ideas and inspiration, ready to imitate what they saw, on however modest a scale. The deference shown by neighbouring landowners, who cut down their own trees to enhance the views from Badminton's roof and windows, was indicative of this attitude and also explains why many small country houses, without being direct copies of them, were reminiscent of the residences being erected in London and elsewhere at this time by leading

Barnsley House, which Brereton Bourchier had built *c.* 1697. Inset: A portrait by Maria Verelst

noblemen and politicians. Two such buildings in Gloucestershire were Fairford Park and Barnsley House. The first was the work of Valentine Strong, and noted by Baskerville as 'a great square new-built house wherre Squire Barker, lord of the manor now lives, who hath the royalty of the river running by the town in which are very good trout.' A later description added that the property included 'gardens well laid out and kept in proper order: a fine plantation along the east bank of the Coln, with pleasant serpentine walks and openings to take in views of the Wiltshire hills and distant objects.' The house has now completely disappeared and its setting is so much altered as to be unrecognizable, but Kip's engraving (*c.* 1700) shows quite elaborate pleasure gardens, a kitchen garden, extensive stabling, a bowling green and tree-lined avenues leading away into the distance. Barnsley House still remains and with enough of its original features to provide a picture of a family home of the period, well-built and comfortably appointed. Brereton Bourchier, its builder and owner, was married to Katherine Brydges, a sister of the future Duke of Chandos, and both were drawn into the London social life of the Brydges family through visits and correspondence and had cosmopolitan tastes. Like others in their circle, they made their house a centre of hospitality where relatives and friends were entertained, and news and views exchanged. It stands on a rise, a short distance from the Burford–Cirencester road, surrounded by gardens and parkland, and in the late seventeenth century must have afforded a welcome stopping-place for members of the family using the difficult and sometimes hazardous routes across the Cotswolds.

Fairford Park and Barnsley House, though civilized and comfortable, were not show places. This description must be reserved for Dyrham Park, the really outstanding gentry house of the period in Gloucestershire. It was built between 1692 and 1704 by William Blathwayt, a newcomer to the county, a man who had achieved success through 'his knowledge of modern languages and his early and steady application to business.' He had been a clerk of the Privy Council under Charles II and James II, and Secretary at War and Secretary of State to William III. It was the profits of these offices and of his marriage to Mary, heiress to the fortunes of the Wynter family, that financed the creation of Dyrham Park, designed as a symbol of his public success and as a setting for his private life where his many possessions could be housed. Having travelled widely as a diplomat in France, Italy and Germany and served in Holland at the English embassy and under William, Blathwayt was well acquainted with architectural trends in these countries and inclined to emulate them, though his house was designed by Samuel Hauderoy, a French architect living in England, and William Talman, Comptroller of the Royal Works; and the grounds by George London, the most fashionable English gardener of the time. Local supplies of stone went into the basic structure of the house, but marble for fireplaces came from France; cedar, mahogany and walnut for floors, staircases and doors from the West Indies and North America; and leather, silk, satin and tapestry for hangings, curtains and upholstery from Italy and the Far East. Similarly, local labour was used for construction work, but special craftsmen, from Bath, Oxford and London, were entrusted with decorative carving, carpentry, plastering and sculpture. Blathwayt himself was not always on the spot, so he had to rely on others to report progress and to see that his wishes were carried out – a situation far from satisfactory in view of his impatience to have the work completed. His complaints of slowness – 'Hunter intends never to have finished but to wynter in ye Country at my expense' – were met with excuses of workers being discontented with wages, or absent 'because of revels at Bath'; these were followed by threats from Blathwayt that he would dismiss the local workforce and bring replacements from London – surely only bluff in view of how much more labourers from the capital would have had to be paid. And always he was mindful of details, including these in letters and memos to supervisors on the spot:

> The Gilt Leather in the Great Parlour very ill putt up and must be strecht which can only be done in Wett Weather
> The Cover of the Billiard Table to be changed for a more Substantiall Leather
> The Pallet Bed of Printed Calico . . . to be placed within 6 inches of the Wall
> The Window Curtains in the Gilt Leather Parlour . . . to be made to draw up
> The Cage (for singing birds) must be so hung up upon a very strong Pulley as not to deface the Ceiling, nor the Rope to be too much in ye Eye[10]

Dyrham. View of the main block and orangery, designed and built for William Blathwayt in a style befitting his status as adviser to William III

Into this setting was introduced Blathwayt's large collection of pictures, most of them Dutch paintings of birds, flowers, seascapes, landscapes and interiors. Specimens of blue-and-white Delft ware and Chinese porcelain adorned shelves and chimney pieces. Glass-fronted presses, specially made, held the most valuable books in the library which comprised volumes in many languages, 'bound in vellum and marbled paper', dictionaries, collections of maps and prints – all reflecting Blathwayt's many and varied interests. Private and public rooms were furnished with elaborately carved chests and cabinets, richly upholstered chairs and couches, ornamental mirrors, curtained beds and Persian carpets. It was natural that Blathwayt, a close friend and great admirer of William III, should share the latter's chief pleasures (architecture, painting and gardening) and not surprising therefore that Dutch influences should play a large part in the furnishing of the interior, and the making of the garden at Dyrham. 'Every caprice of the Dutch style which could be effected by Art, abounded at Dyrham where such Ornaments were so numerous and sumptuous as to defy both Expence and Imitation' (Bigland). Because the house was situated in a hollow with steeply rising ground on three sides, it was impossible to reproduce a flat Dutch landscape; however, the main features of such were achieved by the introduction and use of water, the hillsides being terraced and local springs exploited to facilitate the making of a huge cascade, many fountains, and a long canal and two lakes close to and on a level with the house. Like

A seventeenth-century bedroom at Flaxley Abbey, satisfying the contemporary desire for comfort and style

Badminton, Dyrham had 'a wilderness of high large trees and where they are many agreable shades', formal parterres and an orangery constructed as an integral part of the house. This was used to shelter delicate trees and shrubs and propagate the seeds that Blathwayt was able to obtain through his connections with Holland and overseas trading companies. Dyrham inspired widespread and uncritical admiration and was soon attracting sightseers. Though the grounds were much altered during the eighteenth century, the details of the Kip engraving included in Atkyns' *Ancient and Present State of Glostershire* are confirmed by the written records of Blathwayt's undertaking, and by a descriptive chapter devoted to the garden by Stephen Switzer, a contemporary horticulturalist and writer on gardens, in his *Ichnographia Rustica*.

Dutch influences were also evident in two other Gloucestershire gardens being laid out at much the same time as Dyrham. One was at Flaxley Abbey where, in the middle of the century, the Boevey family had replaced the Kingstons as owners. William and James Boevey belonged to a second generation of Dutch settlers in England. Made wealthy through trade, they were only slowly becoming Anglicized and entertaining social ambitions, until William, son of James, married Catharine Riches, very much younger than himself, well-educated, cultured, and anxious to turn Flaxley (still largely consisting of the old abbey buildings) into a comfortable family home and give it a contemporary setting. After only a few years of marriage, Catharine was left a widow with very considerable means, which she proceeded to spend on Flaxley. Her Dutch connections explained the introduction of a canal, flower-beds, fountains and an avenue of trees, where before a stretch of grass had covered the site of the monastic cloisters and garden. Catharine Boevey had as a friend and neighbour (and a fellow enthusiast for good works) Maynard Colchester at Westbury-on-Severn, who had succeeded to the manor and estates there in 1696 and immediately set about remaking the garden; and although it is true that Dutch influences spread rapidly throughout the whole country after the accession of William III in 1689, inevitably Colchester must have been aware of the changes that were taking place so near at hand at Flaxley. The design of the garden at Westbury has survived in spite of later alterations and some years of total neglect, and has recently been recreated by the National Trust working on the basis of details recorded in Colchester's account books between 1696 and 1705. As in the cases of Dyrham and Flaxley, there is a Kip drawing that defines the main features of the new layout: an elaborate formal garden near the house with parterres, a pond and a fountain, and a long canal flanked by lines of holly and yew trees planted alternately and near enough to the water to be reflected in it. At one end of the canal was a tall summerhouse with large sash windows commanding wide views and a cupola topped by a gilded copper ball, easily visible from a distance. At the other end of the canal a low wall fronted the high road with a gateway set in to provide a view of the grounds from the road. A nursery garden produced some of the plants needed to stock the garden and, according to the account books, flowering shrubs, fruit trees and hundreds of bulbs – tulips, irises, narcissi, anemones, etc. – were bought and planted to ensure a mass of spring colour.[11]

Not every family had the inclination and means to furnish their houses and lay out their gardens on the scale of Dyrham or Westbury; nevertheless it is clear from household accounts and correspondence that in general the standard of living was improving and many new refinements coming to be accepted as the norm. Having moved away from a feudal relationship with those who were dependent upon them, the gentry no longer had unpaid servants, nor, since the practice had been dropped, could they count on the services of young men from other gentry families being trained as gentlemen in their household. On the whole, households were smaller than they had been a century earlier (a staff of twelve on a yearly wage was fairly common) with servants having clearly defined duties to perform, though these could be multifarious – a coachman being required to double as a footman and vice-versa: a housekeeper being expected to take responsibility for keeping accounts and controlling household stores as well as supervising the maidservants. Seldom were there hangers on qualifying for board and lodging in return for mere attendance or occasional minor services, but this did not mean that the family was without its dependants. Trusted servants were frequently kept on beyond their usefulness and provided with accommodation in the house or somewhere near; they were also remembered in wills. John Dutton (1657) wrote:

> My will likewise is that my household servants be kept together and continue in my house for the space of 2 months next after my decease, in which time they may better provide for themselves for

Westbury Court. The gardens were laid out in Dutch style for Maynard Colchester

> their future livelihood. And that a competent allowance be given to my wife for housekeeping during that time and for payment of their wages.

Some years later his nephew's wife, Mary Dutton, bequeathed:

> To my servant that shall live with me at the time of my death as my waiting-woman, a suit of mourning, and besides a year's wages. To my servant Mary Kirby whom I took as an apprentice, the sum of four pounds.[12]

Such regard on the part of employers seems to have been fairly common, but of course there must have been inconsiderate masters and mistresses as well as unreliable (and perhaps unscrupulous) servants. What were the true facts behind the will of Tryphena Leigh (daughter of Theophilus Leigh and his first wife, Lady Elizabeth Craven) in which her servant Mary Cocks was named as sole executrix, and legatee of almost all her mistress's wealth and possessions? After leaving her father's house and going to live at Painswick with Mary Cocks, Tryphena appeared to drop out of the Leigh circle entirely, no references being made to her in the letters of a normally caring and affectionate family. Was Tryphena herself to blame, or Mary Cocks? A similar situation occurred at Flaxley. In 1686, Catharine Boevey took as her companion Mrs Mary Pope who came to stay for a month and remained forty years. She gradually asserted her authority over the household and ultimately, as sole executrix after her benefactress's death, made off with her books and failed to spend the money entrusted to her for the rebuilding of the parish church for the intended purpose.

As well as regular servants, there were a number of people employed from time to time by gentry households – men to carry messages and packages, women to knit stockings, mend clothes, do extra washing and help in the garden. It is not possible to judge whether their services were urgently needed or whether these jobs were found for them. A 'wash mayd' – Anne King, paid £2 per annum – was one of the staff at Adlestrop, yet other people were paid for 'the scouring of blankets' and for 'the washing of my Lady's white hood'. Again, although there were regular gardeners attached to the households, at Westbury a woman was paid for collecting liverwort, and at Adlestrop for bringing holly and wood sorrel. And then there were the poor and needy, not belonging to the parish or receiving the Poor Rate, and a growing problem to judge by the frequency of entries such as these in household accounts:

A dumb man at Evesham	4*d*.
A poor lame man at the door	6*d*.
A poor Yorkshire woman	6*d*.
A pig bought for a poor family	2*s*. 6*d*.
A poor man that had had losses by fire	2*s*. 6*d*.

This last item crops up in many accounts. Admittedly fires in flimsily built cottages must have been fairly frequent, but was this perhaps a generally accepted formula used by those obliged to beg?

Household and personal accounts, as meticulously detailed as estate records, indicate that food was varied and by no means humdrum. Gloucestershire households clearly benefited from proximity to the Severn because salmon, lobsters, crabs, oysters and lampreys were often mentioned; and the availability of goods being imported through Bristol would explain purchases of lemons, oranges, almonds, spices, wine and currants. Though gardens produced fresh fruit and vegetables, raspberries, strawberries, cherries and gooseberries were bought from time to time. London seems to have been the main source of tea and coffee which were requested, in letters, from friends and acquaintances. Such services were usually acknowledged by gifts of venison, woodcock, partridges, salmon – most acceptable to anyone living or staying in town. Much concern about health was expressed in letters. Reports on, and enquiries after, invalids were taken seriously, but the remedies advocated and tried suggest that the sick who survived them must indeed have been tough. Frequent payments to doctors for attendance on children and for bone-setting would seem to indicate that such professionals were available even in rural areas.

Dyrham. The State Bedroom, furnished sumptuously for the entertainment of royalty though Blathwayt was never called upon to provide this

Clothes were still largely being made at home and mended and renovated there. Materials for these and useful accessories such as buttons, tapes, lace and ribbon were bought for this purpose. Now and again, a straw hat, a pair of gloves, a petticoat or a pair of breeches are budgeted for, but clearly these were not readily available locally. Theophilus Leigh, having asked his son James to buy him a nightgown in London, grew anxious when it did not arrive:

> This carries you a Hue and Cry after my Night Gown wch in yr last to me you had promised to bring in a day or two: and in yrs since to Molly, writ yt you had bought it. I wish you have not sent it by a wrong Carryer. Ours is ye Winchcombe Carryer: his name Isaac Rasthill, he inns at ye Whitehorse near Holborn Brydge and comes out of Town Thursday morning between 10 and 11.[13]

Watches and clocks, silver ornaments and candlesticks must also have been obtained in Bath, Bristol or London, though the mending of them was sometimes entrusted to local workers. Not every household could boast of the up-to-date furniture in foreign woods such as adorned Dyrham, but even if locally made in English timber, beds had attractive hangings and coverlets, chairs were upholstered and there was an abundance of cushions, pillows and bolsters to provide further comfort. The increasing emphasis on the keeping of accounts and the greater amount of letter-writing explains regular expenditure on parchment, ink, quills, wax and sand.

Released from the restrictions imposed on them during the Civil Wars, the gentry became increasingly active in their pursuit of entertainment in the second half of the seventeenth century. Expanding business and family concerns obliged them to travel more than they had done before, but a greater interest in and knowledge of the country inspired a confidence and inclination to travel for pleasure as well. By 1700, Kip had begun to sketch his impressions of gentry houses and their settings, later to be included in Sir Robert Atkyns' *Ancient and Present State of Glostershire*. In gentlemen's libraries there could be found surveys of various counties and collections of maps including Camden's *Britannia* and Ogilbey's *Road Book*; and many households afforded hospitality to friends and relatives on tour and heard their experiences at first hand. During the 1670s Thomas Baskerville in the course of his travels visited Gloucestershire and recorded his impressions of the gentry houses and towns that he passed through. In the 1690s Cassandra Willoughby showed herself an indefatigable traveller, carrying out a round of visits to family connections in the Gloucestershire area – the Leighs at Adlestrop, the Chamberlaynes at Maugersbury, the Somersets at Troy (where they lived prior to moving to Badminton) and the Brydges at Wilton – and keeping a journal of her visits to these places as well as elsewhere. Celia Fiennes, whose uncle lived at Moreton-in-Marsh, also passed through during the 1690s in the course of her *Travels on Horseback through Great Britain*; while shortly after the turn of the century, in 1703, William and John Blathwayt, still only teenagers and perhaps in preparation for a Grand Tour abroad later on, travelled to the north of England in the company of their tutor who recorded their progress. Men who were acting as sheriffs, justices of the peace and deputy lords-lieutenant had to travel round the county frequently on administrative business and members of parliament had to go to London, but these journeys had their social side as well and the visits of officials could stir quite small towns – Gloucester, Tewkesbury, Cirencester – into a whirl of activity that was an echo of what was going on all the time in London. By the late seventeenth century visitors to the capital had formed their own Gloucestershire Society as much for social reasons as for its avowed charitable purpose. In addition to their own legal and financial business, gentlemen carried out commissions for their friends, visited the theatre and listened to coffee-house gossip. Life in London could, however, have its hazardous moments, as reported in a letter sent to Sir John Newton by his son:

> On Sunday last there happened a sad accident to Esq. Thynn who lately marry'd ye Lady Ogle, as he was rideing in his Coach through ye Pall Mall, 3 or 4 outlandish men on horse back came up to ye Coach and one of ym discharged a Blunderbuss at him and shot him through ye body with Severall bullets: whereof 5 or 6 were found in his body so that he died ye next morning. Ye men are since taken and have confest ye fact, ye occasion for this barbarous assassination is not certainly known but it is conjectured to be in respect to an outlandish Count, who, as they say, had received some affront from Esq. Thynn. Ye Count was formerly a pretender to Lady Ogle.[14]

Nearer home there were regular exchanges of visits with relatives and neighbours. From Adlestrop, Theophilus Leigh walked every week to Cornwell to attend a club where local gentlemen met to discuss the news, books and other matters of common interest. He also gave a weekly dinner party for family and friends to which his sons came from Oxford, and seemingly many of his expeditions were also family affairs, often several in one week, according to the record he kept of them:

> We went to Maugersbury to dinner
> With my children to Sir William Juxon's
> I went to Lower Swell to Sir Robert Atkyns
> Went to my cousin Tracy's at Stanway to dinner
> To Mr Hastings at Daylesford where I stood Godfather to his son
> Went with sisters Chamberlayne and Bourchier to Heythrop
> To Mr Knight at Daylesford to see his new house.[15]

Families enjoyed having meals together, playing cards, discussing news. Almost every house had its own bowling green which came into use on these occasions, and newly laid out gardens must have been of interest to visitors. Making and listening to music always afforded pleasure. As well as being visited by mummers, waits and 'The Musick' – local talent that visited gentry houses – members of the family were able to perform themselves. Many households had musical instruments and Thomas Baskerville, while visiting the widow Castleman at Coberley, noticed in the parlour 'a fair organ, viols and violins'. Edmund Chamberlayne, an ungracious curmudgeon in many ways, became an amiable host under the influence of music. Early in the next century, Lady Freeman of Batsford, considering the suitability of an Oxford graduate as a tutor for her family, noted with satisfaction: 'He also understands Musick being a performer upon the Bass Violl and Flute which will be a great advantage to the children in their Musick.' When renovations to houses and gardens were discussed, no doubt the craftsmen responsible for the work were either praised or criticized; and if a landscape or family portraits were required, then it was helpful to look at examples of a painter's work and receive a recommendation. To judge by inventories, most houses had their quota of pictures, including family portraits by fashionable artists. Blathwayts, Bourchiers, Leighs and

Brydges, for instance, were painted by Kneller, Simon and Maria Verelst, Michael Dahl and John Taylor.

For the really energetic, outdoor sports came into their own again after the wars, especially once estate owners were able to replace their stocks of weapons and horses. Hawking was not as much practised as in the previous century, but fowling continued along the banks of the Severn. The coursing of hounds and deer-hunting were popular with Cotswold landowners, many of whom still maintained their deer parks. The best known of these was at Sherborne where John Dutton had built up his herd during the Commonwealth period, employed staff to manage this, and provided comfortable accommodation for spectators in a lodge in the park. Not only did Dutton provide entertainment for his friends, but any owner of hounds, on paying a fee of *2s. 6d.* and tipping the keepers, was free to make use of the facilities in the park to try out his animals. As a family the Duttons loved sport, had an inherited predilection for gambling and were very fond of their horses. This is reflected in the bequests made by William, nephew and heir of John Dutton:

> I give and bequeath to my truly real friend Sir Denis Harper my young brown horse. I give and bequeath to my loving friend Sir Will Juxon my chestnut horse with my brown foal colt that comes 3 years old. I give to my very true friend Mr Rutter my pad nag, my little yearling colt to be kept till he be fitting to be backed. All the rest of my horses I leave to my truly loving brother.[16]

Theophilus Leigh was another keen horse breeder, having in his stables Turkish steeds, Arabian greys and Galloways, while one of the mares reared by Brereton Bourchier at Barnsley was lent to James Brydges for breeding purposes. During the second half of the seventeenth century, for betting men and those interested in horses, the major attraction was Bibury Races. Held on Aldsworth Downs, between Bibury and Burford, these drew crowds from all over the country, were patronized by Charles II and his brother James, and afforded occasions for the local gentry to entertain on a lavish scale, and either improve or diminish their fortunes.

CHAPTER EIGHT

THE CLOSING YEARS OF THE SEVENTEENTH CENTURY

In the course of the seventeenth century the gentry had become more aware of how much their lives could be affected by the central government, and of the impossibility of remaining immune from the consequences of its policies. This meant that, especially after the Civil Wars, they were conscious of the importance of having political knowledge, whether they were actively involved in administration or not, and of being able to work out for themselves the possible trend of future events. Through newsletters, contacts in London and correspondence with friends abroad, they had the means of assessing the wider implications of what was happening, both for themselves and for the county community as a whole, and to feel the more confident or fearful accordingly. Education, experience and ambition drew a number away from the county into the wider sphere of national affairs, but most of those concerned with leading an active public life were content with assuming local responsibilities and trying to safeguard the interest of the Gloucestershire community, which loomed as large in their estimation as the whole country. There were also those who remained parish gentry, concerned only with the affairs of their own families and dependants and their immediate locality, sharing many of the interests and pleasures of the more important families, but avoiding wider commitments which lack of means or inclination might prevent them fulfilling.

As the reign of Charles II continued, with official policy aiming to uphold the restored power of the monarchy and established Church against possible attempts to undermine their supremacy, the old antagonisms that had divided the gentry during the wars continued to exist – not to the extent of open hostility it is true, but nevertheless enough to indicate that people, once roused to political awareness, could not be lulled back into unconsciousness again. Religious dissenters, though still present, were prevented by the Clarendon Code from holding public office, and the opponents of the Stuarts on political grounds were careful not to reveal their opinions unless or until it behoved them to do so; so it was only the occurrence of the Exclusion crisis towards the end of the reign that forced men into declarations of sympathy and divided the ranks of the gentry again. Charles's lack of a legitimate heir meant that the succession would pass to his brother James, Duke of York, but this prospect was unacceptable to those who feared the latter's Catholicism and absolutist tendencies. Charles, who had no illusions about James, was determined that he should succeed to the throne, come what may, and, to defeat the organized move to exclude him, dismissed three parliaments in as many years (1679–81) when opposition members threatened to pass a bill insisting that the next sovereign must be a Protestant. (Charles's illegitimate son, the Duke of Monmouth, and James's elder daughter Mary, married to William, ruler of the United Provinces, were named as possible candidates.) Those members who were present at these sessions were obliged to take sides and to vote on the issue. It was at this point that the opposing sides christened each other by hurling insults that came to be adopted as party labels – the Exclusionist Whigs being named after the stubborn Presbyterian opponents of the Stuarts in the Scottish lowlands; the Tory supporters of Charles after the native clansmen who had resisted the establishment of English rule in Ireland. On the whole, Gloucestershire gentry representing the county and other places, while in favour of Exclusion, were not prepared to attend in order to express their views, Richard Howe (sitting for Wiltshire) and Henry Powle (for Cirencester) being among the exceptions who both attended and voted against Exclusion.

It is doubtful whether any of the members of the Exclusion Parliaments could have foreseen the lengths to which James – once he became king – was prepared to go in pursuit of his aims, but Sir John Guise left the country in 1685 and took refuge in Holland rather than stay to find out. The abortive attempt by the Duke of Monmouth to sieze the throne in the first year of James's reign (1685) did not affect Gloucestershire directly though he had some covert sympathizers there – Sir John Dutton and Sir Robert Atkyns for example. However, the retention of the army that had subdued the rebellion, and James's subsequent attempts to introduce Catholics into key positions at Oxford, to bludgeon judges into acknowledging his right to suspend or dispense with established laws, and to force the clergy into upholding his Declarations of Indulgence (designed to extend toleration to all nonconformists, Protestant and Catholic alike) inevitably aroused resentment even among those who, until then, had believed that true loyalty to the monarch was synonymous with non-resistance. After all, a large number of the gentry had been at Oxford and felt some kind of allegiance to their own college, if not to the university as a whole; many had trained in the law and had helped to pass statutes in parliament; others were patrons of livings, had relatives in the church, or just felt that their loyalty to the Anglican establishment overrode all other considerations. Active opposition to the royal policy became apparent when the deputy lords-lieutenant refused to complete a questionnaire regarding their own political opinions and those of other leading men in the county; and when newly appointed judges (James's nominees), arriving in Gloucestershire to conduct the assizes, were met by the sheriff alone and boycotted by the gentry who customarily would have turned out to greet the visiting dignitaries and offer them hospitality.

In 1688, as leading politicians were considering how James could be brought to see the error of his ways, his second wife, the Catholic Mary of Modena, gave birth to a son, thus opening up the prospect of a continuation of James's policies into another reign. So, in order to safeguard the Protestant Church and the laws of England, an invitation was sent to Mary, James's daughter in Holland, to take his place. Up to this point, though openly disapproving of James's policy, the Gloucestershire gentry had been 'trimming' in the hope that a major crisis might be averted somehow. However, when it was known that Mary's husband William of Orange had embarked for England to claim the throne and James had issued orders to the lord-lieutenant to summon the militia, the old instinct to obey their anointed king came into operation again; the Duke of Beaufort had no difficulty in getting his deputies to muster troops at Cirencester to stop William in his tracks should he land at Bristol (as was expected) and try to proceed through Gloucestershire to London. In the event William landed on the south coast and came nowhere near the county, though one of the few violent affrays that occurred during the so-called *Bloodless Revolution* took place at Cirencester, where several members of the militia were killed by the followers of Sir Richard Lovelace, while the latter were trying to make their way to Bristol to join William.

The flight of James left the way clear for his daughter and son-in-law to succeed him, and turned the question of loyalty into an unavoidable and, for some, an insoluble issue. The generally accepted justification for the Revolution Settlement – namely that the throne was left vacant by James and that it was incumbent on parliament to appoint his successor – was not sufficient to salve the consciences of those who regarded an oath of allegiance to an anointed king as absolutely binding until that king should die. So when it came to all public officials having to pledge their loyalty to William and Mary, some chose to relinquish their posts and retire into private life. Prominent Gloucestershire gentlemen who were prepared to acknowledge the new rulers were Sir John Guise, who had returned from Holland, Sir Ralph Dutton, John Grobham Howe, Thomas Master and Sir Robert Atkyns. Those who did not take an oath of allegiance, and thus became Non-Jurors, included members of the Leigh, Chamberlayne, Blomer, Bourchier and Bathurst families, and Edward Atkyns, whose post as Judge of the Exchequer was transferred to his brother Robert. Thus while retaining social links and continuing to share many interests and pleasures with each other, the gentry became markedly divided on national political issues. As far as county interests were concerned, they presented a united front, but when it came to seeking public office or promoting their public image then all might depend on which party was in power at Westminster, and their own relationship with it. To hold public office at any time was costly in terms of time, money and effort, and during the eighteenth century it came to involve commitment to a particular way of life as well. To be out of office left a man free to devote himself to the affairs of his family and estate, but also demoted him to the ranks of the parish gentry.

At the close of the seventeenth century the number of gentry in Gloucestershire had changed little, though the fortunes of some families had been affected by circumstances and certain names had either become less prominent or disappeared altogether, being replaced by those of newcomers. In the next century Wynters, Pooles and Kingstons, Hungerfords and Cliffords no longer played a leading role in county affairs, while Atkyns, Colchesters, Blathwayts and Boeveys did. Those who had managed to survive and surmount the vicissitudes of the period had moved with the times, shown enterprise in managing their affairs and had sufficient acumen to avoid political pitfalls. Of the newly eminent among the ranks of the gentry, the Atkyns and Colchesters had legal training and experience behind them; the Clutterbucks were successful clothiers and had married into the long-established Clifford family; the Boeveys had a mercantile background; and William Blathwayt, diplomatic training and marriage with the heiress of the Wynters. A few families without previous roots in the county acquired a landed interest there for a limited period, but disappeared in the next century – the Courteens at Swell and the Castlemans at Coberley. Men like John Crofts and Sir Edward Massey, who came into prominence only as a result of the wars and Commonwealth, achieved no lasting fame in county affairs. The latter might have done, perhaps, had he married and had a son to succeed him, for he was a born winner in many respects; but lack of an heir was one of the rocks on which even an ancient family could founder, as John Clifford wrote on the occasion of the Heralds' Visitation in 1682:

> I was forct to huddle up that small entry your Clark took out of my pedigree which had I had longer notice of your coming should have bin better prepared. . . . Unless it may add anything to your compleating of your record, 'tis indifferent to me whether it be entred or not, the name of Clifford in this Country dying with me for want of issue male after 600 years continuance in the same place. Kingdoms and Familys have theyr periodes.[1]

Of course there must already have been in this century some prototypes of the bucolic squires of the eighteenth century novels who damaged rather than enhanced the family reputation and fortunes. Those disinclined to write letters or keep accounts have left no records by which to be judged; the black sheep who turned up from time to time in many families were outnumbered by more worthy souls. Occasionally though, we are made aware of them. Theophilus Leigh's long and patient struggles with his eldest son James, as revealed in his letters, are highlighted by the latter's marked lack of appreciation and response. In spite of having life made easy for him, James was querulous, demanding and difficult. His dealings with a fellow-officer from whom he withheld 'forrage money' seem to have been high-handed in the extreme, and it is not surprising that they ended in a duel. James's irritation that his father should want to know about 'so trifling an affair' is typical. Anthony Kingscote, too, felt that he had good reason to disinherit his eldest son Christopher: 'He is and hath been a very disobedient sonne unto mee and his Mother, and hath rejected and scorned both our Councells and alsoe the advice and councells of all his best friends.' Other faults included prodigal spending, cheating his brother, getting into debt and 'that he was never married to this Woman that liveth with him.' It may be, however, that the father was carried away by his extreme puritanical views in judging a son who had adopted and clung to a royalist outlook and life style. Edmund Chamberlayne was another whose ways were deplored by his family. Capable of being charming to his friends, Chamberlayne was consistently inconsiderate towards his wife whom he kept short of money, and to his sons who might well have remained uneducated but for the generosity of his brother-in-law. Nor did he endear himself to local people when he shot one of his tenants whose wife he had seduced and managed to escape punishment. Family exasperation was summed up in a letter from Lady Chandos, his mother-in-law, to Theophilus Leigh (1703):

> Son Chamberlayne went away and never took leave of ever a one of his wife's relations and stayed almost a fortnight in town after he told his friends his business was done and he was to be gone next morning. I do give you to be so kind as to tell him I hope he will not forget his promise to let his wife come up to town and see her friends. I think 'tis very hard after 7 years' time he should grudge it, considering what a wife she has been to him: and pray, son Leigh, let him understand for his own reputation's sake, he might be a little kinder to her.[2]

On the whole, though, Macaulay's description of the gentry in the late seventeenth century as gross, uneducated and untravelled was not true of the majority of

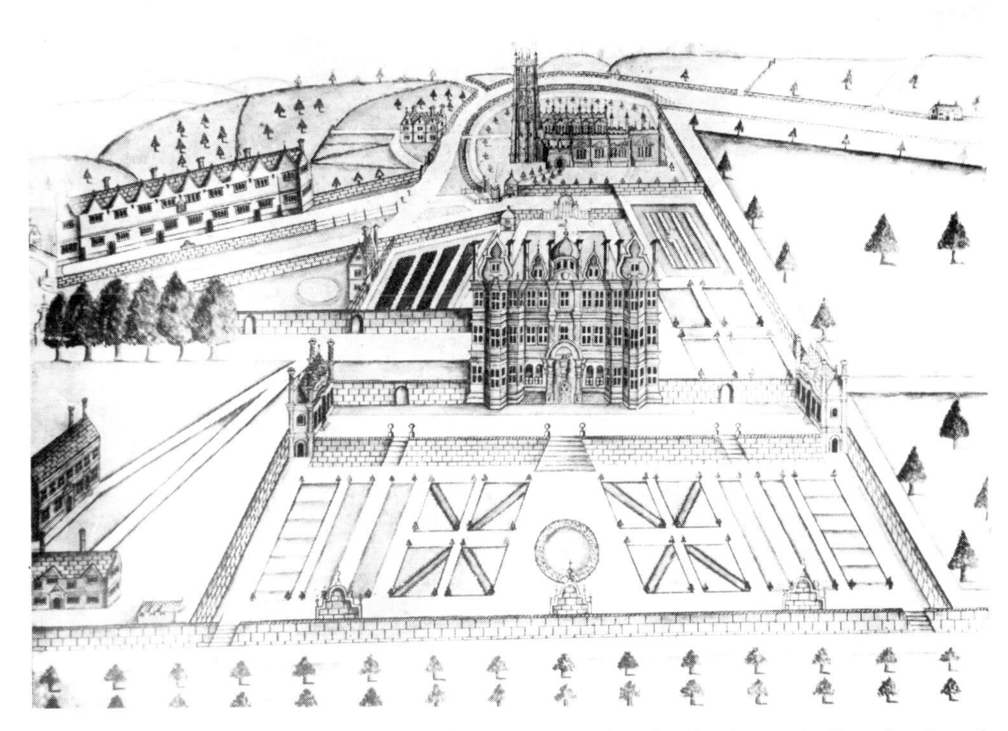

Chipping Campden: showing the home of Sir Baptist Hicks, the almshouses built and endowed by him, and the church where he and his family were buried. A seventeenth-century watercolour

Gloucestershire families which, so far as existing records can reveal, appear to have been reasonably well-read, conscientious in fulfilling private and public commitments, well-meaning towards their fellows and genuinely concerned with the interests of the county. Either by the appointment and support of an incumbent or by contributing to its upkeep they helped to maintain the parish church and tried to ensure its continuing usefulness to the community. Sir Robert Atkyns, finding the situation in Lower Swell outside his control, in a letter dated 1683 drew the attention of the Bishop of Oxford to:

> the ill condition of our chancel . . . and the cold air, the wind and wet that blows in upon us. We seldom have any communion and not till we invite our minister to afford it to us. We have some hasty prayers in the morning every Sunday and a few notes read to us in the afternoon, for Mr Callow is minister too of Stow and is in haste still to ride away from us thither and it is no wonder if of those few that belong to us, some are Quakers and some Anabaptists and very few of the rest care for coming to church. We earnestly entreat your care for us and help us to one that will take pains among us and faithfully and diligently watch over our souls, catechise our children and servants and visit our ignorant people . . .[3]

Gentry families continued to finance almshouses founded during the previous century and to establish new ones, such as the Hicks and Perry foundations at Chipping Campden and Wotton-under-Edge respectively, and the Dutton almshouse at Northleach. By the end of the century too, they had been responsible for endowing in many villages benefactions of food, fuel and clothes. Evidence of a new and more constructive attitude to alms-giving can be seen in the growing number of trusts to finance schools and forms of training for the poor. Some of these schools provided elementary education for both boys and girls, and instruction in useful skills; Sir Thomas Rich's Hospital at Gloucester (founded 1666) also arranged apprenticeships for boys, with London masters. Grammar schools, like Sir William Romney's at Tetbury (1610) and William White's at Thornbury (1642), it was hoped, might give a start in life to worthy poor scholars; and the link between Gloucestershire and Oxford University was recognized and strengthened by the foundation of scholarships by George Townsend to enable eight scholars from schools in Cheltenham, Northleach, Chipping Campden and Gloucester to study for degrees at Pembroke College.

Whether the gentry understood the economic forces behind the changing times or not, they certainly recognized their symptoms and reacted to them; they also realized that, for some, the changes were for the worse and not the better. We have mentioned the increasing number of beggars in the countryside, somehow escaping the net of the Poor Law and dependent on charity for subsistence; and the church at Lower Swell was probably not the only one that was affording shelter to the homeless. 'There is in our little church an aisle that is ready to fall and it is called by the people the knaves' house and some beggars have heretofore made it their dwelling.' Those who stepped in with money and bequests at this point could not have known that what they saw as a worrying problem was a mere trickle compared with the overwhelming flood of poverty and unemployment that was to affect the whole country in the next century; and that, even in the late seventeenth century, their efforts to make the existing Poor Law work, and to implement it with charitable gestures whenever possible, had minimal effects; nevertheless they tried.

Interlude

POLITICAL BACKGROUND TO THE EIGHTEENTH CENTURY

The coronation of William III and Mary as sovereigns in place of James II, while calming the nation's fears of the establishment of a military despotism and a dominant Roman Catholic Church, was not a lasting settlement in itself. The terms of the Bill of Rights (1689), accepted as binding by the new rulers, limited the monarch's power to set himself above the law, established his financial dependence on parliament and safeguarded the supremacy of the Anglican Church. The future remained uncertain though, as William and Mary had no children at the time of their accession and, following Mary's death in 1694, William's obvious unwillingness to consider remarrying meant a direct heir was unlikely. The death of James II in France in 1701 and the recognition of his son, James Francis Edward, by Louis XIV as rightful successor to the English throne threatened the country with further anxiety as to who was to be the next ruler. Members of parliament, determined to keep this decision in their own hands, drew up and passed the Act of Settlement (1701) fixing the succession on Mary's sister Anne, the younger daughter of James II, a Protestant married to a Protestant, Prince George of Denmark. The Act also provided that should Anne die without an heir, which now seemed only too likely in view of her having no surviving children after seventeen pregnancies, then the throne was to pass to Sophia of Hanover and her heirs, direct descendants of James I's daughter Elizabeth and her husband Frederick of the Palatinate.

William III disliked and distrusted the English political parties and would have liked to ignore them, but he needed the support of parliament to finance his government in England and his wars against Louis XIV. These were begun initially to defend the United Provinces, but arguably also, after James II's friendly reception in France, to safeguard England against foreign invasion. Necessarily therefore, he sought the co-operation of the Whigs who had invited Mary and himself to rule, while accepting that the Tories and Non-Jurors, who could not reconcile their consciences with accepting the new régime, would oppose him. When Anne came to the throne in 1702 she should have been able to count on universal support since she was a Stuart in the direct line of succession, and a Protestant. However, she was not a strong enough personality nor sufficiently independent of her ministers to reconcile the two parties which continued to take opposing views of the war with France (which could be regarded as either a necessary measure of defence or a pointless extravagance), and of the question of the succession – supposedly decided by the Act of Settlement, but still a source of concern to the Tories who had doubts about the morality and legality of accepting the Hanoverians when a son of James II was alive and available to succeed. Those who thought along these lines were encouraged by the willingness of the queen herself to contemplate the succession of her half-brother, but in the event their opponents were more determined and better organized to ensure that the objectives of the revolution of 1688 should be realized. Anne's death in 1714, though it came as no surprise, nevertheless found the Tories still pondering what moves to make, while the Whigs, who had been poised for action for some while, promptly sent off an invitation to Sophia's son, George Elector of Hanover, to assume the government of England.

Because they were German born and bred and made no secret of their deep fondness and concern for Hanover, the first two Georges were not popular as sovereigns. Both were by nature shy, with a preference for leading their lives in private rather than in public, rigid in their habits and by no means inspiring company. Neither was particularly cultured and except for music had little interest in the arts. George I had no wife to preside over his court (she had been divorced and left imprisoned in a castle in Germany) and his immediate entourage consisted of German servants and mistresses, an unaccustomed and unacceptable arrangement in English eyes. Another unusual feature of his family life was the bitter hatred which he displayed publicly towards his son – creating an ambiguous situation for those wishing to serve at Court or seek favours, for loyalty to the reigning monarch precluded loyalty to the heir to the throne and vice versa. When he succeeded his father in 1727, George II – though he had a charming and cultured wife – showed the same reluctance to surround himself with an interesting and scintillating court, and indulged in the same hostility towards his son and heir, Frederick, Prince of Wales.

Like William III, George I and George II were well aware of their indebtedness to the Whig party for their position and power, and of the potential danger to them of the Jacobite Tories. Thus for the first two decades of their rule, Whigs held all posts of responsibility in the government, had the controlling influence in both houses of Parliament, and exercised power even in the provinces by cultivating 'interest', that is, a following on whose support they could count at elections and in carrying out government policies in return for the granting of favours or merely a known connection. The leader of the Whigs was Sir Robert Walpole, more perhaps of a country squire than a polished statesman, but trusted by George I and his son and sufficiently well regarded by the people as a whole to reconcile them to the Hanoverian succession. Even more importantly, he kept the country at peace until 1739, thus giving it a chance to recover from the expenses of the recent wars against France and to exploit the gains secured by the Treaty of Utrecht (1713) which ended them, namely: extended trading rights and possessions in the New World, and recognition for Britain as the leading power in Europe.

The outbreak of war with Spain in 1739, which ran counter to his policy of peace, marked the first stage of Walpole's decline. In 1742, he was forced to resign, having lost control of a majority in the Commons, the essential factor of his political supremacy. Thereafter, the situation between the two parties remained confused until the accession of George III in 1760, with both Whigs and Tories split into self-centred groups. All were concerned with the pursuit of wealth and prosperity but with differing views as to the best way to achieve these: most of the Whigs were in favour of protecting commercial and colonial interests by means of war if necessary, whereas most of the Tories, with landowning interests at heart, believed that peace and low taxation were the best means of safeguarding the status quo.

By 1760, when George II was succeeded by his grandson George III, Jacobite hopes had finally faded, and with them the reservations that some Tories had had about accepting the Hanoverians. Even the masses now were prepared to regard the third George as 'their' king, for he had been born and brought up in England and was anxious to identify himself with the interests of his subjects. That he succeeded up to a point was indicated by the nickname he was given – 'Farmer George' – and by the warm reception he and his family received when they made royal visits, for instance, the one to Cheltenham in 1788. Much though he would like to have reassumed the constitutional powers of the early Stuart monarchs, George was too willing to be influenced by other people to assert his authority effectively most of the time. When he did the results were usually unfortunate, exemplified by the stand he made against the American colonies which provoked war and ultimately the loss of part of Britain's overseas empire, plus the alienation of most European countries that sympathised with the colonists' repudiation of English rights to control their trade and inhibit their industrial development.

To the English people, the loss of the colonies was primarily of economic rather than political significance since it affected both imports and exports and domestic occupations connected with these, and caused a slump in trade and employment. In the long run, however, it was the political implications of the Declaration of Independence that had the most far-reaching effects, since the definition of personal rights contained therein had an instant appeal for anyone who believed he was suffering oppression or injustice. The success of the Americans in putting their principles into practice helped to spark off an already combustible situation in France and precipitated the revolution of 1789. In England, though the romantically inclined and the helpless poor viewed events in France with excitement and approval, those in charge of government were filled with apprehension and took immediate steps to check the spread of subversive ideas among the disaffected; they then declared war on the French to prevent them spreading revolution by force to Britain and elsewhere in Europe.

CHAPTER NINE

PUBLIC SERVANTS

The gentry network in Gloucestershire was comprehensive and close, a fact that becomes particularly clear during the eighteenth century when the names of those involved in civil administration are considered. Successive generations in a family, close relations and connections by marriage were all involved in one capacity or another, and to judge by their letters, they were aware of each other's commitment to public service. Fathers recommended their sons, uncles their nephews, and there seemed to be no lack of eligible aspirants when offices needed to be filled, except perhaps in the case of the shrievalty. This was now so shorn of power and burdened with responsibility and expense as to be undesirable to most, though to any who could afford and were undismayed by the difficulties involved, this could prove a useful step to higher office.

Ultimate responsibility for the conduct of county affairs, and in particular for its security from external and internal dangers, was in the hands of the Lord-Lieutenant: a Tudor creation no longer regarded as an innovation but the established perquisite of the county aristocracy. The post was usually held by a member of either the Beaufort or the Berkeley family, but during the eighteenth century two newly created peers, Lord Ducie and Lord Chedworth, held it for a while. In the case of Lord Ducie, it is unknown whether he took his duties more earnestly than most or whether he was not as readily acceptable as a Berkeley or a Beaufort would have been, but whatever the reason he sought to be relieved of his responsibilities after only a few years in office. The demands made on the lord-lieutenant were not onerous: an exalted life-style and an impressive presence probably counted for more than executive ability when the appointment was made. The work connected with the lord-lieutenant's responsibilities was largely done by his deputies, chosen for their reliability and social standing from among the leading gentry families of the county. To organise the militia (the one safeguard against enemy attack or rebellion), to transmit official information to the public, to judge the potential seriousness of signs of unrest: all called for practical good sense, an accurate knowledge of their neighbourhood and understanding of the current situation – qualities which seem to have been handed down from one generation to another in certain leading families like the Tracys, the Duttons and the Leighs.

The major threats to the stability of the country and of the county during the eighteenth century were the activities of the Jacobites, economic troubles which sparked off unrest among the poorer classes and, in the 1790s, the spread of revolutionary doctrines aimed at bringing about social and political upheaval. The Jacobite danger was not a continuous one and died down after Prince Charles Edward's last visit to England in 1750, but from time to time and more particularly in the years of rebellion, 1715 and 1745, popular suspicion of Roman Catholics bound up with the fear of a Stuart restoration came to the surface and necessitated official action. Orders from the lord-lieutenant – that the houses of known and suspected Catholics should be searched and any arms removed – had to be obeyed, but the deputies probably used discretion as to how officiously these were carried out: there were some Tories among the gentry, opponents of the Whig policies of the Hanoverian government, who, while unwilling to commit themselves to rebellion, nevertheless retained Stuart sympathies that were known to their friends and neighbours. Whenever searches were conducted, insignificant numbers of arms were discovered, making the whole exercise seem unnecessary in one way, though popular fears had to be allayed. A typical haul found at Great Barrington amounted to '1 ffowling Gunn, 1 Blunderbus, 2 Bullett guns, 1 Screw'd gunn, 1 Birding gunn, 1 Silver hilted sword, 3 Hangers'. There were no active signs of support in the county for James Francis Edward in 1715 or Charles Edward in 1745, and thereafter an opportunity did not occur; it is clear, however, from their correspondence and friendship with Stuart supporters in exile, that families like the Leighs had reservations about making a wholehearted commitment to George I or George II, and even Whig sympathizers were alarmed by and not wholly confident of the failure of the rebellions. Lewis Moreton, serving under Lord Cadogan in the army sent to subdue the rebels in Scotland in 1715, wrote home to his family in Tortworth in reassuring tones as if he were aware of their fears:

> It is allways with a great deal of pleasure that I write to Tort: but particularly now since I can wish you joy of the defeat both of the English and Scots rebells. I have not had the pleasure of a letter from you nor any body else since I left London, butt I don't wonder att it, for I hear you and my Brother have been too busy and I conclude the Ladys have been too much frightn'd to write.[1]

The economic troubles of the century that occasioned hostile demonstrations among the labouring poor were the result of agricultural and industrial changes, understandably regarded with suspicion at first, even though in the long run they proved beneficial. The centres of potential unrest in the county were always the Forest of Dean and the Kingswood area near Bristol, where mining communities customarily asserted their independence of laws that others regarded as binding; also the clothing districts where adverse fluctuations in trade led to immediate unemployment, and any attempted innovations to hostile reactions; and towns like Gloucester and Tewkesbury where bad harvests could cause food shortages among people almost entirely dependent on market supplies. Primarily it was the responsibility of justices of the peace to do what they could to nip any incipient trouble in the bud; but where there was only one magistrate resident in a wide area, or where the extent of the unrest proved beyond their powers to contain, then it was usual for an appeal to be made to the lord-lieutenant and for him to order his deputies into action – that is, to call out the militia. This had to be done in 1756 and 1792 when the clothworkers rose against their employers; in 1792 when the miners in the Kingswood area went on strike for higher wages and tried to get fellow workers to join them; and in 1795 when serious shortages in many districts drove the poor to take the law into their own hands, seize supplies of food in transit on the roads and the River Severn, and sell it at low prices to those in need. By the 1790s the numbers involved in the rioting and the vehemence of their demands made the situation serious, and even terrifying, for the authorities and employers whose lives and property were threatened, and no doubt it was reassuring that the appearance of the militia on the scene was usually enough to disperse the rioters (though had it come to the actual use of force, the soldiery might well have shown some reluctance to fire on people of their own kind with whom they had more in common than with the officers commanding them, and when in any case they felt that their job was to protect the country from invasion, not from internal strife). The deputy lords-lieutenant, many of whom were militia commanders and magistrates, also found themselves in an ambiguous situation, ready and willing to use their judicial powers to quell riots, but by no means as keen to resort to the use of force. Lord Ducie, in resigning as lord-lieutenant, gave as one of his reasons the impossibility of finding enough volunteers among the deputies to act as militia officers: 'Fourteen or fifteen I think have offered to be Officers from the County. . . . We want in all, 36 Commission Officers for there can't possibly be less than 12 Companies, our own number being 960.'

The spread of revolutionary doctrines in Europe and England's declaration of war on France in 1793 coincided with the food shortages of the 1790s, so the situation became all the more confused and threatening. At no time during the century had any effective leader appeared among the rioters and their demands were always specifically concerned with wages and conditions of work, but such was the terror of revolution among the governing classes in England after 1789, that they suspected ulterior motives in any signs of unrest and regarded as all the more serious the chances of invasion by the French. Under these circumstances it was deemed necessary to increase the numbers of the local militia so that, should any attempt be made to land French troops, enough trained fighting men could be assembled quickly to defend strategic points in the county. The response to the emergency was such that, as well as extra men joining the militia, bodies of volunteers were formed by local gentry, who not only trained and drilled the men but also bore a proportion, sometimes all, of the expense of equipping them with arms and uniforms. For the Dyrham Volunteers, William Blathwayt bought military feathers, swords and sword knots, silk sashes and suits. Among the clothiers, Philip Sheppard took great pains to see that his men were well turned out; and Nathaniel Winchcombe supplied the Frampton Volunteers with epaulettes and stars, but ensured that behaviour matched up to such finery by enforcing a code of discipline admired and copied by other organisers. In the north Cotswolds the troops based at Stow-on-the-Wold had a banner and badges made for them by the women of local gentry families, primarily Leigh, Dutton and Howe, and were also financed largely by the latter; having had their intentions approved by the clergy at their initiation, they thereafter attended church services regularly during their training sessions. Seemly behaviour as well as a seemly appearance was expected of all the volunteer forces, which were raised in most small towns throughout the county at the instigation of local landowners, who then assumed responsibility for them.

As deputy lords-lieutenant and militia officers, Gloucestershire landowners combined service to the county with service to the country as a whole. In another role, as members of parliament, they also undertook to safeguard local interests while dealing with matters of wider and graver concern. Since the sixteenth century, when membership of the Commons began to recommend itself as a symbol of status and prestige, the gentry had shown increasing eagerness to seek election either as knights of the shire or borough members. Events of the seventeenth century and the revolution at the end of it had resulted in the transference of the mainspring of governmental power from the monarchy to parliament, thus confirming the relevance of membership to anyone who wished to play an influential part in national affairs. The terms of the Bill of Rights and the Act of Settlement ensured that, when George I ascended the throne in 1714, he was hampered not only by his foreign ways and devotion to Hanover, but also by the statutory limitations on the use of his power and influence; and since the Hanoverian succession had been brought about by the Whig members of parliament and their supporters who opposed the despotic tendencies of the Stuarts, it followed that these same people should be upholders of the new régime and should predominate in its administration. Here, by covert insinuation and overt accusation, they kept known Jacobite sympathizers out of office and succeeded in making Toryism synonymous with treason, thus obliging its adherents to keep a low profile. Members of the Leigh, Chamberlayne, Guise and Tracy families did not seek public office during the first decades of Hanoverian rule, and Sir Allen Bathurst after the death of Anne in 1714 relinquished his post as Royal Treasurer and retired to Cirencester to concentrate on the development of his estate. Those who in due course were able to distance themselves convincingly from the Jacobite cause found their way back into parliament and public office. Two of Bathurst's sons became members of parliament and the elder, Henry, also held appointments as Attorney General, Justice of the Common Pleas and Lord Chancellor; and Thomas Tracy and Sir William Guise appeared among the knights of the shire in the second half of the century.

Throughout the country during the eighteenth century, the results of parliamentary elections were determined primarily by aristocratic influence; in Gloucestershire, this was shared by the Beaufort and Berkeley families who between them controlled the county seats, and occasionally some borough seats as well. Townsfolk traditionally showed independence when it came to choosing their parliamentary candidates, but at times the expense of sending representatives to Westminster seemed so considerable that they approached members of the landed gentry with a request to stand, because the latter would be prepared to waive their fees; on these occasions the backing of one aristocratic family might well prove decisive. As a result of Whig domination of the central government, the county seats from 1714 to 1734 went to Whig candidates unopposed. Of these, Henry Berkeley was the longest sitting member (1714–34). A trained soldier and an officer of the Foot Guards and Grenadiers, he had served at the court of Queen Anne, became an Equerry and finally Master of the Horse to George I. Those who sat with him in turn during these years were Edmund Bray of Great Barrington, a deputy lord-lieutenant and magistrate and the last of his family to serve the county; Kenard De la Bere of Southam, a trained lawyer helped in his political career by his relative Thomas Stephens who had been a knight of the shire 1714–17; and Sir John Dutton who, having inherited debts from his father, would have lacked the financial means to get into parliament, but for his marriage to an heiress, Mary Cullen, who brought with her a settlement of £12,500.

The waning power of Walpole and the Whigs during the late 1730s, and the return of

Sir Allen Bathurst retired from public office to concentrate on the development of his estate at Cirencester. A portrait by Sir Godfrey Kneller

the Bathursts to the political scene, redressed the balance in favour of the Tories for the next three decades. Thomas Chester of Almondsbury, who secured a seat in 1734, held it until his death in 1763. The last of a family that had originally made money through trade, then enhanced their status by marriage into the Denys family of Dyrham, the acquisition of an estate at Knole Park and public office, Chester had been an avowed Jacobite earlier on, credited with the power to raise a regiment of foot soldiers from among the workers on his land; though he never actively supported the cause, he now openly set it aside in favour of 'the most inflexible Attachment to what he thought the true interests of the Country.' According to his epitaph in Almondsbury church he made an exemplary member of parliament: 'Never prevailed on to swerve, nor . . . by one vote, or conniving Absence to desert or disappoint the Expectations of his Constituents.' Chester was joined in succession by Benjamin Bathurst, who owed much to the support and influence of his elder brother Allen; and Norborne Berkeley of Stoke Giffard, a younger member of the Berkeley family who had escaped their inherent Whiggism and was prepared to accept Beaufort support. He undertook personal service to George III as Groom of the Bedchamber and public office as Keeper of St Briavel's Castle and Constable of the Forest of Dean.

During the 1770s the Tory hold was broken and for a while elections were contested so vehemently, acrimoniously and with such great expense that in 1783 the Beaufort and Berkeley factions agreed to nominate and support one candidate each. This pact continued effective throughout the period of the French wars and until the movement for parliamentary reform challenged such aristocratic monopoly of power. The first of the Whig candidates was Sir William Guise, a Berkeley nominee, educated at Oxford and Lincoln's Inn. He was something of a dilettante, having spent two years abroad on the Grand Tour, part of the time sightseeing in the company of the historian Edward Gibbon, who thus described his fellow-traveller: 'a very sensible, well-bred man who has seen a good deal of the world and without being a profound scholar is far from wanting either parts or knowledge.' In due course Guise was followed by the Hon. George Cranfield Berkeley, a younger brother of the infamous fifth earl, who was more interested in his career in the navy perhaps than in domestic affairs, for his parliamentary commitments necessarily took second place to his responsibilities as Commander-in-Chief during the wars. He had strong support in the Forest of Dean because of the family's traditional connection with St Briavel's Castle and, during the seven months' campaign before the notorious election of 1776, his followers – 'Resurrection men with holly in their hats' – had demonstrated vociferously and menacingly (though not successfully) on his behalf. Of the Beaufort nominees, William Bromley Chester died after holding his seat for only four years (1776–80). More active in county affairs than in parliament, he had many friends among his fellow landowners in Gloucestershire who showed their respect for him by making a collection to help meet the expenses of his election (between £20,000 and £30,000) which seemed excessive even for those days, and some of which were still outstanding at his death. Thomas Master, who held the Tory seat from 1784 to 1810, belonged to the family that had acquired the abbey lands at Cirencester under Elizabeth I and thereafter assiduously served the interests of the town. Strong Tories in the late seventeenth century and potential Jacobites under Anne and George I and II, they had throughout retained the support of the townsfolk; Thomas's grandfather and father had represented them in parliament from 1712 to

1749, and his son was to do likewise from 1785 to 1792. Thomas, as well as inheriting the family estate at Cirencester, also acquired through his heiress mother all the properties belonging to the Chester family in the vicinity of Almondsbury. Thus were united the resources of two lines that had already served the community well for two hundred years, and they were to continue similarly as Chester-Master for another two centuries.

As has been said, townsfolk, when they could afford to do so, preferred to have their own burgesses as representatives, but at Cirencester, for instance, Bathurst influence was strong enough to ensure that, whenever a member of the family was available and willing, he would be elected. Similarly, if one of the Master family offered himself as a candidate, he was sure to be accepted. Attempts by outsiders to intrude were usually defeated, though the existence of an independent element in the town could result in a contest if any rivals appeared on the scene. Because no Bathurst was of age in 1755, and the family backed two other candidates instead, there was so much dissension that a Whig, John Dawnay of Ampney, succeeded in getting in; and Rudder commented in 1779: 'Frequent oppositions in the borough and in choosing their representative in Parliament, have made the poor inhabitants more licentious and less industrious than they formerly were.' To him, an undisputed dictatorship was preferable to democratic processes that were bound to lead to trouble. Another instance of gentry representation of a borough occurred at Gloucester where from 1727 until 1780 successive members of the Selwyn family of Matson were elected. The Selwyns had been active in county affairs since acquiring their estate in the late sixteenth century and, though the independent townsfolk of the city may have deplored the family's espousal of the royalist cause during the Civil War, it was not expedient to hold this against them since the reservoir supplying Gloucester with water was situated on Matson land.

Gloucestershire was no more immune than other counties to the irregularities and corruption that attended parliamentary elections during the eighteenth century. Richard Freeman of Batsford declined an invitation to stand as a candidate for Tewkesbury in 1722, 'finding there is no hope of success but upon very expensive terms. I perceive money will not be less prevailing in this corporation than in others and that therefore whoever emptied his purse most freely need not fear carrying his election.' Tewkesbury was still markedly susceptible to money fifty years later when Nicholas Hyett tried to insinuate his son into the seat there. 'If they pursue their old schemes and a certain sum would do and that sum did not exceed £1,500 I should be willing to stretch as far as that.' Writing to the candidate Matthew Ducie Moreton about his chances of success in 1714, Henry Creswyck asserted: 'Bribery will abound. If I were you I would be very lavish wherever voting takes place. What Mr Dutton means about the management of Mr Ireton's and Mr Barker's intent, is MONEY. Three guineas put into Mr Hart the parson's hands will go further than six in Mr Storey's.' The church was evidently worth cultivating! And Thomas Chamberlayne thought Creswyck's methods sound. 'Mr Creswyck has computed the votes in his division and is of the opinion we shall have 150 voices in it out of 300. I must do him the justice to say that he takes true pains and spends a world of money.' He also sent a word of caution in a postscript, that eminent landowners liked to be wooed for their support and not taken for granted. 'I forgot to tell you that my Lady Freeman of Batsford is a little disgruntled that neither you nor Mr Stephens have solicited her vote either in person or by letter for her interest.'[2] Not only local people but anyone with electoral rights in the county was approached. Thus, in 1739, Sir John Dutton wrote to Jonathan Blackwell of North Hall in Hertfordshire:

> I do myself the honour, though unknown to you, to acquaint you that my cousin Tracy of Stanway and Mr Stephens of Lypiatt have been nominated candidates for this county at the next election upon Whig interest. I am informed you have a considerable estate in this county and I take the liberty to desire the favour of your vote and interest for these gentlemen . . . I am informed also you have three tenants in the Parish of Awre in the Forest of Dean who will vote as you direct them if you are pleased to insist upon their doing so.[3]

The support of influential landowners was worth securing because they were able to control the votes of their tenants and employees – or at any rate expected that the latter would do as they were told. A letter from William Whitmore made this clear:

> I am sorry your servant's trouble was increased by my being several miles from home but am much more concerned to hear of the disobedience of my agent for whom I always had an esteem because I thought him a good servant and faithful. I will send him a letter and use all other means that I can anyways think may be for your service. I shall very much resent if any person that I have any interest in should vote against you.

There is a similar hint of menace in a letter from William Young, Lord Berkeley's secretary, to Sir John Dutton in 1740:

> I did by his Lordship's direction write to Mr Harris, one of the Keepers of the Forest and told him that it was expected he should make use of all his interest and use his utmost diligence in serving Mr Tracy and Mr Stephens . . . This I hope will engage him to act as he ought for the future, but should he do otherwise, some other course must be taken with him. . . .

Those who were subjected to pressure needed the tact and firmness of Prideaux Sutton, writing to Sir John Dutton in 1739:

> No one can be more ambitious of obeying the commands of Sir John Dutton than myself but my misfortune it is not to be now at liberty so to do. I am under the command of some great men and therefore cannot do what otherwise I should be desirous of . . . I sent to my cousin Sheldon to secure the votes at Sherrington but he cannot promise because of his obligation to Lord Leigh who gave him the living.

Candidates who were successful, thanks to the support of obedient voters, might be expected to deal with the repercussions of loyalty. Matthew Ducie Moreton, elected in 1714, subsequently received the following letter:

> On the request of John Hall, the bearer thereof, an honest civil young man and a proficient in the Mathematics, now out of employ. We humbly entreat your recommendation of the said young man to the Office of Excise, or some other post. The said John Hall . . . some years since undertook the teaching of a school in a neighbouring parish whereby he gotten reasonable livelihood; but by reason of his parents voting at an election for Parliament men in an interest espoused by us, was turned out of that parish and never since well settled in business.[4]

As well as ownership of property to qualify him for membership of parliament, a prospective candidate needed much more besides – ready money to cover the current expenses of election, a solid corps of voters whose loyalty was not to be shaken, and friends among the neighbouring gentry who would be willing to influence the votes of their dependants also. Once elected, a member had to pay for his journeys to Westminster and back, for lodgings and other outgoings while in London. That there was never any shortage of candidates for nomination indicates that a number of the gentry were prepared to meet all the costs involved and believed these to be worth while in view of the prestige, importance and influence that accrued to membership. From the point of view of those who elected them also, the returns were considerable. The bulk of legislation enacted during the eighteenth century consisted of private bills in respect of enclosure, turnpikes, canals and the like, and it was the county and borough members who undertook to steer these through the Commons, using their contacts with Gloucestershire members in the Lords to complete the passing of the bills by the Upper House. When legislation of more general purport was introduced, involving issues that might incidentally affect Gloucestershire – for example, the regulation of wages or of trade in goods such as cloth or cider – then it was useful for the county to have representatives in parliament who knew, understood and sympathized with local views. The process might also be reversed. The bill that embodied Sir George Onesiphorus Paul's suggested reforms for Gloucestershire prisons, a measure of purely local significance initially, led to further legislation that extended the reforms to the whole country.

For some of the gentry, the expense, demands and publicity attached to being in parliament was uncongenial. While anxious to serve the county community, they preferred to do this on their own ground and so contented themselves with being justices of the peace. Not that this was any less time-consuming or exhausting, but at least they were free to live at home, to look after their estates and remain in continual contact with the people for whom they felt responsible. Except for the expenses (four shillings a day) he could claim for attendance at sessions and the assizes, a justice was unpaid for his work which customarily took up a great deal of his time. Lesser matters could be dealt with in a room at his own home, but he would also have to travel to join other magistrates in more formal meetings at some convenient rendezvous like a local inn; and of course he was obliged to attend the quarter sessions whenever they were held, and the assizes at Gloucester. The latter took place twice a year in March and August, and were occasions of great ceremony – when the judges arrived and proceeded to court each day beneath waving banners and attended by javelin men and drummers; of solemnity – when serious cases were presented by the grand jury and subsequently tried; and of light-hearted social activity – when wives and daughters who accompanied local justices to the assizes graced the dinners and assemblies that were held at the time, friends exchanged hospitality, and fellow landowners discussed their dogs, horses and estate matters.

We have mentioned that magistrates were responsible initially for dealing with any major crises that affected the county – strikes, riots or threatened invasion – on which occasions they had either to quell the trouble themselves or take the initiative in calling for help from higher authorities, that is, the deputy lords-lieutenant or the militia. (Some of the justices were militia officers also and, during the 1790s, members of the

James Leigh, of Adlestrop, with his family: a portrait by Thomas Beach: Leigh's notebooks throw considerable light on his work as a JP

volunteer forces that were formed to defend the county in the event of a French invasion.) Most of their work, though, was concerned with the everyday problems of the neighbourhood, and from the notebooks of James Leigh, who kept an informal record of his magisterial activities, we can get some idea of the state of the countryside and the people living in it.[5] Petty thieving was a commonplace, explained partly by want but more often cupidity. Clothing, food, tools, hay, household goods were stolen daily; animals, timber, farming equipment less often. Like most of his fellow magistrates, Leigh was anxious that the value of the items involved should, if possible, be fixed at less than a shilling, so that the crime could be dealt with locally instead of meriting referral to a higher court and a sentence of transportation or death. Magistrates knew local people and their circumstances, and clearly used discretion in handling accusations and complaints which could vary from the frivolous and spiteful to the really serious. We are not told what happened to John Wilks, charged with 'feloniously milking a cow and stealing a pint of milk', but where more material evidence was forthcoming, a warrant would be issued to a plaintiff allowing him to search for the missing property. Children were as numerous as adult offenders in respect of stealing money and food, and it is understandable that a humane magistrate would be very reluctant to refer any to the assizes with the near certainty of a sentence of execution hanging over them.

A whole range of cases concerning non-fulfilment of obligations came regularly before the justices: paternity suits wherein care for the mother was combined with a desire to prevent her and the child becoming a charge on the parish rates: the ill-treatment of apprentices and non-payment of agreed wages leading to an employer being summoned to appear to explain his behaviour. Assaults were frequently reported and, in the absence of impartial witnesses, the settlement of these cases must have called for some knowledge of the people concerned. Mutual recriminations between husbands and wives were patiently heard, and in some cases Leigh reported success: 'The affair was made up to the satisfaction of both parties.' Quarrels between neighbours could involve physical violence and damage to property, and if recurrent, as they often were, would be referred to the quarter sessions. Matters regularly dealt with in local petty sessions were drunkenness, Sabbath-breaking, illegal trading and neglect of duty by constables. Before turnpikes were introduced, the justices had to see that local people carried out their obligatory work on the upkeep of the roads; after the establishment of turnpikes they punished travellers who tried to evade the tolls, harnessed too many horses to their carts, or used vehicles with wheels narrower than the statutory two and a half inches. Cases of dangerous driving were reported and punished:

> Upon the information of Richard Smith . . . that Samuel Huckfield and William his son . . . did interrupt the free passage of his chaise in coming down Adlestrop Hill, driving his wagon against it: damaging it and frightening Mrs Smith and Mrs Jane Oldershaw who rode therein: and all this through negligence and willful misbehaviour. . . . Upon the appearance of the said Samuel and William Huckfield and their having nothing material to urge in their defence, I convicted them and made them pay the penalty of 14 shillings.

Equally dangerous, were highwaymen:

> Richard Carey charged upon oath on suspicion of being a Highwayman, two loaded pistols with powder, lead, bullets and shot having been found in his pockets and a hanger under his coat.

and

> Edward Bate, John Dixon and William Fenton charged with unlawfully and maliciously assaulting Thomas Rolph and James Merryman his servant, on the highway with pistols loaded with gunpowder and lead slugs, and with menaces in a forcible and violent manner demanding money from them and one of them firing a pistol at them to their great terror, danger and fear.

Perhaps the most difficult tasks of all were the enforcement of the Game Laws and regulations connected with the Poor Law. The former must have exercised the consciences of magistrates considerably, because where the offenders were their own tenants or labourers they were reluctant to charge them, yet failure to do so provoked the wrath of fellow landowners anxious that the laws should be enforced as rigorously as possible. After 1670, the qualification for owning dogs and guns for hunting purposes was the possession of property worth £100 or more, and in addition, after 1785, a stamped certificate costing 10*s*. 6*d*. had to be taken out. That considerable numbers of men were indicted for illegally carrying guns, hunting with dogs, setting traps and being found in possession of hares, game and occasionally deer and 'unable to give a satisfactory account of how they came by them' indicated that the Game Laws were a challenge to the daring and frequently ignored. Humane landlords were conscious of the fact that often the returns from such illegal sorties made all the difference to the larders of the less well-off. They must also have known that sometimes the offerings on their dinner tables resulted from back-door negotiations with poachers that made their own servants accessories after the fact.

As the century progressed, the problems of poverty, unemployment and homelessness grew steadily more serious. Because Gloucestershire was linked by road with so many areas – the South West, Wales, the Midlands, the Thames Valley – many wayfarers passed this way and not a day went by but the magistrates had to investigate where they were going and whether they had a pass for their journey. This particular duty seems to have disturbed James Leigh more than any other because many of the wayfarers, required by law to return to their place of birth or last employment in order to qualify for regular relief, were unfit to travel any distance at all, let alone the miles between Adlestrop and their destination. There was Sarah Davis, *en route* from Hemel Hempstead in Hertfordshire to Kineton in Hereford: 'Her husband was included in the pass but ran away at Oxford'. Ann Groves was making her way from Weatherby in Yorkshire to the city of Bristol. William Freestone, a discharged soldier, Hannah his wife, Hester and Mary their children were 'passed from Adlestrop to Kemble in their way from Newcastle-upon-Tyne to Frome in Somerset.' Christian Peters, a widow, and her five children were trying to get from Uxbridge in Middlesex to Sedgeley in Staffordshire. For some of these cases Leigh arranged conveyance over the next stage of their journey, directing the High Constable of the next place of call to pay for this, or else bearing the expense himself. He also gave them money.

In comparison with the vagrants, the local poor receiving relief from the parish were better off, though Leigh received a constant stream of complaints from them that they were getting too little money or being refused it altogether. Invariably, he would summon the overseers concerned to explain their decisions and then arrange that these should be amended. In the case of a man whose wife was 'lying dangerously ill of a cancer and he not able to provide for himself and family', the overseer was made to promise 'to pay the complainer for the summons and his time and to pay likewise for a nurse to attend his wife.' In the case of Hannah Day, a widow with a son 'out of his mind and not able to work', the overseers were advised to pay a shilling a week for the son and 'to provide some cloaths for the said Hannah Day (who is in a very poor ragged condition) and a pair of shoes for her son.' To William and Mary Welcroft 'very poor and impotent and unable to support themselves, it was arranged that two shillings a week should be given in summer and three shillings a week in winter.' Over a considerable period, James Leigh's charitable disposition was rarely misguided. On one occasion though, James Aires, a boy of twelve, claimed relief on the grounds that he was an orphan, with no friend in the world, and had come to Stow hoping to find work at the fair. To Leigh he seemed 'a remarkable sensible lad of his age'; however, after the overseers and Leigh's fellow magistrates had investigated his case, 'the said James Aires was committed to the House of Correction till the Quarter Sessions as a rogue and vagabond strolling and lodging in barns and outhouses and giving no good account of himself.' Inevitably, listening to and taking notice of such instances of distress drew the justices into the midst of the community they were serving and very close to its problems. Each day they were at home, such business had to be dealt with and, even when they were away attending quarter sessions or the assizes or occupied with other responsibilities as commissioners for enclosures, turnpikes and the like, it was only left in abeyance for their future attention. It could not be forgotten; it did not go away.

Persons who were indicted for serious offences and subsequently found guilty (except of capital crimes) were held in local gaols and the county prison at Gloucester, an experience little better than transportation or execution since conditions in these places were universally deplorable – crowded, insanitary and inhumane. All prisoners, men, women and children, healthy and sick, guilty or otherwise, were herded together (and sometimes chained up to prevent their escape from insecure quarters) in conditions guaranteed to corrupt in every way, with little hope of any amelioration however urgent their need. This state of affairs was not peculiar to Gloucestershire: it occurred all over the country and at intervals during the eighteenth century engaged the attention of a number of reformers. However, it was not until John Howard started his movement for prison reform in the 1770s that any constructive measures were seriously considered. Howard's tour of gaols all over the country led to his meeting with Sir George Onesiphorus Paul when he came to Gloucestershire and to finding in him a fellow reformer who was prepared to accept Howard's criticisms of the county prisons and do something about them. Paul's election to the shrievalty in 1780 gave him the responsibility as well as the opportunity to visit these places, observe conditions for himself and then draw up his own proposals for reform. Already known socially in gentry circles, and in his official capacity as a magistrate, Paul was regarded with amused tolerance rather than respect, but before long his complete sincerity and single-minded devotion to whatever cause he undertook earned him serious esteem and widespread support. Undeterred by fears of unpopularity he seized every opportunity to propagate his ideas – through public meetings, the writing of pamphlets, and bringing personal influnce to bear on important people; and though his harangues were lengthy, ponderous and hard-hitting, they made an impact and were heeded, to the extent that it was *his* ideas for improving Gloucestershire prisons that were embodied in legislation in 1784.[6]

While giving priority to the physical and moral welfare of the prisoners through the provision of suitable quarters, proper care and supervision, Paul believed that imprisonment should serve a dual purpose of punishment and reform, to which end he advocated solitary confinement, to give prisoners a chance to consider the error of their ways, and regular occupation to introduce some discipline into their lives. Thanks to his unceasing efforts, the county gaol at Gloucester and four other prisons were rebuilt and the material circumstances of the inmates immeasurably improved – his plans for the layout of the buildings and the ordering of daily routine there providing an exemplar that was, in due course, copied in other parts of the country; these were also embodied in a pamphlet *Rules, Orders and Regulations for the Control and Government of Prisons*, which was widely read and acclaimed, establishing Paul as one of the leading authorities on prison reform at the time. Like all reformers, he was subjected to criticism by many who were ready to admit the evils of the existing system, but not prepared to take any steps to remedy them; and even the inmates of the prisons rebelled on occasion against the discipline, some seeming to prefer their previous state of apathetic misery. Opponents of the reforms labelled the county gaol *Gloucester Bastille* and painted lurid pictures of the effects of solitary confinement on prisoners, but Paul was firm in his resolve; he must have been encouraged by the way in which national reforms followed the lines he had laid down, and as late as the 1820s and 1830s had recourse to them as 'the model of the best system of criminal discipline . . . reconciling humanity with punishment and the prevention of crime with individual reform' (part of the epitaph on Paul's tomb).

Having rallied his fellow magistrates behind him over prison reform, Paul next proceeded to rouse their concern for lunatics who, at that time, except for a few housed in private asylums, were either confined with criminals in gaol or left to wander like vagrants at the mercy of an unfeeling public. According to a law of 1774 all asylums were supposed to be licensed at the quarter sessions and inspected regularly by two justices and a doctor, but this was widely disregarded and therefore ineffectual. Paul, inspired by a visit to one of the few existing asylums in the country at York, returned home with ideas for building a similar institution at Gloucester and for ensuring more humane care of lunatics in the county in the future. Largely as a result of his efforts among the justices in Gloucestershire and politicians at Westminster, another act was passed in 1808, empowering magistrates to set up asylums according to local needs and to supervise the management of them. This added a further responsibility to those already being shouldered by the justices, but Paul's tireless energy and unquenchable enthusiasm were matched by the conscientious support of other members of the bench and the willingness of the public to subscribe to the upkeep of such necessary institutions.

Paul's manner and methods were used on occasion to bludgeon people into backing his projects, and there is no denying that on the Gloucestershire Commission of the Peace he was the most articulate and active member for nearly forty years. However, his fame and achievements, both local and national, must not be allowed to obscure the devotion to duty of many others of the county justices. The prestige of being on the bench undoubtedly appealed to some aspiring newcomers to the landowning classes, who – having been elected – thereafter gave only minimum attention to their judicial responsibilities; but such men were in a minority, and some new members as well as representatives of families traditionally associated with the magistracy, for example, Hyett, Clutterbuck, Codrington, Blathwayt, Boevey, Leigh, Dutton, Chamberlayne and Guise, were unfailingly conscientious in carrying out their duties. A few were hated and feared because of their ruthlessness in enforcing the Game Laws or quelling riots, but most of them were respected and trusted not only because of their official standing and judgments but also for their willingness and ability to help local people, support local projects and identify themselves with local interests.

At the time of the Dissolution, many of the gentry in adding monastic lands to their estates also took over advowsons previously held by the monks. Thus was established a link between manor and parish church that in some cases became a family tradition, since whenever a son or nephew was available for ordination, the living automatically went to him. It also meant that a number of the clergy ranked as gentry and therefore qualified for service as justices of the peace and commissioners; occasionally too, they inherited family estates and became landed proprietors in their own right. The de la Beres at Southam, Lloyd-Bakers at Hardwicke and Leighs at Adlestrop were families owning the advowsons of neighbouring parishes; the Haywards, settled at Forthampton since the sixteenth century, enjoyed the continuing patronage of the Ducie family there.

The Lysons were both patrons and incumbents of Rodmarton during the eighteenth century; then in 1800 the Revd Daniel inherited the Hempsted estate of Daniel Lysons his uncle and thereafter both lands and living were held by his heirs. The Revd Charles Coxwell, who held the livings of Barnsley and Bibury, also owned a considerable amount of land in the area and was a keen manager of his estates and presumably a successful one, as he was able to leave £20,000 to his family when he died. The Revd Thomas Leigh, rector of Broadwell and Adlestrop while his brother James was in control of the family estate, shared the latter's zeal for agricultural reform, and later acting as a trustee for James's son furthered the progress of enclosure at Adlestrop and recorded the results with satisfaction. It was due to his awareness and speedy action that in 1806 he secured Stoneleigh Abbey (a lawful bequest to himself) in the face of cousinly counterclaims, and was in due course able to hand it on to his great-nephew, thus uniting for the first time since the sixteenth century all the Leigh family lands. In their official capacity as justices, etc., the clergy were in no way less effective than their lay counterparts, nor were they neglectful of their spiritual responsibilities. They administered the affairs of their parishes conscientiously, caring for the congregation and for the fabric of the church that sheltered them on Sundays; many were responsible for starting Sunday schools and elementary schools for the children of the parish poor; they administered charity bequests designed to provide bread, clothes and fuel for the needy. The Revd Thomas Leigh, having in his lifetime seen that other people's money was disposed of as intended, himself left a bequest of £4 annually to each of the Sunday schools in Broadwell, Longborough and Adlestrop.

Other ways in which the gentry might be said to have served the public during the eighteenth century were as officers in the army and navy, and as colonial administrators. Until the French wars begun by William III and continued during the reign of Anne, the armed forces – because they were not permanent establishments – held no career prospects nor would service in them have been acceptable socially or professionally. However, the prolonged fighting between 1689 and 1713, and intermittent hostilities later, made the existence of a standing army and skeleton naval force essential to the security of the country, and with the recognition of this fact opportunities for long-term employment and promotion became more promising and desirable. They also offered certain advantages in the case of young men in search of careers, because the expenses involved in qualifying for a lieutenancy in the navy or purchasing a commission in the army were considerably less than for several years at university and/or the Inns of Court. Prejudice against both army and navy was strong to begin with, but since the politicians never succeeded in excluding servicemen from parliament (as they had civil servants) and the younger sons of gentry families began to make successful careers for themselves in the armed forces, so gradually they came to be tolerated, then accepted in county and London society, and as members in the Commons. A letter from Lord Paget to Captain Brudenell Rooke (in 1740) reflects the changing attitude of the older generation:

> I take for granted you are by this time in Town and consequently in the way of hearing what passes in the military world. If there should be any vacancy in an old marching Regiment of Horse that is to be purchased, I should be glad to know, together with the Price, that I may endeavour to place my son to his own liking for he still is fond [of] the army. For my part (tho I should not have chose that profession perhaps for him, according to the usual and it may be silly notions of our country) yet since

Christopher Codrington of Dodington: colonial administrator, philanthropist and patron of learning

> he desires it so much I must own I think it best complying with his inclinations that it may not be my fault that he does not make some figure in life if that be his fortune.[7]

For those joining the army an initial outlay of between £150 and £200 was needed for a commission and twice that much for a place in a first-rate regiment. Thereafter, though commanders had to take responsibility for the welfare of the men under them, there were few opportunities for making money, so a young officer was dependent on his salary and what his family could allow him, to meet the expense of uniforms, maintaining his weapons, travelling, etc. If he took pride in the appearance of his men, what he was allowed to subtract from their pay for uniforms might not meet the expense of these and would have to be subsidized out of his own pocket. General Whitmore's papers covering the mid-eighteenth century include a number of bills for his own outfits and those of the men he took to Ireland on service. The prices of footwear, coats, etc., rose according to which rank these were for: a basic outfit for a private £1 18*s*. 5*d*.; for a drummer £2 14*s*. 7*d*.; for a sergeant £3 9*s*. 0*d*.; for a fife sergeant £3 15*s*. 0*d*. The regimental band evidently merited special consideration. Several members of the Rooke family served in the Coldstream Guards and among their papers are copies of regimental regulations, one of which would certainly have no bearing today:

> Officers to oblige their men to let their hair grow, for no soldier must appear with a wigg except such as are bald who must have one that cannot be distinguished from their own hair.

Young men quickly got bored when not actively engaged in fighting and readily sought diversion in excessive drinking, gambling and light-hearted dalliance. Theophilus Leigh warned his son, James, in Portugal during the Spanish Succession War, 'Bacchus and Venus are two deities you must take care to avoid committing idolatry with.' However, military men stationed in England must already have found a social role for themselves by the 1720s when Macky, writing about assemblies in provincial towns, commented:

> These [assemblies] are very convenient for young People, for formerly the County Ladies were stewed up in their Father's old Mansion Houses and seldom saw Company but at an Assize, a Horse Race or a Fair. But by the means of these Assemblies, Matches are struck up and the Officers of the Army have had pretty good success where Ladies are at their disposal.[8]

Naval men were worse paid than soldiers and later than them gained the right to be kept in reserve on half pay when not needed for fighting. Even so, when hostilities ceased some preferred to join merchant ships where pay and conditions were better than in the navy. That discipline in fighting ships was pointlessly harsh for those on whom it was imposed, and dehumanizing for those involved in enforcing it, is indicated by the mutinies in the fleet at the end of the century. In his journal, General Sir George Whitmore throws light on conditions abroad Lord St Vincent's flagship during the siege of Cadiz (1798):

> To relieve the tedium of the blockade and amuse the sailors who showed signs of mutinous tendencies, the Admiral had visitors on board and two of the ship's boys dressed as Mercurys with wings painted on their caps acted as pages to the ladies on board. It was also their business to keep the quarter deck clear of such small litter as bits of rope, yarn, feathers, etc., and they were always employed in picking up something. If they neglected their duty, they were subject to be tied by the thumbs to the poop deck till my heart ached for them.[9]

While on active service, however, all seamen and particularly officers had chances of boosting their basic pay with prize money and fees for convoy protection or the carrying of freight. Promotion was more strictly governed by seniority than in the army, but even so, influence could be useful in finding ways round the regulations concerning the qualifying service for lieutenants and for facilitating progress up the promotional ladder. Theophilus Leigh hoped that a ship might be found for his son through the good offices of the boy's uncle James Brydges, at the Admiralty. In 1792, the Revd Thomas Leigh wrote to Lord Hawke on behalf of his cousin, Cassandra Austen (mother of Jane):

> My wife has just received a letter from Mrs Austen in which she mentions the great loss her son Frank has sustained in the death of Sir Henry Martin by whom he expected to receive promotion. He is a lieutenant on board the squadron now before Flushing. Mrs Austen asks in her letter whether we could mention him to your Lordship and request if you would be so good as to speak in his favour, should you have any opportunity of recommending him in the naval line. He was trained in the academy at Portsmouth, has been upon the East India section and is an excellent seaman.[10]

Like officers in the army, naval men played their part in the social life of the county. Robert Rooke, a young naval captain stationed at Plymouth, having been sent out to raise recruits, combined duty with pleasure by accepting an invitation to a week's shooting with Lord and Lady Clifford. Part of a letter to his father, Captain Brudenell Rooke, written in October 1757, ran:

> I don't know that I ever spent a week more agreably. We were a hunting or shooting every day. . . . My Lord pressed me to stay but my Party had gone forward so long that I was obliged to go. I have been here a week and we got two good Recruits . . . I did all in my power to avoid going a Recruiting, but as I was the last for going a Board, I was the first for Recruiting. . . . This is reckoned the best country and I am very well known here and all my Party are Gloucestershire men so that I am in hopes to meet with success. I am just now in wright time for the Fairs.

On the whole Gloucestershire gentry families did not produce many professional soldiers and seamen, though in some a service tradition was established during the eighteenth century that continued for several generations. While the eldest sons succeeded to the earldom of Berkeley, younger sons and other members of the family made the navy or the army their career. Two became admirals, James in the early part of the century and George Cranfield, who sat as a member of parliament when he could spare the time from his duties as Commander-in-Chief of the fleet in North American and Portuguese waters during the Napoleonic Wars, and later as Surveyor-General of Naval Ordnance. Members of the Codrington family served as soldiers in the West Indian islands, where there were family estates, and one – Sir Edward – became an admiral in the early nineteenth century. The Moreton family of Tortworth intermarried with the Ducies and the Reynolds in the middle of the century, and produced both soldiers and sailors, as did the Estcourts; likewise the Rookes, newcomers to the county in the eighteenth century, who acquired land at St Briavels as part of the marriage settlement of James Rooke with heiress Jane Catchmay. Earlier in the century Admiral Sir George Rooke had augmented the family fortunes with prize money gained during the French Wars; later generations, with the exception of Robert mentioned above, followed each other in the army where they served with distinction. Two notable members of the Guise family were soldiers. John Guise campaigned in the Low Countries and the West Indies during the wars in the middle of the century and fought in Scotland against the Jacobites in 1745; and Sir John Wright Guise, a commander of the Scots Guards in the Napoleonic Wars, later ranked as the Senior General in the Army List and was specially honoured for his bravery by Queen Victoria. Members of the Whitmore family also made their careers in the army – Lieutenant General William Whitmore in the middle of the century, and General Sir George Whitmore, who began his career during the Napoleonic Wars. The latter served in Gibraltar, the West Indies and Malta, and evidently handed on his keenness for soldiering to his sons, two of whom became generals.

We noted earlier that gentry families were quick to appreciate the increasing importance of overseas trade in the eighteenth century, to invest in joint stock companies and even to apprentice younger sons to serve in company ships or trading stations. Some too acquired estates in the colonies gained by the Treaty of Utrecht, or took posts as government officials in overseas possessions. Richard Master, after serving as a major in the army, became Consul at Algiers, then Governor of Tobago, before inheriting the family estates in Cirencester and taking up public service as a member of parliament. The Codrington family had estates in Antigua and Barbuda from which, as a result of good management, they derived an immense fortune. They pioneered new crops and new methods on their plantations, and always there was at least one member of the family personally supervising what went on; in due course the heir, having learned the business at first hand, would return to England to spend some of his time and the family wealth at Dodington. Christopher, who died in 1702, having served as Governor of the Leeward Islands during his career, could afford to leave £20,000 to All Souls for the furnishing of a new library as well as vast sums for propagating the Christian religion in foreign plantations. The estates in Gloucestershire were added to and Dodington improved with the fruits of the family's colonial activities, so it was hardly surprising that Christopher Bethell Codrington, who inherited the Codrington possessions on the death of his uncle in 1794 and in due course became a member of parliament, was strongly opposed to the abolition of the slave trade.

One of the best known colonial administrators of the eighteenth century was Warren Hastings who belonged to a Gloucestershire family long established at Daylesford. Losses incurred during the Civil War, which they failed to recoup later, obliged the Hastings to sell their original family home, but without relinquishing the hope of getting it back later; this seems to have been one of Warren Hastings' ambitions throughout his career while serving the East India Company in India, and then the British Government there as Governor-General (1772–85). Like all nabobs, Hastings made money while he was in India, but not by such corrupt means as his traducers later made out, since his term as Governor-General was spent mainly in trying to find a viable solution to the problems of the country's administration rather than in lining his own pockets. It must therefore have been a bitter blow on his return to England to be denied a quiet retirement in the familiar, friendly surroundings of Daylesford and to be obliged instead to face the glaring publicity of a seven-year trial, answering charges that were based on either spiteful misconstruction of his actions or deliberate falsehoods. Many of his Gloucestershire friends rallied round Hastings during his trial, and in particular his near neighbours the Leighs at Adlestrop were deeply concerned for him. Their relief must have been almost as great as his own when they received his message at the close of the trial: 'Dear Friends, I am acquitted.' Before the start of the impeachment in 1788 Hastings had already embarked on the building of a new family home at Daylesford designed for him by Samuel Pepys Cockerell, architect to the East India Company; and in spite of having to spend most of his money on legal fees, he was able to complete the house, one of its main features being a boudoir for his wife, with a domed ceiling painted and lit to represent the night sky in India. Hastings spent the remainder of his days in quiet seclusion at Daylesford, enjoying the company of friends and, with the Leighs, planning the landscaping of their respective estates where they marched together along the line of the Chipping Norton turnpike.

The willingness of the gentry to assume responsibility in connection with local and national affairs had become one of their outstanding characteristics during the course of their rise to significance. As the demands of public service expanded with the increasing elaboration of government, so the gentry applied their abilities to fulfilling these, in many cases showing unexpected talents and application in the process. In some families a tradition of public service was already firmly established by the eighteenth century, their names recurring with foreseeable regularity in the lists of sheriffs, justices of the peace and members of parliament. During the century new names appeared, partly as a

Daylesford House. It was Hastings' lifelong ambition to buy back the family estate at Daylesford and rebuild the house there. Inset: Warren Hastings of Daylesford: acquitted of misuse of his powers as Governor-General of India after a trial lasting seven years

result of some of the clothiers achieving landed status (see Chapter 10) and partly because incomers to the county had taken the place of families that had declined or died out, e.g. Boevey at Flaxley, Webb at Hatherop, Blathwayt at Dyrham. Some of the lesser gentry remained parish-bound, running their small estates as efficiently as their more important neighbours and fulfilling obligations to their tenants, the church and local institutions, but never aspiring to prominence because their means were limited and/or temperamentally they were disinclined. Those who were more publicly concerned with local and national affairs tended to have expanding interests in other directions as well, e.g. in commercial and industrial undertakings that gave them a wider perspective on the situation generally. A leading gentry household at this stage can be seen as one where the head of the family was frequently away on business leaving the supervising of the estate to an agent or attorney while he dealt with public affairs. He would be a familiar figure at the quarter sessions and assizes and meetings of commissioners, and if he was a member of parliament, equally well known at Westminster and in London clubs. His sons were not as likely as in the past to remain locally, hoping for a successful marriage to secure their future prospects, but were more probably making their way in a career associated either with family concerns or with public service. Since ownership of land and independent means were still essential qualifications for positions of authority and responsibility, the gentry class continued to predominate in public life and to be indispensable to the successful running of county and national affairs.

CHAPTER TEN

INVESTORS AND INNOVATORS

During the eighteenth century a number of circumstances combined to produce a climate favourable to the advance of the landowning classes. As we have seen, the political situation enabled them to reach the peak of their importance so far as their contribution to the community was concerned, because it was they who shouldered most of the responsibility for local government, and assumed the task of representing Gloucestershire and some of its boroughs in parliament – not new roles it is true, but increasingly comprehensive and prestigious as contemporary problems became more challenging. Economic conditions too favoured and encouraged ability and enterprise, since although the country was involved in foreign wars from time to time, causing heavy taxation and interruptions to trade, these did not constitute major setbacks to her advance; indeed, either in the course or as a result of them, many people profited. Just as the bounds of Britain's overseas empire were being extended by wars and mercantile undertakings, so at home opportunities for invention and expansion in almost every sphere were proliferating, making it possible for anyone with the means and ability to use these to better themselves. Not everyone did, nor was everyone successful; nevertheless a great number of people made profits that enabled them to improve their social status and standard of living, and in some cases to bring them public acclaim as well. Such successes were not exclusive to any particular class: in every walk of life people turned current opportunities to advantage; but inevitably those who started off with some advantage – whether it was education, money or the right contacts – had fewer difficulties to contend with than those disadvantaged on every score. Inevitably also, the outcome in simplistic terms was that the rich got richer and the poor got poorer, until the widening gap roused the consciences of the philanthropists and inspired the political and social movements that in the nineteenth century were to start a reversal of the process.

To the gentry, the ownership and maintenance of estates was still the core of all their activities. The land which was the basis of their power and influence was also an important, even if no longer the only, source of subsistence for them and their families, and at all costs must be preserved. A great help to thrifty as well as potentially profligate owners was the *strict settlement*, a legal device introduced in the late seventeenth century which ruled that the titular owner of an estate was only the life-tenant and therefore could not sell or alienate any of the property outright, but must be able to hand it on entire to his heir. Part of the estate might be mortgaged in the short term for a special purpose, but the family property as a whole could never be used to finance speculations, pay off debts or underwrite gambling – a likely possibility at a time when newspapers were asking: 'How many fair country seats, parks and lordships and manors have been thrown away by the cast of a dye?', and the leading London clubs like Almack's provided a setting where 'a thousand meadows and cornfields are staked at every throw and as many villages lost as in the earthquakes that overwhelmed Herculaneum and Pompeii.' Even those concerned with serious investments in projects that promised to be profitable had to find the means for this in ways other than selling off or mortgaging a piece of land.

However, by the early eighteenth century there *were* other ways of raising capital. Whereas in the past an urgent need for money would have been supplied by London goldsmiths, now it came from the new private banks being established in the capital by men (some of them former goldsmiths) who had contacts with both wealthy men wanting to deposit unused funds and others anxious to borrow on fixed, reasonable terms. Francis Child, Richard Hoare and Andrew Drummond, all founders of new banks, had rich merchants and notable landowners as clients, and enjoyed close friendships with the latter, having themselves acquired estates and built country houses – Child at Osterley Park, Hoare at Stourhead and Drummond at Stanmore. For those with money to invest and willing to take some risks to secure high returns there were the joint stock companies, while the funds of the Bank of England (founded in 1694), because backed by the government, were regarded as safe securities. In spite of the shock waves caused by the crash of the South Sea Company in 1720, confidence in the stock market was soon restored. The totally fraudulent and dangerously speculative ventures disappeared, but the South Sea Company – once its affairs had been sorted out – took on a new lease of life and, along with other companies, it continued to attract investments. Holdings in these and the funds of the Bank of England were regarded as worthwhile assets and often included as such in marriage settlements and bequests, which according to the means of the families concerned might range from several hundred to several thousand pounds.

Nevertheless, whatever his interest in increasing his income from as wide a range of sources as possible, foremost in a gentleman's considerations was always the estate that, either directly in produce or indirectly in rents, maintained him and his family, and this was kept under constant surveillance by the landowner himself or by his agent. Already, before the end of the sixteenth century, most often at the instigation of his tenants though occasionally on the initiative of the landowner himself, some consolidation and enclosure of scattered holdings in the open fields had taken place; the manorial lord benefited in much the same way as his tenants by this move to economise on time and labour, facilitate experiments and improve the quantity and quality of output. After the interruption of the wars in the seventeenth century, landowners had even greater reason to show enterprise in their farming activities and, as we noted, began to make the best possible use of every piece of land available; in fact the so-called agricultural revolution had in many ways been anticipated in Gloucestershire before the eighteenth century started. During the course of this century, however, changes were accelerated and extended very considerably as a result of a second Enclosure Movement; this time, though necessarily with the cooperation of their tenants, the enclosures were usually initiated by the landowners themselves and carried through because of their means, legal expertise and political influence. Lord Hardwicke was left in no doubt as to his tenants' willingness to fall in with his proposals:

> Sir, the generality of the Nation being soe much Improved by Inclosures that I think there was never more Reason for wee at Hardwick to make some to keep up the Rents of our Lands. . . .

Parliamentary enclosures, as the name implied, were achieved by private Acts and, far from being sudden or arbitrary moves on the part of landowners, involved careful preliminary calculations, lengthy conferences with tenants, expensive parliamentary procedures and, after the Act was passed, long-drawn-out attempts to satisfy all the interested parties. It is true that some smallholders suffered as a result of these enclosures, especially if common land was included, losing their semi-independent status and becoming landless labourers, but this was not invariably the fault of their landlord and might be due to a lack of willingness or the means to enclose their allotted piece of land and make it pay. As in many other spheres, those with enterprise and even the smallest of financial resources were able to survive, while those without were helpless in the face of circumstances beyond their control. Indeed these could be beyond anyone's control because the rising population, especially in the towns, and the needs of the armed forces during the wars of the eighteenth century, created an urgent demand for supplies of food quite beyond the actual or potential capacity of old-fashioned subsistence methods of farming.

The expenses involved in bringing about an enclosure were very considerable and not to be undertaken unless likely to be exceeded by the expected returns. James Leigh filled a whole notebook with speculations and calculations before convincing himself that an enclosure at Adlestrop was desirable:

> There is I think no reason to doubt, if all the 32 Yard Lands in Adlestrop Field were fallen into my Hands [i.e. the leases terminated] and that I had money sufficient to spare from other purposes . . . an Inclosure might be safely and advantageously undertaken at Adlestrop: and though it would not be attended with so much profit as in many other places where there are large Tracts of Waste and almost useless Land . . . yet still even here I say, the Improvement would pay very good interest for the whole sum laid out and likewise Yield some clear Gain to the Proprietor, besides the Satisfaction he would enjoy in the Thoughts of having his estate put in the best Condition possible and everything about him right and convenient.[1]

At the outset, most intending enclosers sought the advice of others who had already experimented, and worked out in detail what the project might cost them. This averaged between £1 and 30 shillings an acre. Even so there were some expenses that could not be foreseen. Fees to surveyors, legal advisers and parliamentary officials varied according to how long each phase in the proceedings lasted. The Enclosure Bill for Longborough, from its first being presented in parliament in November 1793, was being handed from one official to another and passed between the Commons and the Lords until the following April before it was eventually read and carried. Meanwhile in addition to the fees expended in parliament, legal advisers were charging for making coach journeys to and from Westminster, sending letters reporting progress (or lack of it) down to Gloucestershire, 'perusing the Bill, adding several New Clauses, making a Fair Copy of the Petition as altered, which took up much time' and 'Mr Master not being able to present the Bill and having referred me to the Hon. Mr Berkeley, attending him with the Bill'. (Mr Master and the Hon. G. C. Berkeley were the county members at the time.)

Once an Enclosure Bill had been passed, and commissioners appointed to put its clauses into effect, the latter's expenses while making enquiries and drawing up their recommendations had to be paid. They usually met to confer at local inns where food, coals, pipes of tobacco, lights and writing materials were provided; even an abortive meeting where some commissioners failed to turn up was charged to the expenses of a clerk who did attend:

Attending the Commissioners as Clerk – the Meeting being adjourned till tomorrow, there not being a sufficient Number of Commissioners to proceed to Business	£2 2*s*. 0*d*.

A tenant, required to give up his land, was usually compensated with an area larger than he had conceded, and might be given some money as well. The owner, hoping to lease farms and lands at an increased rent, had to have new walls or hedges put up; farmhouses and outhouses renovated or rebuilt; roads and paths resited; and though it was usually the landowner who was castigated for being grasping and unreasonable, tenants too could be greedy:

> Mr Leigh to allow the following articles for the intended repairs – bricks, tiles, lime, lath, ceiling nails, tailing nails and glazing for all the common windows and the lower box window casements, hinges for the doors and a lock for the front and back door. The necessary oak and elm timber but no nails for the doors and floors and roof. As the original intention and design of the building to be added to the present farmhouse was only to render the same useful and commodious for the business of the farm to which it appertains, there is no necessity for making it otherwise than a plain farm building. If it is the tenant's humour and will to have it fitted up in a genteeler style, all extra expenses occasioned thereby must be his own.[2]

So whether he planned to finance the enclosure out of his current income or by borrowing the necessary capital, a landowner had to have more cash in hand than even the most careful budgeting called for.

With the exception of diehard conservatives or eccentrics, most landowners in Gloucestershire who had not enclosed their land earlier did so during the eighteenth century as a means of ensuring its continued viability. There were no inventors among them, but many were innovators in so far as in their newly hedged or walled fields they experimented with new crops in rotation, using every available acre every year, and with the breeding of cattle, pigs and sheep that would supply the increasing demands of local and more distant markets for meat and dairy produce, and of local clothiers for special kinds of wool. Edward Sheppard, clothier, landowner and writer, carried out lengthy and complicated trials in the cross-breeding of sheep, and in the best ways to shear sheep and clean their fleeces. (He was a firm advocate of washing these on the animals before shearing.) He was also anxious to establish that breeds of sheep and types of land should be carefully matched if the best results were to be obtained. His findings were published in a paper presented to and much appreciated by the Board of Agriculture. The feeding of animals necessarily improved as more and a greater variety of fodder crops were incorporated into sowing programmes, and in this sphere too individual owners put their own theories into practice, even revolutionary ones, according to a letter from the Duke of Chandos to Henry Perrot at Barnsley:

> Pray did you not tell me that the Mast of the Horse Chestnut if Fried in an Oven and made into a Paste was an excellent feed for Cattle as well as Leys, and that they would grow fat upon it?

During the seventeenth century Gloucestershire landowners had owned an unusual number of horses which they employed instead of oxen for farm work; during the eighteenth century, when farmers in other parts of the country were taking to horses, there was a tendency here to go back to oxen, especially in the Cotswold area, though in the Forest of Dean, too, they were being used by Christopher Bond on his Newland estate. Thomas Estcourt, at Shipton Moyne, carried out experiments for two years comparing teams of oxen and horses for draught purposes and came to the conclusion that oxen were certainly not inferior to, and on heavy soils might be better than, horses. Henry Perrot evidently subscribed to the same view, as this letter to him showed:

> When I was at Barnsley, I observed you ploughed with Oxen and I think you said you found it abundantly cheaper than with horses . . . I shall be obliged to you if you'll let me know how you manage them . . . I mean what you give them in the summer and how you keep them in the winter . . . and what quantity of ground, supposing the soil to be a stiff clay, a yoak or two yoak will be able to Plough in a day. I take it for granted you are obliged to house them in the winter, but I suppose you give them no corn and only a little hay: and pray let me know if there are any to be bought fit for the purpose, about you.

The exchange of ideas, livestock and seeds between interested landowners became a commonplace during the eighteenth century. Correspondence with the Board of Agriculture kept Gloucestershire owners in touch with new developments elsewhere – Joseph Cripps and Thomas Estcourt acknowledged information about new ploughs and asked that papers published by the Board should be sent to them – and at the same time social gatherings and shows arranged by the Bath and West Agricultural Society, 'attended by so many gentlemen of the county that it may almost be considered a Gloucestershire society' (Rudge), also helped to disseminate views and the results of experimentation. Writers on the economy of Gloucestershire – George Turner, Thomas Rudge and William Marshall – while condemning any signs of neglect, such as undrained or weed-infested fields, animals in poor shape, falling yields due to overcropping, were at the same time full of praise for the many landowners who were showing enterprise in adapting new machinery to their particular needs and working out their own schemes of planting, draining and fertilizing. They noticed too, where estates included woodland on the Cotswolds and in the Forest of Dean, that this was being carefully coppiced and replanted when older trees were being cut down. The Leighs at Adlestrop supplied most of the wood needed locally for fencing and building repairs. The Bathursts at Lydney husbanded their basic stock while selling timber for shipbuilding, bark for tanning and ropemaking, coppice wood for burning and withies for baskets. Sir John Dutton's concern for his woodland was reflected in the terms of his will:

> I strictly enjoin and desire every person in whom my estate shall be vested . . . to finish and perfect the plantations I have begun at my new park and all the other works I intended there . . . and when the same are finished, I desire they may be always kept in good order.

The writers' concern was primarily and almost exclusively with satisfying themselves that no opportunities for profiting from the land were being wasted, and no doubt they would have approved of the new leases that were issued after enclosures had been made, defining precisely what use was to be made of the lands involved. It is less certain that they would have been as patient as many landowners, with tenants who ran into difficulties and could not keep up with their rents. Sometimes this was the result of bad harvests or outbreaks of disease in animals generally, sometimes of bad management or bad luck on the part of an individual tenant; whatever the circumstances, landowners were reluctant to lose worthy tenants and so stopped short of terminating leases. Debts were carried over or even waived altogether. James Leigh sent his agent to interview a defaulting tenant, to replace sheep lost through foot-rot and to suggest how the arable land might be made more fertile: mould from cleared ditches mixed with lime, coal ashes, pigeon dung, malt dust and soap boilers' ashes were among the proposed remedies.

Although the profits from enclosure varied according to the extent of land involved, the degree to which it could be improved and how much rebuilding of farms, etc. had to be done, a landowner hoped to, and usually did, make a profit of not less than fifteen per cent on his outlay (i.e. more than twice as much as on any other form of investment) and to double his income from rents. Sometimes the return was even better than expected. The Revd Thomas Leigh recorded that, where his brother James had expected £100 a year from one of his newly enclosed fields, the return had in fact amounted to £190. Quite apart from the financial gains and increased output of crops and yield from stock, landowners must have derived immense satisfaction from the sight of neatly enclosed fields, newly aligned roads and tracks, farmhouses in good repair, 'everything right and convenient' as James Leigh had hoped. However, their own improved circumstances did not blind the majority of owners to the plight of those whose means had been reduced. On a number of estates, new cottages were built for dependent labourers, many of them with enough land attached to enable the occupants to be at least partially self-sufficient. Thomas Estcourt, George Onesiphorous Paul and the Revd Charles Coxwell were among the staunch advocates of helping the working classes to help themselves instead of keeping them in a position of dependency on charitable bounties.

It was not only in respect of agriculture that the gentry branched out during the eighteenth century. We noticed in the previous century that those with coal and iron deposits on their land were exploiting these; now new developments such as the use of engines to drain mines and coal for smelting ore were adopted to improve the quality of output. In the south of the county, in mines belonging to the Whitmores at Pucklechurch and the Newtons at Bitton, and in the Forest of Dean at Flaxley and Lydney, deeper seams were dug and more safely worked because of proper drainage; and though the experiments ended in frustration and disappointment, efforts were made to find and work seams of coal on estates at Barnsley and Wyck Rissington in the Cotswold area. Only landowners with considerable capital behind them to pay for technical advice and the necessary equipment could afford to embark on ventures of this kind with no absolute certainty of a profitable outcome.

With more estate business to be conducted in the county and elsewhere, more journeys to be made in connection with public responsibilities as well as for pleasure, more goods to be moved from estates to local markets, ports, the Midlands and London, landowners necessarily became aware of the inadequacies of existing transport facilities. Roads that were largely unmade and badly maintained, made travel difficult and sometimes dangerous, and the carrying of goods a slow, unwieldy and unsafe procedure: while a lack of signposts to indicate directions and distances could add to the length and hazards of all journeys. In 1735, Lord Lichfield, travelling from Bath to Ditchley (Oxon) along a familiar route, found the way heavy even with two sets of horses, and on nearing Cirencester 'in a very wett night' lost the road completely, 'which hindered us above an hour and one of my horses hung his hind leg in a Deep Rut so that we were forced to digg him out.' Thirty years later, Arthur Young condemned the practice of using pieces of stone 'as large as one's head' for mending the roads which were thus 'rendered most execrable'; while Samuel Rudder reported that, in 1776 near Gloucester, he saw a chaise stuck in the mud and was told 'that a horse was like to have been smothered in the same place two days before, but was luckily saved by some persons coming accidentally to the poor animal's assistance.' In the vicinity of towns and villages, where the influence of civic authorities or of conscientious justices of the peace prevailed, attempts were made to fill in holes and ruts, drain ditches and cut back overhanging trees and branches, but, in country areas especially, it often proved an insuperable problem to find labourers to work on the roads and raise funds to pay for necessary materials. The terms of Inclosure Acts had provided for the realignment of roads and for supplies of stone and gravel to be stored in accessible places, but this did not appreciably lighten the task of local magistrates nor lessen expenses which were often met out of their own pockets. So when a remedy was proposed in the shape of turnpike trusts, it was not surprising that landowning gentry were among those who favoured the innovation.

Three turnpikes, one in Gloucestershire, had been set up before the end of the seventeenth century, but it was during the course of the eighteenth century that most of the main roads in the county were improved, with the result that towns such as Gloucester, Cheltenham, Tewkesbury, Cirencester, Lechlade, Stow-on-the-Wold, and Northleach were linked with each other and with places outside the county – Worcester, Oxford, Birmingham and London – by passable tracks.[3] Landowners who were members of parliament helped to steer necessary legislation through the Commons and the Lords. The routeing of proposed new roads gave rise to as much controversy as modern motorways and ring roads. Colonel Whitmore who was anxious to ensure expeditious transport of coal from his mines at Pucklechurch was urged: 'I hope the Col. will be in London to present the petition the first day of the Parlt. Meeting; and the rather because I am informed the Gentlemen in the Westerleigh Interest have a scheme to draw the Road from Swindon, Wootton Bassett etc. into theirs and a Petition ready for it.' Those keen on investment bought shares in the trusts that were set up to finance the expense of improving road surfaces and setting up turnpikes where the tolls could be collected; or else they made bids for the returns from particular gates when these were auctioned each year. Among the Leigh papers is a plan (dated 1797) drawn up for the rebuilding of a tollhouse at Adlestrop and an estimated bill for this amounting to £34 8*s*. 11*d*. which evidently James Henry Leigh was going to meet, doubtless in the expectation of recouping his expenditure from the tolls. Complaints, whether justified or not, that the roads were not being properly maintained or that tollhouse keepers were acting dishonestly, called for frequent investigations and many landowners served (unpaid) as commissioners for this purpose; those who were magistrates found their work increased, dealing with infringements of the regulations – initially with the rioters who tried to stop the innovations by breaking down gates and threatening the lives of tollhouse keepers, and later on with tricksters intent on evading the tolls. Names that appear in connection with the making and administration of the turnpikes include Leigh, Dutton, Blathwayt, Freeman (of Batsford), Chamberlayne, Selwyn, Guise, Master, Bathurst and Berkeley. Thus, in one capacity or another landowners were associated with the better road services as the century progressed and undoubtedly benefited from them, but one wonders whether some came to have mixed feelings about them, as did the Hon. John Byng who complained that turnpikes 'have imported London manners and depopulated the country. I meet milkmaids on the roads with the dress and looks of Strand misses'; and Arthur Young who noticed that:

> Given the power of expeditious travelling . . . young men and women in the country villages fix their eyes on London as the last stage of their hope; they enter into service in the country for little else but to raise money enough to go to London which was no such easy matter when . . . the fare and the expense ran high. But now a country fellow, one hundred miles from London, jumps on to a coach box in the morning and for eight or ten shillings gets to town by night: which makes a material difference.

Even with improved road surfaces, however, the transport of goods remained expensive, slow and limited, whether carried out by pack-horses or wagons, neither of which were suitable for bulky or perishable goods. As an alternative Gloucestershire had always had river transport – via the Severn, Wye and tributaries of the Thames – to facilitate the movement of local products within the county and to more distant markets in the border counties of Wales, the Midlands and the London Basin. Along these same routes went goods for export to Ireland and overseas, and in return came foreign imports – among them building and furnishing materials and foodstuffs useful for enhancing the standard of country-house living. The proposal to link existing waterways by building canals was a response to the expansion of domestic and foreign trade during the eighteenth century. The use of the rivers for transport, though invaluable to merchants, was not popular with others. Owners of mills depended on a swift current for water power; those with fishing rights and proprietors of riverine fields (tramped over by men and horses pulling barges) continually raised their voices in complaint, to limited effect. Plans to build canals through hitherto untouched land roused even louder protests: some technical, arguing the impossibility of making canals work; some financial, in so far as it seemed unlikely that the initial costs would ever be recovered from tolls; some purely emotive, prophesying the desecration of the countryside, the disruption of farm work and a threat to the safety of men and animals. Three canals were ultimately completed. The Stroudwater, linking the rivers Frome and Severn, afforded the clothiers in the Stroud area (who were the chief promoters of the scheme) a cheap and efficient way of

The Stroudwater Canal linking the Rivers Frome and Severn, promoted and financed by the gentlemen clothiers

obtaining coal and raw materials, and despatching cloth for export. The Gloucester and Berkeley Canal provided a straighter and safer route for large vessels *en route* up the Severn between Berkeley and Gloucester. The Thames and Severn, the most complicated of the three since it involved making a two-and-a-half mile tunnel through the hill at Sapperton, promised, though it did not prove, to be particularly valuable as it completed a continuous waterway between the two great estuaries in the southern half of England.[4] Landowners were not as reluctant as they were later in respect of railways to have the canals directed through their estates. Clearly the usefulness of these and the expected profits from tolls were persuasive arguments in favour of their development, though the rights of land concessionaries were listed and safeguarded carefully in each relevant piece of legislation, for example:

> No building to be injured or garden cut through
> Land cut for the canal to be fenced off to prevent accidents to cattle
> Landowners to be allowed to build warehouses on their own land
> Landowners may use their own pleasure and farming boats on the canal

Those with estates served by the canals were naturally keen to invest in them, and some Gloucestershire gentlemen showed their faith in canals generally by putting money into them elsewhere, especially in the Midlands where some of them had other properties. Some also invested in the Leeds and Liverpool Canal; John Parsons of Kemerton, owner of quite a small estate, was nevertheless prepared to risk £20,000 in this enterprise which promised 'a very unexceptionable security: the interest is 4 per cent . . . and the Principal discharged when required, on giving reasonable notice.' Gloucestershire gentlemen in parliament followed with interest the fortunes of bills promoting the Rochdale, Bury and Swansea canals. Of this last it was reported in 1797: 'the Duke of Beaufort is a great opposer of our Swansea Bill: we expect to carry it in the Commons though fear it will be lost in the Lords.' The faith shown in these cases was certainly needed. All the canals took longer and cost more to construct than was originally envisaged. Two proposed ventures in Gloucestershire never reached completion – the Coombe Hill, and the Hereford and Gloucester – and money put into them was not recovered; of the three that were ultimately finished only the Stroudwater brought immediate returns. Nevertheless, in the long run, not just the proprietors but many others in the county benefited from cheaper goods (especially coal) and, until the railways superseded canals in the next century, the sons and grandsons of the original investors derived some financial profit from the risks that had been taken, and in some cases sacrifices made.

The idea of investing in projects that were new and potentially profitable appealed to forward-looking men with available capital and confidence in their own judgement. Others preferred a safer way of ensuring a return on their outlay and this they found in investment in urban property – either land that could be leased for development or houses that could be rented out. Although some towns stagnated or even shrank in size during the eighteenth century (where local markets or industries had decayed), many were expanding to meet economic and residential demands so that living accommodation and space for building were in short supply and could command high prices. It was in London, where current expansion was phenomenal, that land and property were most coveted. We noted that before the end of the seventeenth century a few Gloucestershire families had acquired a vested interest in these, and during the eighteenth century this trend gathered momentum, as the capital drew to itself a major share of national trade and financial business, and to a greater degree than ever before attracted visitors in search of pleasure. Through marriage settlements, purchase or business connections, families such as the Whitmores, Leighs, Codringtons, Hales, Huntleys and Perrots acquired property and retained links in the city that secured them a regular income. The Lloyd Bakers of Hardwicke received rents from the popular London spas at Sadlers Wells, Bagnigge Wells and Islington. Of course such holdings were not commensurate with the huge estates owned and being developed by aristocrats like the dukes of Bedford and Westminster, but they gave the families concerned a financial stake in the capital, a reason for visits to confer with legal advisers and an interest to be shared with friends and acquaintances.

Also desirable was property in towns nearer at hand, experiencing a similar expansion. Successful merchants from Bristol bought estates in the county and achieved landowning status without relinquishing their interest in the city, while established landed families, concerned with overseas trade, by acquiring property there, hoped to share in the profits of the business boom that was second only to that of London. On a lesser scale, and primarily to secure control of voting rights, properties were held in Tewkesbury, Gloucester, Cirencester and other enfranchised boroughs in nearby counties. The development of Cheltenham as a spa and pleasure centre also attracted investment. The Duttons whose estate stretched from Sherborne to Cheltenham had a quarry at Leckhampton which supplied much of the material for new buildings in the spa. A tramroad carried stone to Gloucester as well, and brought back coal for the domestic use of residents and visitors in Cheltenham. Joseph Pitt, a newcomer to the ranks of Gloucestershire landowners, had a meteoric rise from rags to riches during his life-time, starting as a humble holder of horses and ending up one of the wealthiest men in the county. He bought land and built houses in Cricklade and Cirencester in order to secure votes and qualify himself for membership of parliament. Much of the fortune he amassed through legal and banking business carried on in London and Cheltenham was spent on developing the area of the spa in Cheltenham named, after him, Pittville.

In the sixteenth century opportunities for advancement – through royal favour or official positions – stirred the ambitious gentry to action. In the eighteenth century it was chiefly economic developments that afforded a means of improving family fortunes. The dividing line between landowning and business began to disappear as some of the gentry branched out into commercial enterprises, at the same time opening their ranks to admit some successful entrepreneurs like the clothiers. Shopkeeping was still ruled out, but investment in capitalistic ventures was becoming acceptable. Merchants and landowners with profits in hand had for some time acted as private bankers in advancing loans to friends; now also those who acted as tax commissioners and receivers tended to have large sums of money from time to time which they either deposited locally or remitted to private banks in London. We have noticed that, as well as serving Gloucestershire gentry families, London bankers became their friends, which meant that, locally, gentlemen with sufficient capital to embark on banking business themselves felt they could do so without losing status. Members of the Hale family of Alderley, hitherto successful exponents of the law, and James, son of a leading clothier John Dalloway, were among the promoters of local banks: also Richard Master of Cirencester who, after serving in the army and in the colonies, returned home to assume his family's interest in the parliamentary seat for Cirencester and to take up banking business. Joseph Pitt, mentioned in connection with the development of Cheltenham, was another who turned to banking after a successful business career, using his own and other people's money to profit from loans and investment. Joseph Cripps of Cirencester, an active promoter of agricultural innovations on his estates with considerable investments also in brewing and carpet manufacture, used much of his capital to establish and maintain a bank in Cirencester. Such was his standing locally that in due course he was nominated a justice of the peace and elected to parliament as a member for Cirencester; and his business acumen was reflected in the fortune he had amassed by the time of his death, probably unequalled in Gloucestershire at the time.

Innovators in their own sphere of business and an innovation in themselves were the *gentlemen clothiers* who rose to prominence during the eighteenth century in the economic and social life of the county. They added a new dimension to the meaning of 'gentleman' in so far as their careers proved that landowning was no longer the only way into society and public life, but that success in business might equally well lead to social acceptance and prestige. True, these new families did acquire land, first of all to accommodate their mills and then to build new houses away from their places of work, but even without this their businesslike methods, practical ability and genuine interest in the community would have recommended them for public responsibilities. Not all aspired to these, but those that did made as great a success of them as they had of managing the production and sale of their cloth.

As early as the Civil War the clothiers were emerging as a noticeable group, independent enough to take practical steps to show their support for parliament. When Thomas Baskerville was touring Gloucestershire in the 1670s he commented:

> The clothiers . . . building fair houses because of the convenience of water, so useful for their trade, do extend their country some miles . . . and if a man be able to purchase so much ground as will keep a horse or two, you shall have a house built there to spend £500 per annum: . . . and he that shall take a prospect of places where clothiers live, shall find the sides of the hills and country full of little grounds and paddocks.

Early in the eighteenth century Defoe stated confidently that the area round Stroud was 'famous not for the finest cloths only, but for dying those cloths of the finest scarlets and other grain colours that are anywhere in England; perhaps in any part of the world'; while Brewer, annotating his *Delineations of Gloucestershire*, repeated Baskerville's view that 'as the usual attendant on the successful prosecution of this lucrative branch of trade (clothing manufacture) the scenery in the vicinity is enriched with villas evincing different degrees of affluence and taste.'

By the sixteenth century the medieval wool markets in Gloucestershire and the merchants who dominated them had lost their importance and been superseded by places that had natural advantages for spinning and weaving, access to raw materials, plentiful supplies of water for cleaning, dyeing and fulling processes, and cottage dwellers available and willing to undertake work – for example, the Stroud, Painswick, Dursley and Minchinhampton areas. Here in valleys near running water the first mills were set up, and from here the clothiers operated their system of distributing wool for spinning and weaving in nearby villages and collecting yarn and woven cloth for finishing. Some of the families concerned had like the Pauls and Clutterbucks come into the area as immigrant refugees in the sixteenth century, with skills learned originally in France and Holland. Some were indigenous to Gloucestershire and had started as sheep farmers and wool merchants, the Stephens, for instance, then perceiving the signs of the times had moved from an agricultural to an industrial sphere. Others – the Playne, Pinfold and Sheppard families – had worked their way up from being spinners and weavers themselves to becoming employers and millowners. Already by the end of the seventeenth century the wealth of such families was evident, in their style of living – as witnessed by inventories and wills – and in the making of bequests, money for lending to needy fellow clothiers, for schools and apprenticeships and for gifts to employees, in addition to what was left to the family.

The early eighteenth century constituted a watershed in the development of the cloth industry and trade. Until then spinning and weaving had largely been organised on a domestic basis, leaving the workers with a measure of independence and the scope to combine husbandry with their other ploys. Fulling and dyeing were already being carried out in mills and there was an obvious advantage in having labour near at hand for all processes; so when increasing demands from home and overseas markets necessitated a speedier and larger output, a first response was to build mills to house machines for carrying out preparatory and finishing processes, and to encourage workers to settle nearby to provide labour. Initial opposition to the idea of factory work was overcome by at least two families, the Clutterbucks and Pinfolds, who built cottages for their workers and took responsibility for their maintenance and repair. As markets continued to expand, so production was stepped up by the introduction of machinery to carry out processes hitherto done by hand – Louis Paul originated a machine later perfected in Hargreave's 'Spinning Jenny' – but because of the conservative attitude and fear of the workers, any innovations had to be made carefully. However, by the end of the century, several successful families – Lewis, Clutterbuck, Paul, Playne, Sheppard – had adopted new machines, introduced their own improvements on these, were employing a considerable work force and producing high quality cloth that set a standard for the home market and constituted a large part of England's exports to Turkey, Russia, India, Ireland and America.

Meanwhile, the business acumen of the clothiers was also being applied to the marketing of goods. Instead of doing this themselves they employed agents to travel around Britain selling cloth, collecting orders and registering reactions to the products they were marketing. The sensitivity of the clothiers to these reports in due course led them to experiment with mixtures of wool and different kinds of dyes in order to achieve more varieties and colours in the finished cloth. Coarse local wool was supplemented in the end by finer grades from Spain and Germany, and 'all but common colours such as browns and olives were produced by those who made it their special business.' The willingness of the master clothiers to respond to immediate market demands is illustrated by the kind of advice sent them by their agents:

> I hope you will have one eye to turn some of your most ingenious hand on the fancy trade, which has answered very well in point of profit to any manufacturers.
>
> I cannot help feeling anxious you should get rid of your cloakings more especially as the season will soon be over. I am sorry to say this article, from change of fashion, is becoming less and less in demand.
>
> If there is a chance of selling the Nap Black superfines I will let you know, but the rage for French cloths is so far abated that scarcely anyone will pay the smallest advance for them – but when the town fills at winter they may sell better.[5]

To begin with, the master clothiers lived in houses adjoining their mills so that they could keep a close watch on their workers. As the scope of their business grew and their own fortunes expanded, they wanted to distance themselves, at any rate in their spare time, from their places of work and built new houses in contemporary style in more congenial surroundings. Fluctuations in the cloth trade in the course of the century brought failure to many clothiers, especially the smaller ones, but success seemed to breed success where the larger manufacturers were concerned and it was they who began to share the life-style, leisure pursuits and ultimately the responsibilities of the country gentry who were now their neighbours. Of these, Nathaniel Winchcombe, John Dalloway, Edward Sheppard and Onesiphorus Paul were the most prominent, while the latter's son, George Onesiphorus, achieved nationwide as well as local fame in connection with his work for prison reform. Nathaniel Winchcombe was connected with other clothing families through his mother and his wife, and through them also acquired

Gatcombe House: an imposing mansion built for the clothier Edward Sheppard and designed to reflect his success

considerable wealth. He himself was a specialist dyer, but sufficiently successful to be able to leave much supervisory work at his mills to subordinates and thus free himself for undertaking public duties as a sheriff and a justice of the peace. John Dalloway built himself a fine house near his mills at Brimscombe and in his leisure time wrote and campaigned to promote the making of the Stroudwater Canal, in which venture he was ably supported by his son William. Edward Sheppard, to improve the quality of his cloth, experimented with the breeding of sheep to try to produce fine wool that might replace Spanish imports. He was much respected by his fellow clothiers as 'the person most conversant with the trade in the West of England' and often acted as their spokesman; but his keenness to introduce new machinery to improve the efficiency of his mills was not shared by his workers. To match his success and chosen life-style, he built Gatcombe House, a well-proportioned and spacious mansion set in beautifully landscaped grounds, with an impressive porticoed entrance, a very extensive conservatory adjoining one end of the house, and elaborate ceilings and fireplaces to adorn most of the rooms.

Foremost of all the clothiers were the Pauls. Onesiphorus Paul senior was a skilled cloth-maker who introduced many technical improvements in the dyeing and finishing of cloth. Success and great wealth encouraged him to entertain high social aspirations both for himself and his family. Readily assuming responsibilities in the county, he entertained the Prince of Wales during a royal visit in 1750, and as High Sheriff presented an address to George III on his accession and was knighted in consequence. It was of him that George Selwyn, friend of Horace Walpole, wrote sarcastically: 'Sir Onesiphorus Paul and his Lady are the finest couple that have ever been seen here since Bath was built. They have bespoke two whole length pictures which some time or another will divert us. His dress and manner are beyond my painting; however, they may come within Mr Gainsborough's.' Certainly, all Paul's hopes for his son were fulfilled. George Onesiphorus had a gentleman's upbringing, finishing his education at Oxford, then making a grand tour of European countries including Italy where he bought the first pictures for his future collection. On his return to England he flung himself into a hectic social life – patronizing the most fashionable clubs in London, card parties and assemblies at Bath, musical festivities and race meetings in Gloucestershire where he was on friendly terms with the nobility – the Duke of Beaufort, the Earl of Berkeley and Lord Bathurst – and leading landowners such as Sir John Dutton and Sir William Guise. The family had meanwhile moved from a home near their mills to Hill House, Rodborough – 'a beautiful villa situated on an eminence with a pleasant prospect of the river'; here George Onesiphorus, having delegated his interests in the family business to a cousin, settled down to lead the life of a country gentleman – supervising the management of his properties (in Shropshire, Somerset, Durham and Wiltshire as well as Gloucestershire), building up his library, adding to his picture collection and developing his stables. In 1780 he was made High Sheriff and thus became responsible for the gaols in the county, a turning point in his life since thereafter he was able to devote most of his time and energies to local administration and the promotion of prison reform. However, the amenities of Hill House, the beauty of its surroundings and its owner's capacity for hospitality, all came into their own on the occasion of the visit of George III and his family to the county in 1788, when Paul undertook to organise an expedition for the visitors from Cheltenham to Rodborough, guaranteeing the safety of the royal party as well as arranging for them to be seen by as many local people as possible. The royal party breakfasted at Hill House and then were escorted to the mills at Woodchester where a red carpet (scarlet cloth woven in Gloucestershire) was laid out for the ladies to walk on while they watched machines carried out from the mills into the fields and put into action for their benefit. Paul's horses too were brought into service when they were lent to the visitors because 'the King's driving has killed so many horses on his Tour that no House in Gloster will suffer their horses to go.' The gracious manners, dignified bearing and pleasing personality of the owner of Hill House ensured that no one could have done more for the reputation of the cloth trade and of the county on this particular occasion – an impression echoed many years later by an obsequist who wrote: 'I do not know any individual who gave me a better idea of a respectable English country gentleman than the late Sir George Onesiphorus Paul.'

The economic changes taking place in Gloucestershire during the eighteenth century were symptomatic of what was happening all over the country, but less revolutionary and less far-reaching in their effects perhaps than in the Midlands and the North. Farming in the county, allowing for seasonal fluctuations and periodic setbacks like the Black Death, had always been prosperous, providing a livelihood – directly or indirectly – for the majority of the population. For this reason landowners and workers on the land were eager to get the best out of their holdings and, though instinctively opposed to changes, were prepared to go along with them if they promised to bring better results. It will be remembered that the early enclosures here were instigated by smallholders, not the great landowners. Those made during the eighteenth century mostly involved the remaining open fields, demesne or hitherto unused land, not usually commons, though it was when the latter were threatened that violent opposition was aroused. Responsible landowners, however, ensured that those who lost their rights in the commons (i.e. grazing, furze and fuel gathering) were compensated either with other land or the return on allotments set aside for leasing. As yet, no General Inclosure Acts had paved the way for wholesale seizure of whatever land was still available for enclosing and exploitation, nor had any village been swept away to make new field arrangements possible. The improved quality and increased quantity of output during the century kept pace, except in years of bad harvests, with the growth of population locally and, with the greater demand for supplies in the towns, mining and clothing areas where the workers perforce were beginning to distance themselves from the land and ceasing to combine husbandry with other occupations.

Through the enterprise of men with capital and initiative, there were also some industrial developments in Gloucestershire, especially in connection with mining, the refining of ores, brewing and cloth-making. These involved a move away from home-based crafts and industries to mass production in pits and mills, but such changes were not commensurate with those that had begun and were to reach overwhelming proportions in the Midlands, Lancashire and Yorkshire. Lacking sufficient local supplies of coal and other raw materials and the space for unlimited urban growth, Gloucestershire was not, nor likely to be, an area that could support an expanding industrial population, so having enjoyed a limited profit from the innovations of the eighteenth century, it was spared the problems of mass movements of workers from the land to the towns and of influxes of workless people from other areas. By the end of the century Bristol, Gloucester and even the 'pleasure town' of Cheltenham were acquiring a small deprived population living in poor circumstances, but these by no means compared with the embryonic slums of the new towns in expanding industrial areas elsewhere.

In taking the lead in economic progress during the century, the landed gentry managed on the whole to remain in control of the situation so far as their immediate dependants and employees were concerned. The scale of developments in that area was not yet so great as to outstrip existing administrative machinery which meant that the prestige and power of the gentry were still unchanged. Indeed even as reform movements got underway in the next century, the challenge to traditional authority and usages came not so much from outside the ranks of the landowning classes as from within, members of long established families as well as newcomers taking up with causes such as parliamentary and municipal reform, the need to revise the Poor Law and the protection of exploited workers, any of which if carried through successfully was likely to affect the position of those promoting it. Having survived the first repercussions of contemporary economic changes and of the French Revolution, the landowners were even more strongly placed than in previous centuries, for the sources of their wealth were more diverse and their territorial interests more widely scattered, affording them some control over the local administration of, and parliamentary voting power in, other counties as well as Gloucestershire. Events of the century had proved the capacity of their class to assimilate newcomers from a different background, providing that the latter had the means and inclination to show the same concern for local affairs, share the same personal interests and enjoy the same social pleasures as long established families. Intermarriage, joint business ventures, mutual support in various county undertakings meant that as far as prestige and popular esteem were concerned there was little difference between members of old families like the Guises, Tracys, Duttons, Leighs, and new names like the Clutterbucks, Pauls, Sheppards, Cripps, where they met on the bench, at the assizes, at commissioners' meetings, or while on pleasure bent at race meetings, the spas of Bath and Cheltenham, and the Three Choirs Festival.

CHAPTER ELEVEN

PATRONS AND PLEASURE SEEKERS

In seeking to arrive at a definition of a true gentleman, Defoe commented: ''Tis below him to get money: his business is to spend it'; and certainly the work done and responsibilities accepted by the gentry necessitated their having a regular income that was not obtained by daily labour, as well as spare capital to finance their interests, whether in connection with business or pleasure. During the eighteenth century, those who were successful in their undertakings managed to increase their means quite considerably and, while using part of their money for normal outgoings and investment, the remainder they regarded as a legitimate means of projecting an image of success and beneficence, since a man's status was judged by the style in which he chose to live.

The accession of the Hanoverians with their foreign ways, adherence to rigid German etiquette, and limited means and inclination to give a lead in social and cultural affairs, meant that in the latter respect the role of the monarch and his court now devolved on the aristocracy and gentry. Although there were some of these who frequented the court, waited upon the king and generally played a prominent role under the royal aegis, many more exercised their influence and bestowed their patronage independently, knowing that they were more in sympathy with the inclinations and tastes of their fellow countrymen and therefore more likely to be observed and heeded by them, than would foreign rulers and their entourage. Only the very rich could maintain households and dispense patronage on a scale resembling that of earlier sovereigns – the Beauforts and Berkeleys in Gloucestershire, for example – but a considerable number of the gentry managed to achieve a life-style sufficiently comfortable to be both impressive and influential. Whatever their means – and annual incomes, which rose steadily during the century, might vary considerably from about £1000 to over £5000 – the gentry felt an urge to spend: on material goods that made life easier for them and their families; on fashionable trappings indicating their awareness and appreciation of ideas that were widely accepted; and on patronage, by purchase, commissions and gifts, that satisfied the public expectation of prominent men to supply the generous part.

In order to achieve a suitable setting for his life, a gentleman first gave attention to a house and its surroundings, for this was the hub of his existence, and however long or often he had to be away from home, here he habitually returned, to relax in the company of his family and friends, and enjoy whatever interests and pleasures appealed to him. For the most part gentry families had at various times improved their homes and brought them into line with current fashion. The changes introduced during the eighteenth century were therefore mainly designed to extend accommodation in line with the demands of domestic needs and hospitality, and to enhance the furnishings and decoration according to the owners' tastes. The latter would be determined by education, travel, reading and personal observation of other people's homes and grounds seen in London and elsewhere, perhaps even deliberately visited for the sake of collecting ideas. According to Chesterfield: 'No one can properly be styled a gentleman who has not made use of every opportunity to enrich his own capacity and settle the elements of taste which he may improve at leisure.' Certainly many young men returned from their Grand Tour enthusiastic amateurs of architecture and garden design, ready to augment the drawings and prints they had bought abroad with copies of Campbell's *Vitruvius Britannicus* and Leoni's *Palladio* published during the second decade of the century. From these they derived ideas and inspiration for their own building projects, and standards which secured them a reputation as arbiters of taste. The eighteenth century saw the emergence of professional architects trained in the traditions of the Royal Office of Works, and the growing significance of these is demonstrated by their frequent employment, and recommendation by one client to another. There were as well amateur architects like Lord Burlington, widely esteemed and sought after for his views and practical advice, and Sanderson Miller, a Worcestershire squire, much liked and trusted by the gentry in the Midlands who were prepared to let him make building designs for them.

Whether or not they consulted the professionals, knowledgeable friends or books, many gentlemen were in fact their own architects in so far as they often drew up plans and always made the final decisions about the main features to be embodied in the rebuilding or renovation of their homes. Generally the relationship between patrons and employees was amicable and mutually respectful, but that it could sometimes give rise to problems is illustrated in an exchange of letters (1774) between Thomas Estcourt and an architect, William Donn, who had been asked to draw up plans based on Estcourt's own suggestions, for a new house at Shipton Moyne. Donn was clearly a difficult character, jealous of better known architects and resentful of any criticism of his work. Estcourt's claim that a fee of fifty guineas was excessive for a preliminary survey and sketches that were unsatisfactory anyway, provoked Donn into an angry response:

> Mr Adam charged Lord Fife £75 for his design of one room . . . I cannot suppose you will think fifty guineas too much for mine . . . Plans [are] endless to a Building like yours as every moulding must be drawn at large besides general designs. As you understand drawing yourself you cannot be unacquainted with the long time they have taken. You say they don't come within your ideas of beautiful architecture . . . and that as you disapproved them, you disliked to pay for them. Would you have made such a proposal to any other? Then why to me? The £10 you gave me at Estcourt I thought had been earned by the journey and near a week's stay . . . making Sketches and digesting your ideas with regard to the principal Rooms, which you desired me to do and what none of the aforesaid gentlemen [Adam, Sir William Chambers, Paine, Taylor] would have done for double that sum.[1]

Alexander Pope, advising the owners of great houses and gardens to 'consult the genius of the place' before making plans for them, was thinking along the same lines as Charles

Cotton who had written some years before: 'That which does impart / Lustre far beyond the Power of Art / Is the great owner.' Early in the century gentlemen went away from London with the new buildings they had seen as a topic of conversation to be mulled over with their friends in the country; later on, during their visits to the capital they found that 'A very fine place to talk of in town . . . is the right use of a seat in the country.'

We have seen how important it was to the gentlemen clothiers to acquire land and build on it houses that reflected their success, knowledge of current trends in architecture and their status in the local community. In this they were but following the example of the established gentry who had always regarded their homes as symbols of their importance and adapted them to meet the needs and tastes of each succeeding generation; and who, in the eighteenth century, aimed to extend and segregate the servants' quarters in separate wings and attics; to achieve an impression of spaciousness and grandeur in areas to be used for the reception and entertainment of guests; and to provide the family with rooms where they could enjoy their books, music and other indoor pursuits. While, in general, all those anxious to build or renovate came under the same contemporary influences, many Gloucestershire gentlemen were more particularly informed and advised by well-known professional architects or friends. As no building accounts for it have survived, we do not know the names of the architects and craftsmen responsible for Barnsley Park. However, the kinship and close friendship of the owner Henry Perrot with the Duke of Chandos makes it possible that two of the duke's architects, John Vanbrugh and John Price, were consulted about the plans for the building, and that some of the plasterers and decorators who worked on the duke's house at Canons were employed at Barnsley also. Sir John Rushout asked his friend Lord Burlington to design an imposing frontage and entrance hall for Northwick Park; Lord Talbot followed the example of London friends in employing William Kent at Great Barrington; James Leigh approached Sanderson Miller when he wanted ideas for modernizing Adlestrop; and Warren Hastings involved the architect of the East India Company, Samuel Pepys Cockerell, in the building of Daylesford House. Some owners – Richard Clutterbuck at Frampton and Thomas Cripps at Upton, for example – still preferred to patronize local architects and craftsmen, but John Strahan and William Halfpenny, the architects they employed, were well acquainted with the work of better known men such as John Wood at Bath and Colen Campbell at Stourhead, and so were able to reproduce fair copies of this for their patrons. What does become clear from a survey of building projects undertaken during the eighteenth century is that many Gloucestershire gentry were completely up to date in their knowledge of architectural fashions and had access to the means of achieving these when making improvements to their homes.

One of the earliest and most satisfying of eighteenth century buildings was Barnsley Park, modest in style and proportions, but as perfect as infinite attention to detail could make it. Henry Perrot, son-in-law of Brereton Bourchier who had built nearby Barnsley House about twenty years earlier, moved in fashionable circles in London where he became acquainted with the new trends in building and the patrons and workmen responsible for them; in consequence his own house became a good example of the Baroque style that resulted from close co-operation between moneyed men of taste and the skilled interpreters of their wishes. Visitors, approaching from the main road by a

Barnsley Park. Built by Henry Perrot, in architecture and workmanship it closely resembled the London home of his kinsman the Duke of Chandos

circuitous drive that afforded views of the surrounding parkland, finally drew up in front of a building whose architectural features closely resembled those of the house in Cavendish Square designed for the Duke of Chandos by John Price. Built of stone from a local quarry, it fitted unobtrusively into the landscape, its symmetrical design and restrained ornamentation stopping well short of ostentation. Inside was a lofty entrance hall overlooked by a gallery facing the front door and reached by a wide, well-lit stairway. Rooms on the ground floor and first floor were arranged in such a way that guests could circulate freely during receptions and parties. The walls and ceilings of the entrance hall, adjoining saloon and dining room were decorated with very fine plasterwork which, if not actually done by them, was comparable with the output of the leading Italian stuccoists of the time. Windows at the front of the house overlooked the park; those at the back, a formal garden possibly laid out much as at present in compartments like rooms, outlined and protected by hedges, with pieces of statuary as focal points. The Duke of Chandos who visited Perrot at Barnsley envied him his comfortable yet elegant home probably because it was so different from the impersonal, overwhelming magnificence of his own mansion at Canons.

Great Barrington, after being in the possession of the Brays for 200 years, was acquired by Lord Chancellor Talbot in 1734 and subsequently handed on to his son, who, using the fortune inherited by his wife Mary de Cardonnel, proceeded to build a new house (*c.* 1736) near the site of the old manor. Described as 'an elegant structure in the Doric style', this was situated on a terrace above the River Windrush, here widened to form an ornamental lake. William Kent, master painter and architect, was employed to design both the house and the layout of the grounds. He produced a Palladian

Great Barrington. The seat of Lord Chancellor Talbot. The house and gardens were designed by the fashionable architect William Kent

mansion similar in appearance to those he was building for his patron, Lord Burlington, and others in his circle. Inside, the walls, ceilings, door frames and chimney pieces were decorated with elaborate plasterwork carried out by Giovanni Bagutti, one of the fashionable Italian stuccoists of the day. Outside, in the park, Kent achieved the studied informality that was to become his hallmark, by having lawns planted with trees stretching between the house and the river which was crossed by an ornamental stone bridge; beyond lay a deer park enclosed with a high stone wall pierced by impressive pillared gateways and wrought-iron gates giving on to the two main roads which bordered the estate. Sandby's painting of Great Barrington emphasises the spaciousness and peace of its setting, the sumptuous coach approaching the house seemingly only an insignificant feature in the landscape. This was the country home of a family with London interests and contacts, used as a retreat and for entertaining friends, and intended to impress.

Another newly built and impressive house was Frampton Court, indicative of the importance to landowners of having an up-to-date dwelling and of their prodigality in trying to achieve this, for Richard Clutterbuck completely destroyed the home of his great-grandfather William Clifford, erected only eighty years before, and replaced it (1731–33) on the same site with a mansion of dignified grandeur. His architect, John Strahan, was a Bristol man who employed a team of local masons and craftsmen, all capable of achieving a high standard in both style and workmanship. The entrance to the

Frampton Court. Designed by John Strahan for Richard Clutterbuck, its impressive portico was ornamented with the arms of the Clifford and Clutterbuck families

house was designed to make an immediate impact, with a wide flight of steps flanked by balustrades, leading to a pillared portico surmounted by a pediment adorned with the Clifford/Clutterbuck arms. The interior was remarkable for its wealth of woodwork – the floors and stairway and panelling in the dining room and drawing room all being made of oak; and doors, doorways and chimney surrounds skilfully and effectively carved to show the wood to its best advantage. All the furniture for the new house was specially made in mahogany and walnut, and no doubt the Bristol connections of Clutterbuck and his architect gave them access to timber supplies available in the port and also to the Bristol delft tiles with which the fireplaces were lined. Some years after the house was completed an orangery was built in the grounds in Gothic style, reflecting a new development in taste being sponsored and encouraged by amateur enthusiasts such as Horace Walpole and Sanderson Miller. The architect here was William Halfpenny, Strahan's successor and author of a large number of books on architecture and architectural patterns, who enjoyed both royal and gentry patronage. Though interesting and attractive in itself with arched windows and a battlemented roof topped by a cupola, the orangery was merely a decorative appendage to the solidly-built mansion which represented the wealth Clutterbuck had derived from his heiress grandmother Mary Clifford, from the clothing business of the Clutterbucks and from his own position in the Bristol Customs Office.

Also intended to reflect wealth and status was the house built for Charles Hyett at

Painswick House. The staircase and hall in the house rebuilt for Charles Hyett during the 1730s

Painswick during the 1730s out of the proceeds of his father's successful legal practice and marriage to an heiress. On what had previously been a farm site rose a gentleman's residence, in the architectural style of Strahan, known at first as Buenos Ayres and later as Painswick House. Its rather austere exterior gave no hint of the impressive interior, with lofty reception rooms downstairs and a very fine stairway leading to equally large rooms on the first floor. Though the craftsmen responsible area not known, the ceilings and fireplaces throughout were of a high order. Outside, the extensive grounds were designed in true Rococo fashion, a formal layout near the house giving way to orchards, a plantation and a wide dell with ornamental ponds, a dovecot, a gazebo, garden seats and ornaments. Thomas Robins' painting of the garden represents it as it was in the eighteenth century and as its present owners, Lord and Lady Dickinson, have now restored it.

Without being completely rebuilt many houses were renovated during the course of the eighteenth century. In some cases new wings and outbuildings were added; in others, exterior and interior appearances were improved to bring them into line with contemporary fashions. One such scheme brought William Kent into the county even before he was commissioned by Lord Talbot. In 1730, Sir John Dutton, with a view to improving the facilities for hospitality at Sherborne, decided to remodel the reception rooms and add a new saloon and more bedrooms; to this end he paid £31 10*s*. 'to Mr Kent for his trouble making Plans for me at my House and Lodge'. This was an undertaking guaranteed to appeal since the architect was left free to produce a scheme integrating furnishings with interior decorations and involving him in close collaboration with carvers, gilders, painters, glaziers and furniture-makers in order to achieve pleasingly harmonious effects. Kent had already worked in association with the elder John Moore on furniture for Kensington Palace; now he renewed the alliance with John Moore's son, cabinet- and chair-maker to the Prince of Wales. Some of the new furniture went into the dining and drawing rooms at the lodge for the greater comfort of the guests who gathered there to watch the famous Dutton hounds being coursed. Major redecoration was also undertaken at Highnam Court some time after 1755 when John Guise came of age. Perhaps to celebrate this, and to mark the inheritance of the estate that had been divided between his mother and his aunt, he embarked on enlarging the entrance hall and rebuilding the main staircase which was enhanced with a wrought-iron balustrade. Fireplaces, doorcases and ceilings were in the style of Adam, newly coming into fashion at that time, and the plasterwork on walls and ceilings, which was of a very high standard, was probably carried out by Franceso Vassalli, a well-known Italian stuccoist. Particular attention and expense were lavished on the music and drawing rooms where the owner and his guests relaxed and were entertained.

Interesting alterations to the outside of buildings were made at Lower Slaughter, Northwick Park and Adlestrop. At the first, General Sir William Whitmore had a new block of stables built, well equipped and topped with a gilded cupola. In all it was a more expensive undertaking than the redecoration of the interior of the house being done at the same time, since the horses were important to the General and his family who travelled regularly between London and Gloucestershire as well as making visits to relations and friends. At Northwick Park, with the help of, and perhaps persuaded by, Lord Burlington, Sir John Rushout improved the façade and front rooms of his house so as to satisfy his friend's Palladian preferences. The embellishments also served to impress visitors as they approached across the park and were received into a high-ceilinged entrance hall, where the doorways to other rooms and elegant curved stairway closely resembled features in Burlington's own house in London. Fashionable guests would have felt at home there and had no cause to consider their Gloucestershire host out of touch with the ambience of life in the capital. The changes made at Adlestrop by James Leigh (1759–62) were the direct result of his friendship with Sanderson Miller, who had already acquired a reputation because of the Gothic buildings – sham castles, picturesque cottages and summerhouses – he had designed for himself and others. All his work was light-hearted and fanciful, but evidently appealed to those for whom it was devised. Most of the original building at Adlestrop was pulled down so that a new front could be added. This had three double-storied bays with floor-to-ceiling windows lighting the interior. The tops of the bays were decorated with stone balustrades and pinnacles; and above them was a gabled roof sheltering the attic rooms where the servants slept. Narrow octagonal buttresses capped with miniature chimneys were

Northwick Park: remodelled for Sir John Rushout by his friend Lord Burlington to afford suitable accommodation for London visitors. A water colour by Anne Rushout (1804). The Royal Commission on Historical Monuments

introduced between the bays and at the corners of the building. The success of the innovations was perhaps due partly to the very good relationship that existed between the Leigh family and Miller. The contracts made with the workers responsible for the building indicate that patron and architect were in complete agreement as to what they wanted done, and letters exchanged between the Leighs and Miller while the work was in progress reflect the good humour and tolerance that characterised all their dealings.

The detailed care with which building plans were worked out was matched by the attention given to procuring just the right materials and fitments to achieve the desired effects in refurbished rooms. Marble chimney-pieces, table-tops and pediments were obtained from statuaries' yards in London; chandeliers, girandoles and other lighting fitments were specially commissioned, as were metal handles and catches for doors and windows; London was still the main source of glass for windows and mirrors. The cost of transport for bulky goods might be considerable whether by water or by road, if special packing cases had to be made, and when towards the end of the century turnpike fees were added to porterage. In 1731, Sir John Dutton paid

Carriage of 4 loads of Goods from London by Water	£ 5 5*s*. 0*d*.
For Deal Cases, Matts etc. for Packing up ye things for Water Carriage	£11 19*s*. 6*d*.

Adlestrop. The architectural style reflects Sanderson Miller's fondness for Gothic features

When he wanted special hearthstones for the new parlour, dining room and study, he sent teams of horses twice to Woodstock to collect them.[2] James Leigh, during the rebuilding of Adlestrop, used local stone and estate timber as far as possible, but obtained from Oxford 'a Gothic Chimney piece for the Room over the Hall: a Chimney piece with an Ovolo for Lady Caroline's Bedchamber and one for Lady Caroline's Dressing Room'; to the cost of which was added £1 0*s.* 2*d.* for packing cases and nails, and 16*s.* 8*d.* for the expenses of '2 Men, four days each'. The fashion for having niches made in halls and libraries to accommodate busts and statues was followed in Gloucestershire homes – Barnsley Park, Sherborne, Painswick House and Alderley, for instance. Sir John Dutton paid £20 'to Signor Vassalli' for making 'the busts and pedestals in my hall' and Robert Hale bought '2 busts of Homer and Cicero finished very neat and bronzed in dark copper £1 12*s.* 0*d.* Ditto of Francis Bacon £1.' Another innovation during the latter part of the century was the water closet and, though exclusive to London at first, this amenity was appearing in Gloucestershire in the 1790s. James Henry Leigh obtained from Joseph Bramah:

Water Closetts from London forwarded by Waggon	£18 4*s.* 2*d.*
Installing	£34 6*s.* 1*d.*
Ball Cock etc.	£ 1 11*s.* 0*d.*

The contents of the above were forwarded by the Worcester coach directed to be left at Adams, the George Inn, Chipping Norton. But to judge by the Dyrham accounts, plumbers were no more efficient then than they are now, because there are frequent payments to 'a man setting the Water Closet to work.'

As with architects and craftsmen, so with painters: Gloucestershire families connected with fashionable circles became acquainted with the work of artists being employed most widely. The eighteenth century was primarily an age face-painters dependent on the patronage of those who wanted family portraits to adorn the walls of their homes, at the same time as recording images of success for posterity, and all those who could afford it spent money to this end. We noted that already by the end of the seventeenth century Sir Godfrey Kneller, Michael Dahl and members of the Verelst family had painted some portraits of Gloucestershire gentry, and these artists continued to be popular. Kneller was of course the best known and most accomplished, tending to be commissioned by leading families like the Bathursts and the Blathwayts; but during the early eighteenth century Dahl became a contender with Kneller in popularity because of his genial character, very considerable ability and thoroughness in carrying out whatever he undertook. Though much of his work was for the royal family and the nobility, his rather old-fashioned, conservative style appealed especially to the county gentry, and not surprisingly examples of his portraiture were to be found in the homes of the Leigh, Blathwayt, Bourchier and Dutton families. In 1726 Sir John Dutton paid him sixty guineas for three portraits, and in the following year: 'for painting my picture £15 15*s*. and for my sister's picture half length £31 10*s*.' Harman Verelst and his daughter Maria were also popular with country gentlemen and painted members of the Bourchier family, probably on the recommendation of the Duke of Chandos who employed them, as he did Dahl.

A painter of a different kind was Bernard Lens, who combined teaching and the copying of works by well-known artists with undertaking commissions for painting miniatures on ivory. Popular with the royal family and prominent nobles, he was also engaged by the Whitmores, who owned one of his likenesses of George I as well as fifteen miniatures of members of their own family. A minor figure in the middle years of the century but much appreciated by the gentry was Arthur Devis, whose puppet-like figures, dressed in exquisitely painted silks and satins, were always surrounded by possessions, either the furnishings of a room or the features of an estate, which sought to convey the sitters' sense of ownership and pride in their property. His portrait of Lady Caroline Leigh shows her fashionably dressed in a straw bonnet, satin gown and gauze scarf, fishing in the stream at Adlestrop, with a glimpse of a waterfall, trees and parkland in the background. Two artists who trained under Sir Joshua Reynolds but thereafter worked in the provinces, touring country houses in the Midlands and South West, were Thomas Beach and Tilly Kettle. Both tended to produce rather mannered individual and group portraits, but were patronized on a number of occasions by Warren Hastings and members of the Leigh, Dutton and Chamberlayne families. One interesting work commissioned by Naper Dutton from Thomas Beach and entitled *The Hand that was not Called* showed a group of local friends playing a memorable game of cards in which Dutton, with a recklessness typical of his family, had wagered, and narrowly avoided losing, the whole of his estate.[3] Contemporary with the foregoing, but much better known and with superior talent, was Johann Zoffany; a versatile painter of

Portrait of Lady Caroline Leigh by fashionable artist Arthur Devis. Her great-aunt, Mary Brydges, was also her husband's grandmother

portraits and of theatrical and conversation pieces, he was much patronized by the fashionable world in London and was also commissioned to paint the Duttons who were portrayed in what was clearly one of the family's favourite pursuits, namely card-playing. While on a search for work in India during the 1770s, Zoffany was employed by Warren Hastings to produce official portraits of himself and his wife and scenes of contemporary events. Some of these were brought back to England to adorn the walls of Daylesford House.

As well as portraitists, the eighteenth century produced painters of landscapes and of animals. John Wootton, accomplished in both these genres, was paid £30 10*s*. by Sir John Dutton 'for a landskipp for my drawing-room chimney', presumably to hang on the wall above the mantelpiece in the frame he later obtained for it at a cost of £6 10*s*. 6*d*. George Stubbs, the famous animal painter, was commissioned by Warren Hastings to portray his favourite horse and some of the animals that roamed the park at Daylesford. On the whole though, after portraits, the Gloucestershire gentry wanted pictures of their houses and estates. This explains their readiness to co-operate in and subscribe to publications such as Atkyns' *Ancient and Present State of Glocestershire* and other surveys containing engravings and prints of gentlemen's seats in the county, for example Brewer's *Delineations*. Canaletto, one of the best and best-known topographical painters of the middle years of the century, had the Duke of Beaufort for a patron but did not work for any other Gloucestershire landowner. Paul Sandby, a trained draughtsman and surveyor who later turned to landscape painting in watercolours, produced some pleasing scenes of country houses, including one of Great Barrington for Countess Talbot, who doubtless heard of him through her husband, Steward of the Royal Household while Sandby was living and working in Windsor Great Park. Gloucestershire also produced its own depictor of country houses whose career owed everything to the patronage of local gentry. Thomas Robins senior was born at Charlton Kings and worked for most of his life in the neighbourhood of Cheltenham and at Bath. He was commissioned by Benjamin Hyett to paint his town house in Gloucester and country seat at Painswick; by Charles Prinn to paint Charlton Park; and by Henry Brett, Sandywell. At Bath he received patronage from, and became a close friend of, Sir Ralph Allen and here, as at Cheltenham, he sketched views of the spa and public buildings. Almost primitive in their lack of perspective, intimate detail and lively interest, Robins' pictures nevertheless reflected the current craze for the Rococo and had a unique characteristic in that they were framed in a painted border of flowers, shells, butterflies, birds and miscellaneous garden tools, most delicately drawn and coloured.

That patrons valued pictures for their own sake and not just as wall coverings is evident from the care they bestowed on them. Rarely were local craftsmen employed to deal with them; instead, as payments in household accounts reveal, men were sent for from London to clean, restore and reframe, and to make frames for new acquisitions. In 1727 Sir John Dutton paid £152 6*s*. to a Mr Colliver to come from London 'to view my pictures and mend them and to supply 13 gold frames.' Later, in the 1780s, William Blathwayt had frames for his pictures made in London; one, 'carved and gilt in Burnished Gold', cost £3 10*s*. and was specially cased and packed at a cost of 7*s*. Another, perhaps for a miniature to be worn as a jewel, cost £76 to be 'set round with Brilliants and a Gold Buckle'. The wife of James Henry Leigh also had special frames made for some of her favourite portraits. Pictures made talking points when shown to visitors, and sometimes copies of admired pieces were ordered and presented as gifts. Dutton had his sister's portrait copied and framed for his brother-in-law; the Leigh and Bourchier families received paintings of their relatives, the Duke and Duchess of Chandos. Inventories show that in many houses pictures were hung on stairways and in passages as well as in the principal rooms, so that there must have been quite a number of them acquired over the years and regarded as an integral part of the household furnishings. During the course of the century painting became part of the currency of conversation in polite society. Although, except for the Whitmores and the Hales, the gentry in Gloucestershire did not aspire to employ Reynolds or Gainsborough to paint their portraits, nor Canaletto their houses, they had a discerning eye for merit among the artists whose work was available to them: and by employing the latter, they fulfilled the role of patrons quite as much as royalty or the nobility.

In a regular fashion also, the gentry were bestowing patronage when they engaged the services of tradesmen to supply their domestic and personal needs. Although estates were still self-sufficient to a certain extent, an improved and more sophisticated standard of living called for a greater variety in food supplies and more elaborate household equipment and furnishings than had seemed satisfactory in the past. Where families lived in the vicinity of a town, however small, they used local shops and markets for basic goods for the kitchen, stables and garden, just as they employed local workmen for ordinary jobs about the house and grounds. The value of such patronage, and its marked loss when owners were away from home, was remarked on by Rudge in his survey of the county:

> The inns are well supported by the great and the shopkeepers and retailers have very considerable dealings with the inhabitants of the circumjacent villages but they very seriously feel for the absence of the gentry from their usual places of residence . . . and have to lament the want of housekeeping in their respective manor houses. In most of these, within memory, the tradesman found a valuable customer, the farmer a friend and adviser, and the poor inhabitants hospitality and charity.

Not only local tradesmen, but suppliers much further afield, as far away as London in fact, began to receive regular orders from Gloucestershire families during the course of the century – some recommended by friends in the capital, some dictated by fashion. The use of such sources was made feasible by the increasing number and regularity of carrier services that operated along the main roads to inns in places such as Chipping Norton, Cirencester, Winchcombe and Tetbury, where goods could be directed and then picked up by household servants. Bulky goods might also be sent by sea via Bristol or Gloucester. A special point seems to have been made of careful packing in boxes or baskets, for which a surprisingly reasonable charge was made; and though sometimes they might be despatched by the wrong carrier and left at an unexpected destination, there are few recorded complaints of purchases arriving in an unsatisfactory state – even wine, about which many clients were extremely particular. Regular customers were frequently allowed a discount off the usual prices, but might need to be reminded of this when money was in short supply as during the wars of the 1790s. At the bottom of an account (1797) for furnishing materials – 'White Callico: Moss Rose Chintz: Rose and Jessamine Bordered Cotton' – was appended a note to Mrs Leigh:

> Madam, You was so kind to say you would pay ready money for the above in consequence of my charging them low; having some very heavy payments to make and finding money very scarce if convenient to you to favour me with settling, it would very much oblige.[4]

For unusual foods, the gentry necessarily went beyond local sources of supply. Tea – 'Imperial Green and Bohea' – coffee and chocolate were usually sent from London, wines from Bristol, fish from Gloucester, though families like the Leighs, Duttons, Blathwayts, Colchesters and Guises might on occasion spread their custom differently. The Blathwayts dealt with a Bristol merchant who could supply several kinds of cheese, and both they and the Leighs ordered wines and mineral waters from London. Quite frequently the Duttons paid for 'a Barrell of Oisters', and 'the Carriage of a Basket by coach' which might contain game from Norfolk, lobsters from London or fish from Bath; and once, 'a Parcel from London to Poison Rats by Coach 1*s*.' In the Leigh accounts there are payments to men and women bringing a Cheshire cheese from Crickhowell; 'Lettices' from Warwick; 'asparagrass and spinnage', rabbits and roasting pigs from Evesham; salmon and sturgeon from Worcester: all presumably ordered from known sources. Even in wartime families expected their special needs to be met, though they might be disappointed, as was Mrs Blathwayt in 1794: 'Madam, There's no pruins (prunes) in ye Kingdom, nor French Plums.'

Country houses seem to have been well stocked with linen: fine damask cloths and napkins, linen sheets and bolster cases for the family: coarse cotton cloths and sheets for the servants' use. Ticking and coarse materials could usually be obtained locally, but linens as well as the more luxurious fabrics wanted for curtains, hangings and upholstery – chintz, damask, lace, silks, velvet, taffeta – were ordered from London dealers, whose lists of wares opened up an Aladdin's cave of temptation to moneyed purchasers. The growing fashion for papering walls reached Gloucestershire during the later years of the century and from then onwards orders for paper were placed with London firms. From one of these, offering decorating and paper-hanging services, the Leighs ordered striped, flowered and Chinese patterns and evidently wanted to make sure that the papers were hung correctly, because included in the bill were 'Travelling Expenses for Man, and Lodging'. The Blathwayts also paid for a man to come from London to hang the paper they had ordered. Reflecting the increase in entertaining in country houses, a large amount of fine china was bought and breakages replaced regularly. The London showroom of Josiah Wedgwood and the warehouses (in London and Worcester) selling the Worcester ware of Flight and Barr supplied dinner and tea services in plain white, and blue-and-white patterned china for use at Dyrham and Sherborne. From the factory at Worcester the Leighs ordered in brown and gold Berry Pattern: 12 breakfast cups and saucers, 18 tea cups and saucers, 12 coffee cans and stands, 12 breakfast plates, 4 large plates, 6 egg cups, 2 muffin plates and covers, 2 slop basins, 2 sugar baskets, 2 cream ewers, 6 extra plates: which, with packing at 5*s*. 6*d*., came to a total of £14 8*s*. 6*d*. Cutlery, silver table-ware and ornaments usually came from goldsmiths and jewellers in London, as special designs and the addition of crests might be required. The Whitmores had gold and silver models of Queen Anne, George I, George II and Queen Caroline. At one time Sir John Dutton ordered: 'An elegant Globe Tea Vase, with arms and crest on cover and stand: an elegant Festoon Ewer Coffee pot with crest: a Festoon Sugar Bowl, cream pail and ladle with crests: 3 Festoon Vases and ladles: 2 Elegant Cut Cruets ornamented with Festoons of silver'. William Blathwayt likewise was specific and detailed in his demands: 'An elegant plated Urn with silver threads: a large size plated Top Dish with silver gadroon edges: 12 threaded plated water plates with silver edges': all of which had to have arms engraved on them.[5]

Inventories show that gentry houses were fashionably furnished during the eighteenth century with chairs, tables, chests and book-cases of imported woods like mahogany and walnut that must have been made by skilled cabinet-makers with access to pattern books and the necessary raw materials. Where up-to-date styling did not matter so much – in shelves, cupboards and fitments for the servants' bedrooms – local craftsmen were commissioned to make these; but new furniture that was to grace rooms used by the family and seen by visitors was ordered from London. In 1731, when William Kent was redesigning the interior decorations and furnishings of Sherborne House, Sir John Dutton commissioned from John Moore matching settees and stools in mahogany and two table frames, carved painted and gilded, for the lodge; also:

9 Carved Mahogany Chairs for my Hall
12 Walnut Chairs with Stuffed Backs and seats for my best Bedchamber
12 Walnut Chairs Frames with Banister Backs for my Drawing Room upstairs. French feet
A best Damask Bed

In 1756 Robert Hale bought six chairs and two elbow chairs to match in walnut; two square tables, a large bookcase, a writing table, a tray and knife box, all in mahogany. The items supplied to William Blathwayt in 1797 were much more elaborate:

6 very neat white and gold Chairs with Caned seats and Caned Tabled backs
A pair of neat Fire screens Japaned, the panels covered with Crimson & Blue Silk
A neat Sattin wood Ladies writing Table, the top to fall over a private Drawer
A very handsome sattinwood Octagon Table on Pillar and Claws banded with Purple wood varnished and on good brass Sockett Castors

These were despatched in a specially made wooden case and packed 'with fine paper' to stand the journey by road to Dyrham. Indicating an improved standard of living and more leisured existence, most houses had several musical instruments including harpsichords and pianofortes and these too came from London. The Whitmores hired their pianoforte at a cost of 10*s*. 6*d*. a month. Another sign of increasing affluence and of the importance of keeping up appearances was a family's acquisition of its own means of transport. Although the men still made local journeys on horseback and sometimes used public coach services over longer distances, the tendency was to purchase some kind of carriage that could be used by the women and children as well. In 1728 Sir John Dutton had 'A new Coach with springs, lined with Cafoy, gilt and painted with mosaic work' costing £145 9*s*. Four years later he exchanged his coach (whether this purchase or an earlier is not clear) for 'a new chariot machine'. In 1791 William Blathwayt received an estimate for 'a neat new Chairback half pannel'd Phaeton made of the best Materials – line with Drab Cloth Livery Lace . . . the Body neatly Painted and Varnished pattent Yellow: the Carriage Vermillion picked out Yellow and Black.' James Henry Leigh in the following year was sent a list of charges for the making of a new carriage 'lined with fine cloth, Trim'd with Best Raised Lace to Pattern, Plate Glasses, Mahogany Shutters,

Spring Curtains with Silver'd Caps and fasteners . . . the Body covered with Best Neats Leather Jappan'd to a High Gloss, Painted any Colour you may Chuse with Arms etc. on the Pannels.' This was to cost £125; or for £18 15*s*. 'extry' could be made as a landau, which – as the maker urged – 'is as serviceable as a Coach if your Coachman takes care to keep the Leather Suple with Oil'. It is noticeable that in these estimates and in bills for coach repairs, the materials used and parts like springs and axles were described as 'town-made', this clearly intended as a mark of superiority.

Some individual preferences as regards dress, jewellery, etc. will be dealt with in Chapter Twelve, but it should be mentioned here that many of the Gloucestershire gentry placed regular orders with fashionable tailors, wigmakers, dealers in guns and fishing tackle, perfumiers, tobacconists and stationers. Since appearance was an important factor in establishing a favourable impression and commanding respect, as a family moved upward socially, so it became expedient – on public occasions at any rate – for them to progress beyond what could be made at home or locally, into clothes that were cut and finished in up-to-date styles and increasingly expensive materials; that accessories such as fans, snuffboxes, wigs, shoes, etc. should come from well-known or recommended sources; and that a gentleman should be equipped for sport in a manner equal, if not superior, to his neighbour. Similar attention was given to the appearance of their servants. Most employers provided their men servants with new clothes once a year, but some like James Leigh hoped that with care these might be made to last longer:

> 1769 If the men can make their things serve handsome for 2 years I allow them for the livery coat and waistcoat £1 1*s*.: for the frock and waistcoat 12*s*.: for the breeches 10*s*. 6*d*. for the hat 5*s*. Paid William Bickley for George's breeches made in January last £2 2*s*. NB. These breeches though made in January are not to be worn till June which is the time for all George's things, but he will then be entitled to 10*s*. for having no breeches since June 1767.

The Dutton family dressed their servants in green livery, the Blathwayts in scarlet and the Whitmores in blue, and the last two had the uniforms made by their own tailors to very specific orders. Concern for the servants' appearance even extended to a willingness to pay the tax for them to use hair powder. Sir James Dutton's return for 1798, as well as naming himself and his wife, included his butler and under-butler, footman, groom, housekeeper, lady's maid and his son's servant.

Households remained much the same size as they had been in the past century though they seem to have been more formally organized with the wages and duties of each servant carefully defined. The increased amount of entertaining in gentry houses during the eighteenth century threw an extra burden on the domestic staff whose responsibility it was to look after the visitors; and since some of them were left in charge of the house in the absence of their employers, reliability and adaptability were all-important. The wife of William Leigh, advertising for a cook in 1740, required someone who, in addition to her work in the kitchen, could supervise the maids, sew and mend, keep accounts and take charge of supplies in the larder when her mistress was not available. Joseph Jackson of Sneyd Park, seeking a coachman on his sister's behalf, specified that he must be able to drive a coach and four horses, to look after the latter, 'be about the house to wait at table', and 'when he had nothing else to do, he'll be employed in the garden'.

Charles Edwin's letter (1791) on the state of the household when he returned home after an absence revealed what could happen when trust was misplaced:

> My whole family keeping open house in the Housekeeper's Room, Laundry and Servants' Hall, each giving entertainments according to their Rank which cost me eleven hogsheads of liquor, Ducks, Fowls, etc. as the entertainments consisted not only of Tea but Supper . . . I am sorry to add that both William and his Son has been frequently detected in robbing my Granarys of Corn and other things.[6]

Domestic servants on yearly salaries were frequently paid above the statutory wage rates and given an allowance besides so that they need not be dependent on vails (tips) from visitors – a situation which would have reflected adversely on the dignity of the household and its owner, though it is noticeable that Gloucestershire gentlemen when visiting other people's houses either as viewers or visitors distributed tips as a matter of course.

In addition to patronizing tradesmen and recruiting household staff in the neighbourhood, the gentry helped to finance local entertainers. It is uncertain to what extent they took the initiative in inviting musicians, dancers, etc., to perform for them and to what extent they were sitting targets for anyone who liked to call: the latter seems most likely. At holiday seasons, especially Whitsun, harvest time and Christmas, gentry families were necessarily drawn into the festivities of local communities, both as spectators and participants. According to Macky, writing in 1724, 'here in England during the twelve days of Christmas, the Nobility and Gentry retire to their respective seats in the country, and there with their Relations, Neighbours and Tenants, keep Carnivals in their own Houses, Hospitality, Musick, Balls: and play as much during this season all over England as in any kingdom whatever.' Where there were special celebrations at the family home – a birthday, a marriage, a coming-of-age – local people expected to be invited to show their respect and to share in the rejoicings. The ringers at Adlestrop, Longborough and Stow churches were frequently rewarded by the Leigh family for celebratory peals; and a Stow fiddler was a regular attendant at Adlestrop entertainments as were Morris dancers from neighbouring villages. At Sherborne too the Stow fiddler turned up; Morris dancers from Bledington and Barrington; 'Lady Talbot's servant that came over to Sherborne to play the fiddle'; the Cheltenham Drummer; 'ye Musick at Mead mowing'; and 'a poor man that play'd on the Back pipe'. At Sherborne Church the ringers never failed to perform when there was a birthday in the Dutton family. To the members of gentry families who were undoubtedly capable of providing their own music had they so wished, and in any case enjoyed professional entertainments when they were in London or at the spas, the standard of local talent must have been barely tolerable, but the idea of turning away its exponents unthinkable. Maybe the entry in the Dutton accounts in 1792 was not the only occasion when performers were paid *not* to demonstrate their expertise: 'Richard the Fiddler for two days coming over to Sherborne but did not play to the Ladies 4*s*.'

It had always been a characteristic of the gentry, since most of them accepted it as a natural duty, to respond to the needs of those less fortunate than themselves – whether the latter were the local poor, chance beggars at the door, or more remote worthy causes such as the ransoming of prisoners, the repair of decaying churches, the rebuilding of towns destroyed by fire. Payments of this kind continued to feature in personal expenses during the eighteenth century, and it will be remembered that Gloucestershire justices of the peace regarded poverty and vagrancy as the most serious of the problems they had to deal with. As the century advanced and more local charitable institutions were established – asylums, hospitals, orphanages for instance – most families subscribed to these on a regular basis, while continuing to finance schools and almshouses begun by their forebears. Endowments for these and for new schools featured in wills, as for instance that of Anthony Collett (1716) whereby rent from land at Bourton-on-the-Water was to be used to pay a master to teach twelve boys to 'read, write and cast accounts'; and that of Anthony Pleydell at Ampney Crucis, ordering £65 to be spent annually on the maintenance of a school master in the village and on apprentice fees for fifteen village boys. Many clergy and laymen were prepared to give their backing to the movement for Sunday schools initiated by Robert Raikes, owner of the *Gloucester Journal*, during the last decades of the century; and Colonel Maynard Colchester of Westbury and his neighbour Catharine Boevey at Flaxley were prime movers in inaugurating the Society for the Promotion of Christian Knowledge and schools connected with this at Westbury, Wotton-under-Edge and Stroud. It was also largely thanks to the joint efforts of these two philanthropists that the informal annual meetings of the cathedral choirs of Hereford, Gloucester and Worcester became, after 1724, the regular Three Choirs Festival (still held today) organized to raise money for helping needy clergy and their families. On a much larger scale was the munificence of Christopher Codrington, who 'by his will (1702) gave £20,000 to All Souls' College: £6,000 thereof was appointed to build a library and the remaining £14,000 to buy books to furnish it. Moreover he gave a noble library of his own to the same use and did further settle great revenues for propagating the Christian religion in foreign plantations.'

The other charitable concern of the clergy was their parish church. Sometimes this served as the family chapel as well – as at Barnsley, Adlestrop, Dyrham, Alderley, Sapperton and Great Barrington – where the family worshipped regularly, were ultimately buried and their virtues recorded for posterity on marble memorials; but even if they had a private chapel in their own home, they were no less assiduous in helping to maintain the local church. As well as weekly offerings they made larger contributions at Christmas and Easter, and gifts of bibles, communion plate, candlesticks and furnishings. Sir John Dutton's accounts include payments for:

Cleaning the Monuments in the Church	£37 3*s*.
Guilding a wrought Flaggon for ye Communion Table	£ 4 16*s*. 6*d*.
A green Cloth Pulpit cushion and carpet for the Communion Table and Fringe Lace for both, a present to ye Church	£ 9 11*s*.

James Dutton, his son, paid 12*s*. 10*d*. for a panel of Irish oak, and a further four guineas to have the commandments painted on it for display in Sherborne Church. James Leigh, having already paid for plastering and tiling in 1739, wainscotting, pewing and repairs to the pulpit in 1759, also bore most of the cost of major structural repairs to Adlestrop Church in 1764–5. Catharine Boevey endowed a curacy at Flaxley, provided religious books for the poor and bequeathed enough money to rebuild the parish church, though this was spent in other ways by her unscrupulous executrix. Sylvanus Lysons of Hempsted left an estate 'charged with the payment of £20 a year each to nine clergymen's widows: 2 guineas for a sermon in Hempsted church, £5 for an entertainment on Ascension Day.' Often, of course, the lord of the manor was the patron of the living and, though the situation described by Addison may sometimes have arisen (where the squire stubbornly stayed away from church while the parson inveighed against his sins in his absence), because the chosen incumbent was often a member or a friend of the family, the cooperation between the church and the manor usually resulted in a shared feeling of responsibility for all matters concerning the parish.

Having spent a considerable part of their income on commissioned work and purchases designed to improve their standard of living, and on charitable undertakings, the gentry still had enough money left to indulge in personal diversions and pleasures. As young men many of them had been sent on tours of England or the Grand Tour of the continent, partly to round off their education and become acquainted with current trends in art, architecture and music; and partly so that they could meet others of their own class and share their social activities. Some undoubtedly came back from Europe with undesirable habits such as a taste for gambling and card-playing, but many more developed a genuine liking for and interest in paintings, sculpture, antiquities and architecture and thereafter cultivated these as serious pursuits. Touring abroad was by no means unadulterated bliss, the discomforts and dangers of the journey at times threatening to outweigh the pleasures to be experienced on arrival. Bad weather in the channel was always a hazard that could delay the traveller at the onset or end of his journey for a week or more. James Leigh, who went abroad for nearly a year 1747–8, started off badly by having to wait to set off from Harwich and then being seasick for twenty-four hours during the crossing. He travelled through Holland, the Rhine states, Austria and Italy and formed unfavourable opinions of many of the people he met. The Dutch 'endeavour as much as possible to impose upon strangers' and while they 'excell so much in neatness, they fall much short of their neighbours in Common Honesty'; the people of Germany 'seem generally poor, yet where Popish tyranny is exercised, the generality of the People go half-naked and every House of tolerable appearance is inhabited either by Monks or Nuns.' His Protestant prejudices were allied to nostalgic patriotism. At Leyden 'we had only time to see the Physical Garden which is indeed a very fine one but in my judgment inferior to that of Oxford.' At Nijmegen 'upon the banks of the Waal we had a prospect (of the city) beautifully situated, something like the prospect of Westminster Abbey from the Bridge in Kensington Gardens.'

As compared with foreign expeditions, travel in England – though tedious at times – must have held few terrors. Individuals and whole families made sightseeing tours of stately homes, inspected churches and viewed landscapes currently being extolled by enthusiasts for the picturesque. They also visited London on pleasure bent; the spas at Buxton, Bath, Tunbridge Wells and Cheltenham for the sake of their health; and coastal resorts to indulge in the growing fashion for sea-bathing. About the latter, at Weymouth, Lord Caernarvon enthused to James Leigh in 1767:

> Our situation is truly Romantick and we seem to be fairly at sea. Here is the finest Beach I ever saw and I do believe the Bathing is in greater perfection here than anywhere. There is little or no company: there are however Balls once a week.

They kept diaries and journals, sketched and painted the places they visited or commissioned others to do this for them, and wrote about their experiences in letters to their families and friends. Many kept detailed expense accounts from which it is possible to follow their itineraries from inn to inn, and to note the cost of meals and refreshments, post-horses and payments to ostlers, coachmen and turnpike keepers. James Dutton (later the first Lord Sherborne) and his family were tireless travellers. They went to London, Paris, Scotland, Ireland, Brighton, Holkham and Lymington, as well as to the spas at Matlock and Bath, and presumably for the racing to Epsom, Newmarket and Ascot. They took a number of servants with them, at least two coaches and paid generously for extra help when it was needed: 'To three servants twice to Ranelagh *6d.* each, each night *3s.*', and 'To two Chairmen that went to Court with Lady Sherborne 21*s.*'; and when mishaps befell: 'Paid David for a Hackney Coach called for when in London, when Lady Sherborne's Coach wheel broke 1*s.* To the carriage of my Lady's stick from Shrewsbury to Cirencester 2*s.* 10*d.*' Members of the Leigh family travelled regularly between Adlestrop and London, went to stay with friends, and like the Duttons visited the spas and the seaside. The Revd Thomas Leigh (brother of James) made a habit of stopping at Woodstock and Headington on journeys to and from London. At the former he once lingered to skate on the lake in the park which cost him 6*s.* 6*d.*, while at the second he bought plants for his garden and in season ate strawberries for 1*s.* or 1*s.* 6*d.* with cream. A stay of nearly two months at Southampton in 1765 cost James Leigh, his wife and small son £157 19*s.* 6*d.*, which included bathing thirty-one times 'with a Guide at the Sea Bath', the regular services of a hairdresser for Lady Caroline and a purchase 'at Tredwells' Toyshop in Oxford 4*s.* 6*d.*' on their way home. A two-month visit to Buxton in the previous year, for Lady Caroline to benefit from the waters, had turned into quite an elaborate undertaking. Two servants accompanied James and his wife, and Nanny followed in her own carriage. Although it was early summer an extra charge was paid for the servants to have a fire and rushlights in their room. On the journey there and while at Buxton, the family visited the churches at Stratford and Burton-on-Trent, Lichfield Cathedral, Castleton, the Peak District, the Duke of Devonshire's house at Chatsworth where they were shown round by the housekeeper, the silk mills at Derby, and the Marble Mill near Buxton where they bought three urns for £1 9*s.*[7]

During the course of the century the growing attraction of the spas was matched by the eagerness of those who could afford to spend some time there, ostensibly to benefit their health, but in fact quite as much to savour the social life and mingle with the fashionable élite. As early as 1703 Mary, wife of Theophilus Leigh, in Bath for the sake of her ailing niece Emma, wrote home:

> There's an abundance of company here more than has been known so early in the year for several years. The Queen intending to come to the Bath in August makes people flock down, that came for health before. There's Plays three times a week and Musick in the Grove the other nights, but no Balls yet.[8]

At the end of the century a similar account was given by Henry Tracy:

> I have pleasure of finding a great many of my acquaintance here. . . . We have been at one Subscription Concert where we were highly gratified by the warbling of our favourite Madam

Mara. . . . We have not made our appearance at a Ball yet but intend doing so on Monday night . . . I believe once or twice more of that species of amusement will be all we shall partake of during our stay here as we are none of us fond of dancing especially in so great a crowd and shall therefore prefer the Plays and Concerts which are infinitely more to our taste.

Since the waters seem to have been equally distasteful whether bathed in or drunk, their efficacy was surely questionable and any improvement in health experienced by the partakers attributable to faith as much as to therapeutic processes. Nevertheless the visitors' first appearance each morning would be at the Pump Room in obedience to their doctors' orders and only after that would they feel justified in giving time to less serious pursuits. Writing about Tunbridge Wells in the 1720s, Macky remarked: 'The Manner of Living at Tunbridge is very diverting for one Week; but as there is no variety but in new Faces, it soon becomes tiresome.' The majority of visitors to any spa, however, stayed for several weeks, and if they became fatigued it was not from boredom but because of the demanding routine of activities they engaged in. Some went to the Pump Room more than once a day; then there was attendance at church, walking in parks or gardens and shopping to occupy the early part of the day, followed after dinner by the theatre, assemblies, balls and card-playing. It was important to be dressed in the height of fashion when seen in public, therefore much time was spent in patronizing tailors and dressmakers, milliners and 'toy shops' (sellers of trinkets and jewellery), some of whom were London tradespeople who moved to Bath and Tunbridge in the season especially to acquaint the provincial world with the latest modes. Frequent references in letters to what was being worn indicate that this was a subject of commanding interest; for instance, in 1784 Jane Parsons received this description from Dr Dark in Bath:

The fancy dresses of this place are very various, the ladies in a morning walk out with greatcoats something like a coachman's about the cape which are 3 and 4 deep. The other part resembles much the old Joseph that my mother used to wear 40 years ago, buttoned down to the toe and a black girdle 2 inches wide. But their heads are in ten thousand different forms: it is impossible to give a description of them and they are so wide and high 'tis impossible without an importation (by the present appearances) there can be hair enough grown in this island to support this small but pleasant city.[9]

William Leigh and his wife Mary, Sir George Whitmore and his wife Elizabeth, favoured Cheltenham for short visits during the late 1740s; the Blathwayts, James Dutton and family, James Leigh and Lady Caroline went to Bath. In the 'Accompt of Expenses at the Bath' kept for Sir William Blathwayt in 1710 were bills for sweetmeats, wine, corn and hay for the horses, and 'the Pumper, Serjeants and Chairmen', 'Cook, Servants, Musick, Ringers, etc. at your Entertainment'. In 1756 the Leighs spent nearly three months there, staying in furnished lodgings and hiring what they needed in the way of crockery, cutlery and glasses. They took some servants with them and had extra help for washing and 'dressing of dinners'. Recurring expenses were for doctors and apothecaries, payments to 'the Pumper for Lady Caroline' and for 'gifts to the Pump Room'. They attended balls and concerts, subscribed to the bookseller and coffeehouse, often lost and sometimes won money at cards. Provisions bought for the table included fish, pork, fowl, geese, asparagus, cucumbers and spinach; buns, pastry, cheesecakes and chocolate; port, brandy and mineral water. Plentiful and varied supplies of food occur in all accounts and it would appear that rigid dieting was not part of the medical treatment advocated, though possibly no one in the above-mentioned families was seriously ill.

Bath was the nearest and therefore most convenient spa for Gloucestershire families to resort to, and while it received the patronage of gentry and nobility from all over the country it continued popular. After the visit of George III and his family in 1788, Cheltenham began to compete with Bath, especially as residential accommodation, shopping facilities and entertainments developed to meet the specialised demands of moneyed people in search of diversion and relaxation. On the whole though, in this century, except for short visits, it never became as popular with Gloucestershire people as Bath; nor did the more limited attractions of the springs at Bristol and Gloucester and Stow-on-the-Wold, which would seem to confirm that those who resorted to the spas wanted a complete change of surroundings and an opportunity to escape into a kind of theatrical world, where for a brief spell, dressed in their best clothes and against a background of music, they elegantly acted out the parts of leading men and ladies.

But for those in good health and primarily seeking the utmost in sophisticated pleasure there was nowhere to compare with London. Whether they travelled in their own coaches or hired transport, the length and discomforts of the journey did not deter them and at any rate were forgotten once they reached the capital which was the hub of the nation's political, economic and social life. For several generations now the heads of gentry families had been used to going there in an official capacity or on estate business, but during the eighteenth century they were much more often accompanied by their wives and children and, though calls of business might still occupy the men for part of each day, all succeeded in spending some of the time enjoying themselves. Their point of view was expressed by George Embury, writing to John Parsons in 1792:

> London is at present full and last night at the theatre in the Haymarket I met with so many of my acquaintances from all quarters of my connexions. From your neighbourhood alone [i.e. Kemerton] I saw Mr Barwick, Mr Jackson, Mr and Mrs Wells, Mr and Mrs Parkhurst and Sir George Paul our associate in the grand inquest who did me the honour to know me again. Business and pleasure have each their attractions and I wish the latter did not desire to intrude so often: the former is rather jealous of such control. Ranelagh and routs suit me best as they are amusements which do not intrude upon the day and only abridge us of a few hours sleep. Tomorrow night there are to be grand doings in honour of the Duchess of York's birthday.[10]

As when they visited the spas, a house would be rented for the season and the whole family, accompanied by servants bringing linen, silver and other necessities, would move up to town. Depending on the size of the estate and the extent of its self-sufficiency, food supplies might also be taken, though by the middle of the century some goods were regularly being obtained from London shops anyway, and this was an opportunity to explore their potential further. Leases and inventories in respect of the properties rented indicate that they were adequately furnished and that compensation had to be paid for damages or losses incurred. Whether the lessees were able to make reciprocal claims is uncertain, though such would have been justified when, for instance, the Duttons paid a man *3s. 6d.* 'for taking down a bed in Grosvenor Street, cleaning same from Buggs and Refixing'. A full programme of activities was planned to take advantage of the opportunities the capital offered. The men frequented coffeehouses and clubs where English and foreign newspapers were available for reading, and 'where there is Playing at Picket and the best of conversation till Midnight' (Macky). James Leigh was a member of Almack's Club, and James Dutton belonged to this, White's and Boodle's. The ladies spent much of their time walking in St James's Park or Kensington Gardens where they could see what was being worn in fashionable circles, and shopping for clothes, hats and accessories so that they could pose as leaders of fashion themselves when they went back home. To judge by their trade bills, London shops were now catering for an affluent and increasingly sophisticated clientele, in offering a wide range of imported dress and furnishing materials, the latest fashions in dress, and exotic foodstuffs; and although it was the women primarily who took pleasure in shopping, the men were equally anxious to acquire the newest styles in wigs, snuffboxes and watches.

The evenings might be spent at assemblies in private houses where guests drank tea or coffee, played cards and sometimes danced. Families with friends and acquaintances in London would be sure to receive invitations to these. During the 1720s and 1730s members of the Leigh and Chamberlayne families, who were related to him by marriage, were invited by the Duke of Chandos to spend evenings at Canons, his magnificent house at Edgware; here they supped, played cards and listened to music performed by the duke's private orchestra. Alternatively there were entertainments at Vauxhall and Ranelagh where, to the accompaniment of music, the public could walk, eat light refreshments, watch masquerades and firework displays. Other attractions were the plays, operas and oratorios performed at Drury Lane, Covent Garden and the Haymarket. After their initial failure earlier, Handel's oratorios were becoming fashionable in the 1750s, and during one short visit to London the Revd Thomas leigh attended performances of *Judas Maccabeus, Esther, Samson*, and the *Messiah*. Shakespeare's plays, the *Beggars' Opera, Comus* and *Love in a Village* seem to have been favourite entertainments and were sometimes seen more than once in the course of a stay in the capital.

The sights of London were invariably visited – Hampton Court, the Mint, St Paul's, the Tower, the British Museum, Westminster Abbey, Greenwich Hospital; and minor spas like Sadler's Wells and Bagnigge Wells were popular venues for afternoon picnics. Unusual diversions also delighted out of town visitors – glimpses of the royal family, or processions and receptions arranged for foreign dignitories, the waxworks, a live crocodile, Johnson's equestrian feats, electrical experiments, 'seeing a man play tunes upon glasses'. Firework displays, whether at Ranelagh and Vauxhall or special occasions, such as the Royal Fireworks in St James's Park in 1749, were always a great attraction especially if there were youngsters in the party, though to judge by a letter from Lord Beaufort to Captain Brudenell Rooke the experience could work out expensive:

> You have never given me your advice about applying for a Place to see the Fireworks, which as they don't often happen may be a sight worth seeing: or if they are fixed for a day in January we may possibly continue our journey on purpose to be there time enough for a sight of them. I imagine we may see what passes in the Air from our own house but that perhaps may not be sufficient. In short, I will not give Fifty Pounds for a place to see them from.[11]

That no time was wasted, once London had been reached, is indicated by these extracts from the diary of Edward Bisse Hale, who spent five weeks there in 1763:

April	19.	Saw the King go to the House of Lords. Somerset Apartments, the Cloth laid and the Dessert for the Venetian Ambassador. *Love in a Village* at night.
	20.	Went shopping, Ranelagh at night.
	21.	Shopping. Lord Mayor's Dessert in the evening.
	22.	Shopping. *Romeo and Juliet.*
	23.	Visited Hampstead and Highgate. Saw State Coach.
	24.	Went to St Paul's. Dined in the Strand. Walked in the Park.
	27.	Took a walk to Westminster Abbey and dined at George Adey's.
	28.	Saw my Aunt: and *Cymbeline* in the evening.
	29.	Saw Bridewell: and *Hamlet* in the evening.

and so it went on, until having stayed in on 14 May and 15 May he had a final fling on 16 May:

Saw the Charter House, Christ's Hospital and St Bartholomews. Supped at home.[12]

To return to a country existence after the glamour of life in the city might have seemed an anticlimax for some, though it was their own homes that provided a stable background in the lives of the gentry. Assuredly for short spells they thoroughly enjoyed the social whirl in Bath or London about which they wrote enthusiastically to their friends, but few would have foresworn for long the satisfaction and assurance to be derived from familiar surroundings and a routine over which they had control instead of one that was imposed on them. The marked difference between the town-dweller and the countryman tended to become blurred during the course of the century as the latter gradually assimilated urban manners, fashions and standards; and although on the stage the country bumpkin continued to be mocked and humiliated by his cleverer town counterpart, there was far less justification for this than there had been a century before. No element of patronage influenced the attitude of the Duke of Chandos towards his relations and friends from Gloucestershire; they stayed at Canons on equal terms with the duke's political and business associates and London acquaintances; he sought husbands for their daughters and appointments for their sons as if for members of his own family. Gloucestershire gentlemen were accepted as members of London clubs and attended functions in London with no fear of being thought inferior. George Selwyn scoffed at the behaviour of Sir George Onesiphorus Paul and his wife it is true, but then both the parents and their son were rather larger than life and, while exciting a certain amount of amusement, nevertheless commanded respect for their achievements. On the whole, the country gentry, whether engaged in public duties or not, were neither less knowledgeable nor less experienced than those with whom they mixed in London or the spas, and just as capable of making their mark socially. Many had a circle of friends and correspondents that stretched far beyond the boundaries of the county, as is clear from surviving collections of family papers in the County Records Office. The Leighs were widely known for their hospitality and, while Dr Theophilus Leigh as Master of Balliol, wielded a certain influence at Oxford. The Duttons had a national reputation for their expertise in greyhound- and horse-breeding. The Atkyns family produced outstanding lawyers and, in Sir Robert Atkyns III, one of the earliest county historians. Catharine Boevey regularly spent winters in London and summers at Flaxley entertaining notable personalities, including bishops and the writers Steele and Addison, who are said to have

Catharine Boevey of Flaxley. A friend of the writers Addison and Steele who portrayed her as 'the perverse widow' wooed unsuccessfully by Sir Roger de Coverley

portrayed her in *The Tatler* as the perverse widow wooed in vain by Sir Roger de Coverley; she ultimately achieved a monument in Westminster Abbey designed by James Gibbs. Colonel John Selwyn, after a distinguished career as aide-de-camp to Marlborough, became a friend and supporter of Sir Robert Walpole and held a series of Court appointments, ending up as Groom of the Bedchamber to George II and Treasurer to Queen Caroline, whom his wife also served as Woman of the Bedchamber. Their son George carried on the family tradition of representing Gloucester in the House of Commons, but was much more interested in the social round than politics. He spent much of his time in London and Paris in the company of his close friend Horace Walpole whom he frequently visited at Strawberry Hill and entertained in return at Matson. Members of the Lysons family were known and liked by the royal family; Samuel was a particular favourite and perhaps owed his appointment as Keeper of the Records at the Tower of London to this. His elder brother, the Revd Daniel, became chaplain to Horace Walpole who encouraged him in his writing and illustrative work, some of which was printed on the press at Strawberry Hill and achieved wide recognition. The seriousness with which the gentry regarded themselves, their status and their responsibilities were indeed reflected in other people's estimation of them.

CHAPTER TWELVE

PERSONAL MATTERS

Although a large part of their lives was spent under the critical gaze of the public, the gentry also had a private side to their existence. This in most cases mattered more to them than winning acclaim and approval, since it was from the comfort and security of their homes that they derived the confidence and freedom of mind so necessary to the successful fulfilment of their official responsibilities and duties.

In spite of so many marriages being arranged with a view to enhancing family fortunes and estates, a majority of these led to satisfactory and affectionate relationships that ensured stable households where children could grow up happily, servants work willingly and guests enjoy hospitality. The obvious advantage of a young man's marrying an heiress, and joining her possessions to those he already owned or hoped to inherit, appealed in an age when large estates were more viable than small ones; when consolidated properties could be worked more economically than scattered holdings; and when it seemed right and desirable to secure for a future generation the combined resources of two established estates. Matches such as those between Thomas Master and Elizabeth Chester, John Howe and Joan Grobham, Henry Guise and Mary Cooke, Sir John Webb and Mary Blomer, averted the break-up and sale of lands that had been acquired and valued over a long period. The paperwork involved in marriage arrangements ran into dozens of pages, and many doubts and ambiguities had to be resolved before a final settlement was reached. This was usually precise, detailed and foolproof, securing the rights of both partners and of whichever should outlive the other, particularly important in the case of the wife whose fortunes had been merged with those of her husband, though sometimes things might go awry even for the men. It must have been galling for Sir John Dutton to have to record in his accounts:

> To the Attorney General for his opinion concerning the £5000, part of my first wife's jointure which was to be paid to me after Sir Richard Cullen's death: which sum I lost through Lord Lechmere's negligence in drawing the writings: £3 8*s*. 6*d*.[1]

Most parents were ambitious for their children and prepared to further their marriage prospects with land for boys or dowries for girls, but this was not always possible in large families or, if it was made so, might seriously diminish the resources of the estate.

Christopher Bond, on inheriting his modest estate at Newland, was obliged to sell part of it in order to provide dowries for his two sisters, and later on for his two daughters as well. The Duke of Chandos, out of his great wealth, delighted in being generous to his young relatives among the members of the Leigh, Chamberlayne and Atkyns families who, in turn, were invited to stay at Canons where suitable marriage partners were paraded for their benefit. In the case of the girls, Chandos augmented their dowries to enhance their chances; but though he prided himself on achieving satisfactory matches for his protegé(e)s, he was nevertheless anxious not to force the issue.

Once a suitable partner had been found, everything was done to expedite the marriage. Two of Theophilus Leigh's daughters, Mary and Emma, were married in Chandos's parish church at Edgware with all the excitement of a London wedding. To speed the marriage of his son William with Mary Lord in 1721, Theophilus:

Lent him on his Bond without interest towards a present to his wife	£100
Gave him for his wooing and expences	£100
Gave him to buy a pair of Coach Horses	£ 40
Paid for my son to Mr Jones ye Lawyer for ye Marriage Settlement	34 guineas
Paid to Mr Jones's clerks for Engrossing ye Settlement	£ 20[2]

When he married his second wife Mary Keck in London in 1728, Sir John Dutton arranged for the Bishop of Ely to conduct the service, paid for numerous attendants, ringers and musicians, bought a new sword and lace ruffles for himself, and, while providing only a modest wedding ring for his wife (15*s*.), gave her as well, a handsome pair of diamond earrings costing £350. Then, having shown her some of the sights of London and the houses and gardens belonging to Lord Castlemain and Sir Gregory Page, he took her home to Sherborne, sending housemaids, chambermaids and cooks ahead by stage-coach to be ready to receive the new bride, and arranging for welcoming peals of church bells to be rung at Barrington, Windrush and Sherborne. Possibly the worst fate that could befall a gentry family was the lack of an heir, so at a time when high infant mortality still prevailed, it was hoped that every marriage would produce a number of children, some of whom at least would survive. Mary Keck's death in childbirth and that of the baby as well, only a year after the marriage, was a sad event for her husband; he made elaborate and expensive arrangements for the bodies to be brought from London to Sherborne for burial, bought twenty-two mourning rings to distribute among his wife's closest friends, and hired a mourning coach for his own use during the following year.

There was a noticeable relaxation in the attitude of parents towards their children during the eighteenth century, less stern formality and more affection and sympathetic understanding being shown than previously; and extending beyond the immediate household to all relatives, however remote, family ties were strong and consciously strengthened by an unfailing interest in and concern for each other. Enquiries after the whereabouts, health and fortunes of members of the family were regularly included in letters or formed postscripts to these; and periodic visits kept everyone up to date with each other's circumstances. As soon as a child was born, godparents were sought and easily found since relatives were always ready to serve in this capacity, to subscribe to the expenses of midwife and nurse, and to arrange for a proxy at the christening if they were unable to attend themselves. Thereafter, they continued to take their commitments seriously, remembering birthdays and acknowledging special occasions with gifts and often leaving bequests to their godchildren in their wills.

Except when there was serious illness in the household or their mother was producing another baby, children were mainly kept at home while young, giving pleasure to their parents by their presence. All gentry households had one or more nursemaids, and sometimes 'Nanny' was an important member of the establishment, being kept on from one generation to another. The Leighs entrusted her with an allowance for herself and the children, and, though expected to keep careful accounts, she was left to decide what was needed and to make the necessary purchases. It is noticeable in the accounts of all families how often children's shoes had to be bought and repaired:

> Your little Baby's new shoes 2*s*. Cass's shoes and clogs 5*s*. Pumps for Tommy 2*s*. Miss Leigh's new purple shoes 4*s*. 3*d*. Miss Leigh's shoes soled, heeled and patched 1*s*. 8*d*.

Hands, too, were protected, in the case of the Leigh children with 'a pair of muffs', 'a fingered pair of kid gloves and a pair of lamb mittens', while one of the Miss Whitmores had 'White Grained Kid Gloves and a pair of Green Lamb Gloves'. Items in the expenses for William Leigh's children mark the stages in their growth. Molly progresses from a robe to stays (£1), a riding habit (£1 11*s*.) and a hoop petticoat (10*s*); Betsey, a young lady ready to emerge into society, has her hair curled (1*s*.) and then is given 10*s*. 6*d*. 'for the Ball'. Harry has regular hair-cuts to begin with, until achieving a peruque, though this was seemingly unsatisfactory: 'To a Peruque maker to take back a Peruque which he made for my son Harry which he wore 5 or 6 times (the wig he valued at £4) paid him to take it again £1.' There are few references to toys, but girls were often given silver thimbles, ribbons and lace, presumably to encourage them in useful ploys.

Before regular schooling started, the children were supplied with aids to learning – copy books, spelling books and 'counters to learn to cast with'; and though the boys, and even some girls before the end of the century, were sent away to school in due course, they would already have had some instruction at home. In the case of Molly, daughter of William and Mary Leigh, this seems to have started early with a payment for £3 3*s*. 'to begin to teach Molly to speak plain'. Arabella, daughter of John Colchester, presented an even greater problem as she was both deaf and dumb, and her mother sought advice on methods of teaching her. Most often, the teachers were women, like Betty Andrews who was paid 8*s*. 6*d*. for nineteen weeks' schooling for the two children of James and Lady Caroline Leigh; but young men from Oxford and Cambridge awaiting preferment in the Church or other posts might be appointed as tutors. Dr Theophilus Leigh, while Master of Balliol College, was asked on occasion by his friends to recommend suitable applicants, and Lady Freeman of Batsford was pleased to have a reliable teacher introduced to her:

> This morning, a Friend called on me who is a Fellow of a Colledge in Oxford, and understanding the children's Tutor was gone, told me of one who was a fellow of the same Colledge whom he could recommend upon his own knowledge – he says he is an extraordinary good scholar, speaks Italian, is a very sober man, and though of foreign birth, yet comeing over young, had his education here, which will be the more agreeable because I shall be sure they will be taught after the English manner.[3]

This young man was particularly useful because as well as academic ability he also had an understanding of music and could teach this; in other households music and dancing lessons were given by special teachers. A Frenchman, M. Charles Jansen, presented bills for 'Lecons de Danses aux Demoiselles Dutton'. James Leigh engaged John Palmer, a dancing master from Liverpool, for fourteen lessons at 15*s*. each, the stated terms being; '1 guinea per day per visit: 4 hours teaching: expenses of conveyance to house from nearest point on coach road.' It would be interesting to know how many other families employed John Palmer to make it worth his while to come so far afield to work.

As in previous centuries some gentry families favoured good grammar schools for their sons if such were available; thus the Revd Samuel Lysons sent Daniel and Samuel to Bath Grammar School where both received a grounding adequate enough to enable Daniel to proceed to Oxford to take Orders and his brother to be trained as a lawyer at the Inner Temple. Theophilus and Thomas, sons of Theophilus Leigh, went to Christ Church School at Oxford before entering the university. The Hon. James Dutton was sent to a private school in London where board and tuition cost £52 10*s*. a year and extras included fees to French, writing and dancing masters, and 'a Sergeant of the Guards for attendance, a fusil and accoutrements'. The young man also had accounts with a leather breeches-maker, a shoemaker, a hatter, a hosier and a tailor. Thomas Master, William Chester, Henry Somerset and Benjamin Hyett were educated at Westminster; sons from the de la Bere, Talbot, Chamberlayne and Whitmore families went to Eton. General William Whitmore bought a special account book costing 1*s*. 2*d*. to record the expenses involved. George Whitmore was allowed £80 a year while at school (1725–32) and managed at first on less than this. However, by his fourth year, he was needing considerably more, although his father paid for his place in the Worcester coach when he came home for the holidays, gave him an occasional present – 'a pair of Buckels, two Silk Handkerchiefs, a pair of Garters, a Perrywigg and a Nightcap' – and settled 'Several Bills to your Aunt Jones when you were ill of ye small Pox at Eton'. Gifts to the headmaster and the undermaster also featured at intervals, as they did in the expenses of James Lennox Dutton for his son William while he was at Eton (1765–8). The need to be on good terms with his contemporaries as well as in the good graces of the masters was reflected in one of William's letters home:

> I wish you would be so kind as to let me have tea and sugar here to drink in the afternoon, without which there is no such thing as keeping company with other boys of my standing.[4]

Among the girls who were sent away to school was the daughter of James Henry Leigh, whose fees for board, tuition, music and dancing amounted to £20 for a half year, to which were added expenses for gloves, stays, paper, silk-tape and lace and a seat in church. On behalf of his eldest daughter, in addition to 'board and education' James Lennox Dutton paid for haircutting and pins; a tooth-drawer; the apothecary; a drawing master; gold and silk thread for sewing purposes. For his youngest daughter the extras included a French spelling book and a French prayer book; a history of England; a children's geography book; thread, tape, bobbin and cotton; a wash ball; gloves; and a seat at chapel.

The final stages of boys' education remained unchanged during the eighteenth century – namely foreign travel combined with university and/or the Inns of Court.

Until the accession of George III in 1760 restored the old rapport between Crown and university, Oxford – customarily favoured by Gloucestershire students – lost some of its attractions for those in search of future patronage and preferment because of its prevailing Jacobitism and High Churchmanship. Also, in spite of regulations to curb excessive spending on dress, gambling, drinking parties and trips to London, university life was markedly expensive and thought by many parents to be corrupting. George Selwyn, sent down for blasphemous behaviour after only a few terms at Oxford, seemed to exemplify all that was undesirable in undergraduates – reckless extravagance, excessive drinking and a total disregard for authority. The number of boys going up from Gloucestershire decreased slightly in the first half of the century, though families with Anglican and Jacobite leanings continued to send their sons as before, with Christ Church favoured by the Lloyd Baker, Hale and Clifford families; Exeter by the Clutterbucks, Coxwells and Talbots; Oriel by the Sheppards and Pitts; and Balliol by the Bathursts, Masters, Whitmores and Leighs. Family links often explained these choices. For instance, three nephews of Dr Theophilus Leigh were enrolled at Balliol during his mastership, and several connections of Dr Henry Brydges, Visitor to the College and related to the Leighs by marriage. Institutional connections were also influential, though the Townsend Scholarships available from four Gloucestershire grammar schools did not always ensure a representative quota of Gloucestershire men at Pembroke.

For the most part these gentlemen commoners spent only a couple of years at the university and then departed for the Inns of Court or the Grand Tour without taking a degree. Those intending to enter the Church or practise medicine stayed longer. Many family archives contain detailed accounts of university expenses, kept by either the undergraduates themselves or their parents. Matthew Hale made a list of 'Washing Things carried to Oxford the first time' (1742):

> 9 Ruffled Shirts 4 Plain Ditto 10 Socks 3 Pr of White Stockings 6 Pr Worsted Stockings 9 Handkerchiefs 4 Night Caps 2 Waistcoats 2 Pr of Sheets 2 Pr Pillow Drawers 2 small table cloths 2 towels.[5]

James Leigh, 'being much at Oxford and some time at London', admitted that such visits more or less doubled his expenses, normally about £48 for half a year, but 'I am not at a certain allowance and cannot tell exactly what money I spent as I did not pay for every individual thing myself. My father pays to my tutor every half a year £5 5*s*. as likewise I have had a pair of velvet breeches which I did not pay for myself and perhaps some shirts and stockings which amount to £5.' James's younger brother Thomas was more meticulous about his accounts and kept a detailed record of his progress through bachelor's and master's degrees (1755–58), Deacon's and Priest's Orders (1758–60), becoming a Fellow of All Souls (1762) and taking an additional degree in Law (1763). Over and above his tuition expenses he paid a chambermaid, a laundress, who also received a Christmas box each year, a bedmaker and a tailor for the hire of gowns, hoods and a cassock. He kept a horse from the time of his first becoming an undergraduate, but, unlike his brother, did not start making trips to London and elsewhere until after taking his master's degree. He married in 1762 and thereafter his accounts include payments to his wife for housekeeping – £3 3*s*. a month. Throughout his career he was most concerned to balance his yearly budget or to satisfy himself that an imbalance was justifiable.

1761 The reasons of my expenses amounting to so much this year hath been the great deal I have spent in extraordinaries as in the purchase of a lottery ticket (£11 12*s*. 0*d*.) and a horse, besides the expenses of a tour to Winchester and the Isle of Wight which amount at least to £30 extraordinaries.

1773 We have spent this year about £50 more than our clear annual income, accounted for by having had much more company in our house than usual, and by having journeyed about more than usual.

It was still expected of gentry families that they would fill the ranks of the justices of the peace and members of parliament, so time spent at the Inns of Court was regarded as a necessary preparation for such public service. Some Gloucestershire names appear in the register of the Middle Temple – Stephens, Codrington, Colchester, Dutton and Brett, for example – but Lincoln's Inn seems to have been the most popular, with brothers joining each other there, succeeded by members of the next generation – Hale, Tracy, Howe, Talbot, Kingscote, Guise, Whitmore and Estcourt among them. Like the university, the Inns of Court became increasingly expensive as the century progressed and young men entered there necessarily came from families with the means to support them. Even so, their allowances did not run to vast extravagance, especially if more than one son had to be financed. Perhaps because it cost less and because the young man would be under more controlled surveillance, they were sometimes apprenticed to an established attorney for part or all of their training. Samuel Lysons worked under a lawyer at Bath before completing his legal education at the Inner Temple. Peter Leigh was apprenticed to a Stow attorney, Richard Jervis, who contracted 'to inform and instruct him in the Profession of Law and Practice of Attorney . . . and at the end of five years endeavour to procure the said Peter Leigh to be admitted one of the Attorneys of the Court of Common Pleas.'[6] Thomas Stephens, himself a product of the Middle Temple, arranged for his son George to study for five years in London under the guidance of a well-known and successful King's Bench attorney. The parents of both Peter Leigh and George Stephens saved themselves several thousand pounds by these arrangements since, after the initial expense of indenture, they paid only for clothes, washing and lodging, while the attorneys provided tuition and 'competent and sufficient meat and drink'. Peter Leigh evidently kept his part of the contract to give honest and reliable service because, before the five years were up, he was being entrusted with work to carry out on his own.

From the sixteenth century onwards, the law had been an accepted route to financial and social success, and it still afforded career prospects for gentry sons who were not going to be directly responsible for running the family estates. It was reported of the Atkyns family in the eighteenth century that 'There has always been one of them presiding in some of the Courts of Judicature of this kingdom above 360 years.' The Hale family too and the Stephens of Lypiatt tended to produce at least one lawyer in each generation; while Benjamin Hyett, a trained attorney living in Gloucester, made enough money from his large practice and marriage to heiress Elizabeth Morwent to found a fortune. He thus enabled his son Charles to buy the site of Painswick House, the future family home, and his grandsons Benjamin and Nicholas, both trained lawyers, to devote their lives to public service. The Yorkes, newcomers to the county when they bought the Hardwicke estate in 1726, had phenomenal success not only as lawyers: Philip and his son Charles both became Lord Chancellor and the latter's son Home Secretary; Philip also achieved a knighthood, a barony and an earldom during his lifetime, Hardwicke providing him and his family with a local habitation and a name. Richard Jervis, mentioned above in connection with the training of Philip Leigh, was an interesting example of an attorney who became *persona grata* among the local gentry without actually aspiring to join their ranks. He lived and owned land in Broadwell, styling himself esquire, and acted as an agent for the estates of a number of local families, members of which sought and acted on his advice in both personal and legal matters. Officially he rubbed shoulders with them at meetings of Turnpike Trustees and Enclosure Commissioners; socially, he dined with them and met their friends. In emergencies they trusted him to come to the rescue, as did Henry Danvers Doughty when he sent this urgent appeal:

> As I was coming this morning through Chipping Norton for Broadwell, I was arrested for a debt of £42 by Mr Lipscomb, the Sheriff of Oxfordshire's officer. . . . Now as I don't doubt of your assistance in this affair, I would be glad if you would come over immediately to the White Hart, or if that does not suit your convenience, if you will be so kind as to send the money by my servant; or security for such and by so doing will confer a lasting obligation upon your obedient and humble servant. . . .

Although it became a commonplace during the eighteenth century for writers to decry the value of the Grand Tour as an educational experience, nevertheless at this time it reached the height of its importance and popularity among the gentry. Evidently enough young men went abroad and behaved in a reprehensible manner for some parents to doubt the wisdom of exposing their sons to temptation; but for the majority, this was a risk they were prepared to run in order that their heirs should acquire sophistication, an acquaintance with foreign languages and first-hand knowledge of Classical art and architecture. Those who set off on their travels straight from school were perhaps too young to profit as much as they should have done, however serious and conscientious their ciceroni; those in their early twenties, who went after being at the Inns of Court or university, were more likely to benefit and it is clear from what they brought back in the way of books, prints and pictures and what they added to their libraries and picture collections later, that their aesthetic awareness had been heightened by what they had seen. When they were in Rome, John and William Blathwayt were painted by Pompeo Batoni, a fashionable painter who catered for the wishes of English travellers to bring away with them mementoes of their tour; he specialized in portraying well-dressed figures posed nonchalantly against a background of Roman antiquities. Benjamin Hyett, described as 'an elegant scholar, man of the world and a polished gentleman', developed a lasting love of painting while visiting galleries in the Low Countries and Italy and returned home with the nucleus of his future collection – his own portrait, the works of Piranesi and several views of Naples. George Onesiphorus Paul too bought books and pictures and acquired the ambition to become a serious collector in due course. Folios of prints and pieces of statuary collected abroad came to be features of the libraries and reception rooms in houses like Dyrham, Adlestrop and Lower Slaughter. Often lasting friendships were started when travellers were thrown into the company of congenial spirits – Sir William Guise with Edward Gibbon for instance, or George Selwyn with Horace Walpole, who thereafter drew him into his own social circle and band of aesthetes. William Leigh spent three years abroad with Lord Cornbury, benefiting from the latter's introductions to foreign courts and wide circle of acquaintances. He sent home regular accounts of the political state of the countries he visited and was entrusted with quite responsible commissions by his relatives and friends, such as tracking down pictures and supplying descriptions of them to his uncle James Brydges, and buying materials for the trousseau of the latter's bride-to-be. Acquaintance with English ambassadors and agents sometimes ripened into lasting contacts and led to their being used in the future as a means of obtaining works of art that might come on the market. A few years abroad could indeed determine the future direction and development of a young man's tastes, friendships and interests.

Without being able to go back in time and overhear their conversations *en famille* and when entertaining their friends, we cannot be sure whether the effects of education and travel were absorbed by the gentry in the eighteenth century to the extent of becoming an integral part of their nature, but in most cases this must have been so. Their letters, which after all were not intended for publication, indicate that they read their books, recommended and lent them to others and valued them sufficiently to have them protected by good bindings; for example, George Whitmore had his copies of *Paradise Lost and Regained* 'new-bound and gilt'; and a *History of Modern Europe* put into 'binding, neat in Calf, lettered and figured'. That they discussed knowledgeably and to good effect the skills of architects, artists and craftsmen can be inferred from their building projects and the way they embellished their houses. Enthusiasm for antiquities, fired by visiting ancient sites in Italy, was maintained on their return by a continuing interest in the archaeological past of Gloucestershire. Atkyns and Rudder, though primarily concerned with the contemporary state of the county, included in their accounts any matters of archaeological or genealogical interest that might enhance the image of the people and places they were writing about. Not only clergy were concerned with the history of their parishes, though they undoubtedly led the growing number of antiquarians as the century progressed. Landowners, too, wanted to find out and preserve any evidence of the past on their estates. There were many references to archaeological discoveries in the letters of the Rooke family of St Briavels. The Estcourts too were alive to the interest of the past, as Thomas Estcourt revealed:

> Our repair of the church goes on very well: we have discovered some curious and beautiful pavement under the Pews when we took up the floors, from which it appears that the Church was founded or beautified by some of the oldest families in the county. . . . Matthew Wyatt, a great Antiquarian and Herald . . . was in Raptures with the Beauty of this old Pavement though much defaced and damaged, as he says they are Norman tiles and much more perfect and more beautiful than any which the Antiquarian Society possesses. We are in hopes to save enough of these tiles to pave a small compartment somewhere in the Church.[7]

Members of the Lysons family made themselves the leading experts on the antiquities of Gloucestershire. The Revd Samuel Lysons of Rodmarton and his sons the Revd Daniel and Samuel were all Fellows of the Society of Antiquaries, and the two younger men spent most of their lives collecting, illustrating and publishing information of antiquarian interest. The Revd Daniel, while chaplain to Horace Walpole, produced

Environs of London and *Magna Britannia* illustrated by himself and then, after inheriting the family estates, wrote on a Gloucestershire subject: *A History of the Three Choirs Festival*. Meanwhile his brother Samuel was proving his artistic skill by exhibiting work at the Royal Academy and contributing etchings to Daniel's works. Eventually he took up the study of antiquities in Gloucestershire and published three definitive works on these: *Views and Antiquities in Gloucestershire; A Collection of Gloucestershire Antiquities*; and *The Roman Antiquities of Woodchester*.

On public occasions gentlemen presented themselves formally dressed, radiating self-confidence and an aura of competence and reliability. What was the reverse of this image, seen only by family and friends? Undoubtedly appearance mattered as much in private as in public life, since in both, as well as proving their own success, gentlemen were concerned with giving a lead to others in dress and behaviour – a role largely relinquished by the Hanoverian monarchs and now being assumed by the nobility and gentry instead. A number of the Gloucestershire gentry, as a result of seasonal visits to London and the spas, kept abreast of the latest fashions themselves and in due course informed others of them. Only a minority now were parish gentry never stirring beyond their own locality, but even those who went no further than the county town had contacts with the capital and subscribed to national newspapers and periodicals which carried commentaries on the passing scene as well as news. All who could afford, and there were few who could not, affected mourning on public occasions (a death in the royal family for instance) as well as in private grief, and even if outfits had been worn before, they were given a fresh look with new trimmings and accessories. In 1727 Sir John Dutton bought 'a mourning suit for the King, waistcoat lined with silk' which cost him £9 12*s*. A death, whether near or remote, inevitably produced a spate of letters of condolence with the bereaved, and replies to these written on mourning paper and sealed with black wax. Receipted bills and entries in personal account books reveal trends in fashion as well as personal preferences in dress and adornment. In February 1777 William Blathwayt ordered from his London tailor 'a light colour Bath Coating Great Coat, double Breasted and bound round the Edges and Button holes'; also 'a Superfine Brown Cloth Suit, the Coat and Waistcoat lined with Shalloon, with Silver Plated Buttons.' In May he had made 'a Superfine Olive Colour Cloth Coat and an Ash Colour Corded Silver Waistcoat laced with narrow Silver French Braded Lace and Black Silk Stocking Breeches, the Coat faced with Cloth, the waistcoat lined with Silk Serge, the Breeches interlined and lined with Fustian.'[8] Men in the Whitmore, Leigh, Dutton and Blathwayt families affected campaign wigs, bagwigs, bobwigs and peruques as the century progressed, and then in the last decade took to dressing their own hair, ordering 'hair powder, sticks of hard pomatum, and pots of soft pomatum' for this purpose. Hats, whether to be worn or carried, were ordered from London as were riding boots and, for the Revd Thomas Leigh, an umbrella. Silk and cambric were bought for handkerchiefs and neckerchiefs (evidently made at home) and infinite yards of lace for ruffles. Silk stockings were obtained ready made, but woollen ones were knitted at home. Even after he gained his title, Lord Sherborne thriftily held on to familiar wear: 'For three pounds of worsted to new foot some of Lord Sherborne's stockings 12*s*.' William Leigh also liked woollen stockings: 'Given to widow Bradford to buy wool to make stockings for me, 6*d*. Given to her for making up my thick stockings. 3*s*.' Being something of a dandy, William Leigh was likened by his family to Will Honeycomb of the Spectator Club, but he was capable of changing this image completely when, during summer vacations, he put on his oldest clothes and, with his brother Theophilus similarly clad, set off on long country walks during which they were in danger of being taken for and treated as tramps. Perhaps it was for these occasions that he wanted his thick woollen stockings.

Almost all men had some jewellery – a gold watch, a ring, a jewelled pin, enamelled or jewelled buckles – but it was their wives who owned considerable collections often comprising very valuable pieces. At the time of her death Elizabeth Whitmore had six gold rings; three snuff boxes – gold with an agate lid, tortoiseshell with a gold rim, and silver with an Egyptian pebble; a gold girdle buckle and a pair of gold shoe buckles; bottles for salts and scent with gold tops and chains; 'cornelian seals with the family arms engraved and set in gold'; as well as brooches, earrings and a gold case for tooth-picks. Cassandra, daughter of William Leigh, soon after her marriage to Sir Edward Turner, a soldier of comfortable means, made a list of her jewellery:

A diamond necklace & solitaire A pair of brilliant drop earrings A rose stay hook A brilliant hoop ring Two brilliant roses Three diamond rings One emerald ring set around with diamonds Eleven fancy rings One brilliant pin

In 1775 Lady Sherborne paid £836 to a London jeweller for:

A gold hoop ring A pair of earrings with knots and single drops A pair of earrings with 2 yellow rose diamonds set around with pearls A necklace of 39 brilliants, a chain and a tassel with 266 brilliants Pair of gold lockets A Shagreen case with lock and key 648 very fine pearls for a bracelet @ 5*s*. 9*d*. each

Although much of their clothing was still made at home, the women like the men had some garments made specially, or bought them from retailers in London and Bath – stays, hoop petticoats and quilted petticoats, mantuas, wrappers and aprons. New bonnets and hats were ordered for special occasions; feathers were dyed and recurled to be used again. Increasingly too, fashionable shoes were ordered, in leather and with ties instead of buckles, as by Mrs Blathwayt from a dealer in Bath in 1794:

Pair of Spanish Poppy Heels and Binding Pair of Green shoes and Bands Pair of Black and Blue Sandals Pair of Black and Yellow Sandals Pair of Elastic Clogs

Fur tippets and muffs appear among the belongings of women in the Dutton, Leigh, Whitmore and Blathwayt families, but there is no way of knowing whether the purchase of these was determined by personal taste or a desire to be in the fashion.

As is evident from their correspondence, men and women alike in the eighteenth century were much concerned with matters of health. Not only did they expatiate on their own ailments and those of the rest of their household; they also wanted to know how other people were, what remedies they resorted to and with what success. They took an almost morbid interest in the discussion of symptoms and, to judge by the medicines they resorted to, were fearless in their pursuit of cures. Nor were they averse to country remedies. Lord Sherborne paid 2*s*. 'to a man that charmed the warts away', and in many household accounts women were rewarded for collecting herbs and lichens of various kinds – presumably for use in the stillroom. However, an increasing number of trained medical men were available. Some Gloucestershire families, including the Duttons, consulted the eminent London physician Sir Hans Sloane. Mary Leigh was also treated successfully by a London doctor, according to a letter from her husband William:

> My Dearest, My dear daughter's letter by this post has given me no little satisfaction, observing by it that Dr Addington pronounces you better and that you did eat a Flounder for your dinner with a good Appetite. I persuade myself you have in Dr Addington a safe, careful and skilfull Physician. He told me you would be better for your late, very painfull Disorder.[9]

Locally, in the county, Daniel Lysons combined private practice with work in the hospitals at Gloucester and Bath; Charles Trye acted as surgeon to the Gloucestershire Yeomanry and the Gloucester Infirmary; while in the Stow-on-the-Wold area, Anthony Compère and his sons served a number of gentry families, setting broken bones, drawing teeth and dealing with childish ailments as well as more serious adult complaints. Lysons came from a gentry family with lands at Hempsted; Trye had inherited and ran the family estates in Gloucestershire and elsewhere; and one of the Compère sons married the heiress to the Chadwell property at Broadwell – all indicating that the medical profession was now achieving a social as well as a professional status equal to that of the law. Edward Jenner, discoverer of vaccination, was initially encouraged in his work by the Berkeley family and thereafter received considerable support from leading county families who had faith in him. To judge by the frequent references to it, toothache was a common complaint. William Leigh called in the Compères, father and son, to deal with his dental troubles and once a woman, Mrs de la Mar, was paid 2*s*. 6*d*. 'for filing a tooth'. The Revd Thomas Leigh evidently believed in taking precautions:

> Toothpick case of toothpicks 2*s*. Dragons root for the teeth 8*d*. Powder and brush for the teeth 1*s*. 6*d*. For sealing my teeth 5*s*. Balescot's Electuary for the teeth 3*s*.

Because they were away from home more frequently than in previous centuries and had wider interests and the means to cultivate these, gentry families during the eighteenth century had little difficulty in filling their leisure time. Even though they had staff to cope with domestic work, wives organized and directed this and often did some of it themselves, because as entertaining became an increasingly regular feature of family life, the smooth running of the household was all the more important. Wives checked the household accounts, conducted much of the family correspondence as well as handling business letters for their husbands from time to time, and usually it was they who kept track of family events – births, marriages and deaths. They embroidered trimming and material for their clothes, sewed and knotted purses and other trifles for gifts, and improvised decorations for their bonnets. Even the wealthy were thrifty in their habits and, having spent a lot of money on clothes or accessories, they tended to look after them well and find ways of giving them a new look from time to time. As the century went on, periodicals and magazines for women appeared and these were subscribed to, as well as libraries from which novels and histories might be borrowed. Lady Sherborne belonged to a library in London for which service she paid an annual subscription of three guineas, 1*s*. for a catalogue, and 15*s*. 2*d*. for the carriage of books sent to her. Card games, chiefly quadrille, piquet and whist, were as popular with the

The Dutton family at home engaged in playing cards, one of their great pleasures. A portrait by Zoffany

women as with the men, but though the former made and lost small sums of money in play, they were usually prudent enough not to run risks. The Dutton family were notorious gamblers, but other families too produced young men who got into debt and even ran through fortunes in the space of a few years. Philip Sheppard claimed to have run through £100,000 in thirteen years. Even the soberest of men, not given to dangerous gambling, found the odd wager irresistible – whether on the outcome of a race, some political issue, or purely social speculation – for instance, the sex of an unborn child or someone's marriage prospects. 'Lady Charlotte Montagu to receive a guinea if she marries before this day twelvemonth' (James Leigh).

Most country gentlemen spent some of their leisure time in the open air and this necessitated their having all the facilities for sport. As well as riding clothes and boots, they bought guns, fishing rods, saddlery, etc. from London specialists. One order from James Dutton included:

8 Best hunting whips with silver nails	£4 4*s*.
10 doz. best hunting Cord lashes	15*s*.

4 natural look holly walking sticks	1*s*.
5 hunting thongs with hunting cord lashes	10*s*.

After receiving his title he bought new harness for the horses he used in town, and those he used for travel purposes, with specially engraved crests to be attached. 'Dogs chiefly occupy the thoughts of a Country Squire,' wrote a cousin to John Parsons and certainly to judge by correspondence they were often the subject of enquiries and exchanges. The Duttons were perhaps the best known for the size and excellence of their pack, but their enthusiasm was shared by numerous other families including the aristocratic Beauforts and Berkeleys. Richard Berkeley assured John Parsons:

> I think recollecting you asking me to assist you with some hounds as I shall always be happy to help a Brother Sportsman. I can now supply you with a Couple of young ones and one old Hound, a very good dog and well-bred. If you will send a carefull Person for them next week, my Man will deliver them.[10]

Brudenell Rooke was one of the sporting fraternity, also ready to oblige, in this case the Duke of Beaufort, who acknowledged:

> The Dogs and Fowls arrived very safe on Friday, being left where my things always are, within a little mile of the house. The former are very pretty and one of them seems sociable, the other at present far otherwise. The Partridges are beautifull and agree with the Chinese Pheasants with whom they at present keep Company.[11]

On occasion, Rooke acted as the intermediary, for instance, between Beaufort and the Duke of Marlborough:

> I have conversed with my Keeper about the Deer which the Duke of Marlborough is to have and you may with my Compliments acquaint his Grace that when I know what sort of Deer he would like to have, we could then better settle the time of catching them. . . . I have a favour to ask of his Grace in return which is that if he has any large hounds proper to Park Hounds I should be very glad to have a Dog and Bitch.

Although the Game Laws protected the privileges of those entitled to own dogs and to hunt, legal enforcement of these was still lenient and patchy rather than strict, since paternalism and justice tended to override considerations of class interest in the minds of justices. That feelings sometimes ran high between the 'haves' and the 'have-nots' is shown by the following letter sent by a tenant to Mr Parsons of Kemerton:

> On Sunday last . . . a Dog belonging to you came in my House and taken away with him a Joint of Meat from the Table that wee had cooked for Dinner and Went of with it, and one Time before this, a Dog belonging to you killed Three couple of Ducks for me for which Reason I asked you to Give me a Hair [hare] and you promised me one but never Give me Tho you have presented them all over the Neighbourhood and to the Next Door. You forgot your promise to me. You ordered my Dog to be Shot for no trespass at all. Pray what must I doo to your Dogs for trespassing of mee.[12]

The Leighs, Whitmores and Duttons always kept a number of horses, for drawing their coaches, for riding, and for their children to use; and we have noted that George

Shooting, a popular outdoor pastime in the eighteenth century. A scene on Minchinhampton Common

Onesiphorus Paul's stables were drawn upon when extra horses were needed for George III and his family during their visit to Cheltenham. Whether they did much riding themselves or not, almost all the gentry flocked to race meetings at local venues such as Bibury, Cirencester and Tetbury; many entered horses for the races; some rode themselves, and almost all bet on the results. So sure were they of seeing their friends on these occasions that frequently political and business matters were discussed and settled there and disappointment expressed if someone failed to turn up.

Another outdoor interest that gathered momentum during the course of the century was the improvement of gardens and grounds. Already by the end of the seventeenth century there were writers on gardening, botanists studying the nature and use of plants, and practical gardeners who were satisfying the demands of landowners anxious to create new settings for their homes that would mitigate the formality of existing surroundings. The establishment of nursery gardens, first in London and later in the provinces, made it possible for garden-makers to obtain plants and trees to achieve the effects they wanted; and anyone connected with trading companies was able to have exotic specimens brought back for them from overseas. The fact that the Dutch were far ahead of other European nations in horticultural practice was also a help, in that regular travellers from England were commissioned to bring back from Holland bulbs, seeds and plants not available here. The Duke of Chandos asked William Leigh to send him full particulars as to how the Dutch heated their greenhouses and to arrange for the despatch of 10,000 turfs to be used at Canons for this purpose. During the eighteenth century, Gloucestershire landowners had some magnificent examples of planned gardens not too far away to provide them with inspiration and ideas even though their own efforts would be on a much more modest scale. The building of Blenheim and landscaping of the grounds there must have interested and influenced all those who travelled through Woodstock and stopped in inspect the work of Vanbrugh, Charles Bridgeman and Capability Brown. The successful accomplishment of William Kent's layout at Rousham would also be known, as well as the new effects at Cirencester Park, initiated by Lord Bathurst with the help and encouragement of his friend Alexander Pope. These consisted of ten long avenues of trees radiating out across the park from the house and culminating in views of village churches, Cirencester Church providing the vista at the end of the main Broad Avenue. Bathurst had practical knowledge and a love of shrubs and trees, and while arranging the new avenues contrived to leave a number of woods and copses growing naturally to break the rigidity of his design. He also introduced a number of fanciful buildings in the park including a sham castle, a rustic pavilion, an ivy-covered Gothic lodge, and a Doric column capped with a statue of Queen Anne. There was a serpentine lake with a meandering path round it, and a terrace with flowering shrubs and evergreens near the house which commanded a view across much of the park. In due course Bathurst's ideas were to become outdated; nevertheless in the 1770s when the Revd J. Sullivan was travelling round the county, he reported: 'According to modern ideas, there are too many unbroken avenues in the wood of Cirencester. As it is indeed, it possesses a great deal of beauty; nor do I ever remember to have enjoyed a more pleasant ride in any of the countries I have traversed.'

Cirencester Park was the work of two amateurs. Some landowners, lacking the inspiration and expertise of Bathurst and Pope, had to consult professionals about their garden plans. As we have seen, William Kent was commissioned to introduce improvements at Great Barrington and, being primarily a painter, he brought artistic features into the landscape there. In 1729 Sir John Dutton 'paid Mr Bridgeman of Oxford for journeys and a plan of the Park £71 4*s*,' and a few years later had serpentine walks made behind the lodge. Like Bathurst, Dutton was a lover of trees and shrubs, and ordered a large yew tree, 700 wych elms and 25 oaks for his garden, as well as 100 honeysuckles, 100 sweet briars and 2 'foreign jessamines'. As natural landscaping became more popular, flower-beds, the kitchen garden and fruit trees were given less attention; nevertheless at Sherborne there was a large orchard with pears, cherries, peaches, nectarines, apricots, plums, figs and vines, and orange trees grown in pots; nor were flowers entirely absent since Spanish brooms, polyanthus, bellflowers, roses and hollyhocks appeared in a nurseryman's account. A sundial engraved with the Dutton arms was set up with 'a tin cover' to protect it. At Dyrham, too, William Blathwayt had an orchard with variations on Dutton's choice including apples, damsons, quinces, mulberries and sweet almonds; his range of flowers included 'scarlet horse-shoe geraniums, double hyacinth, Van Toll tulips, and double white narcissi'; and his kitchen garden was stocked with several kinds of peas and beans, turnips, radishes, savoys, cauliflowers, onions, carrots, endives, 'early York cabbage and Sugar Loaf Cabbage'. In the 1790s Humphrey Repton was called in to improve the grounds, which had not been changed since they were first laid out at the turn of the century. His proposals led to a new entrance and approach road being made and masses of earth being

Cirencester Park. The new house of Sir Allen Bathurst with avenues of trees converging on it

moved to lessen the slopes round the house, followed by extensive planting of beeches, elms, limes, oaks, sycamores, planes, chestnuts, hornbeams, spruces, willows and poplars. To these were added flowering trees – laburnums, acacias, syringas, amelanchier and lilacs. All the plants at this point came from Miller and Sweet, nurserymen at Bristol.

Although no traces remain of the gardens that they made, it is known that the Keytes of Ebrington, the Tracys of Toddington and Powell Snell who had bought an estate at Guiting Power in 1720, all bought plants from Henry Clark, a gardener of Chipping Campden who also undertook business as a nurseryman and acted as agent for a number of landowners in the area. He seems to have obtained some of his stock from London because costs of carriage from there are included in his accounts, though he was able to offer quite a wide range of plants on his own account. He mainly supplied flowers, shrubs and seeds of annuals, but some fruit trees and evergreens were also listed in his bills. None of the above-mentioned landowners had vast parks that called for landscaping, so it is likely that the grounds round their houses were left as pleasure gardens for the immediate enjoyment of their families, and that suggestions for planting came from Henry Clark himself.[13]

From the mid-seventeenth century when William Leigh and his wife Joanna started to improve the grounds at Adlestrop, members of the Leigh family took a continuing interest in the immediate surroundings of their house. In 1752 James Leigh embarked on a major reorganization, inviting Samuel Driver, a nurseryman from London, to propose changes in the layout. Subsequently Driver himself and two helpers came down to Gloucestershire for three weeks to start on the improvements, which were to include the making of a walled kitchen garden, an orchard and flower borders. Driver was paid at a rate of five shillings a day and his helpers at a shilling, but local workers received only between threepence and tenpence. All the necessary plants and trees came from Driver's nursery at Lambeth and Leigh continued to deal with him for at least fifteen years. In 1765 a head gardener, William Bricknell, was appointed at Adlestrop and a contract drawn up between him and James Leigh, outlining their respective responsibilities. In return for a yearly salary of £38, diet and lodgings, Bricknell was to look after all parts of the grounds, 'cut the grass as often as is proper; furnish large quantities of flowers in the borders; keep the kitchen garden fully cropp'd with phisical Herbs and also plenty of Melons and Cucumbers', though 'Mr Leigh will not insist that any large quantities of Turnips shall be produced from the Garden when Field Turnips are in season.' The terms of the contract covered two pages and evidently proved satisfactory to both parties as Bricknell remained at Adlestrop for many years, continuing to buy plants and seeds from Samuel Driver. The garden borders in the summer must have looked colourful, as a typical order for seeds included: 'Affricans marygold, Hollyhocks, Double larkspur, Sweet scented Pease, Nasturtion, Love lies ableeding, Viola Tricoler, Yellow Lupins, Candy Tuff, Stript Columbine'. It seems doubtful that Bricknell gained any advantage from the clause which stated: 'Mr Leigh will give up the tools he now has and an Inventory thereof to be taken and the same sort of tools in the same Condition to be left by Wm. Bricknell when he quits his master's service', since the list included:

3 large Rakes one broken head
1 Dutch How Broke
6 Scythes and 3 Spades only 2 usefull
12 Hand Glasses very much Broken
1 Dunge Forke mising.[14]

During the 1790s, James Henry Leigh consulted Humphrey Repton about further improvements in the grounds at Adlestrop. The suggestions included the damming of the stream in the park to make cascades and the planting of clumps of trees to add interest to the sweep of lawn between the front of the house and the Chipping Norton road. The orchard and kitchen garden remained untouched, also the flower garden for which Repton designed 'a Bath and Seat'. No payments for the latter's services are recorded except by the Revd Thomas Leigh in his bank book, where the entries read:

Humphrey Repton's design for a bath house in the garden at Adlestrop

April	1799	Pd to H. Repton	£100
Nov	1800	Mr Repton	£ 60 19*s*. 0*d*.
	1801	Subscribed to Mr Repton's book	£ 2 3*s*. 0*d*.
	1808	Mr Repton £10 His book	£ 5 5*s*. 0*d*.
	1809	Mr Repton	£ 10

The last two entries may have been in respect of plans for the grounds of Adlestrop Rectory which the Revd Thomas improved, and may explain Jane Austen's knowledge of Repton's work and fees, since she and her mother (the Revd Thomas's cousin) stayed at Adlestrop while the grounds were being altered.

Affection for his family and home, the pride he took in his estate and the pleasure he derived from his garden, all combined to set a limit to the time a country gentleman was prepared to be away from them, but sometimes there might be reasons for absence beyond his control. William Leigh, when he succeeded his father in 1727, found the estate heavily burdened with debts, largely as a result of Theophilus's generosity to his family and friends. The situation was so serious that William had only two courses of action open to him – to sell some land or to economize drastically. Rather than reduce his son's inheritance he chose the second alternative, arranged to let the house at Adlestrop and went abroad with his wife and children, leaving an agent to handle the estate in his absence. The latter's success in this, together with the family's frugality while living in Holland, recouped their fortunes sufficiently for them to return to Adlestrop in 1732 and resume the life they had enjoyed before. William Leigh's earlier trip abroad in the company of Lord Cornbury had enabled him to make many friends, and their hospitality undoubtedly eased the lot of the family during their enforced exile. It was at this time that William Leigh's help was conscripted by Lord Blandford (grandson of the Duchess of Marlborough) who was wooing Maria de Jongh, a burgher's daughter, in defiance of his parents' wishes. He used to include notes (very badly written and expressed) in his letters to Leigh with a request that they should be handed on to the lady. After the marriage in 1729 Leigh and his uncle, the Duke of Chandos, offered to act as mediators between Blandford and his father to smooth the way for the return of the couple to England.

Another reluctant exile, later in the century, was George Whitmore, who for reasons of both health and economy left Lower Slaughter with his wife and daughter in 1782 to stay at St Omer in France. They were still there when the Revolution broke out in 1789, but continued to feel safe until England's declaration of war on France in May 1793 made them enemy aliens in the eyes of the French. Immediately they were plunged into a nightmare which lasted for seventeen months and led to George Whitmore's death. Lulled into a false sense of security by an official decree that 'all strangers resident in France were under the protection of the Law', they lingered until the Channel ports were closed and postal services with England cut off, when it was too late to make a move. Almost immediately St Omer was occupied by French troops, the English residents put under house arrest and their papers seized. Then, on the grounds that a plot to destroy the town had been discovered with evidence of English implication in it, the men were taken away from their families and imprisoned separately from the women and children, who were also forced to leave their homes. They were not allowed to retrieve any of their possessions and, but for the loyalty and generosity of French servants, would have been completely destitute. Moreover, as well as being terrorized by their captors, they were aware that only the latter stood between them and the mobs which, as the Reign of Terror spread across France, went about seeking victims to send to the guillotine. As the war progressed and an English army drew near to St Omer, the prisoners were moved and forced to trek to Arras and then to Amiens, still short of money and clothes and constantly harassed by their captors. George Whitmore's health grew steadily worse and Mrs Whitmore was torn between anxiety for him and for their daughter Mary, who was only fifteen and very frightened. Not until November 1794 were the prisoners allowed to return to St Omer, by which time George Whitmore had died and been buried in an unmarked grave for fear of its being violated. It was another four months before Mrs Whitmore and the other English exiles were able to get back to England. Among the Whitmore papers is a diary of their sufferings kept by Mrs Whitmore, also a number of facts that she jotted down about the family – whether as a proof of identity because all their papers had been taken, or for Mary's information, in the event of anything happening to both her parents, one cannot tell. There are also some engraved visiting cards bearing the names of titled French people, presumably friends who visited the family at St Omer in the days of peace. It would be interesting to know whether these survived the Terror or not.[15]

The circumstances of George Whitmore's death and burial were not what he or his family would have anticipated or wanted, since the gentry regarded the manner of their leaving this world with as much seriousness as their life in it. The terms of a will, arrangements for the funeral, the design of a tomb or memorial were all matters that preferably they aimed to settle well beforehand. The making of a will was necessarily a solemn undertaking since the handing on of the estate intact and in good heart was a responsibility that a landowner had in mind throughout his life. Where there was a direct heir the task was simple and straightforward, unless for some reason the father had taken against the son and chosen another relative to succeed him. Lack of an heir might mean property being left to a daughter or some other connection, and the family name threatened with extinction unless it was laid down that the inheritor must take on the name with the property. The descendants of Thomas Master who married heiress Elizabeth Chester inherited both the estates and bore the name Chester-Master. Michael Hicks after his marriage to Henrietta Beach attached his wife's name as well as her lands to his own and became Michael Hicks-Beach. John Ackerley added Chamberlayne to his name on succeeding to the estates of that family: and John Mitford became John Freeman Mitford when he took over Batsford from his uncle Thomas Freeman.

The commitments of marriage settlements had to be honoured and often a man felt responsible as well for other members of his family, like unmarried sisters, so that a will might not just involve the payment of legacies but also burden the estate for some years to come with regular charges on its revenue. Unmarried daughters also had to be catered for, both before and after marriage, the choice of a suitable partner sometimes determining whether the payment of an allowance should be continued or not. William Selwyn ordered:

> If any of my said daughters shall bestow herself in marriage contrary to the liking and consent of their mother and without her advice therein and approbation thereof, then my will is that such daughter of mine so carelessly casting away herself in marriage shall lose and forfeit her portion of all my said estate . . . and what should have been the portion of such an undutiful daughter shall become the proper estate of such other of my daughters that shall behave themselves. . . .

As has been said before, it was the habit of the landed gentry to make charitable bequests to churches, schools, almshouses, colleges – and to remember faithful servants and the local poor. Cassandra, daughter of William Leigh, returned to Adlestrop to live after being left a widow and, as well as making general bequests to the poor there and in a number of neighbouring villages, was clearly aware of particular individual needs when she drew up her will:

> To John Newman the Clerk £1 1*s*. To John's son who is blind £1 1*s*. To the widow Newman, his mother, for shoes, shift and a blanket £1 1*s*. To Mary his idiot sister £1 1*s*.

Usually detailed instructions were left as to the time and place of burial with an emphasis being laid on privacy and economy, though most of the gentry were prepared to pay the necessary fine in order to be buried in something better than the statutory woollen shift:

> Samuel Cooke, Rector of Cottesford in the county and diocese of Oxford saith that the body of Cassandra Turner . . . was buried in crepe and sarcenet contrary to the Act of Parliament made for burying in woollen only.[16]

Top: The memorial to William Guise (d.1716) in Elmore Church. Below: Great Barrington Church. Memorials to members of the Bray and Talbot families who in turn owned the manor there

Only the very rich and eminent were buried with public pomp and ceremony, but there were rigid conventions as to mourning that had to be observed and that overrode any personal opinion or feeling. (The very poor sometimes requested and were supplied with mourning in preference to more obviously useful attire.) However, it did rest with the family to decide what other signs of respect should mark the death of a relative. Earlier in the chapter we noted the concern of Sir John Dutton to have the bodies of his young wife and child brought from London to Sherborne for burial in the family vault. The funeral of William Guise in 1716 took place at Elmore Church, with the minister and clerk in attendance, and a bellman to ring the Great Bell and the crypt bell. Coachmen and servants were supplied with black hatbands, members of the family with mourning rings; escutcheons and a hatchment were painted and a brass plate for the coffin engraved. Wine was provided for those who came to the funeral. In due course a stone costing £4 was placed over the tomb. This was a gilded tablet, carved with heraldic devices, made and signed by John Ricketts of Gloucester, a well-known local sculptor. Elmore, like many parish churches, served also as a chapel and a burial place for the local family the Guises, as did Adlestrop for the Leighs, Blockley for the Rushouts, Great Barrington for the Brays and Talbots, and Sherborne for the Duttons. Although burials might be conducted modestly, the memorials erected afterwards were usually designed to afford fitting regard for the dead. At Great Barrington, for example, there are two striking monuments in marble: one of the Bray children (1720) – lifelike effigies being conducted to heaven by winged angels, the work of Christopher Cass, a master mason of the Royal Ordnance who worked for many prominent people; the other to Countess Talbot (1787), a more restrained piece of work by Joseph Nollekens, an eminent sculptor much favoured in fashionable circles at the time. Sapperton has a suitably magnificent memorial to Sir Robert Atkyns (1711), the earliest historian of the county. This was the work of Edward Stanton, a sculptor attached to Westminster Abbey, who portrayed Atkyns reclining, book in hand, and sheltered by a highly ornate canopy. The Rushout monuments at Blockley were the work of John Moore, who received commissions from a number of well-known people in London and the West Country, and of John Rysbrack, acknowledged as the leading sculptor of the mid-eighteenth century. Rysbrack was also responsible for the statue of Sir John Dutton in Sherborne Church, which contains the work of other eminent sculptors: Richard Westmacott, who specialised in chimney-pieces adorned with life-size figures and inset panels designed by him for Wedgwood, made the more than life-size angel holding a medallion with the likenesses of James Lennox Dutton and his wife in relief; and John Bacon, another employee of Wedgwood, who carried out commissions for the royal family and for Warren Hastings at Daylesford. Family memorials, in the same way as portraits, make it clear that the Gloucestershire gentry were knowledgeable about the leading craftsmen of their time, could afford to employ them and were recognized as worth-while patrons by men used to working for leading social figures.

For the average gentleman it was enough – in challenging and often precarious times – if he could hand on his estate intact, make adequate provision for his family and die solvent. Many however were able to take pride in having improved the condition of their lands and the lot of their tenants, raised the family standard of living and left the local church, school and charities better off. A few during the eighteenth century could also boast of having achieved social honours and a higher status which, though these

Memorial to Sir John Dutton in Sherborne Church. His two marriages brought considerable riches to the Dutton estate

involved considerably greater expenditure on keeping up appearances and dispensing hospitality and largesse, seemed well worth while. The Yorkes of Hardwicke rose rapidly to an earldom and clearly gained satisfaction from the high offices that accompanied their improved status. To Allen Bathurst, the barony granted in 1712 made little difference since his staunch Toryism kept him out of public life and office for the next thirty years – though during that time he encouraged his two sons into politics. The earldom, bestowed in 1772 and handed on to his heir in 1775, helped the latter into important government appointments as Lord Chancellor and Lord President of the Council, and *his* son the third earl into equally prominent positions in the next century. John Howe became Baron Chedworth without this making much difference to his role in county affairs, as was the case with Mathew Ducie Moreton's title of Lord Ducie. John Freeman Mitford of Batsford, 'the best equity lawyer in the profession,' was knighted in 1793 in recognition of his services as Assize Judge and Solicitor-General; his subsequent appointments as Attorney-General and Lord Chancellor of Ireland led to his being made first Baron Redesdale in 1802. Though a genial host and welcome guest when he was in Gloucestershire, his legal interests and political commitments kept him away from the county much of the time, so his ennoblement did not appreciably alter the pattern of his life. James Dutton, raised to the peerage as the first Lord Sherborne in 1784, lost no time in having his crest engraved on family silver and painted on the panels of his coach, and, evidently anticipating an increased amount of paperwork, ordered from a London stationer:

A thousand of printed visiting cards	10*s*. 6 *d*.
A quarter of a hundred pens	1*s*. 1 *d*.
A stick of Sealing Wax	1*s*. 1 *d*.
Half an ounce of wafers	3 *d*.
A pint of Ink	8 *d*.
Four ink Bottles	1*s*. 1 *d*.
Silver sand for writing paper	2*s*.
2 sheets of blotting Paper	1 *d*.
Some tape to tie the bills together	2½*d*.
2 quires of mourning writing paper	2*s*.
2 Sticks of black Sealing Wax	1*s*.

Thereafter, whether at home or away, the Duttons lived in considerable style – travelling in several coaches accompanied by a number of servants, expecting the best of meals and service *en route* or wherever they stayed, and dispensing even more lavish hospitality to their friends than heretofore. Lord Sherborne, because of shared interests in horses, dogs and racing, was already on familiar terms with the aristocratic Beauforts and Berkeleys, but though he took evident pride in his new status, he remained on an easy and friendly footing with gentry, neighbours and acquaintances, and continued to play an active and useful part in county affairs. Gloucestershire society never had been overawed by aristocratic influence and, though not disrespectful towards its titled members, tended to judge and value them by their character and behaviour rather than their social standing.

The gates to Elmore Court showing the Guise crest

Interlude

Political Background to the Nineteenth Century

The Revolutionary and Napoleonic wars which dominated British politics until 1815, while proving successful against invasion and subjection by the French, had disastrous effects on finance, the economic state of the country and social conditions. Problems arising out of poverty and unemployment, and bad living and working conditions, already serious issues in the late eighteenth century, remained in abeyance until hostilities ended, but they then came to a head with increased ferocity, aggravated by the demobilisation of troops, the difficulty of switching from war- to peace-time production on the land and in the factories, and an acute shortage of money. Throughout the century, from 1815 onwards, successive governments and well-meaning reformers outside parliament had perforce to face difficulties unprecedented in their proportions and address themselves to finding solutions. The old differences and rivalries between Whigs and Tories continued to determine the fortunes of those connected with the central government and the progress of reform, for, while increasing numbers in both parties acknowledged the need for social and economic measures that would benefit those unable to help themselves, they disagreed as to how and at what rate these should be introduced. However, the steady growth in population, the superseding of agriculture by industry as the country's chief source of employment and revenue, and the downward spread of education, political awareness and power to the middle classes, would in themselves have forced changes in the way the country's affairs were managed, regardless of the willingness or unwillingness of political parties to go along with them.

At the same time, the structure and principles of society were also changing. The landowning classes, having dominated the national scene for so long, while still retaining their property and wealth, were gradually outnumbered and outstripped in respect of means by successful businessmen; the political power they had once wielded was whittled away by successive Parliamentary Reform Acts, as was their administrative role by other reforms which transferred the business of local government from amateur volunteers to professional bureaucrats. In small agricultural communities it had been possible for a communal conscience to operate, everyone recognizing the need to subscribe to the rules and to accept some responsibility for the public good – even the lord of the manor might be cited for anti-social behaviour, such as turning his sheep on to the stubble before the appointed day. In large industrial communities, however, it would have been impossible for society to work along these lines, for here among many and diverse interests, the profit motive prevailed and it was a case of every man for himself.

And by comparison with earlier centuries, everything now was larger in scale. The towns of the sixteenth and seventeenth century were mere villages when set against the urban sprawls that grew up in the Midlands and the North during the nineteenth century. The landless poor and unemployed, still maintained by parish authorities and resources until the mid-eighteenth century, were now to be found throughout the country in their thousands and called for all the resources of the state to deal with them. A large part of the population no longer had links with agriculture, was no longer self-sufficient, and depended to a great extent on overseas trade for the raw materials of their work and to satisfy many of their domestic needs. Problems too assumed the same scale as needs, whether they were connected with taxation, water supplies or the maintenance of law and order; nor could any be regarded as purely local, since all communities now, for administrative purposes, had become integral parts of the network imposed by the central government. Improved communications, especially the establishment of the railways, had the effect of minimising the significance of provincial boundaries and differences, making people less parochial in their outlook and their communities more open to outside influences. Nor was it possible for provincial communities to cut themselves off from and remain oblivious to national crises. Outbreaks of cholera, the food shortages of the early 1840s, the repercussions of revolutions abroad, or wars, now assumed proportions that called for nationwide remedies.

In such circumstances a comfortable county-based gentry class was likely to become something of an anachronism. The monarchy, once a source of favours and inspiration of loyalty and service, had lost much prestige during the years of George III's mental decline and, though George IV as a king tried to create for himself a more favourable image than he had done as Prince Regent, neither he nor his brother William IV were popular. Their niece Victoria made a dignified and serious-minded sovereign who commanded respect among her subjects, but she never became a powerful figure in politics. As parliament became more democratic, the administration more bureaucratic, and as positions in the army, navy and civil service opened to competition and promotion by merit, the capacity of the sovereign to advance the fortunes of place-seekers was curtailed and the attraction of the royal court as a place where favours might be bestowed grew less. The gentry were thus thrown back to an increased extent on their own efforts to maintain their position. That many were able to do so, in a society that could no longer identify with the standards and values that had characterized their class in the past, was a measure of the strength of their hold over the situation, and their continuing ability to discern and exploit favourable factors in contemporary events, and to retain the liking and respect of the local community that had always been the natural setting for their achievements.

CHAPTER THIRTEEN

POWER AND PRIVILEGE IN DECLINE

As the nineteenth century advanced, political and economic circumstances began to change at a rate hitherto unknown. Whereas in the past any new situation would have taken a considerable time to develop and become established, and even longer for public awareness of it to spread, now more channels of communication, quicker means of travel and transport, and thus the gradual foreshortening of distance between the capital and the provinces, all ensured a greater uniformity in ideas and attitudes than there had been before. Differences in class, family means and interests continued to exist, but in times of a mass increase in population, mass production of consumer goods, mass employment and mass recreation, individuality tended to count for less; personal enterprise such as might have been recognized and acclaimed in the sixteenth or eighteenth century was now less likely to achieve success unless backed by money and influence. On the whole, for several centuries, circumstances had favoured the outstanding traits of the gentry's character, just as the overwhelming importance of land had ensured their power and influence; now their personal inclinations and resources were not enough in themselves to enable them to prevail. Of course, legends of rags to riches were still being created and families rose socially in the course of a couple of generations. However, with less land changing hands, it was difficult and costly to acquire an estate and, even if landowning status was achieved, opportunities for public service were not as numerous as they had been, so at every turn the scope of the gentry as a class was being reduced. In some parts of the country, the rearguard action of the aristocracy to retain their power and prestige was a further curb to ambitious gentry, but in Gloucestershire the old aristocratic families of Beaufort and Berkeley, while influential, had never been stiflingly powerful; newly ennobled ones such as Dutton, Ducie and Freeman were too close to their gentry past and commitments to be antagonistic.

Although, thanks to favourable economic circumstances, some families in Gloucestershire were moving upwards and acquiring wealth and importance, not all aspired to or achieved gentry status. To become a member of parliament or a justice of the peace, it was still necessary to own land worth £100 a year, but this qualification had to be complemented by adequate means and leisure to carry out the duties of office as well as acceptance into county society: this last was not a foregone conclusion even if other

Sezincote: its Mogul architecture fits surprisingly well into the Cotswold landscape. Inset: Sir Charles Cockerell whose new house at Sezincote inspired the Prince Regent's Pavilion at Brighton

requirements had been met. The advent and acceptance of some of the clothiers into county affairs in the eighteenth century had widened the ranks of the gentry, as had the rise of families connected with the law, banking and medicine; but by the time they assumed the habits and cultivated the interests of estate owners, members of these families had distanced themselves somewhat from the original sources of their wealth though they might still be benefiting from them. Those who had made money through colonial ventures or overseas trading found it easier to be accepted than brewers, mine owners or tradesmen who, though they might try to forget their backgrounds themselves, found it difficult to persuade others to do likewise. Among the newcomers who moved into Gloucestershire during the early part of the nineteenth century, acquired estates and became accepted socially, were Sir Charles Cockerell, who had made a fortune in the East India Company and settled at Sezincote; the Ducarels of Newland, whose wealth had also been derived from that company; Charles Hanbury of Toddington, whose family owned the Pontypool Ironworks and who married a Tracy, adding that name to his own; and the glove-making family Dent, who acquired the long neglected castle and grounds at Sudeley and proceeded to make them habitable again.

Elsewhere, while new families were taking their place in the county, some older families through shortage of money, ill fortune or simply lack of a male heir were being brought to the point of extinction and might only be saved by propitious marriages, or the transference of estates to a daughter or a distant relative equal to the situation, able to keep the lands together and make them pay. In 1778, Sir James Musgrave had inherited Barnsley Park from Cassandra, last of the Perrots, and then when the Musgraves were without a male heir in the 1830s, Caroline Musgrave married Wenman Wykeham of Thame and their descendants the Wykeham Musgraves became owners of Barnsley Park. Benjamin, last of the Hyett family of Painswick, lacking an heir, left his fortune and estate to Frances Adams, his wife's cousin, whose son then took and handed on the name Hyett to his successors. The Tracy estate at Stanway had perforce passed to a daughter, Viscountess Hereford, in 1767 and then to her sister Lady Elcho in 1817; her son, Francis Charteris, in due course, became heir to the estate.

For those who were landowners, either by inheritance or acquisition, the sound management of their estates was just as important as it had been to their predecessors, but made more complicated by market competition and the intervention of political factors and controls. No longer could the owner of an estate monopolize a local market in order to sell his own products, or even count on being able to dispose of them elsewhere. Nor could he continue to exploit his land according to the same pattern year after year. Even the rotation of crops, the combination of arable with pastoral farming, more efficient methods and transport – innovations that had ensured success in the previous century – were an insufficient hedge against the urgent need for cheap food among the growing mass of non-agricultural workers, the fluctuating demand for secondary products from industry, the increasingly competitive output of farmers in Europe and the Americas, and parliamentary measures affecting trade and taxation. To a greater degree than ever before, an estate had to be run as a business, with economic considerations superseding traditional usages, family loyalties and even human sympathies. Those who had additional sources of income, whether from commercial and industrial undertakings or profitable investments, undoubtedly had an advantage because these could tide them over periods of falling prices and unstable market conditions. On the whole, it was the older established families who still gave their lands primary attention and regarded their investments as no more than a necessary adjunct; all the same, it should be noted that whereas during the eighteenth century they put their money into trading companies, banks, government securities, and tentatively into canal companies and town properties, they were now much more likely to go into new ventures like railways, shipping companies and large-scale urban development.

One family always deeply concerned with and dependent on its estates was the Leigh family. When the younger branch that had been based at Stoneleigh died out in the early nineteenth century, descendants of the older branch who had made their home at Adlestrop since the sixteenth century inherited the Warwickshire lands and began to divide their time between the hubs of the two estates. On the whole they preferred Adlestrop where they had a wide circle of friends, but they realized the advantages of giving personal attention to estate business and of enjoying the amenities of both places, which, for instance, included two different hunting grounds. In their absence, overall responsibility for supervision was in the hands of stewards who, though left with some initiative, were nevertheless expected to carry our implicitly whatever orders they were given. The need for vigilance became clear before the Adlestrop Leighs took up their inheritance, when the report came from the steward at Stoneleigh:

> I believe it will be best to discharge most of the servants at the Great House for they all seem to be dissatisfied and to have expected to live in idleness the rest of their lives. There is a poor deaf housemaid. I fear a little disordered. She says Mrs Leigh promised she should not go to service again but should have a maid to wait on her. Some others are almost as unreasonable.[1]

From Adlestrop detailed accounts were sent to Stoneleigh of the sale of produce and livestock at nearby markets and fairs; of any failure on the part of tenants to fulfil their obligations; of repairs that might be needed or had been done. Although families in the Stow area usually found extra work to supplement their regular wages, in times of shortages and high prices they might find it hard to manage and the Leighs were always ready to ensure that any of their tenants were protected from need. In 1839, when there was a food shortage in Stow and bread cost 10*d.* a loaf (the average wage of a labourer was 9*s.* a week) Lord Leigh bought bread at this price and sold to the poor at 6*d.* a loaf. He also arranged to make allotments available to his cottage tenants. His agent further reported:

> I have made a particular enquiry amongst the large families as to which would be most desirable to them – coals or bread. They one and all replied 'Coals will be better for us than bread; as we have plenty of potatoes, we can manage for food.' I have also had conversations with some of the most deserving and from whom I find that linen and clothing for their children seem to be the leading articles of their wants.

These needs were forthwith supplied by a Stow draper at Leigh's expense. A few years later the situation had improved:

> All piece work has undergone an advance in price amongst the agricultural labourers. The best men are now at 10*s.* a week and one happy thing is that there are no men out of employ. The women and their largest children are bountifully supplied with silk from Blockley. On the whole we are not so badly off.

Although some landowners viewed the coming of the railways with suspicion and even dislike, others realised that they were in a strong position to benefit from them. The Leighs made considerable profits from sales of land and compensation money on both the Stoneleigh and Adlestrop estates, they had shares in at least six railway companies, and gained an unexpected bonus, as reported by their Adlestrop agent:

> I have just received from the auctioneer the enclosed detailed account of the timber sale which went off wonderfully well, making several hundreds more than we expected. I believe we had a great advantage in having a considerable quantity to offer making it worth while for strangers to travel a long distance to buy; there were several such present. Another advantage was that the railway from Banbury to Cheltenham is just beginning to be made, for which a good deal of the larch was bought.

Another family largely dependent on the returns from their estates were the Estcourts. When innovations and improvements were being made towards the end of the eighteenth century, Thomas Estcourt was an enthusiastic advocate of new techniques in cultivation and animal breeding, and until he died in 1818 continued to take an interest in and to promote new developments. He was much concerned for those who worked on the land, but mistrusted indiscriminate benevolence, and with neighbouring landowners and farmers worked out a scheme whereby the needy would be helped, with subsidized rents, the loan of tools and carts, fuel supplies etc., to make themselves independent of relief from the Poor Rate. For his own tenants he built cottages, provided allotments and introduced a system of rewards for those who worked hard for him and tended their own plots satisfactorily. Careful guidelines were laid down for his steward to follow in managing the estate, farm, pleasure ground and plantations, and in directing the workers under him. Estcourt was prepared to pay good wages, but insisted on work being done to his satisfaction; to ensure this, he ordered the steward 'to attend in my room every Monday morning at 10 o'clock, produce his accounts for the preceding week with receipts and disbursements; produce a list of all the workmen employed, and settle with me what they are to do for that week that I may know where to find them in my rides or walks.'[2]

The Curtis Haywards too, having amassed property in the Quedgeley and Tewkesbury areas, in Worcestershire around Pershore, in Bristol and overseas, were determined to keep their estates intact and to profit by them, and so were markedly careful in their administration of them. Their estate books are models of clarity and precision in the way they lay out details of work done, repairs effected, produce and cattle sold, improvements made, the value of hay, seeds, etc., in store, and of sheep, pigs, cows and horses (the last two listed by name). Every effort was made to ensure that, as far as possible, the estates were self-supporting and expenditure kept to a minimum. At Quedgeley annual unavoidable expenses were estimated at £1,690, with more than two-thirds of this going on taxes, rates, tithes, annuities, charities and interest; compared with which the £600 for housekeeping and £30 for doctor and medicine were quite modest outlays. Thrift seems to have been the keynote at Quedgeley: on the farm and in the stables nothing was thrown away that might be useful elsewhere or at another time; when Quedgeley House was being rebuilt at a cost of £5,376, chimney-pieces, hearthstones and floor timbers were saved from the old building to be incorporated into less prominent and less important quarters of the new one. The architect was also obliged to use Lombardy poplar and Scotch fir trees cut down at Quedgeley for scaffolding, and to save the timber afterwards for future use.[3]

However, as the century progressed, even the most careful management of estates and husbanding of resources could not ensure continuing prosperity for landowners. Imports of wheat (especially after the repeal of the Corn Laws in 1846) and of fodder crops, at prices much below home production costs, and a greater demand in the domestic market for meat and dairy produce, meant that the profits from arable farming were steadily decreasing. The need to improve the pitifully low rate of some labourers' wages, highlighted by riots and threats to farms and private property in times of distress, though acknowledged by decent employers, was disconcerting when future prospects were considered. Tenants and those farming on a small scale, insufficiently cushioned against variable returns, quickly found themselves in difficulty in bad years, and even when landowners were willing to abate rents rather than lose good tenants, this could not always save the estate. Although agriculture continued to employ a large proportion of the population at least until the middle of the century, as a money-making

Thomas G.B. Estcourt, MP for Devizes

Sir Berkeley William Guise, MP for Gloucestershire

proposition it was gradually being superseded by other ways of exploiting the land as well as by industry, so that the demand for farm land and the value of it went down. Even the owners of large estates and the most enlightened agriculturists found themselves increasingly in need of other sources of revenue, and were therefore willing to profit from making concessions to railway and mining companies, or if any of their properties lay near towns, from the sale of land for urban development. Any decline in the importance and profitability of land ownership threatened to erode the basic strength of the gentry class, but here their characteristic realism and opportunism came to the rescue. The tide of change could not be turned back nor even halted, so it was expedient to go along with it, and though some of the land and estates that had to be sold were bought by industrialists and businessmen, this did not mean that the traditional gentry way of life was under threat; the newcomers proceeded to take over or rebuild country houses and lost no time in adopting the way of life that went with them. Anxious to be accepted into county society, they also began to take on the responsibilities that had customarily been the mark of gentry status. Ironically, this was happening when the scope of the gentry for giving public service was being diminished, though in one sphere at least their influence and pre-eminence continued – that is, in providing members of parliament, primarily for the shire and sometimes for the boroughs as well. Probably the most important factor in favour of a prospective candidate was still his willingness and ability to bear the expenses of an election, followed by journeys to and from London and residence there while parliament was in session. Until the passing of the Secret Ballot Act in 1872 it was impossible to cut out the bribery and intimidation that were customarily widespread at election times, though it was hoped that the widening of the franchise by successive Parliamentary Reform Acts would make it increasingly difficult for any one candidate to exercise enough influence over the election to determine its outcome. However, old practices died hard and, once an election was announced, established procedures were put into operation, reliable strings pulled and the expected largesse handed out both before and after voting had taken place. During the 1835 election, Thomas Grimston Estcourt had accounts with a number of local inns to supply beer to potential supporters and his agents distributed hundreds of satin ribbon bows and bought dozens of yards of ribbon for making more favours and 'sewing silk for flags'. A fly was hired to convey voters, hay supplied for the horses, and '14*s*. was given away about the streets at sundry places'. Evidently things got rough at times because special constables were employed, a certain Thomas Webb was compensated with 7*s*. 6*d*. 'towards a coat annihilated in a shindy' and another man was given 2*s*. for a cap. Once the election was won, special dinners, bowls of punch and tobacco were provided for faithful supporters.

By education, inclination and means, members of gentry families were still the most obvious potential candidates and until the 1870s, even after the county had been subdivided (in 1832) and four members instead of two were needed, scarcely any new names appeared among those elected. The pact that had been made between the Berkeleys and the Beauforts during the eighteenth century, to nominate one candidate each, held good until the 1820s but not without some opposition from rising families who, after the turn of the century, grew increasingly impatient of this aristocratic domination – partly for reasons of personal jealousy and partly because they were genuinely interested in and committed to ideas of social and political reform. Even during the 1820s the members – Sir Berkeley William Guise and Lord Robert Somerset – continued to reflect the Berkeley/Beaufort influence and only after the Reform Act of 1832 did the electoral contest begin to turn on the personalities and policies of the candidates rather than the strength of their backers. This development took place at the same time as the conception of the role of members was also changing. Improved communications and the spread of education downwards in society were ensuring that the whole country, regardless of distance from the capital, was better informed than ever before; it was more aware of national issues and of the fact that these might be just as vital to the local community as parochial ones, even if only because social and economic problems were becoming too large and complex for local authorities to solve, and called for remedies on a national scale. Thus perceptive and conscientious members no longer went up to Westminster with class and county interests superseding any other considerations. Although necessarily they promised service to the local community in their hustings speeches, they were just as likely to be elected on the strength of the attitude they took to contemporary issues such as the slave trade, political reform or the Corn Laws, or of their support for leading Whig or Tory politicians with whose views they sympathized. William Bethell Codrington, who sat as a member for Tewkesbury, was exceptional in refusing to bow to his constituents' support for the abolition of the slave trade. The family's long-standing connections with plantations in Antigua and Barbuda drove him to pronounce:

> The opinions I hold have been formed in the midst of those slaves and I will assert that if the inhumanity so profusely heaped on the planter or the supposed horrors of the negroes in the West Indies can ever have existence, then they will be the fruit of the bill in question.

Old family names found among nineteenth-century members of parliament were Guise, Berkeley, Codrington, Hale, Kingscote and Estcourt. Sir Berkeley William Guise was in the Commons from 1811 until his death in 1834. Educated at Eton and Oxford, and with firm roots in the country through being a warden of the Forest of Dean and a lieutenant-colonel in the Gloucestershire militia, Guise was a reformer who, in spite of benefiting from it himself, strongly opposed the aristocratic power over elections in the county. He was described as being 'friendly to moderate and temperate reform of abuses but against the dangerous spirit of innovations' and, while supporting Whig policies in parliament, he dissociated himself from public agitation and violence, seeing danger in the destruction of established practices until better alternatives had been found to replace them. Several members of the Berkeley family sat either for the county or for Gloucester city during the first half of the century: of these, George Fitzhardinge Berkeley was the most colourful personality. Like Guise, he supported the Whig interest in parliament, and like him too was cautious, because of a strongly developed streak of realism. In a letter to a friend on the subject of slavery (to which he was opposed) he wrote:

> I have seen Lord Ducie today and am sorry to find that he will not join us in our proceedings respecting the Colonial Slavery. If we have not a great many respectable names, we shall only be laughed at and do no good. I am still ready to go on with you if you think it desirable but I should like to see the form of the requisition as I well know that this subject is one on which a great deal of cant is made use of.

Trained as a soldier at Sandhurst and holding a commission as lieutenant in the Coldstream Guards, Berkeley cut a figure in the sporting and literary world of his day rather than as a politician. Christopher William Codrington, a son of William Bethell Codrington (quoted above) and one of the beneficiaries of the Codrington estates in the West Indies, was a Tory and no doubt confirmed in his loyalties by marriage into the Somerset family. As a captain of the Gloucestershire Yeomanry and a deputy lord-lieutenant, he was much concerned with the preservation of order in the county; as a justice of the peace with the enforcement of the law. The troubled years of the 1830s and 1840s, when shortages of food, high prices and unemployment led to disturbances in Gloucestershire, meant that men like Codrington were continually walking a tightrope, preferring to uphold the law through the action of the courts while being pressurised by terrified farmers and mill-owners into resorting to force. Codrington's attitude to contemporary problems evidently satisfied his constituents since he managed to keep his seat for East Gloucestershire from 1834 until 1865. Evidence of popular enthusiasm for Codrington was noted by the Revd F. E. Witts when he visited the potteries at Cranham in 1834:

> The master and his men bore striking marks of the practical zeal with which the Blue interest had been supported: black eyes and a broken nose disfigured the potters, master and men.[4]

Although each generation produced lawyers, the Hale family had not provided any members of parliament for a century or more until Robert Blagden Hale was elected in 1837. Educated at Winchester, Oxford and Lincoln's Inn, he then became a justice of the peace and Surveyor of the Highways in Gloucestershire. An enlightened Tory and concerned landowner, he was an active patron of schools and charities in the county and would perhaps have fitted happily into an eighteenth century context. When he retired from parliament in 1857, he continued to take an interest in the affairs of the county but devoted himself more particularly to the 'life of a country gentleman . . . living among his tenantry and enjoying his manorial estates'. Another family, long associated with the county gentry but not with national politics, was that of Kingscote. Firmly established in Gloucestershire since the mid-twelfth century, when marriage into the Berkeley family brought them their estate as a wedding gift, the Kingscotes had given priority to the care of their lands rather than to seeking great wealth and social pre-eminence, and by limiting their ambitions and commitments had kept their fortunes stable even through troubled times. It is interesting therefore to find Nigel Fitzhardinge Kingscote offering himself successfully as a Liberal parliamentary candidate in 1852. A trained soldier, an officer in the Scots Guards and an aide-de-camp to Lord Raglan, his experience so far had been military rather than political, though he must have been acquainted with county affairs through his father, who was a justice of the peace. Having fought creditably throughout the Crimean War, Kingscote thereafter devoted himself to parliamentary duties which he combined with acting as a justice and deputy lord-lieutenant in Gloucestershire, and at Court, as Groom in Waiting to the queen and then equerry to the Prince of Wales. In addition to breaking with family tradition in pursuing a public career, Kingscote also took an interest in industrial developments both in the county and elsewhere, and was a director and shareholder in the Great Western Railway. Other representatives of an old-established family in nineteenth-century parliaments were Thomas Grimston Estcourt and Thomas Sotheron Estcourt, son and grandson respectively of Thomas, who had been one of the pioneers of agricultural progress in the county. Both were Tories and for more than sixty years between them held a borough seat for Devizes. To judge by their correspondence and activities both inside and outside the Commons, they were knowledgeable and very competent men whose services were much in demand. Thomas Grimston seems to have been a loyal colleague of Sir Robert Peel and, as chairman of several committees concerned, to have done much to promote the latter's Metropolitan Police Force. In due course he also supported the Tory leader over the repeal of the Corn Laws. An assiduous committee man, he chaired enquiries into such varied matters as the state of prisons, the management of the British Museum, and the regulation of assize circuits. The presence in parliament and political support of Thomas Sotheron Estcourt were also greatly valued and reflected in his appointment as a privy councillor, and for a short while as Home Secretary. He served on committees of enquiry into the working of the Poor Law and of the savings banks, and was responsible for introducing a bill relating to the security and management of the latter. To a greater extent perhaps than his father, he concerned himself with the problems of agriculture and agricultural workers locally, and was interested in the promotion of the Wiltshire and Gloucestershire, and Great Western railways, the economic and social significance of which he considered more important than their potential for profits on investments.

Some of the new names that appeared in national politics during the nineteenth century were Pitt, Cripps, Price and Rolt. These four are interesting in that, though the families acquired property in order to qualify for public office and establish their influence locally, they continued to be directly dependent on business interests to finance their life-style and activities. Joseph Pitt, whom we have already noticed in connection with his legal and banking ventures in Gloucestershire and London, and the development of Cheltenham, drew money from these and from his investments in colonial enterprises. As member of parliament for Cricklade, Wiltshire, his political commitments lay outside the county, but he was thrown into the company of Gloucestershire representatives in the Commons and with members of the county community who flocked to social events in Cheltenham during the first decades of the century. One of these, the Revd F. E. Witts, described him as a man 'elevated from a very humble to a very prosperous situation in life. His enterprises as attorney, banker, speculator in land and many other ways of gaining or losing fortunes, have been eminently successful.' Joseph Cripps had deeper roots in the county than Pitt; he came of a clothier family settled in the Dursley area for several generations, and he himself owned an estate near Cirencester where he practised improved and experimental farming methods. His business interests were varied – banking, brewing and carpet-making – and marriage to the heiress of an East India Company proprietor added to his already considerable fortune. In due course his heirs were to establish themselves at Ampney Crucis on the estate formerly owned by the Dawnays and to assume prominence in local affairs. William Philip Price who had an estate at nearby Tibberton was a member for Gloucester city (1852–68) and first and last a businessman. The son of a timber merchant, who had risen high in civic affairs, Price worked in the timber trade himself, was chairman of the Gloucester Banking Company, of two railway companies – the Midland and the Gloucester and Dean Forest – and of the Gloucester and Berkeley Canal

Company. In an earlier age, his overt attention to and interest in business would have excluded him from county society, but his standing in Gloucester and his political activities led to his nomination as a justice of the peace and deputy lord-lieutenant, and inevitably to his sharing, in some degree at any rate, the social life of those whom he met on the bench and at the assizes. John Rolt, member for West Gloucestershire (1857–67), was another self-made man. Born into a merchant's family in Calcutta, he was left an orphan, sent home to England and apprenticed to a woollen draper. Educated by his own efforts, he was promoted to clerical work and finally gained admission to the Middle Temple where he qualified as a barrister and Queen's Counsel. Having acquired an estate at Ozleworth, he became a justice of the peace and deputy lord-lieutenant. His legal knowledge and ability were recognized by his appointment as Attorney-General and Lord Justice of Appeal, and crowned by a knighthood and being made a Privy Councillor.

Other new names, for example Hanbury-Tracy, Holford, Hicks-Beach and Cockerell, belonged to families that, although comparative newcomers to the county, had established themselves as landowners there and, while continuing to draw revenue from business sources and investments, intended to lead a country-house life based on their estates. Charles Hanbury-Tracy, whose marriage into the Tracy family and acquisition of the manor of Toddington gave him the entrée to society, gained additional status from the impact of his building projects at Toddington, carried out to his own architectural designs at a cost of more than £150,000, and of his appointment as chairman of the commission that decided on the plan for the building of the Houses of Parliament in 1835. He sat in the Commons as a member for Tewkesbury, a borough that continued to favour country gentlemen as representatives well into the century. The Holford family had acquired the Westonbirt estate late in the seventeenth century, but continued to be more concerned with the sources of their wealth – legal work in Chancery and the New River Company – during the following century. When Robert Stayner Holford succeeded early in the nineteenth century a start had already been made on transforming the house and grounds. This was a project that was to absorb much of his time and attention, but not to the exclusion of his commitments to the county as justice of the peace, captain in the Yeomanry and deputy lord-lieutenant, and as a Tory member for East Gloucestershire from 1857–72. Michael Hicks senior, who attached Beach to his name after his marriage to Henrietta Beach, bought Williamstrip in 1785 and made it his chief residence. This fact, and his service as sheriff and captain in the Militia, recommended him as a prospective member for Cirencester in 1794 at a time when no Bathurst was eligible. His son, Michael Hicks-Beach, succeeded to the estate and his father's standing in county affairs. Educated at Eton and Oxford, he was quickly drawn into county affairs as a justice of the peace and deputy lord-lieutenant, and subsequently elected as a Tory member for East Gloucestershire in 1865. He quickly made his mark in parliament and in due course was appointed to responsible posts in connection with the Poor Law, Ireland and the Colonies, ultimately becoming Chancellor of the Exchequer and President of the Board of Trade. Sir Charles Cockerell, member for Evesham from 1819 to 1837, was another newcomer to the county who owed some of his fame to his building achievements at Sezincote. Befriended by Warren Hastings, he had had a successful career in the East India Company working his way up as a factor and merchant until he achieved a place on the Board of Control. On his return to England he took over Sezincote from his brother and married Harriet, daughter of Sir John Rushout of Northwick Park, and through the latter's influence (the Rushouts had sat as members for Evesham for over 70 years) acquired a seat in the Commons.

Thus, established and more recent members of the gentry class were involved in politics at a national level during the nineteenth century and achieved varying degrees of prominence so doing. Although some, like George Fitzhardinge Berkeley, contributed little to parliamentary debate, others were active not only in the Commons and on committees, but also outside the House, campaigning for the causes they supported. Their knowledge of affairs generally, understanding of the state of opinion in their constituencies and capacity for objectiveness, enabled them to assist usefully in whatever matter was under discussion, even though they must have realized that some of the bills they helped to promote and pass would in the long run undermine their own power and status in the county. The Repeal of the Corn Laws for instance, a necessary step to easing the sufferings of the labouring poor, was one that would inevitably affect the profits to be derived from agriculture; measures of parliamentary reform that enfranchised large numbers of people in the towns and countryside created a class of voters, in theory at any rate, outside the landowners' sphere of influence; and moves to bureaucratize various aspects of local administration relieved the gentry of responsibilities that for generations their families had shouldered voluntarily. It was in this last respect, as justices of the peace and lynchpins of local government, that the gentry must have felt their activities and discretionary powers most diminished – not because they were any less well trained or suited to the work than their predecessors, but because the size and intricacy of contemporary problems called for uniform and comprehensive solutions applicable to the whole country. That new machinery and policies designed to deal with the contemporary situation did not seek to destroy the existing structure of local government, but to build and improve on it, was a measure of the efficiency of the justices as well as of the conservatism of public opinion. Any move to substitute national for local control would have been regarded with suspicion and met with opposition because, especially in rural areas, respect for the justices was based on local loyalties rather than fear, a judicial authority largely exercised with sympathetic understanding rather than tyranny. Even during the years 1803–28 when the severity of the Game Laws was heightened so that death or transportation became the usual punishment for poaching and armed resistance to gamekeepers, and when some landowners raged and demanded that the full penalty of the law be visited on anyone who was caught, a great number of justices found ways of avoiding this; they incurred the wrath of their neighbours, but at least they demonstrated their recognition of the desperation of the lawbreakers who, during the postwar period from 1815 onwards, were prepared to risk the gallows rather than let their families starve.

One of the chief responsibilities and concerns of the justices since the sixteenth century had been the relief of the poor and unemployed, and the control of vagrancy; as this problem was magnified during the eighteenth century beyond the capacity of the Elizabethan Poor Law to deal with it, justices throughout the country adopted the system of outdoor relief devised by their colleagues at Speenhamland (Bucks.) in 1794 to subsidise the underpaid workers, this in addition to initiating their own ways of enabling the local poor to remain independent of help from the Poor Rate. It was with the intention of lightening the burden of those who contributed to the Poor Rate and discouraging those who might too easily become dependent on it that the Poor Law Amendment Act of 1834 was passed, removing the administration of relief from the hands of the justices and making it the responsibility of Boards of Guardians who were to set up workhouses as the only source of food and shelter for the needy. However, the immediate effect of the new legislation was to increase hardship, to stiffen the determination of the poor and unemployed to keep out of the workhouse at all costs, and to leave a great number of the gentry – whether in their capacity as justices or as landlords – still subsidizing the needy out of their own pockets. In due course they allowed their names to go forward for election as members of the Boards of Guardians; visited and inspected the workhouses in their neighbourhood; provided medicine and suitable food for the inmates if there was an outbreak of sickness; and always at Christmas time supplemented the spartan workhouse provisions with gifts of seasonal fare and clothes.

Further discretionary powers that the justices had exercised, but which were gradually whittled away from the 1830s onwards, concerned the licensing of alehouses, the inspection of prisons and asylums, the upkeep of highways and local policing. Responsibility for these was now transferred to elected bodies acting under governmental supervision, which left the justices still feeling responsible for local matters but shorn of initiative and official power to intervene; thus when the County Councils Act was passed in 1888 (largely to satisfy the masses enfranchised in 1884 and now anxious to be in complete control of local government) its terms virtually amounted to a recognition of the status quo. Only in the judicial sphere did the justices continue through the middle years of the century with undiminished powers, to hold the petty and quarter sessions and form the grand jury at the assize. During this time the names in the list of Gloucestershire magistrates were not very different from those of a century before, the few new ones being of clothiers and business men who had come to the fore in the late eighteenth and early nineteenth centuries; but because all shared the same educational experience of grammar or public school, university and/or the Inns of Court, the same commitments to the county and comparable life-styles, they formed as in previous centuries a united and socially compatible body. In addition to those already mentioned among the members of parliament, there was the Hon James Henry Dutton, heir to the estates and wealth of Sherborne; Sir James Musgrave, a cousin of and successor to the Perrots of Barnsley Park; Thomas Chester Master, offspring of a marriage between two old county families; and Joseph Chamberlayne of Maugersbury, current representative of a family that had been prominent in local affairs in the Stow area since the sixteenth century.

Among the clothiers who by now had joined the ranks of the county gentry were William Playne and his son William, the former having made a name for himself by his outstanding enterprise in business and unfailing success in handling money, so that for instance in 1825, when the Tetbury Bank was threatened with closure, he could travel to London, borrow gold from the bankers there, bring back enough to satisfy the depositors and stave off collapse. Robert Paul, one of the third generation of his family to profit from their success in the clothing industry, was following in the footsteps of George Onesiphorus Paul, senior and junior, who both socially and politically had made their mark in county society; and Lewis Clutterbuck too, because of his wealth and family's standing, was considered worthy of the magistracy. Some of the new names representing business interests were Sir Thomas Crawley, who had added Boevey to his name on succeeding to his cousin's estate at Flaxley; Philip John Ducarel, descendant of a Protestant refugee family that had settled at Newland and subsequently made money through investment in and service with the East India Company; Henry Norwood Trye, whose father, a very eminent surgeon, had drawn a considerable income from properties in Cheltenham, London and Ireland; and Thomas Lloyd Baker, whose family wealth, gained from investment in and management of land, had enabled him to settle in the county at Uley and then to purchase Hardwicke Court from the Yorkes to make it his family home.

Of the other official responsibilities that had been the perquisite of the gentry in the past, there remained the shrievalty. This had been steadily diminishing in significance since the end of the Middle Ages and, except in relation to the conduct of elections and the assizes, was more an honorary than a power-bestowing appointment. Nevertheless, though acknowledged to be an expensive and even tedious experience, it was a useful step on the political ladder for those seeking advancement. During his year in office, even if there was no election, the sheriff represented the county on ceremonial occasions and thus became a well-known figure in the public eye. Henry Norwood Trye kept a detailed diary of his activities while he held the post (1837–8) and seems to have had little time to spare between his official duties and looking after his estate – 'Cow calved last night. Hardwicke bull. Wrote for plough shares, all ploughs being disabled'; business commitments – 'Railway Board at Cirencester but did not go, being obliged to go to Painswick to receive my interest on Turnpike Bonds £125 12*s*.'; domestic concerns – 'In Cheltenham all afternoon enquiring for a servant'; and social occasions – 'A grand ball at Lord Ellenborough'. His expenses in respect of the assizes amounted to £420 including the employment of all the necessary servitors for twenty days, the hire and keep of horses, and wine for the judges – £21.[5] Maynard Colchester, who was sheriff two years later, seems to have run into much greater expense over clothes. All the javelin men, bailiffs, footmen and coachmen had new hats, gloves and hose. The javelin men had complete sets of new livery too, costing £5 10*s*. each: 'Claret cloth coat edged with yellow. Yellow Waistcoat and Drab Kerseymere Breeches and Garters.' The coachman also was re-outfitted at a cost of £5 7*s*., in 'Claret Cloth Coat lined throughout with yellow Shalloon. Yellow waistcoat and Black Breeches. A pair of Shoes.' The new sheriff either thought the uniforms were looking dingy when he took over, or else he wanted to make a particularly good impression on the judges and the spectators.[6]

The education and training that the gentry had in common fitted them equally well for careers in politics and the law. Some managed to combine the two – Joseph Pitt, John Rolt, Algernon Whitmore and members of the Estcourt and Hale families. Others chose not to go into politics and concentrated on the law alone. As a result of increasing prosperity during the nineteenth century more people acquired property, businesses expanded and became more complicated, thus making more work for the legal profession. County towns, assize towns and spas could always provide work for trained lawyers and even quite small market towns had at least one practising attorney. John Parsons of Kemerton was apprenticed to two solicitors at King's Stanley and, when both died before the five years' term was up, he was able to complete his training under another solicitor in the same place. The gentry appreciated that members of their own class were available to help them professionally in confidential matters like wills,

General Sir George Whitmore of Lower Slaughter. A trained soldier and gifted amateur architect and artist

marriage settlements and leases, and often made contact with their advisers when the assizes were in session or at race meetings and dinner parties. One of John Parsons' clients wrote to him: 'I was in hopes of meeting you at our Shop, the Quarter Sessions, where we had many Gentlemen and spent a very agreable time during my stay there.' Quite a lot of their legal business was therefore dealt with locally, but complicated issues such as disputed entitlement to property, mortgages and investments might be referred to London lawyers, often relatives or acquaintances, who would be assumed to have wider experience. Charles Whitmore and his son Algernon, both Queen's Counsels, acted for their Gloucestershire friends both in the county and in London.

If the law had no attractions for them, young men tended to go into the army or navy, and as in the previous century a family attachment to one or other was often established. Now that the government had assumed responsibility for the defence of a large empire, forces had to be kept overseas and a navy used to transport and supply them as well as to safeguard merchant shipping and English nationals in the Mediterranean, the Baltic and other areas where British trading interests extended. The nineteenth century also saw Britain involved in three major wars – Napoleonic, Crimean and Boer – as well as holding a watching brief over other struggles such as those for Greek and Italian independence which afforded opportunities for fighting to idealistic individuals even if not to a whole army. The Codrington family produced two admirals: Sir Edward, who served throughout the Napoleonic Wars and was Commander-in-Chief in the Mediterranean during the Greek War of Independence; and his son, Sir Henry John, who also fought during the Greek War and later served in the Baltic. In the Chamberlayne family, Charles rose to the rank of admiral and his son John to that of captain, establishing a tradition that was continued in the family until the First World War. In defence of the Empire Henry Berkeley served as a naval captain in East Africa, Gerard Ducarel as an officer in the Indian Army, and General John Estcourt in Canada. A number of Gloucestershire men were involved in the Crimean War – General William Codrington was a Commander-in-Chief, Nigel Fitzhardinge Kingscote, General John Estcourt, and two Whitmores, Francis and Sir Edmund, who were both generals and the first of whom became well known later as the Commandant of Kneller Hall. Their father, Sir George Whitmore, attached to the Royal Engineers, had served throughout the Napoleonic Wars and later in the Mediterranean area until the 1830s. According to his own journals, he was never involved in much fighting, but he undertook responsible work in connection with the defence of Britain during the invasion scare of 1803–1805. He also designed and built barracks and military installations at Gibraltar and on Malta, and later, while serving in an administrative capacity in the Ionian Islands, earned the title of *Colonella della Fabrica* for the impressive public buildings he erected in Corfu and which are still standing today.

The passing of the Poor Law Amendment Act in 1834 did not immediately, nor altogether, solve the problems of poverty and vagrancy, nor did it absolve the gentry from their feeling of responsibility for relieving whatever kind of distress manifested itself in the countryside. Whether as Poor Law Guardians or members of the governing bodies of schools, hospitals, asylums and orphanages, they continued to give their service voluntarily and to regard annual subscriptions to such institutions as unavoidable commitments. As landlords, while fulfilling their responsibilities towards their tenants, they provided the latter with allotments to enable them to grow their own vegetables, and encouraged industriousness by awarding yearly prizes for the best-kept cottages, gardens and plots. At Maugersbury in 1800 Edmund Chamberlayne built the Crescent, a row of four cottages each with one acre of land; in the centre of the block was a large room designed to be used as a Sunday school, and underneath this a public oven, a furnace and a coal store. Chamberlayne hoped that this experiment would be copied elsewhere as a means of enabling poor tenants to be self-sufficient; and although other landowners did not make as much provision as he was prepared to do, they did ensure that the cottages on their estates were kept in decent repair. Half of the village of Sherborne was rebuilt by the Duttons in the early nineteenth century; similarly Great Barrington by the Talbots, and Eastleach by Sir Thomas Bazley who acquired the Hatherop estate in the middle of the century. Indeed, in most estate villages, old cottages were either renovated or else pulled down and replaced with better ones at the expense of the landowner. Always too, whether times were especially hard or not,

Thomas Lloyd Baker whose family bought Hardwicke at the end of the eighteenth century. A popular sportsman and a philanthropist with a keen interest in local affairs

landowners were aware of their tenants' need for fuel. The making of enclosures, while it facilitated more efficient and economical farming, had involved the loss of copses and commons where the poor customarily collected furze and wood; and although all enclosure awards included compensatory arrangements for providing money in lieu of fuel, this did not necessarily prove adequate. The coal clubs started in Adlestrop and Longborough by Chandos Leigh provided one remedy. Those who could afford, paid a subscription of two pence and this then entitled them for a period of fifteen weeks during the winter to buy coal at eight pence instead of fourteen pence a hundredweight, the price difference being paid by Chandos Leigh himself, who also gave five hundredweights each to all people over seventy years old. The Longborough poor were supplied with clothes, sheets and blankets too, costing on average £40 per year. The lists of those receiving help are long and pathetic; 'old, poor'; 'very ill for many months'; 'wife a cripple'; 'blind, unable to work'; 'orphan' are some of the explanations for their needs. An element of censoriousness is offputting: 'bad character: given nothing'; all the same, a 'not good character' was given clothes for her children, and a number of people who did not belong to the village at all, but appeared destitute, were given help.[7] Another form of aid, introduced by the Estcourts and copied by other landowners, was to pay a doctor for attendance on the poor and to meet the expense of any medicines they might need.

It was characteristic of the Victorians to strike moral attitudes and the gentry were no exception. Not only in Longborough, but in other places as well, where lists of the needy poor were drawn up, the latter's worthiness to receive help was decided according to whether they were of good character and regular church-goers – a lingering reminder of the Elizabethan Poor Law which had ruled that allowances to the poor should be handed out after church service on Sundays. Reports of agents to landowners very often contained mention of cases among tenants and villagers meriting special consideration for relief, and few were refused. On occasion, there was much less charity and kindness shown between neighbours than between landowners and dependants on their help. All the same, the bestowers of charity hoped that in due course the recipients might become more self-sufficient; and those who subscribed to orphanages and charity schools did so with the idea of training young people to be capable of leading useful lives later on. It was certainly a widespread belief in the Devil's ability to find work for idle hands that lay behind the strong support given to Sunday schools, and to Thomas Lloyd Baker's Reformatory for Boys, established at Hardwicke, where the inmates were trained in farming skills to fit them for work on the land. But however overt the moral tone, the generosity was there too. Sunday schools were invariably financed by landowners or incumbents of the parish church who might well be members of the same family and, before the introduction of universal state education, local church schools were helped with subscriptions from the local gentry, their wives and families. The Revd Thomas Leigh listed regularly in his annual expenses contributions to the Sunday schools at Broadwell and Longborough, and the day schools at Adlestrop, Longborough and Broadwell; and the subscription list for Stow school was always headed by the names of members of the Chamberlayne family and the current incumbent of the church, and from time to time included other families with local connections, the Whitmores, Hastings and Duttons. In some villages, lending libraries (largely stocked from the Society for the Propagation of Christian Knowledge it is true) and reading rooms were set up and teachers employed to run evening classes. During the 1840s Chandos Leigh paid the Longborough schoolmaster ten shillings a week for taking evening pupils, and enlisted a promising young boy to help him. Such experiments met with a mixed reception and their effects were merely local, so we must concede that they represented genuine good will on the part of those who provided them.

Nevertheless, from the middle of the nineteenth century onwards, although still willing and able to contribute in spheres where formerly they had been autonomous, the gentry were no longer officially the managers of county affairs. The Enclosure Acts of the eighteenth and early nineteenth centuries had enabled a number of tenants to become independent farmers in their own right and more economical and mechanical methods had made many labourers redundant, so on the land there were fewer people directly dependent on and therefore subservient to estate owners. As a result of the extension of political rights and education, the middle and working classes generally became better informed; at the same time they tended to emancipate themselves from any recognition of social superiors and to believe in their entitlement to a wide range of services once given voluntarily by individuals, but now provided under the aegis of the state. Improvements in transport and communications, and especially the growth of a network of local railway lines in the county, made it possible for people even of limited means to get to markets further afield for business purposes, and to a wider range of venues for entertainment – fairs, the assizes and public executions at Gloucester, race meetings, social occasions in Cheltenham. Parish revels centred on the village inn, or the celebratory events of a local family to which people of the neighbourhood were invited, no longer constituted the only sources of pleasure in rural areas. Thus socially, as well as in local politics and economic affairs, the gentry were being eased out of a position where for centuries they had been depended on to take the initiative and assume responsibility.

Combined with the fact that their public service was no longer needed as much as in the past, the gentry landowners were increasingly being forced to look for additional sources of revenue. By the end of the century, although those who still owned them had trimmed down their estates and were running them as economically as possible, members of the gentry were resorting to careers in other spheres or investing in business interests as necessary safeguards. Some of the newcomers to the county, who had come from business backgrounds and retained their links with these, were much better placed than older established landowners to survive the vicissitudes of the times and to have money in hand for meeting the expenses of undertaking official duties and contributing to the social life of the county. Concern with interests outside the county, of whatever kind, meant that many owners were absent from their estates to an unprecedented extent and therefore distanced from the people living on them – a gap that even the most conscientious agent was unable to bridge. So necessarily, the personal commitment that in the past a gentleman had acknowledged towards his home, lands and dependants became tenuous and the occasions for joint family and estate celebrations fewer. When it came to the marking of national events – Queen Victoria's accession and marriage, or military victories – it was still the gentry who organized and subsidized celebratory dinners for adults, parties and sports for the children; and still to a limited extent, people of the neighbourhood were invited to subscribe to an heir's coming of age or his marriage. Funerals too seem to have taken on a more public aspect. Unlike his immediate predecessors who had enjoined the strictest economy, the first Lord

Sherborne was buried in 1814 with considerable pomp and circumstance. There was a funeral procession, consisting of members of the family, close friends and county dignitaries; the church was draped with black hangings and the coffin 'covered with crimson silk velvet, adorned with Glory and Urn, 12 cherubs and 3000 brass nails.' The arrangements for the funeral of Thomas Estcourt in 1818 were also elaborate and comprehensive since, in addition to family and friends, dependants were expected to attend and encouraged to do so by the provision of suitable items of mourning. Among the orders given were:

Silk hatbands and gloves for all who attended
Mr Dixon, Tailor of Tetbury, to make all the clothes and to provide the following – A Great Coat, Drab Cloth, Black Cape and Collar and livery buttons for each of Five Old Labourers, and to procure for each of them a pair of Black Gloves.
The Charity Schools of Newton and Shipton to be provided with the following: To each of the Three Mistresses – Black Mittens, Black Silk Handkerchiefs and Gloves
To each girl Black Bonnet and Tippet
To each Boy – Black Neck Cloth[8]

In sport, staghunting and foxhunting still tended to be exclusive to the gentry because of the expense involved. Those who could afford to keep packs of hounds and maintain deer parks were in a position to control activities since they decided where and when their packs should run, and even moved deer to other districts to oblige friends without quarry of their own. They could also be the reverse of helpful. In 1847, because his favourite candidate was defeated in a by-election, George Fitzhardinge Berkeley refused to allow his deer to be hunted to show his disapproval of the county electorate. The coursing of hares, determined by the whereabouts of a plentiful supply of animals, was a less expensive and therefore less exclusive activity, shared with the gentry by farmers and sometimes town dwellers as well. Racing perhaps more than any other sport was affected by changing circumstances. Until the nineteenth century, small places such as Tetbury or Bibury had been the most popular venues, to which the gentry came on horseback or by coach, from far and near. At Bibury it was reported: 'There was a galaxy of gentlemen riders who alone rode at this Meeting which has never been equalled'. The coming of the railways put an end to this exclusiveness, and in due course enabled Cheltenham to supersede other places in popularity and importance, both as a trading centre and as a racecourse, attracting visitors of all classes not only from the county but from wherever cheap rail tickets were available.

Other occasions that in the past would not have concerned any but the gentry were now being patronized by a wider public. In Bath and Cheltenham during the season there had always been aspirants to gentility sharing the amenities of the spas with those they were trying to emulate, but as the nineteenth century progressed, in Cheltenham at any rate, there was less and less distinction between those who came to benefit from the waters, walk in the gardens and attend the theatre and concerts. Cobbett could not find enough words of opprobrium to describe the place 'to which East India plunderers, West Indian floggers, English tax gorgers, together with gluttons, drunkards and debauchees of all descriptions, female as well as male, resort', but he set out with only condemnation in mind. For the rich and not so rich, free and endless entertainment was afforded by the tree-lined streets, the pleasantly laid-out parks, nursery gardens,

Bibury Races. Nationally famous from the seventeenth to the nineteenth century, they were patronized by royalty (on this occasion by the Prince Regent), as well as by the local gentry who rode their own horses there

attractively dressed shop windows, street musicians, orchestras playing out of doors at the Pump Room and Pittville. Cheltenham had its slums by the mid-nineteenth century, but if the prospect generally had been as unattractive as Cobbett made out, the town could never have achieved its prosperity and a popularity that surpassed that of Bath with the local gentry and with visitors from all over the country. Certainly, for clothes, household goods, books and stationery, many found that they could do as well here as in London. Mr Selden's 'elegant shop in the centre of the High Street' offered 'all the Nick Nackery of Bond Street' and claimed that 'greater civility and more showy display of articles is rarely seen in the first rate repositories of the metropolis'. Gownshops, milliners and drapers according to their advertisements obtained their fashionable wares straight from Paris and London; and the libraries, in addition to books, offered 'French and Irish papers, which together with the London and Provincial are taken in regularly for the use of subscribers', and one also hired out harpsichords, pianofortes and other musical instruments and provided persons to tune them. The theatre, concerts and balls added their quota of entertainment and made a visit to Cheltenham the equivalent of a season in Bath. Small wonder that some of the gentry invested in houses in the fashionable quarters of the town, which they leased or kept for their own use. The Revd F.E. Witts reported in 1839 that the Chamberlaynes were staying in Cheltenham, allegedly to escape from the cold winds in Stow, but really (thought the writer) because 'Mrs Chamberlayne is dreadfully ennuyée with the solitude of the old mansion near Stow . . . and sighs for the society to be enjoyed only in or near a public place.'

As the county town, Gloucester had always been a rendezvous for the gentry at such times as the assizes or a parliamentary election and, since the early eighteenth century, in each third year when the Music Festival (the Three Choirs) was held there. As the chief officials and protagonists, the gentry had taken the lead in all these events, with others merely looking on. But as the nineteenth century progressed, more people were able to get to Gloucester and any interesting happening attracted mass support. At the assizes, for instance, it was reported that 'vehicles of all sorts poured in with the curious on the tiptoe of expectation, and the doors of Shire Hall were besieged by a dense mob, chiefly of well dressed persons, and lawyers' wigs curiously mingled in the throng of white beaver hats and Leghorn bonnets.' At election times, gentlemen's wives and daughters watched processions from windows along the route, while in the street 'all manner of vehicles made up the train, from the gentlemen's private carriage to the hired phaeton or fly'. The Music Festival, as it became better known, also became competitive in that more performers hoped for a platform whence to display their talents and a much larger audience sought admission to the cathedral to hear the music, not at all deterred by having to pay for seats. 'It was a brilliant concert, the rank, beauty of fashion of the ladies, the very elegant dresses, the throngs of gentlemen of considerable station in the county, and the unusual numbers attracted from a distance . . . were very gratifying to the stewards.' Later, at a dance in the tea rooms 'a high born fastidious group' rubbed shoulders with 'a less well bred but equally satisfied Attorney's Clerk pointing a fantastic toe opposite some rosy, good humoured country girl, a belle from Stroud or Tewkesbury to whom the Music of the concert had been something lengthy.' The stewards in charge of the festival, often alarmed by the growing size and enthusiasm of the audience, were nevertheless well pleased at the way in which the profits from entrance fees and collections rose each year for the benefit of the widows and orphans of distressed clergy of Gloucester, Worcester and Hereford dioceses.

Perhaps because so many of their leisure activities and sports were now being shared by people of other classes, the gentry became that much fonder of those that they enjoyed with members of their own circle. Their homes had always been places where the family entertained themselves and each other, and this was still true in the nineteenth century. By this time, most houses had well-stocked libraries and these were augmented by regular library subscriptions to shops in Cheltenham, Bath and London. Music was even more popular than in the past, possibly because it was easier and cheaper for families to obtain instruments. The Leighs, Duttons and Blathwayts were still patronizing London dealers for some purchases. In 1821, Chandos Leigh ordered 'a neat Flute Stop Organ in Mahogany case, gilt front – 1 barrel 10 tunes – £5 5*s*.'; in 1848, Lady Caroline Leigh obtained a 'Boudoir Grand Pianoforte in Rosewood' from Broadwoods for £89 5*s*.; but the shops in Cheltenham would not have been offering to hire out and service musical instruments unless there had been a demand locally for these. The large number of diaries that has come down to us from the nineteenth century indicates that the keeping of journals was a widespread and ingrained habit both when people were at home and on holiday. The Revd F. E. Witts (whose mother was a Tracy) bought the manor of Upper Slaughter in 1852 and, though much of his time was taken up with parochial duties, he was quickly drawn into the social life of the local gentry because of his being a justice of the peace and a member of several commissions and Boards of Guardians. With family, parish and official commitments to be fitted in, his days were fully occupied, yet he found time to keep a very detailed diary of all his activities, together with comments on the people he met and places he saw. Members of the Whitmore family too, both men and women, were assiduous writers and amateur artists as well, making sketches and watercolours of places they visited locally and on holiday. Some of these are especially valuable as they pictured scenes that have now changed beyond recognition. Many other collections of family papers contain records of war experiences, accounts of journeys of exploration overseas, and travel journals. The latter show that, while in England at any rate, some of the Gloucestershire gentry were among the early railway enthusiasts, saving time on their journeys to London and ensuring themselves of greater comfort when they went on holiday.

As well as keeping diaries the Victorians wrote stories and verse and often put these together in the form of a family magazine. They were also much addicted to amateur theatricals, sometimes performed merely for their own benefit, but sometimes put on in a village hall for the benefit of the neighbourhood. To judge by the publicity for these, the plays were usually rather light, and one wonders how entertaining the villagers found them – except as opportunities to see the gentry dressed up and behaving with somewhat less than their usual decorum and responsibility. At home, hospitality was still an essential part of family life. Especially in country areas, dinner parties were a way of keeping in touch with friends, and even in wintry weather people walked or rode quite long distances to keep engagements. Dinner parties meant evenings of talk, listening to music, playing cards or billiards, the consideration of a host's new picture or improvements in the house. Weekend parties or longer visits might be centred on a shoot, a hunt ball or some family celebration, and these would afford opportunities for exploring the neighbourhood, admiring the grounds of the house, meeting old friends and making new acquaintances. Guests of the Bathursts at Lydney were shown the flower garden and shrubbery 'beautifully laid out and rich in fine trees', the groups of deer and fine timber in the park – 'noble chestnuts, oak, stately ash trees, gigantic thorns and yew trees, lime and maple'; they were also invited to inspect the Roman sites excavated by Mr Bathurst's father, and the coins, jewellery, weapons and pottery that had been found in the course of digging. At Hardwicke they admired Thomas Lloyd Baker's new house and the way in which he had disguised its flat surroundings by planting shrubberies and building a greenhouse, an aviary, a flower garden and a rockery. Lord Northwick at Northwick Park showed his picture gallery and art treasures brought back from foreign travels; Sir James Musgrave at Barnsley Park had a wonderful collection of books (once owned by Sir Isaac Newton) housed in a library newly decorated by John Nash, who also built the orangery adjoining the back of the mansion and the octagonal lodge at the rear entrance to the park.

Whatever their circumstances or the trend of the times, maintaining their homes as centres of hospitality was an enduring characteristic of the gentry for they believed that the ownership of a house and estate carried with it an unavoidable obligation to share their good fortune. Of course there was an element of pride and self-congratulation in being able to claim that, as one generation succeeded another, buildings had been enlarged and brought up to date, and grounds laid out according to current fashions, but even more, gentry owners derived satisfaction and pleasure from providing a home for members of their immediate and extended family, and hospitable entertainment for friends and neighbours. When business or pleasure took a family away, they were missed in the locality both personally and as patrons; and whether as a cynosure for sightseers, a source of help for those in need, or a symbol of family achievement, a fitting home has remained until this century all-important to a gentleman's status. By the nineteenth century the old-established families in Gloucestershire were no longer the wealthiest in the county and found themselves obliged to husband rather than expand their resources. Thus they repaired and renovated their houses instead of rebuilding them; added billiard rooms, ball rooms, enlarged libraries and picture galleries, replaced graceful eighteenth century furniture, silk hangings and Chinese wallpaper with heavier Victorian pieces, curtains of velvet and heavy wall coverings. At Dodington, Christopher William Codrington employed James Wyatt to replace the eighteenth century interior, designed by Adam, with Regency-style features, and in particular to redesign the portico, entrance hall and grand staircase to achieve a maximum impact, though even before they reached the house visitors were guaranteed to be impressed by the new lodge gates (also designed by Wyatt) at the two main entrances to the park. At Hardwicke, Thomas Lloyd Baker engaged Sir Robert Smirke to modernise and improve the main part of the house; while at Highnam Lewis Vulliamy was responsible for the additions and alterations. As in the eighteenth century, Gloucestershire gentry knew of and were able to interest the leading architects of the day in giving their houses a new look.

Although there was now an even greater need for skilled gardeners to look after the fashionable conservatories, shrubberies and rockeries being introduced, many owners like those in the eighteenth century took a keen personal interest in their gardens, collecting plants for them while on their travels, devoting exclusive areas to their favourite species and buying plants from specialist nurseries. Evergreens were taking the place of the more delicate flowering shrubs favoured a hundred years earlier, and these were used to create new features in stretches of lawn and overlooking lakes. At Adlestrop, with the exception of some rose trees and some jasmine, almost all the plants introduced were evergreens – spruce, box, holly, rhododendrons, laurel, phillyrea, privet and laurestinus – coming from a nursery at Burford that specialized in these. Nigel Fitzhardinge Kingscote concentrated on his kitchen garden and roses and ferns. He employed three gardeners; one earned £4 a month, the others £2 each. Plants were ordered from Kew, from Guernsey and from Kent and arrived by road and rail. A consignment of ferns from Robert Sim of Foots Cray in Kent had certain items annotated 'examined before packing to see if safe' and 'mice are fond of the crown of this fern', and was despatched 'by Great Western Railway Goods Train'. The order included a copy of Moore's *Handbook of British Ferns*, and the twenty-one items, book, a large hamper and packing and carriage only came to £4 18*s*. in all.[9] That Kingscote was buying a book on ferns reflects the seriousness of his interest and the increasing availability of periodicals and other publications designed to inform and instruct keen gardeners; *The Gardeners' Magazine* and *The Gardeners' Chronicle* supplied popular reading matter for country dwellers and townsfolk alike, and publications on alpines, ferns and roses catered for the dedicated specialist. The Horticultural Society of London, later the Royal Horticultural Society, was mirrored with varying success in local societies all over the country, and in Gloucestershire these were supported both financially and administratively by local gentry families. Concern for those who had worked in gardens was shown in the establishment in 1839 of a Benevolent Institution for the Relief of Aged and Indigent Gardeners to which gentry families subscribed.

Of the new houses built in Gloucestershire during the nineteenth century, three of the most outstanding belonged to comparative latecomers to the county scene. All were

Sezincote. An early example of cast iron being used for an interior staircase

extremely wealthy, independent of their estates for revenue and, like the newcomers in the sixteenth century, anxious that their houses should reflect contemporary values of architecture, lack nothing in respect of comfort and decoration and make the success of the owner very clear. The earliest of these was Sezincote, built *c.* 1805 for Sir Charles Cockerell on the side of the Cotswold hills near Moreton-in-Marsh. Cockerell, with a fortune made in the service of the East India Company and a continuing income from his investments therein, could well afford to indulge his fancy on his return to Gloucestershire, to live in surroundings reminiscent of his time in India. The house and gardens at Sezincote were the result of the combined efforts of Thomas Daniell, the Indian topographical artist who portrayed in his work some of the buildings that Cockerell most admired; of Humphrey Repton, who studied Daniell's paintings excitedly and produced architectural sketches based on them; and of Cockerell's brother the architect Samuel Pepys Cockerell, designer of nearby Daylesford for Warren Hastings. Built of Cotswold stone, but in a style totally alien to the locality, the house nevertheless blends with its setting in spite of the exterior architecture being essentially Indian. The main block, surmounted by an onion-shaped dome, has a curved wing on one side in the form of an orangery, and on the other a pavilion that was once the bedroom of Sir Charles Cockerell who seemingly preferred airy to cosy surroundings. Inside, the house is more English in style, clearly designed for formal entertaining with

Toddington. Designed and owned by Charles Hanbury Tracy, chairman of the commission that decided on the plan for the new Houses of Parliament in 1835

lofty and spacious reception rooms on the first floor reached by a divided staircase, its unusual balustrade and supports being made of cast iron. More homely, low-ceilinged rooms for family use are on the ground floor. Repton also helped to design the gardens round the house, with one of his favoured terraces in front, commanding an uninterrupted view down the hillside, and an Indian-style bridge carrying the entrance drive across a valley, at the head of which is an Indian shrine built into the hillside and reflected in a pool. The Prince Regent visited Sezincote in 1807 and was so taken with its design that he asked Repton to produce a similar one for the Pavilion at Brighton. Though the latter was in fact built according to plans drawn up later by John Nash, it is clear that Repton's ideas had supplied the inspiration.

The second new house was Toddington Manor, built between 1820 and 1835 by Sir Charles Hanbury-Tracy on the strength of wealth derived from the family's ironworks at Pontypool. While at Oxford, he had developed an interest in architecture and through his pursuit of this became a talented and respected amateur architect. The buildings at Toddington reflected his fondness for the Gothic style, and incorporated features adopted from Oxford colleges, such as a tower resembling that of Magdalen College and vaulted cloisters like those at Christchurch. The exterior presented an array of pointed windows, a battlemented parapet and a wealth of pinnacles and turrets making it easy to accept that Hanbury-Tracy had some influence over the design for the rebuilding of the Houses of Parliament in 1835. Details of the interior were also Gothic, the library especially resembling that of Horace Walpole at Strawberry Hill; yet in spite of so much stony excellence, the house was markedly warm and comfortable. No trouble or expense was spared to achieve the right effects – fireplaces being made of marble with mirrored overmantels, much gold leaf used to highlight carved decorations in ceilings and cornices, and medieval glass imported from Europe for the windows. The Revd F. E. Witts visiting the house in 1833 commented on 'the pheasantry . . . well arranged in an umbrageous corner . . . trees, walks and lawns well grouped, affording an enjoyable promenade and a striking view of the most enriched front of the building.' Later, he praised the very high standard of workmanship throughout and attributed this to 'the personal superintendance of Mr Tracy'. There is no doubt that the latter managed to get good service from his local craftsmen and that this, combined with his own imaginative designs, inspired David Verey's claim that 'in the history of English domestic architecture, the house stands alone'.

In conception Toddington was a prodigy house, like those built by Elizabethan courtiers with the dual aim of inspiring contemporaries and, in the event of a royal visit, affording the monarch accommodation and facilities not inferior to those of her own residences. Yet another new house built in Gloucestershire during the nineteenth century had the same quality of a dream being realized, an undertaking only to be entertained by a multi-millionaire such as Robert Stayner Holford. Like his predecessors who had owned Westonbirt for over a century, he was a trained lawyer and a Master of Chancery with many professional and social ties with London; but unlike them, he decided as a young man to live mainly in the county and make a position for himself there, and this required a more impressive setting than the existing house and grounds. His father had already begun to make some improvements in the estate, but Robert Stayner was more sweeping in his approach, having some houses in the village of Westonbirt pulled down and rebuilt further away from the proposed site of his new mansion, before turning his attention to the latter. His favoured style for this was Elizabethan and his model Wollaton Hall, the Nottinghamshire home of the Willoughbyfamily. Lewis Vulliamy, who had already designed a house for Holford in Park Lane, London, was asked to produce plans for a Gloucestershire home, according to suggestions made by the owner. Local stone and craftsmen were used to produce in the late 1860s a dwelling closely resembling its sixteenth century model, with an elaborate and impressive façade dominated by a five-storey tower, and a forest of pinnacles and chimneys at roof level. The interior was arranged around a high-ceilinged, sky-lighted saloon, and everywhere the finest materials, including imported stone and woodwork, were used to prduce aesthetically pleasing effects. Into this setting was then introduced a collection of pictures and works of art exemplifying another of Holford's interests.

Holford was a keen builder, but an even more enthusiastic gardener and plantsman and, in order to make pleasure grounds suited to the new house, he had its immediate surroundings terraced and Italian-style gardens laid out there. Then, beyond the formal garden he embarked on an arboretum, bringing his knowledge of shrubs and trees into play and drawing on his vast wealth to obtain, from all over the world, specimens whose colours and shapes would produce pleasing effects in every season of the year.[10]

Westonbirt was the product of a rich man's imagination, but also of well-informed taste and, though work on the arboretum continued into the twentieth century, even at the time of Holford's death in 1892 it was already established and becoming a source of wide interest.

Sezincote was modestly proportioned as compared with Toddington and Westonbirt, but all three represented a grander and more impersonal way of life than had characterized gentry homes in the eighteenth century and than the average old-established family could or would have aspired to in the nineteenth. There were exceptions, it is true. Lord Ducie built a large new Gothic dwelling at Tortworth in the 1850s and Lord Redesdale replaced an old manor-house with an Elizabethan-type mansion at Batsford in the 1890s, but they were now peers in high office and committed to a way of life and scale of entertaining that was characteristic of the aristocracy rather than the gentry. Cockerell, Hanbury-Tracy and Holford, conscious perhaps of being newcomers to the county, though persons of importance elsewhere, may have felt an urge to do everything on an impressive scale since they had the means to do so; but though their building and gardening projects were viewed with interest and admiration by their neighbours, it was not these so much as their warm hospitality, generous patronage and capacity for public service that identified them with other county families for whom such undertakings had always been an integral part of their life.

Conclusion

Had he been alive today Robert Atkyns would certainly have been proved wrong in his assertion that 'few families flourish beyond three generations', since some of the gentry families long established in Gloucestershire in his time are still extant, as are comparative newcomers of the seventeenth and eighteenth centuries. In the first group there are descendants of the Guise, Clifford and Estcourt families; in the second, the Whitmores, Leighs, Wynters, Blathwayts and Chester-Masters. In a few cases, representatives still live in homes that have belonged to their families for centuries – a Guise at Elmore, a Clifford at Frampton Court, a Southeron-Estcourt at Estcourt Court, and until fairly recently there was a Dutton at Sherborne, a Whitmore at Lower Slaughter, a Leigh at Adlestrop, and a Chamberlayne at Maugersbury. Other gentry houses remain but different families regard them as home, and many have been converted to other uses – as hotels, schools and flats.

The most outstanding characteristic of the gentry has always been an instinct to survive; the houses and records of Gloucestershire families prove that they have also had the *capacity* to do this. As succeeding ages demanded different qualities in those who wished to hold their own in society, so the gentry managed to respond to the needs of the time. Physical courage and a stubborn determination to withstand the difficulties and dangers of medieval life enabled the knights to maintain their position in the feudal hierarchy and to develop a new capacity – namely to manage, as well as to own, land. The beginning of modern times in the fifteenth and sixteenth centuries brought unprecedented opportunities for the enterprising, though challenges were accompanied by hazards, daunting for any but the totally self-assured. Those who sought honours and favour in royal service needed the qualities of a courtier combined with patience and a willingness to accept setbacks that might be as frequent as rewards. Those who hoped to achieve wealth and repute nearer home showed a different kind of enterprise and imagination in enlarging and profiting from the estates, undertaking administrative duties and setting themselves up as leaders in the local community.

The political disruptions and ideological clashes of the seventeenth century called for immense confidence in one's convictions and intellectual rather than physical toughness, though, as in the previous century, those engaged actively in national and local affairs were called upon to show courage, especially in the face of threats that struck at the heart of gentry life – the interruption and sometimes break-up of family life, the loss of lands and revenue, powerlessness to do anything to preserve the stability and well-being of the local community. Few if any families emerged from the Civil Wars unscathed; some were irreparably damaged; others survived in reduced circumstances but with enough hope and determination to recover lost ground when the times allowed.

If the sixteenth century saw the gentry take their first steps along the road to success, the eighteenth century brought their ambitions to complete fruition. Energy, inventiveness and aesthetic appreciation came into their own in this period of political opportunism, economic expansion and artistic achievement; many families enjoyed a fuller, more comfortable and more cultured life than ever before. As in the sixteenth century, when royal officials, lawyers and new exploitive landowners joined the established gentry in the county, the ranks of the latter opened once again in the eighteenth century to admit clothiers, bankers, investors, doctors, soldiers and naval men. Some of the newcomers to the gentry way of life, like all converts, tended to be more gentrified than their exemplars, but they were no less sincere in their desire to stand well with the local community and display those qualities most likely to inspire respect and liking. The only significant difference between the new gentry and the old was perhaps that, because of interests independent of estates, they were often away from the county at regular intervals.

The absence of landowners from their estates on business or in pursuit of political or service careers was one of the factors that helped to bring to an end the traditional paternalistic role of the gentry in the countryside. Whether they belonged to old-established or more newly arrived families, lack of contact with the local community necessarily limited opportunities for contributing to its affairs; at the same time, political and economic changes were emancipating many rural workers from their former dependence on landlords and, even if it meant less security, they preferred to stand on their own feet, choose their own way of making a living and of enjoying themselves.

The industrialization of Britain during the nineteenth century established capitalism as an economic force and success in business as a prime factor in the competition for social recognition and distinction. What the ownership of land had done for a man in the past could now be achieved by a healthy bank balance and financial credibility. Admittedly, fortunes and fame waxed and waned more quickly when founded on such quicksands as speculation and investments, but there was no doubting the reputation that wealth could win for a man nor the lengths to which it would carry him.

Until the period between the two world wars, in some remote areas traditional values and attitudes died hard, with tenants and villagers continuing to look up to the family at the manor and, in spirit if not materially, remaining dependent on it; but in the long run circumstances of the twentieth century have dealt a final blow to the social structure of the county which had lasted for so many centuries. Death duties, the scarcity and expense of domestic and farm workers, the loss of heirs in two wars, have resulted in the breakup of most large estates; only compact holdings run on strictly business lines can now survive, and even these may need revenue from other sources – investments, public opening, the use of houses and grounds for conferences or leisure pursuits. In many houses, visitors are shown round by the owner or members of his family, as hospitably as if they were guests, and momentarily drawn into the way of life of a gentry home; but whereas in the eighteenth century, visitors cast a critical gaze on their surroundings with the idea of emulating what they saw, nowadays there is little envy or desire in their attitude, only relief that they do not have to meet the bills for heating and lighting and cleaning so many rooms, or live under the constraint of maintaining such an establishment.

The outward signs of gentility as understood in the past – landed estates, a way of life that provided for both an immediate and an extended family, the pursuit of a career as much in the public as in a personal interest – are now regarded as something of an anachronism. The legacy of the gentry is implicit rather than definable, but a well-known name at the head of a subscription list for some good cause can add cachet and inspire trust; or on a plaque denoting a gift to a village hall or a school, may spark off another gesture of generosity; and in times when everyone is under pressure and more self-absorbed than ever before, even those who affect to set little store by them, acknowledge that good manners, good humour and civility are the marks of a gentleman – indeed nowadays, as in the sixteenth century, 'Whoever will bear the porte, charge and countenance of a gentleman, shall be accounted one'.

Appendix

SOME OF THE GLOUCESTERSHIRE GENTRY AND THEIR MAIN PROPERTIES IN THE COUNTY AND ELSEWHERE

Origins: 1. Medieval 2. Sixteenth and Seventeenth Centuries 3. Eighteenth Century 4. Nineteenth Century.

		GRO References
2 ATKYNS	of *Sapperton* Oakley Lower Swell Tuffley	
2 BATHURST	of *Cirencester* Bisley N. Cerney Daglingworth Edgeworth Sapperton London Northants. Derby Notts. Yorks.	D 2525
2 BATHURST	of *Lydney* Awre Newent Mangotsfield	D 421
2 BLATHWAYT	of *Dyrham* Barton Bitton Thornbury Henbury Bristol Bath London Berks. Bucks. Cambridge Cornwall Hereford Herts. Middlesex Monmouth Montgomery Oxon. Salop. Somerset	D 1799 D 2659
2 BLOMER	of *Hatherop* Coln St. Aldwyn Quenington Eastleach Southrop Fairford	D 540
2 BOEVEY	of *Flaxley* Westbury Little Dean (later CRAWLEY-BOEVEY)	
2 BOND	of *Newland*	D 2026
1 BRYDGES	of *Coberley* Sudeley Hereford	
1 CASSEY	of *Wightfield* Deerhurst Little Compton	
2 CHADWELL	of *Broadwell* Downington Stow-on-the-Wold	D 1395
2 CHAMBERLAYNE	of *Maugersbury* Prestbury Oddington London	D 621 D 1700
2 CHESTER	of *Knole* Almondsbury Bristol (later CHESTER-MASTER)	D 674
1 CLIFFORD	of Daneway *Frampton* Avening Stroud Tetbury Rodbury Whitminster Somerset	D 149

4 COCKERELL	of *Sezincote* Condicote Bourton-on-the-Hill London	D 536 D 1652
2 CODRINGTON	of *Dodington* Marshfield Sodbury Tormarton Twyning Bristol Bath London Wilts. Barbuda Barbadoes	D 1670
2 COLCHESTER	of *Westbury* Mitcheldean Abenhall	D 36
2 COXWELL	of *Bibury* Barnsley Ablington Dowdeswell Coberley Marston Meysey	D 269 B
3 CRIPPS	of *Cirencester* later at Ampney Crucis Aldsworth	
2 CURTIS HAYWARD	of *Quedgeley* Woolstrop Tewkesbury Bristol Pershore West Indies	D 123
1 DE LA BERE	of *Southam* Prestbury Bishops Cleeve Cheltenham Deerhurst Dumbleton Warwicks. Cambridge Hereford Wilts. Worcs. Staffs. Beds. Bucks. Essex	D 1637 D 2217
1 DENYS	Dyrham, Pucklechurch, Abenhall	
3 DUCAREL	of *Newland* Exmouth	D 2091
2 DUCIE MORETON	of *Tortworth* Cramhall Woodchester Wickwar Thornbury Tetbury London Herts. Yorks. Lincs. Salop. Somerset Wilts. Warwicks.	D 340 A D 1011
2 DUTTON	of *Sherborne* Northleach Bibury Aldsworth Standish Cheltenham Wilts. Somerset	D 678
1 ESTCOURT	of *Shipton Moyne* Arlingham Dursley Frampton Mansell Cricklade Avening Larborough Stroud Tetbury Devizes Malmesbury Dorset Kent Middlesex Monmouth Sussex Wilts. (later SOTHERON-ESTCOURT)	D 1571
2 FREEMAN	of *Batsford* Berks. Northumberland Oxon (later FREEMAN-MITFORD)	D 1447 D 2002
1 GUISE	of *Elmore* Churcham Highnam Rendcomb Brockworth London Wilts.	D 326
2 HALE	of *Alderley* Cam Frampton Kingsbury Maiseyhampton Nibley Ozleworth Sodbury Uley Wotton Yate Bristol Berks. Brecon Dorset Essex Leics. Warwicks. Lincs. Notts. Oxon. Middlesex Somerset Cambridge Wilts. Yorks.	D 1086
4 HANBURY-TRACY	of *Toddington* Temple Guiting Salop. S. Wales	D 2153
4 HICKS-BEACH	of *Williamstrip* Witcombe Badgworth Shurdington Beverston Quenington Almondsbury Bristol London Somerset Essex Herts. Worcs. Middlesex	D 2440 D 1866
3 HOLFORD	of *Westonbirt* Charlton Kings Upton Larborough Wilts. Kent	D 1956
2 HOWE	of Withington *Stowell* Little Compton	
1 HUNGERFORD	of *Down Ampney* Cricklade	
1 HUNTLEY	of *Boxwell* Leighterton Badgeworth Badminton	D 48

	Littledean Newent Didmarton Chipping Sodbury Tetbury Wotton Bristol Berks. Cornwall Dorset Salop. Somerset Warwicks. Wilts.	D 2668
3 HYETT	of *Painswick* Dursley Badgeworth Haresfield Upton Gloucester	D 6
1 KINGSCOTE	of *Kingscote* Avening Horsley Lydney Wotton	D 471
1 KINGSTON	of *Flaxley* Painswick	
2 LEIGH	of *Adlestrop* Longborough Broadwell Oddington. Later also Stoneleigh London	D 670
4 LLOYD-BAKER	of *Hardwicke*	D 3529
3 LYSONS	of *Hempsted* Rodmarton Cherrington	
2 MASTER	of *Cirencester* (Later CHESTER-MASTER)	D 674
3 NEWTON	of *Bitton*	D 1844
1 OLLEPEN	of *Owlpen* Cam Cowley Nympsfield Tetbury Uley	D 456 D 979
3 PARSONS	of *Kemerton* Ashchurch	D 214
2 PATE	of Cheltenham *Matson*	
2 PERROT	Barnsley Oxon Londopn (later WYKEHAM-MUSGRAVE)	D 2388
1 POYNTZ	of *Iron Acton* Newark Alderley	
3 ROOKE	of *St Briavels* Newland Upton St. Leonard Monmouth	D 1833
2 RUSHOUT	of *Northwick Park* Bourton-on-the-Hill Blockley London	
1 SANDYS	of Miserden	D 1042
2 SELWYN	of *Matson* Gloucester Wilts. Dorset	
2 STEPHENS	of *Chavenage* Beverston	D 547 D 1023
2 STEPHENS	of *Lypiatt* Bisley Stroud Cirencester London Brecon	D 745 D 1647
1 TAME	of Stowell *Fairford* Cirencester Cerney Rendcomb	
1 TRACY	of Toddington *Stanway* Hailes Winchcombe	D 2153. D 2311
2 WHITMORE	of *Lower Slaughter* Pucklechurch Cheltenham London	D 45
2 WYNTER	of *Lydney* Forest of Dean Dyrham	D 421

References

Abbreviations

BGAS	Bristol and Gloucestershire Archaeological Society
GRO	Gloucestershire Record Office
SBT	Shakespeare Birthplace Trust
VCH	Victoria County History
HMC	Historical Manuscripts Commission
ROL	Record Office Library

Chapter 1.

1. This and other quotations in the chapter are from the Domesday Survey of Gloucestershire; and from R. Atkyns, *Ancient and Present State of Glostershire.*

Chapter 2.

1. GRO D 456.
2. Smyth, *Lives of the Berkeleys*, 1883.
3. Leland, *The Itinerary of John Leland*, 1535–1543. Bodleian Library.
4. N. Saul, 'Gloucestershire Gentry in the Fourteenth Century', (unpub. thesis), ROL.

Chapter 3.

1. Shakespeare, *Troilus and Cressida*, Act I, Scene III.
2. Act of Supremacy (1534) established the king as head of the Church in England with the power and functions hitherto exercised by the Pope.
3. Background information derived from D. Loades, *The Tudor Court*, 1986.
4. Act in Restraint of Appeals (1533) prevented cases being referred from the English ecclesiastical courts to Rome, since the king was now the ultimate source of appeal in spiritual as in lay matters.
5. The Ten Articles (1536), a summary of the basic principles of belief to which the English clergy were required to subscribe.

Chapter 4.

1. Wyatt's Rebellion (1554). A protest led by Sir Thomas Wyatt against Mary's proposed marriage with Philip II of Spain, a plan disliked by the English on the grounds of his being both a foreigner and a Catholic.
2. B. Rendell (ed.), *The Wynters of White Cross*, 1986, for this and later references to the Wynters.
3. An increasing responsibility as successive Poor Laws attempted to discourage idle vagabondage while providing for the care of the genuinely needy and unemployed.

4. GRO List of Inventories and Wills.
5. GRO Gloucester Borough Records: Chamberlain's Accounts.
6. R. Strong, *The Renaissance Garden in England*, 1978.

Chapter 5.
1. For example, Thomas Stephens of Lypiatt who for many years served as Attorney to Prince Charles.
2. G. Huxley, *Endymion Porter*, 1959.
3. Washbourne, *Bibliotheca Gloucestriensis*, 1825.
4. For comments on the 1640 House of Commons see M. F. Keeler, *Members of the Long Parliament.*

Chapter 6.
1. GRO Civil War Papers CG10.
2. This and other quotations about the Guise family from Camden Miscellany XVI (1936), Guise Family Papers.
3. Quoted in Ollard, *This War without an Enemy*, 1978.
4. M. Toynbee, *Leaders of the Civil War*, 1977.
5. B. Rendell (ed.), *The Wynters of White Cross*, 1986.
6. History of the Leigh family, Bodleian Library, Beachcroft Dep. c. 570.
7. GRO Sherborne Muniments D 678 Barwick MSS.
8. Quoted in H. P. R. Finberg, *Gloucestershire Studies*, 1957.
9. SBT Stoneleigh MSS, Gloucestershire Papers DR 18/20/18.
10. GRO D 45, E17.

Chapter 7.
1. Act of Indemnity and Oblivion (1660) extended a general pardon to those who had fought against the king and entitled those who had bought (as apposed to seized) land during the Interregnum, to keep it.
2. GRO D 1844 C 26.
3. GRO D 1844 C 4.
4. This and other quotations from T. Baskerville HMC Portland II, 1893.
5. For Brydges' efforts to provide for his relations and dependants see J. Johnson, *Princely Chandos*, 1984.
6. GRO 1571 F123.
7. History of the Leigh family, Bodleian Library, Beachcroft Dep c. 570.
8. For this and other references to Cassandra Willoughby see J. Johnson, *Excellent Cassandra*, 1981.
9. Bodleian Library MS English Letters d 77 f 3, 4.
10. GRO D 2659/2.
11. GRO TRS 112.
12. GRO D. 678 Family Settlements.
13. SBT Stoneleigh MSS DR 18/20/18.
14. GRO D 1844.
15. SBT Stoneleigh MSS DR 18/866.
16. GRO D 678 Family Settlements.

Chapter 8.
1. Since 1684, the estates have descended in female line with husbands assuming name of Clifford.
2. SBT Stoneleigh MSS DR 18/20/18.
3. BGAS, *Transactions*, 1962.

Chapter 9.
1. GRO 340a C23a.
2. GRO 340a C 22/37.
3. This and subsequent extracts from Dutton correspondence: GRO D 678 57d.
4. GRO 340a C 22/34.
5. Ensuing paragraphs are based on James Leigh's notebooks, privately owned.
6. E. Moir, *George Onesiphorus Paul*, included in *Gloucestershire Studies*; also *Local Government in Gloucestershire (1775–1800)*, 1968, see also Chapter 10 below.
7. This and subsequent extracts from Rooke correspondence: GRO D 1833 F1/F2.

8. J. Macky, *A Journey through England*, 1723.
9. *The General*, Journals of Sir George Whitmore, 1987.
10. SBT Stoneleigh MSS DR 18/20/18.

Chapter 10.
1. SBT Stoneleigh MSS DR 18/31 Gloucestershire Papers.
2. Idem.
3. *Gloucestershire Turnpikes*, GRO Publication.
4. *Gloucestershire Inland Waterways*, GRO Publication.
5. GRO 149 Correspondence of Packer family; see also E. Moir, *The Gentlemen Clothiers*, incl. in *Gloucestershire Studies*.

Chapter 11.
1. GRO D 1571 E 356.
2. For this and other Dutton family expenses GRO D678 57a.
3. Colnaghi, *English Ancestors*, 1983.
4. SBT Stoneleigh MSS DR 18/31 Personal Accounts.
5. For this and other Blathwayt expenses GRO D1799 A 340–403.
6. GRO D 214 F1/115.
7. SBT Stoneleigh MSS DR 18/31 Personal Accounts.
8. Idem DR 18/20/18.
9. GRO D 214 F1/186.
10. GRO D 214 F1/127.
11. GRO D 1833 F1/16.
12. GRO D 1086 F 105.

Chapter 12.
1. This and subsequent references to Dutton expenses GRO D678 96 A–D.
2. SBT Stoneleigh MSS DR 18/31 Personal Accounts.
3. GRO D 1447.
4. GRO D 678 96D.
5. GRO D 1086 F 105.
6. All references to R. Jervis GRO D 610, 21.
7. GRO D 1571 F 157.
8. GRO D 1799 A 271 A 374–400.
9. SBT Stoneleigh MSS DR 18/31/18.
10. GRO D214 F1 83.
11. This and the following extract: GRO D 1833 F1 18–19.
12. GRO D 214 F1/37.
13. J. Harvey, *Early Nurserymen*, 1974.
14. SBT Stoneleigh MSS DR18/31 Adlestrop Garden Accounts.
15. Papers privately owned.
16. References to Cassandra Turner: SBT Stoneleigh MSS DR 18/31 Turner Papers.

Chapter 13.
1. This and other Leigh correspondence: SBT Stoneleigh MSS DR 18/31/31.
2. GRO D 1571 F 157. Election expenses on p.233: GRO D 1571 X 74.
3. D 123 E1, E9.
4. F. E. Witts, *Diary of a Cotswold Parson*, (ed.) David Verey.
5. GRO D 303 X1.
6. GRO D 36 F 23.
7. SBT Stoneleigh MSS DR 18/31 Longborough Accounts.
8. GRO D 1571 X 14.
9. GRO D 471 A 14 and A 17.
10. Holford's friend, Lord Ducie, had already planted an arboretum at Tortworth and, in the 1890s, Lord Redesdale was to establish one at Batsford. This and Westonbirt can still be seen.

BIBLIOGRAPHY

Manuscript Sources

Family and Estate Papers in the County Record Office, Gloucester [See GRO Handlist]

Stoneleigh MSS. Gloucestershire, Estate and Personal Papers at the Shakespeare Birthplace Trust, Stratford upon Avon

Secondary Sources

Atkyns, R., *Ancient and Present State of Glostershire*, 1712.

Dictionary of National Biography.

Elton, G., *The Tudor Constitution*, 1960.

Finberg, H. P. R., (ed.), *Gloucestershire Studies*, 1957.

History of the House of Commons.

Foster, J.R., *Alumni Oxoniensis.*

Marshall, W., *The Rural Economy of Gloucestershire*, 1789.

Summerson, J., *Architecture in Britain (1530–1830)*, 1953.

Tanner, J., *Constitutional Conflicts of the Seventeenth Century*, 1937.

Transactions of the Bristol and Gloucestershire Archaeological Society, ROL.

Verey, D., *Buildings of England. Gloucestershire*, 1970.

Victoria County History of England. *Gloucestershire.*

Visitations of the Heralds in Gloucestershire, ROL.

Waterhouse, E., *Painting in Britain 1530–1790*, 1953.

Background Reading (arranged in order of chapters)

Mingay, G.E., *The Gentry.*

Postan, M. M., *The Medieval Economy and Society*, 1975.

Johnson, J., *Tudor Gloucestershire*, 1985.

Youings, J., *Sixteenth Century England*, 1984.

Kenyon, J., *Stuart England*, 1978.

Young, P., *The English Civil War*, 1974.

Wilson, C., *England's Apprenticeship 1603–1760*, 1965.

Plumb, J. H., *England in the Eighteenth Century*, 1960.

Porter, R., *English Society in the Eighteenth Century*, 1982.

Thomson, D., *England in the Nineteenth Century*, 1978.

INDEX OF PEOPLE AND PLACES

(Christian names are arranged in chronological order. Illustrations are in italics.)